6TH EDITION

OAHU REVEALED
THE ULTIMATE GUIDE TO
HONOLULU, WAIKIKI & BEYOND

ANDREW DOUGHTY

PHOTOGRAPHS BY ANDREW DOUGHTY & LEONA BOYD

WIZARD
PUBLICATIONS
INC

When the sun goes down, Waikiki will continue to light you up.

OAHU REVEALED
The Ultimate Guide to Honolulu, Waikiki & Beyond 6th Edition

Published by Wizard Publications, Inc.
Post Office Box 991
Lihu'e, Hawai'i 96766–0991

ISBN: 978-0-9961318-6-5   1038
Library of Congress Control Number 2018932113
Printed in China

Cataloging-in-Publication Data

Doughty, Andrew
    Oahu revealed : the ultimate guide to Honolulu, Waikiki and beyond / Andrew Doughty – 6th ed. Lihue, HI : Wizard Publications, Inc., 2018
    316 p. : col. illus., col. photos, col. maps ; 21 cm.
    Includes index.
    Summary: A complete traveler's guide to the Hawaiian island of Oahu, with full-color illustrations, maps, directions and candid advice by an author who resides in Hawaii.
    ISBN 978-0-9961318-6-5
    LCCN 2018932113

    1. Oahu (Hawaii) – Guidebooks. 2. Oahu (Hawaii) – Description and travel. I. Title
DU628.03   919.69'3_dc22

All photographs (except the cover and page 230) taken by Andrew Doughty and Leona Boyd. Photo on page 230 courtesy of Tom Sanders.
Cover imagery courtesy of Earthstar Geographics (www.earth-imagery.com).
Cartography by Andrew Doughty.
All artwork and illustrations by Andrew Doughty and Lisa Pollak.

We welcome any comments, questions, criticisms or contributions you may have, and we will incorporate some of your suggestions into future editions. Please send to the address above or e-mail us at aloha@hawaiirevealed.com.

Check out our website at **www.hawaiirevealed.com** for up-to-the-minute changes. Find us on **Facebook, Instagram, YouTube** and **Twitter**.

Dedicated to the wizard that exists in all of us...

ABOUT THIS BOOK

9

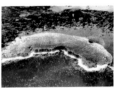

INTRODUCTION

11

11 How it Began
14 The First Settlers
16 Outside World Discovers Hawai'i
18 Kamehameha the Great
19 Modern Hawai'i

THE BASICS

21

21 Getting Here
21 What to Bring
22 Getting Around
26 Getting Married on O'ahu
27 Weather
28 Geography
29 Where Should I Stay?
30 Hazards
34 Traveling With Children (Keiki)
35 The People
35 Some Terms
36 Hawaiian Time
36 Shaka
37 The Hawaiian Language
40 The Hula
40 Books & Music
41 The Internet
41 Farmers Markets
42 A Note About Access
42 A Note on Personal Responsibility
44 Miscellaneous Information
44 Getting In & Out of Waikiki
45 A Word About Driving Tours
45 Smartphone App

WAIKIKI & HONOLULU SIGHTS

46

46 Waikiki Area
60 Honolulu
63 Waikiki & Honolulu Best Bets

EAST O'AHU SIGHTS

64

64 The Coastal Route to Hanauma Bay
68 Past Hanauma Bay to Kailua
76 Kailua Town
79 Kane'ohe
81 East O'ahu Best Bets

NORTH SHORE SIGHTS

82

82 Kualoa
83 Kahana Bay
84 La'ie
86 Kahuku
88 Turtle Bay
88 The North Shore
91 Waimea Bay
94 Surfing Life
96 Hale'iwa
96 Past the Pavement
99 Ain't Technology Grand?
100 North Shore Best Bets

CONTENTS

WAI'ANAE & CENTRAL O'AHU SIGHTS
101

101 Central O'ahu
105 Wahiawa
105 Mt. Ka'ala
108 Pearl Harbor
109 'Ewa
110 Kalaeloa/Barbers Point
110 Wai'anae
114 Makaha
115 The End of the Road
115 Wai'anae & Central O'ahu Best Bets

BEACHES
116

117 Beach Safety
120 Wai'anae Beaches
126 'Ewa & Leeward Beaches
133 Windward Beaches
145 North Shore Beaches

ATTRACTIONS
152

152 Cultural & Educational Attractions
156 Historical Attractions
167 Just-For-Fun Attractions

ACTIVITIES
173

174 Air Tours
178 ATVs
179 Biking
179 Boat Tours
184 Boogie Boarding
184 Camping
185 Escape Rooms
186 Fishing
187 Golfing
189 Gun Clubs
189 Hiking
215 Horseback Riding
216 Jet Skiing
218 Kayaking
222 Kiteboarding
222 Land Tours
225 Parasailing
225 SCUBA
229 Shopping
230 Skydiving
231 Snorkeling
233 Spas
234 Submarine
236 Surfing
239 Waterskiing
239 Whale Watching
240 Zipline

CONTENTS

ADVENTURES
242

ISLAND DINING
254

242 Swim With Sharks
244 Night Snorkeling
245 Rule Your Own Island
246 Paddle, Hike & Jump
246 Night Shipwreck Dive
247 Mermaid Cave
248 Pu'u-ke-ahi-a-Kahoe
    (Moanalua Valley to Haiku Stairs)
250 Wa'ahila Ridge to Mt. Olympus
252 Day Trip to Moloka'i's
    Leprosy Settlement

254 Island Dining Index
257 Island Fish & Seafood
257 Lu'au Foods
258 Other Island Foods
258 Waikiki Dining
270 Honolulu Dining
278 Chinatown Dining
283 East of Waikiki Dining
286 Kailua Dining
290 Kane'ohe Dining
290 Between Kane'ohe & Kahuku
291 Kahuku Shrimp & More
294 Hale'iwa Dining
297 Central O'ahu Dining
297 Ko Olina & Kapolei Dining
300 Wai'anae Dining
301 Island Nightlife
301 Lu'au
307 Dinner Cruises
308 Dinner Shows

ABOUT THE AUTHOR
309

INDEX
310

O'ahu: land of myths. We're not talking about ancient Hawaiian myths. We're talking about the myths that exist about this island, both for visitors and for those who live on the neighbor islands (including me before I moved here to do this guide.) The biggest myth is that O'ahu is Waikiki and Waikiki is O'ahu. Nothing could be further from the truth. O'ahu has all the wonder, adventure and discovery that a person could ever ask for—and far more.

Most travel publishers send a writer or writers to a given location for a few weeks to become "experts" and to compile information for guidebooks. To our knowledge, we at Wizard Publications are the only ones who actually *live* what we write about.

We hike the trails, ride the boats, eat in the restaurants, explore the reefs and do the things we write about. It takes us two years, full time, to do a first edition book, and we visit places *anonymously*. We marvel at writers who can do it all in a couple of weeks staying in a hotel. Wow, they must be *really* fast. Our method, though it takes much longer, gives us the ability to tell it like it is in a way no one else can. We put in many long hours, and doing all these activities is a burdensome grind. But we do it all for you—only for you. (Feel free to gag at this point.)

We have found many special places that people born and raised here didn't even know about because that's *all we do*—explore the island. Visitors will find this book as valuable as having a friend living on the island.

In this day of easy-to-access online reviews from countless sources, you can get "ratings" for nearly every company out there. What you get from our reviews is a single source, *beholden to none*, with a comprehensive exposure to all of the companies. There are two critical shortcomings to online reviews. One is that you don't know the source or agenda of the reviewer. Nearly every company that offers a service to the public *thinks* they are doing a good job. (But as you know, not everyone does.) So who can blame a company for trying to rig the system by seeding good reviews of their company at every opportunity or having friends write good reviews? Many also encourage *satisfied* customers to write favorable online reviews (obviously not encouraging *unhappy* customers to do so). But maybe their enemies or competitors retaliate with bad reviews. The point is, you never *really know* where those reviews come from, and it's almost impossible to reconcile terrible reviews right next to glowing ones for the same company. Which do you believe?

The other problem is a lack of a frame of reference. A visitor to Hawai'i goes on a snorkel boat and has a great time. (Hey, he snorkeled in Hawai'i, swam with a turtle—*cool!*) When he goes back home, he posts good reviews all around. That's great. But the problem is, he only went on *one* snorkel boat. We do 'em all. If only he'd known that another company *he didn't even know about* did a much better job, had way better food, and a much nicer boat for the same price.

We have also been blessed with millions of readers over the years—from our books as well as our smartphone apps—who alert us to issues with companies and places. *Every single message* from our readers is received, placed in a special database that we constantly have available while we're out and about, and we follow up on every observation made by our readers. So when we walk into a business or restaurant, we check to see what our readers say and tips they send us, and we use them to our advantage. (Thanks for the head's up about that incredible coconut cake at such-and-such restaurant—I know what *I'll* be ordering for dessert today.) With such a resource, and after two decades reviewing companies in Hawai'i full-time, there ain't much that's gonna get past us.

A quick look at this book will reveal features never before used in other guidebooks. Let's start with the maps. They are more detailed than any other maps you'll find, and yet they omit extraneous information that can sometimes make map reading a chore. We know that people in unfamiliar territory sometimes have a hard time determining where they are on a map, so we include landmarks. Most notable among these are mile markers. At every mile on main roads, the government has erected numbered markers to tell you where you are. We are the first to put these markers on a map so you can use them as reference points. Where needed, we've drawn legal public beach access in yellow, so you'll know when you're legally entitled to cross someone's land. Most guidebooks have the infuriating habit of mentioning a particular place or sight but then fail to mention how to get there! You won't find that in our book. We tell you exactly how to find the hidden gems and use our own special maps to guide you.

As you read through this book, you will also notice that we are very candid in assessing businesses. Unlike some other guidebooks that send out questionnaires asking a business if they are any good (gee, they *all* say they're good), we've had personal contact with the businesses listed in this book. One of the dirty little secrets about guidebook writ-

ers is that they sometimes make cozy little deals for good reviews. Well, you won't find that here. We accept no payment for our reviews, we make no deals with businesses for saying nice things, and there are no advertisements in our apps or books. What we've seen and experienced is what you get. If we gush over a certain company, it comes from personal experience. If we rail against a business, it is for the same reason. All businesses mentioned in this book are here by *our* choosing. None has had any input into what we say, and we have not received *a single cent* from any of them for their inclusion. (In fact, there are some who would probably pay to be left out, given our comments.) We always review businesses as anonymous visitors and only later as guidebook writers if we need more information. This ensures that we are treated the same as you. (Amazingly, most travel writers *announce* themselves.) What you get is our opinion on how they operate. Nothing more, nothing less.

Sometimes our candor gets us into trouble. More than once we've had our books pulled from shelves because our comments hit a little too close to home. That's OK, because we don't work for the people who *sell* the book; we work for the people who *read* the book.

Oahu Revealed is intended to bring you independence in exploring O'ahu. We don't want to waste any of your precious time by giving you bad advice or bad directions. We want you to experience the best that the island has to offer. Our objective in creating this book is to give you the tools and information necessary to have the greatest Hawaiian experience possible.

We hope we succeeded.

Andrew Doughty

Four million years ago, before the dawn of man, the island of O'ahu emerged from a warm, frothing sea.

As with people, volcanic islands have a life cycle. They emerge from their sea floor womb to be greeted by the warmth of the sun. They grow, mature and eventually die before sinking forever beneath the sea.

HOW IT BEGAN

Sometime around 70 million years ago a cataclysmic rupture occurred in the Earth's mantle, deep below the crust. A hot column of liquid rock blasted through the Pacific plate like a giant cutting torch, forcing magma to the surface off the coast of Russia, forming the Emperor Seamounts. As the tectonic plate moved slowly over the hot spot, this torch cut a long scar along the plate, piling up mountains of rock, producing island after island. The oldest of these to have survived is Kure. Once a massive island with a unique ecosystem, only its ghost remains in the form of a fringing coral reef, called an atoll.

As soon as the islands were born, a conspiracy of elements proceeded to dismantle them. Ocean waves unmercifully battered the fragile and fractured rock. Abundant rain, especially on the northeastern sides of the mountains, easily carved up the rock surface, seeking faults in the rock and forming rivers and streams. In forming these channels, the water carried away the rock and soil, robbing the islands of their very essence. Additionally, the weight of the islands ensured their doom. Lava flows on top of other lava, and the union of these flows is always weak. This lava also contains countless air pockets and is crisscrossed with hollow lava tubes, making it inherently unstable. As these massive amounts of rock accumulated, their bases were crushed under the weight of subsequent lava flows, causing their summits to sink back into the sea.

What we call the Hawaiian Islands are simply the latest creation from this island-making machine. Kauaʻi and Niʻihau are the oldest of the eight major islands. Lush and deeply eroded, the last of Kauaʻi's fires died with its volcano a million years ago. Oʻahu, Molokaʻi, Lanaʻi, Kahoʻolawe—their growing days are over as well. Maui is in its twilight days as a growing island. After growing vigorously, Hawaiian volcanoes usually go to sleep

for a million years or so before sputtering back to life for one last fling. Maui's youngest volcano, Haleakala, is in its final eruptive stage. It *probably* last erupted around 1790 and will continue to sporadically erupt for a (geologically) short time before drifting off into eternal sleep.

The latest and newest star in this island chain is the Big Island of Hawaiʻi. Born less than a million years ago, this youngster is still vigorously growing. Though none of its five volcanic mountains is considered truly dead, these days Mauna Loa and Kilauea are doing most of the work of making the Big Island bigger. Mauna Loa, the most massive mountain on Earth, consists of 10,000 *cubic miles* of rock. The quieter of the two active volcanoes, it last erupted in 1984. Kilauea is the most boisterous of the volcanoes and is the most active volcano on the planet. Kilauea's most recent eruption began in 1983 and was still going strong as we went to press. Up and coming

Ancient forests dripping with life still abound on Oʻahu.

onto the world stage is Loʻihi. This new volcano is still 3,200 feet below the ocean's surface, 20 miles off the southeastern coast of the island. Yet in a geologic heartbeat, the Hawaiian Islands will be richer with its ascension, sometime in the next 100,000 years.

These virgin islands were barren at birth. Consisting only of volcanic rock, the first life forms to appreciate these new islands were marine organisms—algae and microscopic animals. Then fish and mammals discovered this new underwater haven and made homes for themselves. Coral polyps attached themselves to the lava rock, and succeeding generations built upon these, creating what would become coral reefs. A plant called coralline algae also created (and still creates) vast reefs.

Meanwhile, seeds carried by water, wind and birds were struggling to colonize the rocky land, eking out a living and breaking down the lava rock. Storms brought the occasional bird, hopelessly blown off course. The lucky ones found the islands. The even luckier ones arrived with mates or were carrying eggs. Other animals, stranded on a piece of floating debris, washed ashore against all odds and went on to colonize the islands. These introductions of new species were rare events. It took an extraordinary set of circumstances for a new species to actually make it to the islands. Single specimens were destined to live out their lives in lonely solitude. On average, a new species was successfully deposited here only once every 20,000 years.

As with people, volcanic islands have a life cycle. After their violent birth, islands grow to their maximum size, get carved up by the elements, collapse in parts, and finally sink back into the sea. Someday, all the Hawaiian Islands will

Hawaiʻi's First Tour Guide?

Given the remoteness of the Hawaiian Islands relative to the rest of Polynesia (or anywhere else for that matter), you'll be forgiven for wondering how the first settlers found these islands in the first place. Many scientists think it might have been this little guy here. Called the kolea, or

Before they leave for Alaska.

golden plover, this tiny bird flies over 2,500 miles nonstop to Alaska every year for the summer, returning to Hawaiʻi after mating. Some of these birds continue past Hawaiʻi and fly another 2,500 miles to Samoa and other South Pacific islands. The early Polynesians surely must have noticed this commute and concluded that there must be land in the direction that the bird was heading. They never would have dreamed that the birds leaving the South Pacific

When they return.

were heading to a land 5,000 miles away, and that Hawaiʻi was merely a stop in between, where the lazier birds wintered.

be nothing more than geologic footnotes in the Earth's turbulent history. When a volcanic island is old, it is a sandy sliver called an atoll, devoid of mountains, merely a shadow of its former glory. When it's middle-aged, it can be a lush wonderland, a haven for anything green, like Kaua'i and O'ahu. And when it is young, it is dynamic and unpredictable, like the Big Island of Hawai'i, but lacking the scars of experience from its short battle with the elements. The first people to occupy these islands were blessed with riches beyond their wildest dreams.

THE FIRST SETTLERS

Sometime in the first millennia, a large, double-hulled voyaging canoe, held together with flexible sennit lashings and propelled by sails made of woven pandanus, slid onto the sand on the Big Island of Hawai'i. These first intrepid adventurers, only a few dozen or so, encountered an island chain of unimaginable beauty.

They had left their home in the Marquesas Islands, 2,500 miles away. Though some say it was because of war, overpopulation or drought, it was more likely part of a purposeful exploration from a culture that had mastered the art of making their way through the featureless seas using celestial navigation and reading subtle signs in the ocean. Their navigational abilities far exceeded those of all other "advanced" societies of the time. Whatever their reasons, these initial settlers took a big chance and surely must have been highly motivated. They could not have known that there were islands in these waters since Hawai'i is the most isolated island chain on Earth. (Though some speculate that they were led here by the golden plover—see page 13.)

Those settlers who did arrive brought with them food staples from home: taro, breadfruit, pigs, dogs and several types of fowl. This was a pivotal decision. These first settlers found a land that contained almost no edible plants. With

The Last Battle for Supremacy

One of the more popular lookouts on O'ahu is the Pali Lookout on Hwy 61. The view from this precipice is simply glorious. As you soak in the beauty of the lookout, it's difficult to believe that this was the scene of one of O'ahu's bloodiest battles.

King Kamehameha was sweeping across the islands on his way to becoming the first man to conquer them all. When his fleet landed at Waikiki, he steadily drove the O'ahu army farther and farther up Nu'uanu Valley. Once they got to what is now the Pali Lookout, they had nowhere to go but down the cliffs. With the help of western arms and sailors (whom he had captured and then cunningly made into his advisers), Kamehameha's army was turning the battle into a rout. Once at this location some of the enemy tried to scramble down the cliffs. Around 400 others were driven off, their bodies smashing onto the rocks below. This would be the last major battle for conquest in Hawai'i. Kaua'i would eventually surrender, and Kamehameha would at last have his kingdom.

It's hard to imagine, but 50 generations of Hawaiian royalty were born at these sacred rocks in central O'ahu.

no land mammals other than the Hawaiian hoary bat, the first settlers subsisted on fish until their crops matured. From then on, they lived on fish, taro, sweet potatoes and other vegetables. Although we associate throw-net fishing with Hawai'i, this practice was introduced by Japanese immigrants much later. The ancient Hawaiians used fishhooks and spears, for the most part, or drove fish into a net already placed in the water. They also had domesticated animals, which were used as ritual foods or reserved for chiefs.

Little is known about the initial culture. Archeologists think that a second wave of colonists, probably from Tahiti, may have subdued these initial inhabitants around 1000 A.D. Some may have resisted and fled into the forest, creating the legend of the Menehune.

Today Menehune are always thought of as being small in stature. The legend initially referred to their social stature, but it evolved to mean that they were physically short and lived in the jungle away from the Hawaiians. (The ancient Hawaiians avoided living in the jungle, fearing that it held evil spirits, and instead stayed on the coastal plains.) The Menehune were purported to build fabulous structures, always in one night. Their numbers were said to be vast, as many as 500,000. It is interesting to note that in a census taken of Kaua'i around 1800, some 65 people from a remote valley identified themselves as Menehune.

The second wave of settlers probably swept through the islands from the south, pushing the first inhabitants ever north. On a tiny island northwest of Kaua'i, archeologists have found carvings, clearly not Hawaiian, that closely resemble Marquesan carvings, probably left by the doomed exiles.

This second culture was far more aggressive and developed into a highly class-conscious civilization. The society was governed by chiefs, called ali'i, who

If ancient Hawaiian legend is correct, this rock near Ka'ena Point called Leina-a-ka'uhane—
the leaping place for souls—is the last earthly sight that a Hawaiian soul will see
before he joins his ancestors.

established a long list of taboos called kapu. These kapu were designed to keep order, and the penalty for breaking one was usually death by strangulation, club or fire. If the violation was serious enough, the guilty party's family might also be killed. It was kapu, for instance, for your shadow to fall across the shadow of the ali'i. It was kapu to interrupt the chief if he was speaking. It was kapu to prepare men's food in the same container used for women's food. It was kapu for women to eat pork or bananas. It was kapu for men and women to eat together. It was kapu not to observe the days designated for the gods. Certain areas were kapu for fishing if stocks became depleted, allowing the area to replenish itself.

While harsh by our standards today, this system kept the order. Most ali'i were sensitive to the disturbance their presence caused and often ventured out-

side only at night, or a scout was sent ahead to warn people that an ali'i was on his way. All commoners were required to pay tribute to the ali'i in the form of food and other items. Human sacrifices were common, and war among rival chiefs the norm.

By the 1700s, the Hawaiians had lost all contact with Tahiti, and the Tahitians had lost all memory of Hawai'i. Hawaiian canoes had evolved into fishing and interisland canoes that were no longer capable of long ocean voyages. The Hawaiians had forgotten how to explore the world.

THE OUTSIDE WORLD DISCOVERS HAWAI'I

In January 1778 an event occurred that would forever change Hawai'i. Captain James Cook, who usually had a genius for predicting where to find islands, stumbled upon Hawai'i. He had not expected the islands to be here. He was on his way to Alaska on his third great voyage of discovery, this time to search for the Northwest Passage linking the Atlantic and Pacific oceans. Cook approached the shores of Waimea, Kaua'i, the night of Jan. 19, 1778.

The next morning Kaua'i's inhabitants awoke to a wondrous sight and thought they were being visited by gods. Rushing aboard to greet their visitors, the Kauaians were fascinated by what they saw: pointy-headed beings (the British wore tri-cornered hats) breathing fire (smoking pipes) and possessing a death-dealing instrument identified as a water squirter (guns). The amount of iron on the ship was incredible. (They had seen iron before in the form of nails on driftwood but never knew where it originated.)

Cook left Kaua'i and briefly explored Ni'ihau before heading north for his mission on February 2, 1778. When Cook returned to the islands in November after failing to find the Northwest Passage, he visited the Big Island of Hawai'i.

The Hawaiians had probably seen white men before. Local legend indicates that strange white people washed ashore on the Big Island sometime around the 1520s and integrated into society. This coincides with Spanish records of two ships lost in this part of the world in 1528. But a few weird-looking stragglers couldn't compare to the arrival of Cook's great ships and instruments.

Despite some recent rewriting of history, all evidence indicates that Cook, unlike some other exploring sea captains of his era, was a thoroughly decent man. Individuals need to be evaluated in the context of their time. Cook knew that his mere presence would have a profound impact on the cultures he encountered, but he also knew that change for these cultures was inevitable, with or without him. He tried, unsuccessfully, to keep the men known to be infected with vene-real diseases from mixing with local women, and he frequently flogged infected men who tried to sneak ashore at night. He was greatly distressed when a party he sent to Ni'ihau was forced to stay overnight due to high surf, knowing that his men might transmit diseases to the women (which they did).

Cook arrived on the Big Island at a time of much upheaval. The mo'i, or king, of the Big Island had been militarily spanked during an earlier attempt to invade Maui and was now looting and raising hell throughout the islands as retribution. Cook's arrival and his physical appearance (at 6-foot-4 he couldn't even stand up straight in his own quarters) almost guaranteed that the Hawaiians would think he was the god Lono, who was responsible for land fertility. Every year the ruling chiefs and their war god Ku went into abeyance, removing their power so that Lono could return to the land and make it fertile again, bringing back the spring rains. During this time all public works stopped, and the land was left alone. At the end of this *makahiki* season people would again seize the land from Lono so they could grow crops and otherwise make a living upon it. Cook arrived at the beginning of the makahiki, and the Hawaiians naturally thought *he* was the god Lono coming to make the land fertile. Cook even sailed into Kealakekua Bay, *exactly* where the legend predicted Lono would arrive.

The Hawaiians went to great lengths to please their "god." All manner of supplies were made available. Eventually they became suspicious of the visitors. If they were gods, why did they accept the Hawaiian women? And if they were gods, why did one of them die?

Cook left at the right time. The British had used up the Hawaiians' hospitality (not to mention their supplies). But shortly after leaving the Big Island, the ship broke a mast, making it necessary to return to Kealakekua Bay for repairs. As they sailed back into the bay, the Hawaiians were nowhere to be seen. A chief had declared the area kapu to help replenish it. When Cook finally found the Hawaiians, they were polite but wary. *Why are you back? Didn't we please you enough already? What do you want now?*

As repair of the mast continued, things began to get tense. Eventually the Hawaiians stole a British rowboat (for the nails), and the normally calm Cook blew his cork. On the morning of Feb. 14, 1779, he went ashore to trick the chief into coming aboard his ship, where he planned to hold the chief hostage until the rowboat was returned. As Cook and the chief were heading to the water, the chief's wife begged the chief not to go.

By now thousands of Hawaiians were crowding around Cook, and he ordered a retreat. A shot was heard from the other side of the bay, and someone shouted that the Englishmen had killed an important chief. A shielded warrior with a dagger came at Cook, who fired his pistol (loaded with small shot). The shield stopped the small shot, and the Hawaiians were emboldened. Other shots were fired. Standing in knee-deep water, Cook turned to call for a ceasefire and was struck in the head from behind with a club, then stabbed. Dozens of other Hawaiians pounced on him, stabbing his body repeatedly. The greatest explorer the world had ever known was dead at age 50 in a petty skirmish over a stolen rowboat.

KAMEHAMEHA THE GREAT

The most powerful and influential king in Hawaiian history lived during the time of Captain Cook and was born on the Big Island around 1758. Until his rule, the Hawaiian chain had never been ruled by a single person. He was the first to "unite" (i.e., conquer) all the islands.

Kamehameha was an extraordinary man by any standard. He possessed Herculean strength, a brilliant mind and boundless ambition. He was marked for death before he was even born. When Kamehameha's mother was pregnant with him, she developed a strange and overpowering craving—she wanted to *eat* the eyeball of a chief. The king of the Big Island, mindful of the rumor that the unborn child's real father was his bitter enemy, the king of Maui, asked his advisers to interpret. Their conclusion was unanimous: The child would grow to be a rebel, a killer of chiefs. The king decided that the child must die as soon as he was born, but the baby was instead whisked away to a remote valley to be raised.

In Hawaiian society, your role in life was governed by what class you were born into. The Hawaiians believed that breeding among family members produced superior offspring (except for the genetic misfortunates who were killed at birth), and the highest chiefs came from brother/sister combinations. Kamehameha was not of the highest class (his parents were merely cousins), so his future as a chief would not come easily.

As a young man, Kamehameha was impressed by his experience with Captain Cook. He was among the small group that stayed overnight on Cook's ship during Cook's first pass by of Maui. (Kamehameha was on Maui valiantly fighting a battle in which his side was getting badly whupped.) Kamehameha recognized that his world had forever changed, and he shrewdly used the knowledge and technology of westerners to his advantage.

Kamehameha participated in numerous battles. His side lost many of the early ones, but he learned from his mistakes and developed into a cunning tactician. When he finally consolidated his rule over the Big Island (by luring his enemy to be the inaugural sacrifice of a new temple), he fixed his sights on the entire chain. In the 1790s his large company of troops, armed with some western armaments and advisors, swept across Maui, Moloka'i, Lana'i and O'ahu. After some delays in taking Kaua'i, the last of the holdouts, its king finally acquiesced to the inevitable and Kamehameha became the first ruler of all the islands. He spent his final years governing the islands peacefully from his Big Island capital and died in 1819.

MODERN HAWAI'I

During the 19th century, Hawai'i's character changed dramatically. Businessmen from all over the world came here to exploit Hawai'i's sandalwood, whales, land and people. Hawai'i's leaders, for their part, actively participated in these ventures and took a piece of much of the action for themselves. Workers were brought from many parts of the world, changing the racial makeup of the

O'ahu is blessed with more offshore islets than all the other Hawaiian islands combined.

islands. Government corruption became the order of the day, and everyone seemed to be profiting, except the Hawaiian commoner. By the time Queen Lili'uokalani lost her throne to a group of American businessmen in 1893, Hawai'i had become directionless. It barely resembled the Hawai'i Captain Cook had encountered in the previous century. The kapu system had been abolished by the Hawaiians shortly after the death of Kamehameha the Great. The "Great Mahele," begun in 1848, had changed the relationship Hawaiians had with the land. Large tracts of land were sold by the Hawaiian government to royalty, government officials, commoners and foreigners, effectively stripping many Hawaiians of land they had lived on for generations.

The United States recognized the Republic of Hawai'i in 1894 with Sanford Dole as its president. It was annexed in 1898 and became an official territory in 1900. During the 19th and 20th centuries, sugar established itself as king. Pineapple was also a major crop in the islands, with the island of Lana'i purchased in its entirety for the purpose of growing pineapple.

As the 20th century rolled on, Hawaiian sugar and pineapple workers found themselves in a lofty position—they became the highest paid workers for these crops in the world. As land prices rose and competition from other parts of the world increased, sugar and pineapple became less and less profitable. Today, these crops no longer hold the position they once had. The "pineapple island" of Lana'i has shifted away from pineapple growing and is focused on tourism. And the sugar era officially ended in Hawai'i with the demise of the last plantation on Maui at the end of 2016.

The story of Hawai'i is not a story of good versus evil. Nearly everyone shares in the blame for what happened to the Hawaiian people and their culture. Westerners certainly saw Hawai'i as a potential bonanza and easily exploitable. They knew what buttons to push and pushed them well. But the Hawaiians, for their part, were in a state of flux. The mere presence of westerners seemed to bring to the surface a discontent, or at least a weakness, with their system that had been lingering just below the surface.

In fact, in 1794, a mere 16 years after first encountering westerners and under no military duress from the West, Kamehameha the Great *volunteered* to cede his island over to Great Britain. He was hungry for western arms so he could defeat his neighbor island opponents. He even declared that as of that day, they were no longer people of Hawai'i, but rather people of Britain. (Britain declined the offer.) And in 1819, immediately after the death of the strong-willed Kamehameha, the Hawaiians, of their own accord, overthrew their own religion, dumped the kapu system and denied their gods. This was *before* any western missionaries ever came to Hawai'i.

Nonetheless, Hawai'i today is once again seeking guidance from her heritage. The echoes of the past seem to be getting louder with time, rather than diminishing. Interest in the Hawaiian language and culture is at a level not seen in many decades. All of us who live here are very aware of the issues and the complexities involved, but there is little agreement about where it will lead. As a result, you will be exposed to a more "Hawaiian" Hawai'i than those who might have visited the state a generation or two ago. This is an interesting time in Hawai'i. Enjoy it as observers, and savor the flavor of the islands.

A newbie surfer realizes that the learning curve is bit steeper than he thought...

GETTING HERE

In order to get to the islands, you've got to fly here. While this may sound painfully obvious, many people contemplate cruises to the islands. But remember—there isn't a single spec of land between the west coast and Hawai'i. And 2,500 miles of open water is a pretty monotonous stretch to cover.

When planning your trip a travel agent can be helpful, though that method is becoming less and less common. Most people do most of their planning using the internet. Another option is our smartphone app, *Hawaii Revealed*, which has reviews of every resort as well as powerful filters that let you find the resort that has all the features that are important to you. You can get it from the iTunes store or Google Play and the *Where to Stay* section is free.

Also there are large wholesalers that can get you airfare, hotel and a rental car, often cheaper than you can get airfare on your own. **Pleasant Holidays** (800-742-9244) provides complete package tours.

When you pick your travel source, shop around—the differences can be dramatic. A good package can make the difference between affording a *one-week* vacation and a *two-week* vacation.

All passengers arriving on O'ahu land at Honolulu International Airport. If you're going to any of the neighbor islands, interisland flights are done by **Hawaiian** (800-367-5320) and **Mokulele** (866-260-7070).

WHAT TO BRING

This list may assist you in planning what to bring. Obviously you might not bring everything on the list, but it might help you think of a few things you may otherwise overlook:

- Water-resistant sunscreen (SPF 30 or higher)
- Two bathing suits
- Shoes—flip-flops, trashable sneakers, water shoes, hiking shoes
- Mask, snorkel and fins
- Camera with lots of storage
- Junk clothes for bikes, hiking, etc.
- Light rain jacket and sweatshirt or light coat for some occasions
- Mosquito repellent for some hikes (Those with DEET seem to work the longest)
- Shorts and other cool clothing
- Hiking sticks (carbide-tipped ones work best here)
- Cheap, simple backpack—handy even if you're not backpacking
- Hat or cap for sun protection

If you're looking to spend the day at a beach, don't feel compelled to bring everything with you from the mainland.

Hawai'i Beach Time (808-585-1474) rents everything beachy you can think of—from umbrellas to kayaks, beach chairs, surfboards, hammocks, etc. And their prices are fairly reasonable.

GETTING AROUND
Rental Cars

Rental car prices in Hawai'i *can be* (but aren't always) cheaper than almost anywhere else in the country, and the competition is ferocious. O'ahu is the only major Hawaiian island where a sizeable number of visitors stay *without* renting a car. (Waikiki is small and walkable, and many activity companies will shuttle you to their locations, usually for an added fee.) Plus, **Uber** and **Lyft** now both have a large enough presence on O'ahu that you can rely on them to get a ride when you need it, at least around Waikiki and Honolulu, that is. (The same can't be said of the neighbor islands—yet.)

While it's true that you *might* not need a rental if you don't plan to leave Waikiki or intend to let activity companies shuttle

Whether you are an old school longboarder or a young buck on a tiny stick, always take the time to study the ocean before taking the plunge.

you to their offerings, we think it's a big mistake if you don't have a rental car for at least *part* of your stay. Even if you're planning to take tour buses or the county bus, many of the glorious sights described in the driving tours will be unavailable to you. (And it's definitely cheaper to get a rental car than take an Uber to the north shore.) If you're trying to save money and spend much of your trip in Waikiki, get a rental car for at least some *part* of your trip. You won't regret it. Also, make *sure* you don't accidentally get an electronic key wet with salt water. It'll kill the key and kill your budget with the *obscene* cost of replacing it.

Avis, Hertz, National, Dollar, Enterprise and Budget are the most convenient rental car companies due to their return locations. Other companies, such as Alamo, are *outside* the airport. There's a gas station at the airport right before the car rental return, and they charge the usual confiscatory airport prices.

If you are 21 to 24 years of age, most companies will rent to you, but you'll pay about $25 extra for the crime of being young and reckless. If you're under 21, **VIP** and **Paradise** will rent to those 18 and older.

Many hotels, condos and rental agents offer excellent room/car packages. Find out from your hotel or travel agent if one is available.

Below is a list of rental car companies. All the big companies have desks at the airport and in Waikiki. **Discount Hawai'i Car Rental** (800-292-1930) is a Canadian broker that has good prices from the major companies and can also get unusual vehicles and exotic cars.

The Big Guys
Alamo (877) 222-9075
Avis (800) 321-3712

Budget (800) 527-0700
Dollar (800) 800-4000
Enterprise (800) 261-7331
Hertz (800) 654-3131
National (877) 222-9058
Thrifty (800) 367-5238

The Little Guys
JN Rentals (808) 831-2724
Paradise Rent-A-Car (808) 946-7777
VIP (808) 922-4605

4-Wheel Drive
On Kaua'i and especially the Big Island we strongly recommended getting a 4WD vehicle, but you don't need one on O'ahu. (Even if you don't mind the extra cost to rent one, there's just about nowhere to take advantage of a 4x4's capabilities.) If you want to splurge, spring for a convertible instead. They can be fun.

Taxis & Shuttles
If you don't want a rental car (or will be renting one in Waikiki later during your stay), there are plenty of taxi companies around the island. Their meter rates are set. They charge around $35 from the airport to Waikiki. If you call them in advance (instead of hailing them), you can usually get a cheaper rate. For instance, **O'ahu Airport Express** (808-352-1818) charges about $35 for up to four people to get your group into Waikiki. **Aloha 'Aina Cab** (808-944-3400) charges about $27 *for up to four people*. Lastly, **Waikiki Shuttle** (808-544-0004) will take you to Waikiki for $12 per person. Once in Waikiki, cabs can easily be hailed.

Motorcycles
If you think riding a hog is something you do at a lu'au, you may want to skip this section. There's *something* about Harleys. Maybe it's the sound, or maybe

the looks. But riding a Harley-Davidson around Oʻahu is a blast. If you want to rent one to experience things on your own (freedom, after all, is what hogs are all about), you can get them and other motorcycles from these companies:

Paradise Rent-A-Car (808-946-7777) located at 1837 Ala Moana Blvd. has Harleys starting at $129 per day.

Diamond Head Harley (808-791-0870) in Waikiki and **Cycle City Harley** (808-377-4690) near the airport and Nimitz Hwy rent them for $139–$179 per day.

Other two-wheeled options include: **Hawaiian Style Rentals** (808-946-6733) at 2556 Lemon Road rents mopeds from $40–$55, depending on the model.

Big Kahuna (808-924-2736) at 407 Seaside Ave. rents motorcycles for $90–$190 per day. (The latter reflects their top-end Harley.) Mopeds are $40 per day.

Adventure on 2 Wheels (808-944-3131) at 1946 Ala Moana has mopeds for $40 per day or $35 for eight hours.

Be sure to check out the bike before you zoom off. We've seen some pretty bald tires and snotty attitudes at some of these places. We've also had unhappy e-mails in the past from readers who've rented from Big Kahuna and Adventure on 2 Wheels. Small, single passenger scooter rentals don't require a motorcycle license.

Exotic Cars

Oʻahu has lots of opportunities to rent a flashy ride. Ferraris, Vipers, 'Vettes, Porsches and other sexy autos can be had—for the right price. You're looking at around $400 for a Corvette, $1,700 for a Ferrari, etc. That's *per day!* Bear in mind that there are no good opportunities to open them up—we have no empty straightaways on which to throttle these puppies—but if you just want to experience the thrill of driving a fantasy car, and you have a wad burning a hole in your pocket, give it a shot.

Hawaiʻi Luxury Car Rentals (808-222-2277) operates out of a not-so-luxurious gas station at 2025 Kalakaua Ave. They require hefty credit card deposits. If you're 21–24 years old, it'll cost you more.

JN Exotics (808-457-1070) has a luxurious showroom at 888 Kapiolani Blvd. They rent Maserati, Bentley and Ferrari. For deposit they require the pink slip to your soul, and you'll have to pledge your firstborn male child.

Driving Around Oʻahu

Oʻahu has some of the most confusing roads and highways you'll find anywhere in the United States. Roads change names randomly and with no warning, leaving you confused as to where you actually are. Let's use an example. Kamehameha Highway (a major island highway) is also called Hwy 99... until it changes its name to Hwy 80 where Hwy 99 changes to Wilikina Drive, then Kamahanui Road. Then Kamehameha Highway (also called Kam Hwy) becomes Hwy 99 again, then Hwy 83, then Hwy 830 (*if* you remember to turn left at the Hygienic Store in Kahaluʻu), then Hwy 83 again. All this for *one* highway. Or consider Farrington Highway. Look on a map, and Farrington Highway wraps around the western tip. Oh, except for the 6 miles around the tip where it doesn't actually exist. You'll have to go around via Hwy 99... or is it Kamehameha Highway?

Plus when you're on our freeways, you'll find it maddening when you discover that you can often get *off* a freeway... but not back *on* it. Or sometimes you can only get on it by driving in the *opposite* direction you want to go.

While making our maps, we've repeatedly driven the roads with the computer files literally in our laps and tried to mark things as you're likely to see them, not necessarily by their official names. At times we've left off confusing and conflicting names. Nonetheless, though we've gone to considerable effort to make the maps as easy to read as possible, you *will* get confused and lost if you drive around long enough. Hey, don't blame us. We just make the maps; we didn't devise this embarrassing road system.

Remember, Honolulu is a big city, and you *won't* be the only one trying to get somewhere. Although traffic can be bad anywhere at any time, the **basic traffic pattern** is this: *Into* Waikiki and Honolulu from all points in the morning, and *away* from Waikiki and Honolulu to all points in the afternoon. H-1 is backed up pretty often, especially eastbound where H-1 and Hwy 78 meet (called the *Middle Street Merge*). But heavy traffic can occur anywhere and any time of the day.

If you're heading west on H-1, locals call that being *'Ewa-bound*. If you're heading east, it's *Koko Head-bound*.

You may notice construction of a **light rail** going on during your visit. They started work in 2011 with the *frantically* paced goal of being completed in 2025. Yeah, that's a *long* time to build a 20-mile long train using old school steel-on-steel technology. But this is Hawai'i, and you'd be *horrified* to see how things like this get done here. And speaking of horrified, the price tag is (this is not a typo) *$10 billion* and expected to go up. That's double the original estimate and a mind-numbing $100,000 *per foot*. Just wanted to let you know where a chunk of your hotel tax is going.

Seat belt and **child restraint** use are required by law, and the police will pull you over for this alone. It's also illegal for

Some of the things that we consider quintessentially Hawaiian, like coconut trees, were actually imported by Hawai'i's first settlers.

drivers to use a **cell phone** without a headset. Open roads and frequently changing speed limits make it easy to accidentally speed here. Sobriety checkpoints are not an uncommon police tactic on O'ahu.

It's best not to leave anything valuable in your car. **Car break-ins** can be a problem here. Thieving scum looking for anything of value regularly hit rental cars. When we park at a beach, hiking trail or any other place frequented by visitors, we take all valuables with us, leave the windows up, and leave the doors *unlocked*. (Just in case someone is curious enough about the inside to smash a window.) There are plenty of stories about people walking 100 feet to a beach, coming back to their car, and finding that their brand new video camera has walked away. And don't be gullible enough to think that trunks are safe. Someone who sees you put something in your trunk can probably get at it faster than you can with your key.

Buses

O'ahu is the only Hawaiian island with a truly great bus system, cleverly called **TheBus** (808-848-5555). About 30 percent of visitors use the bus system, according to the state. You'll find bus schedules sprinkled in kiosks all around Waikiki. It's $2.75 for a one-way fare (does not include any transfers), or $5.50 for an all-day pass. Ask the driver for the all-day pass before putting your money in the box. It's $70 for a monthly pass.

Bus #8 is the one that circles Waikiki and Ala Moana Shopping Center (there's one every 10 minutes), and we've shown the route on the Waikiki map on page 49. Even if you have a rental car, it might be tempting to jump on the old #8 bus to take you to the other end of Waikiki instead of worrying about parking.

Carry-on baggage is allowed, but, regulations state, "Baggage or carry-on items that will not be admitted on the bus shall include any large, bulky, dangerous or offensive article that may cause harm or discomfort to any passenger." *So there.*

The **Waikiki Trolley** (808-593-2822), on the other hand, is ridiculously over-priced at $45 per person per day, but their *online* price of $70 *per week* is a decent deal and can be combined for discounts on some attractions.

Bikes

Biki (aka Bikeshare Hawai'i) has single-speed bikes strewn around Waikiki and Honolulu. Since this a pretty flat area, riding is pretty easy and convenient. No worrying about parking. No waiting for buses. The drawback is if you have stuff to carry, you'll need a backpack since their "luggage carrier" is pretty small. Plus, you might take a bike to a location one way, only to find that there's no bike available for your return trip. But overall, this feels like a good fit for Waikiki and is a great way to stretch your biking legs. They have lots of pricing structures, from a single ride for $3.50 to $15 for unlimited 30-minute rides for a month and others. They have a map of all the bike locations at https://gobiki.org/map-of-biki-stops/.

GETTING MARRIED ON O'AHU

Hawai'i, with its exotic beauty and nearly perfect weather, is one of the most popular wedding and honeymoon destinations in the world. And sunsets along the leeward side can provide a breath-taking backdrop for your ceremony.

License requirements in Hawai'i are simple. You both must apply to the health department (online is OK) and pay the $65. Your license will be good for 30 days. You'll have to present ID in person

Rainfall Map

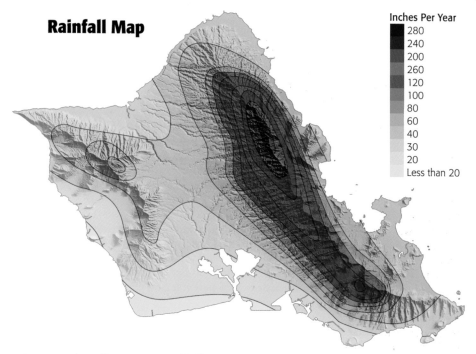

Inches Per Year
- 280
- 240
- 200
- 260
- 120
- 100
- 80
- 60
- 40
- 30
- 20
- Less than 20

to a marriage license agent. (Call 808-586-4544.)

All major resorts can provide planners to assist you with wedding details. They have facilities and sites on their properties along with experienced staff to make the day go smoothly. Resorts can provide chapels, gazebos, waterfalls and lush gardens for your ceremony. Some of the more popular resorts in Waikiki are the Hilton Hawaiian Village, the Halekulani, the Royal Hawaiian and the Moana Surfrider. If you prefer a resort outside Waikiki, consider the Kahala Hotel & Resort or Turtle Bay Resort. Aulani Disney Resort has fairytale weddings that they claim will allow you to live happily ever after. (Prenups are extra.)

There are also many independent coordinators with years of experience helping couples with their wedding plans. Be sure that you and you planner are clear about your budgetary limits and what you want during your wedding day. Also be certain about the amount of assistance you will

receive before the ceremony, so you can relax and enjoy your wedding day.

Be aware of holidays, the popularity of Valentine's Day and the month of June for weddings. By booking far enough in advance, you should be able to arrange a wedding during one of these busy times.

Always be sure there is a backup plan in case it rains. Beaches are public, so you will have other beachgoers present during your ceremony. If you're considering using a state or county park, be sure you have met their permit requirements.

Looking for a different but very Hawaiian reception? Consider holding it on one of the dinner cruises or joining in with one of the island's lu'au (remember that the Polynesian Cultural Center lu'au does not permit alcohol).

WEATHER

One of the biggest worries people have when planning their trip to the tropics is the weather. Will it rain? Is it going to be too hot? What about hurricanes?

Let's deal with the last one first. There have been only three recorded hurricanes in Hawai'i in the past 200 years. One in the 1950s, one in the '80s and *'Iniki* on Sept. 11, 1992, clobbering Kaua'i. None have hit O'ahu, so you should probably spend your precious worry energy elsewhere.

As for rain, it works like this: The prevailing winds (called trade winds) come from the northeast, bringing their moisture with them. As the air hits the Ko'olau mountains, it rises, cools and condenses into clouds and rain. So the mountains and shoreline facing the northeast, called the **windward side**, get the lion's share of the rain. Look at the rain graphic, and it will make more sense. Often by mid-morning, the rising, cooling air causes clouds to form in the mountains, giving them an exotic, mystical look.

Once the air has had its moisture wrung out, it sinks and warms on the southwest side (called the **leeward side**) and often has minimal rain potential. So areas like Waikiki get little rain. The exception is when we get winds from the south or southwest—called Kona winds—where the rain pattern is reversed. These Kona winds only happen about 5–10 percent of the time, most often in the winter.

Waikiki has an embarrassingly equable climate. The average high is 84 °F, and it has *never* gotten above 95 °F since thermometers have been in the islands. Waikiki gets only 20 inches of rain per year, and when it does rain, it's often in the form of short, intense showers.

Average **humidity** ranges from 65–75 percent. And **ocean temperatures** go from 75 °F in February to about 80 °F in September.

GEOGRAPHY

The different Hawaiian islands have different geographic infrastructures. Kaua'i is made up of one giant extinct volcano. Maui has two (one of them still

In the tropics, beautiful weather doesn't always mean sunny skies.

barely alive). The Big Island lives up to its name, consisting of a staggering five volcanoes, only one of which is extinct (though only two of them are active enough for us to see in our lifetime). On O'ahu, it took two now-extinct volcanoes to create this paradise. (The second one is *probably* extinct. See page 61 for more.) **Wai'anae** in the west poked above the water 2.2 million years ago, followed a million years later by its younger sibling, **Ko'olau**, in the east. Ko'olau (called the Ko'olau Mountains locally, even though it's really only one long mountain) is shorter—peaking at 3,150 feet, but it's over 30 miles long. What's most impressive is that it's only half the original mountain. The other half has been erased by ceaseless erosion. The top of the older volcano, Wai'anae, is called Mount Ka'ala and towers 4,025 feet above the ocean.

WHERE SHOULD I STAY?

The vast majority of visitors to O'ahu stay in Waikiki. It's where you'll find the lion's share of all resorts. It's on the world famous Waikiki Beach. It's the home of a zillion restaurants. And it's where the government originally decided they wanted visitors to stay. Yeah, there are a couple of exceptions. One resort out in Turtle Bay near the northern tip of the island. It's a nice place on a pretty cove, but you are a captive of the resort because there are few dining options nearby (mostly in Kahuku). And east of Waikiki is the Kohala Resort. It's also by itself and on a nice beach. It's quiet and pricey and there are additional restaurants not too far away.

Then back in the mid 80s, a local developer backed by a Japanese investor decided to build a new resort area near the southwest corner of the island, calling it Ko Olina. They built four *incredible* manmade lagoons with white sand beaches and a marina and had plans to build a number of resorts. But when the Japanese economy tanked in the late 80s, their money dried up. At the turn of the century new investors resumed building, and today you have several huge, high end resorts around those lagoons, and it's not a bad alternative to Waikiki if you want less bustle.

Finally, you have B&Bs and vacation rentals. Airbnb and HomeAway/VRBO have lots of choices available online.

Detailed Resort & Condo Reviews

O'ahu has it all, accommodations-wise, and as you consider where you want to stay—hotel or condo, by the beach or with a mountain view—you might find it intimidating to wade through the vast number of choices.

So here's what we did. We have *personally reviewed* every resort on O'ahu. We have *exhaustively* cataloged all the amenities, formed opinions on what different properties have to offer and created comprehensive reviews. Sure, you can go online and look at reviews by people who have been to one or maybe two resorts. But none of those sources knows them all and can compare one to the other.

Because this information is so exhaustive, there isn't enough room in our book to include it all. So we have put all of our reviews in our smartphone app, *Hawaii Revealed,* and made that information available *for free.* There you can sort and sift through the resorts in a matter of minutes using our special filters.

Want to book a place to stay and have certain criteria? *I want a hotel in Waikiki that is oceanfront, has a children's pool, fitness room, is good for families and has an outdoor lanai. Oh, and takes service animals.* With the filters in our app, you can cut through the 87 or so resorts and get to exactly what you want, read our in-depth and brutally honest review, and even make a reservation. How's *that* for cutting through the noise?

HAZARDS
The Sun

The hazard that by far affects the most people (excluding the accommodations tax) is the sun. O'ahu, at 21 degrees latitude, receives sunlight more directly than anywhere on the mainland. (The more overhead the sunlight, the less atmosphere it filters through.) If you want to enjoy your *entire* vacation, make sure that you wear a strong sunscreen. We recommend a water-resistant sunscreen with at least an SPF of 30. We use lotions when hiking, and the gel types like Bullfrog when going in the water (because they stay on better). Many visitors who get burned do so while snorkeling. You won't feel it coming because of the water. We *strongly* suggest you wear a T-shirt while snorkeling, or you may get a nasty surprise.

Try to avoid the sun between 11 a.m. and 2 p.m. when the sun's rays are particularly strong. If you are fair-skinned or unaccustomed to the sun and want to soak up some rays, 15–20 minutes per side is all you should consider the first day. You can increase it a bit each day. *Beware of the fact that our breezes will hide the symptoms of a burn until it's too late.* You might find that trying to get your tan as golden as possible isn't worth it. Tropical suntans are notoriously short-lived, whereas you are sure to remember a bad burn far longer. If, after all our warnings, you *still* get burned, aloe vera gel works well to relieve the pain. Some come with lidocaine in them. Some resorts even have aloe plants on the grounds. Peel the skin off a section and

make several crisscross cuts in the meat, then rub the plant on your skin. *Oooo,* it'll feel so good!

Water Hazards

The most serious water hazard is the surf. Though more calm in the summer and on the leeward side, high surf can be found anywhere on the island at any time of the year. The sad fact is that more people drown in Hawai'i each year than anywhere else in the country. This isn't said to keep you from enjoying the ocean, but rather to instill in you a healthy respect for Hawaiian waters. See **Beach Safety** on page 117 for more information on this. For a current surf report call 808-973-4383. Even hardened watermen call for a surf forecast before planning their day.

Ocean Critters

Hawaiian marine life, for the most part, is quite friendly. There are, however, a few notable exceptions. Below is a list of some critters that you should be aware of. This is not to frighten you out of the water. The odds are overwhelming that you won't have any trouble with any of the beasties listed below. But should you encounter one, this information should be of some help.

Sharks—Hawai'i does have sharks. Most are the essentially harmless white-tipped reef sharks, plus the occasional hammerhead or tiger shark. Contrary to what most people think, sharks are in every ocean and don't pose the level of danger people attribute to them. In the past 25 years, there have been so few documented shark attacks off O'ahu—less than one per year—that they haven't been able to create a statistical average. (But the state as a whole had an unusually large number in 2013—14 in all.) When one *does* occur, it's usually tigers attacking surfers. Considering the number of people who swam in our waters during that time, you are statistically more likely to get mauled by a hungry timeshare salesman than be bitten by a shark. If you do happen to come upon a shark, however, swim away slowly. This kind of movement doesn't interest them. *Don't* splash about rapidly. By doing this you are imitating a fish in distress, and you don't want to do that. The one kind of water you want to avoid is murky water, such as that found in river mouths. Most shark attacks occur in murky water at dawn or dusk since sharks are basically cowards who like to sneak up on their prey. In general, don't go around worrying about sharks. *Any* animal can be threatening.

Portuguese Man-of-War—These are related to jellyfish but are unable to

swim. They are instead propelled by a small sail and are at the mercy of the wind. Though small, they are capable of inflicting a painful sting. This occurs when the long, trailing tentacles are touched, triggering hundreds of thousands of spring-loaded stingers, called nematocysts, which inject venom. The resulting burning sensation is usually very unpleasant but not fatal. Fortunately, the Portuguese man-of-war is not a common visitor to most island beaches. When they *do* come ashore, however, they usually do so in large numbers, jostled by a strong onshore wind usually at northeast-facing beaches. If you see them on the beach, don't go in the water. If you do get stung, immediately remove the tentacles with a gloved hand, stick or whatever is handy. Rinse thoroughly with salt or fresh water to remove any adhering nematocysts. Then apply ice for pain control. If the condition worsens, see a doctor. The old treatments of vinegar or baking soda are no longer recommended. The folk cure is urine, and for half the population, it comes with a handy applicator, but you might look pretty silly applying it.

Box Jellyfish—O'ahu is the only island in the chain where these guys are a problem. Once a month, nine or ten days after the full moon, box jellyfish approach the shoreline, especially at leeward beaches, such as Ala Moana, Waikiki and Hanauma Bay, and will sting anything that comes in contact with them. These are *not* the same notorious box jellyfish that kill people in Australia. Although you're certainly *allowed* to swim during that time, we personally choose not to and suggest you do the same. Sting treatments are similar to those for man-of-war, but vinegar *is* recommended for box jellyfish stings.

Sea Urchins—These are like living pin cushions. If you step on one or accidentally grab one, remove as much of the spine as possible with tweezers. See a physician if necessary.

Coral—Coral skeletons are very sharp and, since the skeleton is overlaid by millions of living coral polyps, a scrape can leave proteinaceous matter in the wound, causing infection. This is why coral cuts are frustratingly slow to heal. Immediate cleaning and disinfecting of coral cuts should speed up healing time. We don't have fire coral around Hawai'i.

Sea Anemones—Related to the jellyfish, these also have stingers and are usually found attached to rocks or coral. It's best not to touch them with your bare hands. Treatment for a sting is similar to that for Portuguese man-of-war.

Bugs

Though we're devoid of the myriad hideous buggies found in other parts of the world, there are a few evil critters brought here from elsewhere that you should know about. The worst are **centipedes**. They can get to be six or more inches long and are aggressive predators. They shouldn't be messed with. You'll probably never see one, but if you get stung, even by a baby, the pain can range from a bad bee sting to a moderate gunshot blast. Some local doctors say the only cure is to stay drunk for three days. Others say to use meat tenderizer instead of a brain tenderizer.

Cane spiders are big, dark and look horrifying, but they're not poisonous. (But they seem to *think* they are. I've had *them* chase *me* across the room when *I* had the broom in my hand.) We *don't* have no-see-ums, those irritating sand fleas common in the South Pacific and Caribbean.

Mosquitoes were unknown in the islands until the first stowaways arrived on Maui on the *Wellington* in 1826. Since then they have thrived. A good mosquito repellent containing deet will come in handy, especially if you plan to go hiking. Those with deet seem to work best. Forget the guidebooks that tell you to take vitamin B^{12} to keep mosquitoes away; it just gives the little critters a healthier diet. If you find one dive-bombing you at night in your room and you have an overhead fan, turn it on to help keep them away. **Bees** and **wasps** are more common on the drier leeward side of the island. Usually, the only way you'll get stung is if you run *into* or step *onto*

one. If you rent a motorcycle, beware; I received my first bee sting while singing *Come Sail Away* on a motorcycle. A bee sting in the mouth can definitely ruin one of your precious vacation days.

Regarding **cockroaches**, there's good news and bad news. The bad news is that here, some are bigger than your thumb and can fly. The good news is that you probably won't see one. One of their predators is the **gecko**. This small, lizard-like creature makes a surprisingly loud chirp at night. They are cute and considered good luck in the islands (probably 'cause they eat mosquitoes and roaches).

Snakes

There are no snakes in Hawai'i (other than some reporters). There is concern that the brown tree snake might have made its way onto the islands from Guam. Although mostly harmless to humans, these snakes can spell extinction for native birds. Government officials aren't allowed to tell you this, but we will: If you ever see one anywhere in Hawai'i, please kill it and contact the Pest Hotline at 808-643-7378. At the very least, call them immediately. The entire bird population of Hawai'i will be grateful.

Swimming in Streams

There are opportunities on O'ahu to swim in streams and under waterfalls. It's the fulfillment of a fantasy for many people. But there are several hazards you need to know about.

Leptospirosis is a bacteria that is found in some of Hawai'i's freshwater. It is transmitted from animal urine and can enter the body through open cuts, eyes and by drinking. Numbers are hard to come by, but around 100 people a year in Hawai'i are diagnosed with the bacteria, which is treated with antibiotics if caught relatively early. You should avoid swimming in streams if you have open cuts, and treat all water found in nature with treatment pills before drinking. (Many filters are ineffective for lepto.)

While swimming in freshwater streams, try to use your arms as much as possible. Kicking an unseen rock is easier than you think. Also, consider wearing water shoes while in streams. These water-friendly wonders are available all over O'ahu and allow you to walk in water while still protecting your feet.

Though rare, **flash floods** can occur in any freshwater stream anywhere in the world, even paradise. Be alert for them.

Lastly, remember while lingering under waterfalls that not everything that comes over the top will be as soft as water. Rocks coming down from above could definitely shatter the moment—among other things.

Dehydration

Bring and drink lots of water when you are out and about, especially when you are hiking. Dehydration sneaks up on people. By the time you are thirsty, you're already dehydrated. It's a good idea to take water with you in the car at all times. Our weather is almost certainly different from what you left behind, and you will probably find yourself thirstier than usual. Just fill a bottle or two before you leave in the morning and *suck 'em up* (as we say here) all day.

Pigs

We're not referring to your dining choices. We mean the wild ones you may encounter on a hiking trail. Generally, pigs will avoid you before you ever see them. If you happen to come upon any piglets and accidentally get between them and their mother, immediately bark like

From the air, Kane'ohe Bay's odd-looking reefs appear to be more like giant amoeba than coral.

Don't let anyone tell you there is nothing left to discover on O'ahu. Surprises, such as this natural infinity pool at a place we call Secluded Cove is one example.

a big dog. Wild pigs are conditioned to run from local dogs (and their hunter masters), and Momma will leave her kids faster than you can say, "Pass the bacon."

Traffic

Oh, yeah. Traffic can be a big problem here, especially in Honolulu. See *Driving Around O'ahu* on page 24 for more on this.

Grocery Stores

A decided hazard. Restaurants are expensive, but don't think you'll get off cheap in grocery stores. Though you'll certainly save money cooking your own food if your room has kitchen facilities, a trip to the store here can be startling. Phrases like *they charge how much for milk?* echo throughout the stores. Even items such as pineapples—*grown on this island!*—may cost more here than the ones jetted to you on the mainland. Go figure.

If you're stocking up, consider buying groceries at Costco (808-526-6103) west of Waikiki on Alakawa Street between Dillingham Boulevard and Nimitz Highway, or the massive 300,000-square-foot, 24-hour Walmart/Sam's Club (808-955-8441) just outside of Waikiki on Keeaumoku Street near Ala Moana Shopping Center. Both require memberships.

In Waikiki, the only real grocery store is the Food Pantry (808-923-9831) on Kuhio Avenue at Walina Street. Prices will obviously be higher than other grocery stores, but if you have a kitchen in your room, it's very convenient.

TRAVELING WITH CHILDREN (KEIKI)

Should we have put this under *Hazards*? If you're coming to Hawai'i and bringing the keiki (kids), O'ahu has more kid-oriented activities than any of the Hawaiian islands—some of 'em cheap, some of 'em at *hurt-me* prices.

Hawai'i Children's Discovery Center (808-524-5437) is at 111 Ohe St. It's $12 general admission. Basically, kids up to about 9 will love the interactive exhibits rich with costumes, international cultures, various occupations and science. Kids 10 and up might get antsy. They have an unusually good gift shop.

The *Attractions* chapter is the best place to look for keiki-friendly places. Check out our reviews of Wet 'n' Wild Hawai'i, Sea Life Park, Waikiki Aquarium, Honolulu Zoo and Hawaiian Railway Society.

Hawai'i Pirate Ship Adventures (808-593-2469) is a large pirate ship cruising the water off Waikiki Beach. These guys are mostly geared toward younger children. A 90-minute daytime cruise includes swashbuckling high seas adventures, such as sword fighting, water cannons and treasure-seeking. For adults and kids 13 and over it's $64, 12 and under $54, and kids 2 and under are $10 (though $10 still seems steep for a 2-year-old.) They also do an evening, adults-only pirate-themed cruise for $64, but at press time they didn't have a liquor license, so it's BYOB.

The Dole Plantation (808-621-8408) has a 137,000-square-foot hedge maze that keeps kids occupied for $6 ($8 for adults). (See page 103 for more.)

K1 Speed Hawai'i (808-682-7223) has cool electric race carts that can be a hit with older kids. (See page 170.)

We also discuss swimming with dolphins in our *Attractions* chapter—the kind of adventure kids *dream* of. See Sea Life Park Dolphin Encounter on page 168 for more.

The accommodations reviews describe resorts with good keiki programs. By the way, if your objective was to get *away* from the kids, then maybe these resorts won't be at the top of *your* list. Many resorts have been cutting back on their kids' programs in recent years.

Lastly, you should know that it's a big fine plus a mandatory safety class if your keiki isn't buckled up.

THE PEOPLE

There's no doubt about it—people really *are* friendlier in Hawai'i, even in urban Honolulu. You will notice that people are quick to smile and wave at you here. (Those of us who live in Hawai'i have to remember to pack our "mainland face" when we journey there. Otherwise, we get undesired responses when we smile or wave at complete strangers.) It probably comes down to a matter of happiness. People are happy here, and happy people are friendly people.

SOME TERMS

A person of Hawaiian blood is Hawaiian. Only people of this race are called by this term. They are also called Kanaka Maoli, but only another Hawaiian can use this term. Anybody who was born here, regardless of race (except whites), is called a local. If you were born elsewhere but have lived here long enough to get a driver's license, you are called a kama'aina. If you are white, you are a haole. It doesn't matter if you have been here a day, or your family has been here for over a century—you will always be a haole. The term comes from the time when westerners first encountered these islands. Its precise meaning has been lost, but it is thought to refer to people with no background (since westerners could not chant kanaenae—praise—of their ancestors).

The continental United States is called the mainland. If you are here and are returning, you are not "going back to the states" (we *are* a state). When somebody leaves the island, they are off-island.

HAWAIIAN TIME

One aspect of Hawaiian culture you may have heard of is Hawaiian Time. The stereotype is that everyone in Hawai'i moves just a little more slowly than on the mainland. Supposedly, we are more laid-back and don't let things get to us as easily as people on the mainland. This is the stereotype…. OK, it's *not* a stereotype. It's real. Hopefully, during your visit, you will notice that this feeling infects *you,* as well. You may find yourself letting another driver cut in front of you in circumstances that would incur your wrath back home. You may find yourself willing to wait for a red light without feeling like you're going to explode. The whole reason for coming to Hawai'i is to experience beauty and a sense of peace, so let it happen. If someone else is moving a bit more slowly than you want, just go with it.

SHAKA

One gesture you will see often—and should not be offended by—is the *shaka* sign. This is done by extending the pinkie

Kids will see things, such as Likeke Falls, that they'll never forget.

and thumb while curling the three middle fingers. Sometimes visitors think it is some kind of local gesture indicating *up yours* or some similarly unfriendly message. Actually, it is a friendly act used as a sign of greeting, thanks or just to say, *Hey.* Its origin is thought to date back to the 1930s. A guard at the Kahuku Sugar Plantation used to patrol the plantation railroad to keep local kids from stealing cane from the slow moving trains. This guard had lost his middle fingers in an accident, and his manner of waving off the youths became well known. Kids began to warn other kids that he was around by waving their hands in a way that looked like the guard's, and the custom took off.

THE HAWAIIAN LANGUAGE

The Hawaiian language is a beautiful, gentle and melodic language that flows smoothly off the tongue. Just the sounds of the words conjure up trees gently blowing in the breeze and the sound of the surf. Most Polynesian languages share the same roots, and many have common words. Today, Hawaiian is spoken *as an everyday language* only on the privately owned island of Ni'ihau. Visitors are often intimidated by Hawaiian. With a few ground rules you will come to realize that pronunciation is not as hard as you might think.

When missionaries discovered that the Hawaiians had no written language, they listened to people speaking, then sat down and created an alphabet. This Hawaiian alphabet has only 12 letters. Five vowels: A, e, i, o and u, as well as seven consonants, h, k, l, m, n, p and w. The consonants are pronounced just as they are in English, with the exception of W. It is often pronounced as a V if it is in the middle of a word and comes after an E or I. Vowels are pronounced as follows:

A—pronounced as in *Ah* if stressed, or *above* if not stressed.

E—pronounced as in *say* if stressed, or *dent* if not stressed.

I—pronounced as in *bee.*

O—pronounced as in *no.*

U—pronounced as in *boo.*

One thing you will notice in this book are glottal stops or 'okina. These are represented by an upside-down apostrophe ' and are meant to convey a hard stop in the pronunciation. So if we are talking about the type of lava called a'a, it is pronounced as two separate As (AH-AH).

Another feature you will encounter are **diphthongs**, where two letters glide together. They are **ae, ai, ao, au, ei, eu, oi** and **ou**. Unlike many English diphthongs, the second vowel is always pronounced. One word you will read in this book, referring to Hawaiian temples, is *heiau* (HEY-YOW). The **e** and **i** flow together as a single sound, then the **a** and **u** flow together as a single sound. The **Y** sound binds the two sounds, making the whole word flow together.

If you examine long Hawaiian words, you will see that most have repeating syllables, making them easier to remember and pronounce.

Let's take a word that might seem impossible to pronounce. When you see how easy this word is, the rest will seem like a snap. The Hawai'i state fish is the **humuhumunukunukuapua'a**. At first glance it seems like a nightmare. But if you read the word slowly, it is pronounced just like it looks and isn't nearly as horrifying as it appears. Try it. **Humu** (hoo-moo) is pronounced twice. **Nuku** (noo-koo) is pronounced twice. **A** (ah) is pronounced once. **Pu** (poo) is pronounced once. **A'a** (ah-ah) is the ah sound pronounced twice, the glottal stop indicating a hard stop between sounds. Now, you can try to pronounce it again. **Humuhumunukunukuapua'a**. Now, wasn't that easy? OK, so it's not easy, but it's not impossible either.

Below are some Hawaiian words that you might hear during your visit:

'Aina (EYE-na)—Land.

Akamai (AH-ka-MY)—Wise or shrewd.

Ali'i (ah-LEE-ee)—A Hawaiian chief; a member of the chiefly class.

Aloha (ah-LO-ha)—Hello, goodbye, or the feeling or spirit of love, affection or kindness.

Hala (HA-la)—Pandanus tree.

Hale (HA-leh)—House or building.

Hana (HA-na)—Work.

Hana hou (HA-na-HO)—To do again.

Haole (HOW-leh)—Originally foreigner, now means Caucasian.

Heiau (HEY-YOW)—Hawaiian temple.

Hula (HOO-la)—The storytelling dance of Hawai'i.

Imu (EE-moo)—An underground oven.

'Iniki (ee-NEE-key)—Sharp and piercing wind (as in Hurricane 'Iniki).

Kahuna (ka-HOO-na)—A priest or minister; someone who is an expert in a profession.

Kai (kigh)—The sea.

Kalua (KA-LOO-ah)—Cooking food underground.

Kama'aina (KA-ma-EYE-na)—Longtime Hawai'i resident.

Kane (KA-neh)—Boy or man.

Kapu (KA-poo)—Forbidden, taboo; keep out.

Keiki (KAY-key)—Child or children.

Kokua (KO-KOO-ah)—Help or helper.

Kona (KO-na)—Leeward side of the island; wind blowing from the south, southwest direction.

Kuleana (KOO-leh-AH-na)—Concern, responsibility or jurisdiction.

Lanai (LA-NIGH)—Porch, veranda, patio.

Lani (LA-nee)—Sky or heaven.

When you want to get away, but not too far away, how about visiting an offshore island?

Lei (lay)—Necklace of flowers, shells or feathers.

Liliko'i (LEE-lee-KO-ee)—Passion fruit.

Limu (LEE-moo)—Edible seaweed.

Lomi (LOW-me)—To rub or massage; lomi salmon is raw salmon rubbed with salt and spices.

Lu'au (LOO-OW)—Hawaiian feast; literally means taro leaves.

Mahalo (ma-HA-low)—Thank you.

Makai (ma-KIGH)—Toward the sea.

Malihini (MA-lee-HEE-nee)—A newcomer, visitor or guest.

Mauka (MOW-ka)—Toward the mountain.

Moana (mo-AH-na)—Ocean.

Mo'o (MO-oh)—Lizard.

Nani (NA-nee)—Beautiful, pretty.

Nui (NEW-ee)—Big, important, great.

'Ohana (oh-HA-na)—Family.

'Okole (OH-KO-leh)—Derrière.

'Ono (OH-no)—Delicious, the best.

Pakalolo (pa-ka-LO-LO)—Marijuana.

Pali (PA-lee)—A cliff.

Paniolo (PA-nee-OH-lo)—Hawaiian cowboy.

Pau (pow)—Finish, end; pau hana means quitting time from work.

Poi (poy)—Pounded kalo (taro) root that forms a paste.

Pono (PO-no)—Goodness, excellence, correct, proper.

Pua (POO-ah)—Flower.

Puka (POO-ka)—Hole.

Pupu (POO-POO)—Appetizer, snacks or finger food.

Wahine (vah-HEE-neh)—Woman.

Wai (why)—Fresh water.

Wikiwiki (WEE-kee-WEE-kee)—To hurry up, move quickly.

Quick Pidgin Lesson

Hawaiian pidgin is fun to listen to. It's like ear candy. It's colorful, rhythmic and sways in the wind. Below is a list of some of the words and phrases you might hear on your visit. It's tempting to read some of these and try to use them. If you do, the odds are you will simply look foolish. These words and phrases are used in certain ways and with certain inflections. People who have spent years living in the islands still feel uncomfortable using them. Thick pidgin can be incomprehensible to the untrained ear (that's the idea). If you are someplace and hear two people engaged in a discussion in pidgin, stop and eavesdrop a bit. You won't forget it.

Pidgin Words & Phrases

An' den—And then? So?

Any kine—Anything; any kind.

Ass right—That's right.

Ass wy—That's why.

Beef—Fight.

Brah—Bruddah; friend; brother.

Brok' da mouf—Delicious.

Buggah—That's the one; it is difficult.

Bus laugh—To laugh out loud.

Bus nose—How one reacts to bad smell.

Chicken skin kine—Something that gives you goosebumps.

Choke—Plenty; lots.

Cockaroach—Steal; rip off.

Da kine—A noun or verb used in place of whatever the speaker wishes. Heard constantly.

Fo days—Plenty; "He got hair fo days."

Geevum—Go for it! Give 'em hell!

Grind—To eat.

Grinds—Food.

Hold ass—A close call when driving your new car.

How you figgah?—How do you figure that? It makes no sense.

Howzit?—How is it going? How are you? Also, Howzit o wot?

I owe you money or wot?—What to say when someone is staring at you.

Mek ass—Make a fool of yourself.

Mek house—Make yourself at home.

Mek plate—Grab some food.

Mo' bettah—This is better.

Moke—A large, tough local male. (Don't say it unless you *like beef*.)

No can—Cannot; I cannot do it.

No mek li dat—Stop doing that.

No, yeah?—No, or is "no" correct?

'Okole squeezer—Something that suddenly frightens you ('okole meaning derrière).

O wot?—Or what?

Pau hana—Quit work. (A time of daily, intense celebration in the islands.)

Poi dog—A mutt.

Shahkbait—Shark bait, meaning pale, untanned people.

Shaka—Great! All right!

Shredding—Riding a gnarly wave.

Slippahs—Flipflops, thongs, zoris.

Stink eye—Dirty looks; facial expression denoting displeasure.

Suck rocks—Buzz off, or pound sand.

Talk stink—Speak unkindly about somebody.

Talk story—Shooting the breeze; to rap.

Tanks eh?—Thank you.

Tita—A female moke. Same *beef* results.

Yeah?—Used at the end of sentences.

THE HULA

The hula evolved as a means of worship, later becoming a forum for telling a story with chants (called mele), hands and body movement. It can be fascinating to watch. When most people think of the hula, they picture a woman in a grass skirt swinging her hips to the beat of an 'ukulele. But in reality there are two types of hula. The modern hula, or hula 'auana, uses musical instruments and vocals to augment the dancer. It came about after westerners first encountered the Islands. Missionaries found the hula distasteful, and the old style was driven underground. The modern type came about as a form of entertainment and was practiced in places where missionaries had no influence. Ancient Hawaiians didn't even use grass skirts. These were brought later by Gilbert Islanders.

The old style of hula is called hula 'olapa or hula kahiko. It consists of chants, is accompanied by percussion only and takes years of training. It can be exciting to watch as performers work together in synchronous harmony. Both men and women participate, with women's hula being softer (though no less disciplined) and men's hula being more active. This type of hula is physically demanding, requiring strong concentration. Keiki (children's) hula is charming to watch, as well.

BOOKS & MUSIC

There is an astonishing variety of books available about Hawai'i and O'ahu. Everything from history, legends, geology, children's stories and just plain ol' novels. **Barnes & Noble (808-949-7307)** in Ala Moana Shopping Center has a great selection. Walk in and lose yourself in Hawai'i's richness.

Hawaiian music is far more diverse than most people think. Many people picture Hawaiian music as someone twanging away on an 'ukulele with his voice slipping and sliding all over the place like he has an ice cube down his back. In reality, the music here can be outstanding. There is the melodic sound of the more traditional music. There are young local bands putting out modern music with a Hawaiian beat. There is even Hawaiian reggae. Hawaiian Style Band, the late Israel Kamakawiwo'ole (known locally as Bruddah Iz) and Willie K are excellent examples of the local sound. Even if you don't always agree with the all the messages in the songs, there's no denying the talent of these entertainers.

Meet O'ahu's No. 1 cash crop—after tourists, of course.

THE INTERNET

We have recent updates on our website, **www.hawaiirevealed.com**, as well as links to cool sites, the latest satellite weather shots, a calendar of events and more. You can even check resort reviews right on our site. We also show our own aerial photos of most places to stay on O'ahu, so you'll know if oceanfront *really* means oceanfront.

If you're on-island and need Internet access (to check your mail, etc.), most big resorts have business services available for around $7 an hour.

If you brought your own computer or tablet, nearly all hotels have high-speed internet access. If you're Wi-Fi-enabled, you shouldn't find any difficulty picking up signals in Waikiki. The best place we found with free access is the Waikiki Marketplace at 2310 Kuhio Ave. **Skywave** (800-206-8561) broadcasts wireless Internet throughout most of Waikiki for $9 a day (they may have a stronger signal than your hotel). They service a long list of hotels. Starbucks and McDonald's also have free access.

FARMERS MARKETS

Looking for a taste of local foods? Try one of many farmers markets spread around the island. We've found that the markets sponsored by the Hawai'i Farm Bureau (below) have the best variety.

Saturday—Kapiolani Community College, 4303 Diamond Head Road. From 7:30 to 11 a.m.

Sunday—Mililani High School, 95-1200 Meheula Pkwy. From 8 a.m. to 11 a.m.

Mondays, Wednesdays, Fridays and Saturdays—Kings Village Shopping Center (where Koa meets Kaiulani) in Waikiki has one from 4 to 8:30 p.m.

Thursday—Longs Drugs in Kailua, 609 Kailua Road from 5 to 7:30 p.m. and in Waimea Valley from 2 to 6 p.m.

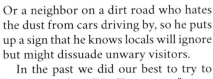

A NOTE ABOUT ACCESS

If a lawful landowner posts a "No Trespassing" sign on their land, you need to respect their wishes. That seems simple enough. But here's where it gets tricky.

It's common in Hawai'i for someone who doesn't own or control land to erect their own "No Trespassing/Keep Out" and "Road Closed" signs. Picture a shoreline fisherman who doesn't want anyone else near his cherished spot, putting up a store-bought sign to protect his solitude.

Or a neighbor on a dirt road who hates the dust from cars driving by, so he puts up a sign that he knows locals will ignore but might dissuade unwary visitors.

In the past we did our best to try to ferret out when "No Trespassing" signs were valid, and when they were not, and we took *a lot* of heat from residents who thought we were encouraging trespassing when we weren't. But the current environment doesn't permit us to do that anymore. So if you're heading to one of the places we describe and you encounter a "No Trespassing" sign, even if you think it's not authorized by the landowner (and even if it's on *public* land), we have to advise you to turn around and heed the sign. All descriptions in our book come with the explicit assumption that you have obtained the permission of the legal landowner, and unfortunately, it'll usually be up to you to determine who that is and how to get it. But please, under no circumstances are we suggesting that you trespass. Plain and clear. Don't trespass…ever… for any reason… period.

The waterfall at Waimea Valley is one of the few on the island that you can swim under.

A NOTE ON PERSONAL RESPONSIBILITY

In past editions we've had the sad task of removing places that you can no longer visit. The reason, universally cited, is *liability*. Although Hawai'i has a statute indemnifying landowners, the mere threat is often enough to get something closed. Because we, more than any other publication, have exposed hereto-

Kuhio Beach, also known as the ponds, offers a safer swim than the open ocean.

fore unknown attractions, we feel the need to pass this along.

You need to assess what kind of traveler you are. We've been accused of leaning a bit toward the adventurous side, so you should take that into account when deciding if something's right for you. To paraphrase a great line from the movie *Top Gun*, "Don't let your ego write checks your body can't cash."

You will probably be more physical during your trip than you are at home, so train up for it. If you plan on doing any hiking, snorkeling or other activities, spend the month before your vacation training. Your body will reward you—we promise.

Please remember that this isn't Disneyland—it's nature. Mother Nature is hard, slippery, sharp and unpredictable. If you go exploring and get into trouble, whether it's your ego that's bruised or something more tangible, please remember that neither the state, the private land owner nor this publication *told* you to go. You *chose* to explore, which is what life, and this book, are all about. And if you complain to or threaten someone controlling land, they'll rarely fix the problem you identified. They'll simply close it… and it will be gone for good.

Sometimes even good intentions can lead to disaster. At one adventure, a trail-head led hikers to the base of a wonderful waterfall. There was only *one* trail, to the left at the parking lot, that a person could take. Neither we, other guides nor websites ever said, "Stay on the trail to the left" because at the time there was only one trail to take. The state (in their zeal to protect themselves from liability at an unmaintained trail) came along and put up a "Danger—Keep Out" sign at the trailhead. Travelers encountering the sign assumed they were on the wrong trail and started to beat a path to the right instead. But that direction started sloping downward and ended abruptly at a 150-foot-high cliff. The hikers retreated and in a short time a previously non-existent trail to the right became as prominent as the correct (and heretofore *only*) path to the left. Not long after the state's well-intentioned sign went up, an unwitting pair of hikers took the new, incorrect trail to the right and fell to their deaths. They probably died because they had been dissuaded from taking the correct trail by a state sign theoretically erected to keep people safe.

Our point is that nothing is static and nothing can take the place of your own observations and good judgment. If you're doing one of the activities you read about in our book or someplace else, and your

Once endangered, green sea turtles are now much more common on O'ahu than they used to be.

instinct tells you that something is wrong, *trust your judgment* and go do another activity. There are lots of wonderful things to do on the island, and we want you safe and happy.

MISCELLANEOUS INFORMATION

Traveler's checks are usually accepted, but you should be aware that some merchants might look at you as if you just tried to offer them Mongolian money. You should also know that Discover Cards seem to be less welcome here than at other destinations. *Many* places don't accept them.

It is customary here for *everyone* to remove their shoes upon entering someone's house (sometimes their office).

If you are going to spend any time at the beach, woven bamboo beach mats can be found all over the island for about $3. Some roll up; some can be folded. The sand comes off these more easily than it comes off towels.

The area code for all of Hawai'i is (808).

Around the island you'll see signs saying "Visitor Information" or something similar. Allow us to translate: That's usually code for "we want to sell you something."

If you want to arrange a lei greeting for you or your honey when you get off the plane at the airport, LeiGreeting.com (800) 665-7959 or Greeters of Hawai'i (800)

366-8559 can make the arrangements for around $30 and up. Nice way to kick off a romantic trip, huh? Since they are made to order, arrange 48 hours in advance.

GETTING IN & OUT OF WAIKIKI

Though Waikiki is the main place where visitors stay, there is no dedicated on-ramp or off-ramp for it from the main highway, H-1. Leaving the airport, the most efficient way to Waikiki is H-1 East. Though the signs *won't* direct you this way, the quickest route is to drive past what they *call* the Waikiki exits, then take exit 24A (Bingham), right on Farrington, right on Beretania, left on McCully, which will take you into Waikiki. Taking the so-called Waikiki exits (exits 22 and 23) is a less direct route. Most visitors erroneously take the Nimitz Highway from the airport and are greeted by heavy traffic most of the way. See the Honolulu map on page 50.)

Leaving Waikiki to get onto H-1, take Ala Wai Boulevard to McCully, and follow the signs if you're heading west (toward the airport), or take McCully, right on Kapiolani and follow the signs if you're heading east on H-1.

An alternative to these is to use the "back door" to Waikiki, namely Kapahulu to the west and exit 25 from H1.

A WORD ABOUT DRIVING TOURS

For directions, locals usually describe things as being on the *mauka* (mao-kah) side of the road—toward the mountains—or *makai* (mah-kigh)—toward the ocean.

Beaches, activities, attractions and adventures are mentioned briefly but described in detail in their own chapters. Sometimes it gets confusing trying to plan which attractions or activities are in the area you'll be exploring.

SMARTPHONE APP

We love books, which are naturally and instinctively approachable. They convey information in a way that is timeless. But at the same time, new technology allows us to do things with smartphones that can't occur in books. Our app, *Hawaii Revealed*, is unlike *any* travel app you've ever seen. All the information from the books is there, but the app costs a little extra because we have also harnessed *and invented* features that will blow you away.

For instance, you want to go for a snorkel at a specific beach today? You can flip to the page in the book and read all about it. But with our app, you tap to the entry and you can read all about it *and* find out that today isn't a good day to get into the water due to high surf. Want to do a hike at a certain windward side trail? Well, the author woke up this morning, saw that the weather was going to be bad on the windward side, circled a part of the map that he thought might be affected and for how long, and every entry in that area that is weather-sensitive will be updated to reflect the bad weather.

Want to book a place to stay and have certain criteria? *I want a hotel in Waikiki that is oceanfront, has a children's pool, fitness room, is good for families and has an outdoor lanai. Oh, and takes service animals.* With the filters in our app you can cut through all of the resorts and get to *exactly* what you want, read our in-depth and brutally honest review, and even book it. How's *that* for cutting through the noise?

There's more—*a lot* more. Visit the iTunes or Google Play store and check out our app, including a free preview.

If the more crowded part of Waikiki gets you down, Fort DeRussy Beach is the widest part of Waikiki, and there are usually far fewer people.

Honolulu is the central hub of the Hawaiian Islands, and Waikiki is the center of tourism. Lots of people work, live and play in this part of the state, and odds are overwhelming that this is where *you'll* be staying. That's because there are around 90 resorts on the island of O'ahu, and all but less than a dozen of them are in Waikiki. At any one time, 44 percent of visitors *in the entire state of Hawai'i* are spending the night in Waikiki.

WAIKIKI AREA

Imagine an area of less than one square mile that has over 30,000 hotel rooms. Imagine that this area is blessed with one of the most user-friendly beaches in the world. Where just about anyone can take a surfing lesson and ride their first wave. A place with more restaurants than most decent-sized towns. A place with limitless shopping. Well, this place actually exists. Waikiki is the essence of carefree. Visitors here tend to feel safe, warm and happy.

Waikiki is about walking and gawking, eating and shopping, surfing and soaking up the sun. You don't come to Waikiki to get away from the action; you come here to get a *piece* of the action. This is the place where you and 4 million of your closest friends each year embrace the tropics and each other. If you're looking for a quiet, out-of-the-way destination, look elsewhere. Waikiki is a humming, happening visitor mecca.

There is almost nothing natural about Waikiki. A century ago the land behind the beach was a swampy sponge. Three rivers emptied into the ocean here, and the beach, though still a great place to swim, was hardly a must-see destination. Then in 1921 they started draining the swamp. People often wonder, *how do you drain a swamp?* Simple—you dig a canal to cut off the source of water and let nature dry it out. This they did by creating the Ala Wai Canal. And the rest is history. Waikiki, now backed by land suitable for development, was ready to take off. Throughout the 20th century, resort after resort sprang up, and visitors began coming here in droves.

As far as the canal itself, local fishermen report pulling out tilapia, jellyfish, pufferfish, and even seahorses. Unfortunately, that's not the only thing you can catch here. The water is contaminated by excessive runoff and people have been known to catch flesh-eating bacteria as well as MRSA from the water, so we'd advise you to observe from a distance.

Early evening is our favorite time to experience Waikiki, when the intensity of the sun is replaced by the joy of people-watching. Stroll along the sidewalks of Kalakaua Avenue (or Lewers, which is also pretty alive at night and considered part of the "Beachwalk" area) and shop, snack and enjoy the warm, secure feeling that dusk in the tropics provides. Incidentally, the main street, Kalakaua, has surprisingly few signs verifying that it's the street you're on.

If you want to stroll along the beach, you can walk from the Hilton at one end of Waikiki all the way to Kapiolani Park at the other. Those few areas that lack sand have other means of traversing the shoreline that will keep you dry. A sunset walk along Waikiki Beach is always a dreamy experience as you listen to music often spilling from the various resorts. If you walk from the Diamond Head side toward Honolulu, you'll be walking toward the sun. During part of the summer, the sun doesn't set over the ocean from most of Waikiki.

Shopping is literally everywhere. One of Waikiki's most iconic shopping Meccas is the International Marketplace. Opened in 1957, this has always been the place to get exotic yet cheap items perfect for souvenirs. It closed in 2014, and the landowners reopened it in 2016. Those who knew it before will be comforted to know that in their attempt to retain the same heritage, the landowners made certain to retain the same—*vowels* and *consonants*—in the new version. That and the glorious banyan tree. Otherwise it bears *no* resemblance. It's now a place to buy $400 flip-flops and other high-end adornments. Those who lust after those flip-flops, rejoice. Those who miss the $2 hula dancers made in China that wiggled on the dashboard, you gotta look elsewhere now.

Though less than a square mile, it's one of those ironies of modern life that the smaller a place is, the more walking you're apt to do. *Forget the car, honey—we'll walk it.* That's the phrase you'll hear and say throughout your stay. Many people who come to O'ahu never even rent a car (which we think is a mistake—see *Rental Cars* on page 22 for more). But for getting around this square mile of activity, odds are you'll either walk, take the bus, take a shuttle or rent a scooter. Driving your car around Waikiki can be a pain because parking is such a problem.

Honolulu's bus (cleverly called TheBus) costs $2.75 one way, $5.50 per day, or you can get a monthly pass for $70. Number 8 is the main Waikiki route, so we've

WAIKIKI RESORTS

Resort Name (alphabetical)	Key	#
Ala Moana Hotel	A2	1
Alohilani Resort Waikiki Beach	M3	65
Ambassador Hotel of Waikiki	F2	12
Aqua Aloha Surf Waikiki	K1	47
Aqua Bamboo Waikiki	L2	54
Aqua Oasis	H3	23
Aqua Ohia Waikiki	I2	35
Aqua Palms Waikiki	D3	8
Coconut Waikiki Hotel	H1	19
Courtyard by Marriott Waikiki	H2	21
DoubleTree Alana Hotel	E2	11
Embassy Suites Waikiki Beach Walk	H4	25
Ewa Hotel Waikiki	N3	69
Halekulani	H5	30
Hawaiian King	J2	39
Hawaiian Monarch Hotel	D1	7
Hilton Garden Inn Waikiki Beach	J2	41
Hilton Hawaiian Village	D5	10
Hilton Waikiki Beach	M2	63
Holiday Inn Express	F2	13
Holiday Surf	J1	36
Hostelling International Waikiki	K3	49
Hotel La Croix	F2	14
Hotel Renew	N4	73
Hyatt Centric Waikiki Beach	I2	32
Hyatt Place Waikiki Beach	N3	68
Hyatt Regency Waikiki	K3	51
Ilikai Hotel & Suites	C4	6
'Ilima Hotel	J1	37
Imperial Hawai'i Resort	H4	26
Island Colony	I1	34
Kai Aloha Hotel	G4	17
Lotus Honolulu	R7	78
Luana Waikiki	F2	15
Marina Tower Waikiki	B4	2
Moana Surfrider, A Westin Resort	K4	53
New Otani Kaimana Beach Hotel	R7	77
Ohana East	K2	48
Ohana Waikiki Malia	H2	22
Outrigger Reef Waikiki Beach	H5	29
Outrigger Waikiki Beach Resort	J4	45
Pacific Monarch	L2	55
Park Shore Waikiki	N4	76
Pearl Hotel Waikiki	J2	40
Polynesian Hostel Beach Club	N3	71
Prince Waikiki	B4	4
Queen Kapiolani Hotel	N3	72
Ramada Plaza Waikiki	D4	9
Royal Grove Hotel	L2	57
Royal Hawaiian	J4	44
Sheraton Princess Kaiulani	K3	50
Sheraton Waikiki	I4	33
Shoreline Hotel Waikiki	I2	31
Stay Hotel Waikiki	K3	52
Surfjack Hotel & Swim Club	H2	20
The Breakers	G3	16
The Equus	B4	3
The Laylow Autograph Collection	J2	42
The Modern Honolulu	C4	5
The Regency on Beachwalk	H3	24
Trump International Hotel & Tower	G4	18
Vive Hotel Waikiki	L2	56
Waikiki Banyan	M2	64
Waikiki Beach Hotel	N4	75
Waikiki Beach Marriott Resort	M3	66
Waikiki Beach Tower	L3	60
Waikiki Beachcomber	J3	43
Waikiki Beachside Hostel	N3	70
Waikiki Beachside Hotel	L3	61
Waikiki Central Hotel	L3	58
Waikiki Circle	L3	62
Waikiki Grand Hotel	N4	74
Waikiki Parc Hotel	H4	27
Waikiki Resort Hotel	L3	59
Waikiki Sand Villa	K1	46
Waikiki Shore	H5	28
Waikiki Sunset	N2	67
White Sands Hotel	J2	38

shown that one on our Waikiki map. The other bus, called the Waikiki Trolley, has a walk-up rate of $45 *per person per day* but a great online rate of $70 *per week*. They can be convenient, but they seem to skip stops at random. The City and County of Honolulu also offers a convenient app (called DaBus2) that will show you just how often the bus is likely to skip your location… and how long you'll have to wait for the next one.

Outrigger canoe rides have been a Waikiki staple for over a century. Aloha Beach Services (808-922-3111, ext. 42341) has rides for $20 (you get to ride two waves—they have a four-person minimum), or you can charter the whole eight-passenger outrigger canoe (includes two captains, extra paddlers are $50 per hour) for $300 per hour. Directly next door Waikiki Beach Services (808-388-1510) rides two waves in a private canoe for $25 per person, four people minimum. Near the Duke statue, Star Beach Boys (808-699-3750) will give you three waves for $20 in a *slightly* bigger canoe. For swimmers, it's worth mentioning that waves don't have brakes, so neither do the canoes. The most you'll get is a shout to watch out before the canoe mows you down.

Picking where to stay in Waikiki is daunting. Price is presumably a factor, and generally, the closer you get to the water, the higher the price. Distance to the heart of Waikiki is also a consideration. If you don't want to walk great distances whenever you want to experience what Waikiki has to offer, the best location is on the ocean side of Kalakaua Avenue between Saratoga Avenue and the Waikiki

The electric energy that you'll find at Waikiki doesn't end when the sun goes down.

Beach Center. The area around the Royal Hawaiian and the Moana Surfrider hotels is usually considered to be the center of Waikiki life.

Waikiki Beach

Nearly every visitor to O'ahu stays in Waikiki, so we described the Waikiki beaches here since it's likely you'll stroll along them at various times throughout your stay.

Waikiki is a swimming and surfing beach, not a snorkeling site, and there are no great snorkeling conditions anywhere along here. If you insist, the best conditions are off the tip of the Kapahulu Groin and the tip of the wall at the south end of Queen's Beach (both of these only if there are no surfers or boogie boarders in the area—they have little patience for snorkelers) and ironically, offshore of the Waikiki Aquarium.

Also remember that although Waikiki Beach is very sandy, the nearshore waters often have lots of rocks and reef that conspire to attack your feet. Smart beachgoers wear reef or water shoes. The sandiest patches are off Waikiki Beach Center (for a little ways), in front of the ultra-pink Royal Hawaiian tower building (although the water there tends to be cloudy) and at the eastern (Diamond Head) side of Kahanamoku Beach) up to the pier in front of the Hilton.

The entire beach is known as Waikiki Beach, but different stretches have different names. Starting in front of the massive Hilton Hawaiian Village, Kahanamoku Beach (named after Hawai'i's favorite son, surfing legend Duke Kahanamoku) is usually very crowded. It's considered a very safe swimming beach due to its protection from a breakwater on one side, a reef offshore and a jetty on the Diamond Head side. There's an easy-to-walk concrete beach path that runs from the Hilton, around Kahanamoku Lagoon and to the far end of Fort DeRussy Beach. If you're looking for a snack, soda or adult beverage, grab one at the Hau Tree Beach Bar behind the beach, or, better yet, use the unexpectedly cheap Happy's Fast & Fresh at the Hale Koa. It's a military hotel, not normally open to the public, but a loophole allows you to wander in from the beach and eat at pool or beachside there. See *Island Dining* for more.

Fort DeRussy Beach is the *widest* part of Waikiki Beach. The sand is also un-

A peaceful morning on Waikiki Beach.

usually firm (in case you brought your dune buggy from home). The southeast end occasionally gets balls of seaweed washing ashore, and the water along the wall—especially on the left side—has cold basal springs that drop the water temperature. But this is a fantastic part of Waikiki and is a bit less crowded compared to other parts of the beach.

Gray's Beach is the one part of Waikiki that has mostly washed away. Waikiki has been enhanced many times over the years with importations of sand, most recently in 2012. Officials tend to be hesitant to bring in more sand, fearing that they'll alter the shape of Waikiki's famous waves. But being bureaucrats, they're also fearful of making a wrong decision, so little has been done in recent years to stop the erosion of sand other than a small project at Kuhio Beach and the strip of beach between Waikiki Beach Center and the Royal Hawaiian. As a result, Waikiki is thin in areas like Gray's Beach. The sand is interrupted twice, leaving only small pockets. This means you'll have to wade through shallow water at this part if you want to walk the full length of Waikiki Beach. It's also much less padded in the nearshore

waters than it used to be, so water or reef shoes are recommended in most parts of the beach.

At Royal-Moana Beach, the beach is at its sandiest, and beach use tends to be high. You won't find a lot of vacant sand here.

Next door is the Waikiki Beach Center. This is the spot for surf lessons and outrigger canoe rides. There are no resorts lining this part of the beach, and Kalakaua Avenue is right next to the park.

Past here is Kuhio Beach, also known as The Ponds. Kuhio has concrete walls forming two separate ponds—perfect for

kids and those skittish about swimming in the open ocean.

When you leave Kuhio Beach, you leave the resort towers of Waikiki behind. The Kapahulu Groin is the jetty extending into the sea where Kalakaua Avenue meets Kapahulu Avenue. This is our favorite place to be in Waikiki when the surf's up—usually in the summer. It extends out into the waves, so you'll feel like you're part of the action. Boogie boarders and body surfers cruise right up to you, then past you. You'll quickly gain a perspective of the waves that's not possible from the shore. Boogie boarders often surf right up to the shore, hop on the groin, run to the end and jump off to start over again. (By the way, *we* always thought a groin was something you pulled playing football. Actually, it's a wall that runs perpendicular to the beach to stop sand migration.)

Though the north end of the groin is usually swimming-pool calm, the south end sometimes provides some of the nicest and longest boogie board rides in South O'ahu. Queen's Beach is named after a long-gone restaurant by that name. It's also a good place to stretch a towel and is usually less crowded than the beaches in front of the resorts. (The section of Queen's next to the groin wall is known locally as *Walls*.) The sand beach ends here.

South of Waikiki

Behind you, Kapiolani Park is a giant, triangular-shaped lawn where people play soccer, fly kites, walk their dogs and jog to their hearts' content. Diamond Head, that iconic volcano crater that defines the Waikiki skyline, seems to tower over this park. The north end is where

A slightly less peaceful afternoon.

you'll find the Waikiki Shell, a seashell-shaped outdoor amphitheater where live performances are occasionally held. There are also four lighted tennis courts on the makai (ocean side) of the park—no reservations needed. And check out the gigantic banyan tree on the Paki Road side of the park. (Yeah, that's *one* tree.)

Kapiolani Park is also where you'll find the Natatorium and the Waikiki Aquarium. (Before you get too worked up over the aquarium, read our write-up in *Attractions* on page 167 to see if it's for you.)

The Natatorium is a WWI memorial built in 1927 to honor Hawai'i's casualties from the Great War. Its 100-meter pool was used by generations of residents for swim meets and recreation, but it was allowed to fall into disrepair. Closed now for decades, this cracked and crumbling blight looks more like a monument to a war that was lost, and forgotten. With the pool deck collapsing, it's now merely a free place to park, and its bathrooms are used by swimmers at Sans Souci Beach next door. There is perpetual talk about tearing it down, but in the mean-time, it's sort of a white elephant that Hawai'i residents, out of embarrassment, kind of hope you don't see.

Sans Souci Beach is a nice but small beach on the south end of the Natatorium. It's semi-protected by one wall of the Natatorium, has showers, restrooms (at the Natatorium) and lifeguards. The sand is fairly coarse and brushes off more easily than the fine stuff, and it extends far enough into the ocean to provide a cushion for your feet. Park at the Nata-torium on Kalakaua Avenue.

Cocktails in Waikiki

It's been our observation that adult cocktails in Waikiki sold next to the beach tend to be a bit weak, especially when served by big resorts like the Hilton, and no amount of coaching seems to make a difference. Perhaps they're counting on multiple purchases. For the record, it's il-

Looks fake, but it's not. Let me tell you about the day I learned that birds don't like drones…

Meet the only royal residence in the United States—'Iolani Palace.

legal to consume alcohol on the beach in Hawai'i. This rule comes as a complete surprise to anyone visiting since restaurants and barefoot bars next to the beach often serve their drinks in plastic cups and sort of wink and nod while they tell you about the law when you ask for a drink to go. The law seems to be little enforced on Waikiki Beach, and a visit to nearly any beach on the weekend will reveal locals with giant ice chests full of beer. From the Hau Tree at the Hilton to Rumfire at the Sheraton Waikiki, drinks in plastic cups are available. At RumFire (no bathing suits allowed) their Hai-Maka Mai Tai (made with my favorite sipping rum, Ron Zacapa) is a pricey but unusual and *super-refreshing* mai tai with a hint of ginger. I review it every time I walk the beach, just to confirm consistency. (No thanks necessary. It's my job.) It's good about 72 percent of the time, but I'm trying to fine tune that percentage. Great rum selection, too—so good, in fact, that they have a dedicated Rum Bible that your server will either bring out on request or deny the existence of entirely. If you're looking for a better deal, check out Koa Oasis at the Hale Koa Hotel (northwest end of the beach). Only 10 steps from the beach and cheaper drinks than most because the military ownership of the hotel shields them from that annoying concept known as taxes. Virtually all permanent beachside venues will serve alcohol.

Freebies in Waikiki

Waikiki is a great place to get rid of all that pesky money you've been earning throughout the year. Everywhere you turn, there are plenty of people and companies that will gladly take your hard-earned cash. If you need a breather, here are a few things that *won't* cost you dearly.

Off Monsarrat Ave. where the zoo meets Kapiolani Park, hanging on the

Cruisin' up to the beach at Waikiki.

chain link of Honolulu Zoo you'll see the weekly Art on the Zoo Fence (808-372-9578), a local display of prints and canvases featuring photographs and paintings of the islands. There's a lot of diversity in what the artists choose to feature, making this open-air gallery worth a stop on weekends between 9 a.m. and 4 p.m. Also in Kapiolani Park, the Royal Hawaiian Band plays free concerts from 2 p.m. to 3 p.m. at the Kapiolani Park Bandstand every Sunday. Their style is usually jazz and pop, but they play interesting renditions of holiday music at various times throughout the year.

There's a nightly sunset Torch Lighting Ceremony at Kuhio Beach, as well as a music and a hula show *most* nights. The music and hula show is certainly worth watching, but the ceremony alone is too brief to make a special trip for. Under the banyan tree to the left of the bronze statue of Duke Kahanamoku. (By the way, don't linger under that tree near sunset. There are thousands of birds in its branches who would love to drop their special brand of aloha on you.)

Sunset on the Beach is that scaffolding you see at Queen's Beach (aka Queen's Surf Beach). Picture a 30-foot screen on the beach, food concessionaires selling the expected junk food, and movies equivalent to recent DVD releases being shown for free. But the screen has been down for a while and calls to 808-923-1094 for listings have led us nowhere. We are told they only do it sporadically now because of "budgetary" reasons, which is a shame, because it was lots of fun (although crowded). Hopefully they will start again before your trip. If there's no movie, you might catch a lively beach volleyball game there.

The Hilton Hawaiian Village (808-949-4321) has a Polynesian show near the pool at 7 p.m. every Friday. Afterward they have Fireworks Over the Ocean. Some boat tours plan their sunset cruises around this event. There may be some exciting fire dancing after the pyrotechnics. Walk as close to the Hilton as possible for the best views.

King's Village Shopping Center (808-732-7736) puts on a small Polynesian Show every Thursday at 6:30 p.m. Drummers, dancers and even a fire knife dancer perform right outside the 50's diner and Burger King. Though the scenery may not be superb, the show is an excellent display. Though not free, also at King's Village is a farmers market every Monday, Wednesday, Friday, and Saturday from 4 p.m. to 9 p.m. Fresh veggies and fruits are commonplace here but the pad Thai, stir fry and other meals are some of the best (and cheapest) you can get on the island.

Street Performers are synonymous with Kalakaua Avenue. The silver guys, in particular, range from talented to just plain lame. With some, the only way to appease them is to give 'em money. In return, they will take their kazoo, make a few mechanical whirring noises, and pick a different position. The Waikiki Bboys are a hip-hop dance group that has a 6:30 p.m. nightly routine immediately across from the Royal Hawaiian Center that does a pretty good job, but we like to leave right before the end because of their preachy (though admittedly well-rehearsed) speech about donating money to their troupe. Some nights street performers are all along Kalakaua. Other nights, hardly any show up.

Sunday Showcase at the Waikiki Beach Walk displays the talents of local entertainers from hula dancers to well-known 'ukulele player Jake Shimabukuro. Shows start at 5 p.m. two Sundays per month on the Plaza Stage, third floor on Lewers Street.

The U.S. Army Museum is often overlooked, located right next to the beach in Waikiki. The building itself is the largest artifact. Battery Randolph used to house two 14-inch guns that could shoot 14 miles into Honolulu harbor. During WWII the battery was made obsolete with the invention of aircraft carriers. They tried to level the building in

Friday night lights, island style.

Fifteen minutes from the asphalt jungle of Honolulu lies a different kind of jungle off Tantalus Drive.

1969, but it was *too tough* for the wrecking ball. In 1976 it was made into a museum. This place is definitely worth your time to see, and the admission is free. (They do accept donations.) Alternatively, they have an audio tour available for $5. Near the beach access across from Saratoga Rd., next to the Hale Koa Hotel. Look for the two old Army tanks sitting in front of the building. If you choose the wrong entrance (to the right) you'll think the museum is simply a monument to the Army Corps of Engineers. The real museum, to warfare since before western contact to the present, runs the whole bottom floor.

HONOLULU

Honolulu is overrepresented when it comes to attractions to visit. It's got so many, in fact, that we have dedicated *Adventures* and *Attractions* chapters you should check out. Look at places like 'Iolani Palace, Punchbowl Cemetery, Chi-natown, Bishop Museum, Doris Duke's Shangri La and Garden Tours.

Driving around Honolulu and Waikiki can be maddening, and no matter how much effort we put into our descriptions, they can't cover up the fact that our road system was created by... well, morons. (Sorry, but it's true.) Having a navigator who's good at reading maps on the fly can help, but you should count on getting lost, irritated and driving in the vicinity of something you're trying to get to only to curse in rage that you can't find it or maneuver to it. Hey... it's O'ahu. After a week or so you'll learn some of its tricks and shortcuts, but the learning curve can be steep. Even living here, we get frustrated at the unintuitive layout. And getting on and off the H-1 freeway can be a joke. We still find it incredible that the primary place where visitors stay—Waikiki—doesn't have a dedicated on-ramp to get back onto H-1 west. From McCully, you're directed though a neighborhood until you wander onto an on-ramp. It's embarrassing, but it's part of our charm, right?

As a rule of thumb, we try to avoid driving into Honolulu from 7–8:30 a.m. and 3–7 p.m. Most traffic goes *into* Honolulu in the morning and *out of* Honolulu in the evening, but traffic can go from calm to disastrous over something as simple as a fender bender no matter where you're going. On weekends, try to avoid driving into Honolulu after 7 p.m.—the traffic usually won't calm down until 10 p.m. or later.

Tantalus

No matter how long you stay in Honolulu, at some point you should take a drive along Tantalus and **NOT TO BE** Round Top. This 10-mile-long road wiggles and winds up the mountains through a pret- **MISSED!** ty forest above Honolulu to the 1,610-foot level, and in the process you'll gain an appreciation of Honolulu's beauty you never really expected.

As a loop road you'll start at one end and finish at another. Take Ala Wai Boulevard, then a right on Kalakaua Avenue, across the Ala Wai Canal and out of Waikiki, left onto Kapiolani, right onto Keeaumoku, up and over H-1, then right on Wilder and left on Makiki. When you get to Makiki Heights Drive, take a left onto it (if it's the afternoon) and go right when it dead ends onto Tantalus to do the loop. If it's the morning, stay on Makiki and go past Makiki Heights Drive, then turn left onto Round Top to begin the loop, turning left onto Makiki Heights Drive when you're done. (This route takes best advantage of the lighting.) See maps on page 51 and 72.

This is a great road to drive in a convertible. Leadfoots may be tempted to take the winding road fast, but you'll actually want to drive this road slowly, or it'll be over too soon, and you'll miss some of the scrumptious scenery. Keep an eye out for pullouts along the way. Several have fantastic views of the leeward side of O'ahu below you, though

When Did the Last Eruption Take Place on O'ahu?

Surprisingly, nobody knows. Ask any geologist, and you might be told with complete confidence that it was 320,000 years ago...or over 100,000 years ago... or maybe as recently as 5,000 years ago. What we do know is that the most recent eruptions have been near the shoreline, from Diamond Head to Kaupo Beach Park. The land that looks the youngest is Kaohi-ka-ipu Island off Makapu'u Beach Park—it's mostly raw lava. These were explosive eruptions where seawater mixed with underground magma and burst to form the hills and craters so prominent along here. The wicked snorkeling at Hanauma Bay, the popular hike up Diamond Head and the massive Koko Crater we all owe to O'ahu's last gasp at island-making. The rejuvenated phase of a volcano can have very long gaps, and technically the island could still be in its final phase of lava flows, though most geologists consider it highly improbable that there will be another eruption here. If one happens to occur during your visit, please just disregard this whole section.

sometimes bad elements may give you second thoughts about stopping. No view, however, can compare to the pure majesty of the view from Pu'u Ualaka'a State Wayside Park. When you pull into this park, stay left at both intersections till the road ends, then walk out a hundred feet to the point. From one corner of the island at Barbers Point all the way past Diamond Head to Kahala, a giant 25-mile swath of O'ahu presents itself. We're only sorry that we don't have a camera lens wide enough to show it all to you. You'll have to see for yourself. The park closes shortly after sunset.

If you want to observe the city lights at night, the Waikiki Starry Skyline viewpoint is 1.8 miles up Round Top. (Plug the address 2845 Round Top Drive into your map app and go past it—there's a wide shoulder with enough room for about a dozen cars to pull over.) Police officers are usually up here after dark to make sure lusty teenagers keep things PG, and the cops will ask people to leave at 10 p.m.

One of the notable Honolulu sights that you won't actually visit is the Punahou School. (It's at the intersection of Punahou and Nehoa—you'll go right past it on your way to the Manoa Falls Trail.) This elite private school was attended by a young Barack Obama. That's a pretty solid claim to fame for an educational institution, but he wasn't the first, *or even second*, president the school churned out. The first was Sanford B. Dole, who went on to serve from 1894 to 1900 as the only president of the Republic of Hawai'i. The second was Sun Yat-sen, a Chinese immigrant to Hawai'i who later played an instrumental role in the 1912 overthrow of the Qing dynasty, ending more than 2,000 years of imperial rule. He then went on to serve as the first president of modern-day China. Three presidents of three different countries from one Hawaiian school. Pretty impressive.

Just outside of Waikiki, Ala Moana Beach provides very protected waters most of the time. Play on the lawn, play on the beach or play in the water. But it's popular, so you won't be playing alone.

Only a couple miles to the south but a world away from Waikiki you'll find Diamond Head and Kuilei Cliffs Beach Parks.

Ala Moana Area

Just outside Waikiki is Ala Moana. If you'd been in Honolulu in the early 1900s, you'd never have wanted-ed to visit the Ala Moana area. It was a nasty, swampy and smelly area of mud flats that also housed the almost continuously burning Honolulu garbage dump. Everyone avoided the area except duck pond owners. Then in 1912 a dredging company owner named Dillingham bought this worthless land. His friends thought he was an idiot, but Dillingham was looking for a place to dispose of all of his dredged earth. In the 1950s a mile of sand was dumped at this park, creating the perfect swimming spot you see today. (But stay out of the ponds in the park, which are still swampy and nasty.) And in 1959, the year Hawai'i became a state, its most prestigious shopping center was built across the street, the 50-acre Ala Moana Shopping Center. Ala Moana went from uninviting wasteland to a beautiful

A REAL GEM

and treasured beach park backed by the largest open-air shopping center in the world in less than 50 years.

WAIKIKI & HONOLULU BEST BETS

Best Former Swamp—Waikiki Beach
Best Sunset Walk—From Kapiolani Park to the Hilton Hawaiian Village
Best Place to View the Most O'ahu Real Estate—From Pu'u Ualaka'a State Wayside Park
Best View at Night—A hotel room in the Waikiki Sheraton above the 20th floor facing Diamond Head
Best Place to See How Royalty Lived—'Iolani Palace
Best Winding Road—Tantalus Drive
Best Place to See Weird Edible Sea Critters—Maunakea Marketplace
Best Dining Deal on Waikiki Beach—Hale Koa Military Hotel
Best Place to Watch Boogie Boarders Close-up—Kapahulu Groin
Best Place to Hear a Crooner Sing Sad Music—Barefoot Bar, Hale Koa

Part of Highway 72 was carved out of the cemented ash of Koko Crater.

Talk about an embarrassment of riches. You have several ways to get to Kailua on the windward side from Waikiki, all of them pretty. Odds are you'll want to take the coastal highway (Highway 72) because there are a number of not-to-be-missed sights along the way. But even if you take the coastal road this time, you should definitely find the time during your stay to take one of the highways that punch though the Ko'olau mountains—the best being the H-3, which is arguably the most beautiful stretch of freeway in the world.

COASTAL ROUTE TO HANAUMA BAY

Leave Waikiki behind by taking Kalakaua Avenue to Diamond Head Road to Kahala Avenue—more scenic than getting on H-1 East right away. You'll pass the lower part of Diamond Head where some pretty scenic lookouts await. Kahala Avenue is where some of O'ahu's richest residents live. There are some truly stupendous mansions along here. In addition, there are some obscenely expensive eyesores on this road, proof that money doesn't necessarily buy good taste.

Turn left at the end onto Kealaolu Ave., which'll turn into H-1 East. (Look for the signs.) The H-1 will become Hwy 72, known locally as the Kalanianaole Highway. (Don't try to pronounce that seven syllable word; you might strain your tongue.)

The beaches along this lower leeward stretch aren't very good (but the waters can have a very vibrant, turquoise appearance), thanks to runoff from Hawai'i Kai, a giant housing subdivision. Don't worry—the beaches will get *much* nicer.

If you're hungry, Hawai'i Kai has lots of restaurants. We've noticed at the Kona

Brewing Company (which has good pizza) an abundance of spotted eagle rays that skim the surface of the water to dine on algae growing along the nearby boat piers.

When an island like O'ahu is nearing the twilight of its volcanic life, the volcanoes usually go to sleep for up to a million years, then sputter back awake for a short time, often creating explosive eruptions near the shoreline instead of the typical drooling type that characterizes most of its eruptive life. Hawaiian volcanoes get hot-tempered in their old age. The results of the volcanoes' last gasp are often cone-shaped mountains of cemented ash called *tuff*, created when seawater seeps into the underground magma, flashing into steam and causing monstrous pressures that eventually explode. Diamond Head and the two giant hills in front of you—called **Koko Crater** (to your left) and **Koko Head** (to your right)—are examples of the volcanoes' final temper tantrums.

The populated section of Koko Head can be reached by taking Lunalilo Home Road toward the ocean. If you drive to the end of Lumahai Road (see map on page 67), there's a little-known hidden gem near a hard-to-see public access corridor that requires a two-minute walk down a steep path to a constantly sloping bluff. But, ahh, what a sight. The **Spitting**

Cave of Portlock is below a gorgeous layered shoreline. Even without the cave, the shoreline is fascinating. Each layer represents a different volcanic explosion in the cliff's history, and you'll see some of the remnants of fallen layers in the exceptionally clear blue water. The spitting cave is where the ocean is chiseling its way inland, attempting to break Portlock in two. As the waves drive into the cave, they rebound off its backside, causing the ground to tremble beneath your feet, and water and mist to explode out of the cave if the surf is

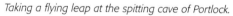

Taking a flying leap at the spitting cave of Portlock.

Snorkelers rejoice—the pool is open at Hanauma Bay.

right. Summer generally brings higher surf to south-facing shores, but even smaller winter waves can cause this effect. Standing right over the cave creates the best tremble; standing to the right of the cave (as you face the ocean) gives the best views. If you want a spectacular spot for your friends and family, look to the right side for the small, raised table. It's the perfect size for a few people to sit on, and with a relatively flat surface, it's excellent for watching the ocean. Some people also visit the natural sea level platform immediately in front of the cave—it provides the best views of the cave (if you're willing to climb down 15 feet of shoreline) and is used by cliff divers as a way to exit the water. For generations, locals have come to the point on weekends to jump off the 65-foot cliff in front of the cave during calm seas, but the injury and death toll has been particularly high, and you'll probably want to refrain from doing it. (You'll see memorial plaques lining the rock for those who perished.) Even if the ocean is flat, the cliff offers spectacular views, and on occasion you can see stray sail boats, kayakers, and even sea turtles rounding this portion of the island.

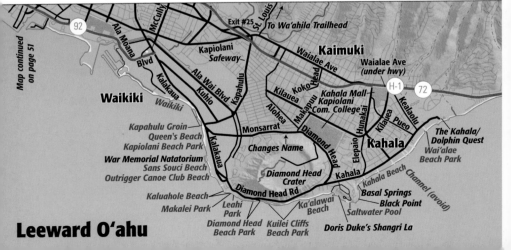

Map continued on page 51

Leeward O'ahu

Back on Hwy 72 you'll start climbing Koko Head and come to one of the island's biggest draws. If you've heard *anything* about snorkeling on O'ahu, you've heard about **Hanauma Bay**. Snorkeling at this underwater nature preserve is one of the most popular activities on the island and shouldn't be missed, but a lot of hype and misconceptions exist. Let's dispel some of them.

The **Hanauma Bay Nature Preserve** (808-396-4229) is actually *inside an old volcano crater* that eroded on one side due to wave action, forming a large crescent-shaped bay that is partially protected from the open ocean, with a wide beach and high cliff walls. In the past, people fed the fish, which actually resulted in fewer varieties. (Bolder species did well, driving out meeker types, so feeding fish is no longer allowed. Conservation efforts are working though, and diversity is returning to the reef.)

But it's full of crystal clear water with tons of coral, right? 'Fraid not. The water tends to be a bit cloudy, and much of the reef is actually made from coralline algae, which *looks* like dead coral, but it's actually a stony material created by plants. It's *supposed*

A REAL GEM

to look like that. And some of the real coral has been damaged over the years.

But what you *should* expect to see are fish... lots and lots of colorful fish of many varieties that are used to people. This is where having a crowd of more than 3,000 people per day works to your advantage—the fish are so tame that they'll often hangout and swim right up to your face. Be sure to bring your underwater camera.

Hanauma Bay is safe most of the time. There are lifeguards, and the inner bay is pretty protected. That said, some years, this is the drowning capital of O'ahu. After all, it *is* the ocean and anything can happen. Besides, if you invite over a million people a year to use *your bathtub*, odds are you'll lose one or two of them. Just remember not to go in the water 9–10 days after a full moon. (See **Box Jellyfish** in our *Hazards* section on page 31.) Also, be wary of swimming over the tops of the reefs. If the water's too shallow, a rogue swell could drop you onto one of the edges. The bay is open from 6 a.m. to 6 p.m. (until 7 during the summer). Closed Tuesdays.

It costs $1 per car and $7.50 per person to get in (ages 12 and under are free).

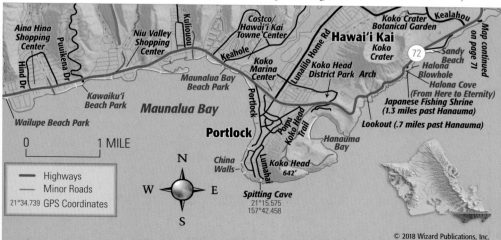

Map continued on page 71

© 2018 Wizard Publications, Inc.

Nearly everyone we've heard at the Lana'i Lookout speculates about which islands they're seeing. And nearly everyone gets it wrong. Here the islands are labeled as we saw them on this wickedly clear morning. Note that although Haleakala is twice as tall as East Moloka'i, it seems shorter due to its distance (100 miles). That's 1/250 of the circumference of the earth, so its bottom portion is below the planet's curvature.

East Moloka'i   West Moloka'i   Maui's Haleakala

Everyone has to watch a nine-minute conservation video before you're allowed to walk down to the bay 150 feet below you. They also have a tram to the bottom for a couple of bucks. Good for hill-haters or those with lots of beach stuff or SCUBA gear to lug. There's a food concession at the top and showers at the bottom. A $16 million "education center" is also at the top. (Though nice, it's hard to see how they spent *that* much on it.)

Snorkel gear is available for rent at the bottom—convenient, though it's overpriced at $20 for cheap-o equipment. (You can buy a decent set at Wal-Mart for not much more than that.) They also have flotation gear. Lockers are $8–$10.

The parking lot is often full by 9 a.m. As groups of cars leave, the park will let small groups of cars in, but you should arrive early if you want to be sure of getting a parking spot and not have to wait forever for your turn to watch the video. And the best snorkeling is early morning when the water is calmer, anyway.

An alternative to driving is **Hawaiian Ocean Promotions** (808-396-1600). For $36 they'll take you to and from some Waikiki hotels to Hanauma Bay. The price includes snorkel gear but you'll still have to pay the admission fee at the bay. Arrange a day in advance. You can also take the number 22 bus from Waikiki if going by public transportation. And this is refreshing: Saturdays are often the *least* crowded, because no tour buses allowed. Beach wheelchairs are available for free.

If you've never snorkeled before, it's probably a good idea to stay inside the reef, but those who are comfortable will want to explore the reef's backside. There you'll find large schools of big fish, and the occasional sea turtle. You may notice a couple of thick cables running through a channel in the reef near the center of the beach. If you try to follow them to the end, you're in for a *looooong* swim—those were the first underwater phone cables to connect Hawai'i to the mainland. There are two of them because each cable could only carry a signal one-way. Before these cables were laid across the ocean floor in 1957, transpacific calls were sent *wirelessly*, by bouncing radio waves off the atmosphere.

PAST HANAUMA BAY TO KAILUA

Continuing on Highway 72, there's a turnout 0.7 miles past the entrance to Hanauma Bay. This is the **Lana'i Lookout**, which is oddly named because if you see an island offshore, odds are it *ain't* Lana'i, it's Moloka'i. (See *Lana'i Lookout Explanation* in photo caption above.)

Lana'i

You'll likely see a few people disregarding the warning signs and climbing over the stone wall, *carefully* working their way down the slippery, sloped terrain to get a closer look at this incredible shoreline. Layer upon layer of cemented volcanic ash is being weathered away, sculpting some interesting and curvy formations.

If you'd like a less precarious way down, cross the highway (easier said than done) and walk about 50 yards east, to the beginning of the guardrail. Hop over it at the green "Scenic Overlook" sign. Go to the bottom of the drainage ditch, turn to the left and walk through the tunnel under the highway. You'll pop out at a magnificent secluded cove about 15 feet above a rock shelf. You can't see the lookout above and to your right (and they can't see you). This area is flatter. Make sure to pay attention to the ocean here and use caution and common sense as to where you amble about. The small tide pools indicate that this shoreline probably sees strong waves at least once a day. Avoid when the ocean is raging. If you're looking for good pictures, morning light is better than afternoon light.

About 1.3 miles past the entrance to Hanauma Bay is a very narrow pullout. (If there is no room park at the next lot and walk back.) There's a **Japanese Fishing Shrine** here with a carving of a Japanese guardian god that was said to preside over dangerous waterways. Originally, there

While everyone else is at the Lana'i Lookout gazing at the shoreline, you're down here at your own private vantage point.

It's impossible to resist stopping on the side of the road above Makapu'u Beach backed by its offshore islands.

was a stone statue installed by a Japanese fishing club, but during WWII it was demolished, and this carving took its place. Though the features of the stone has been weathered over the years, you can still find almost daily offerings of flowers and rice at the base of the shrine.

Walk past the shrine along the ridge for a hundred feet or so, and you're treated to wonderful view of the **Halona Cove** below and Halona Blowhole. Though more distant, in some ways this vantage point is even better than the dedicated blowhole lookout 500 feet up the road. This perspective shows the size of the blowhole eruptions in relation to the people at the lookout platform above. Locals still call this beach *From Here to Eternity Beach* since they filmed what was then (in the '50s) a scandalous love scene here, with the actors kissing and rolling around in the surf. For the record, fooling around on a beach sounds romantic but usually leads to sand in places that do not generally respond well to an abrasive.

Just past the shrine is the parking lot for the **Halona Blowhole.** This is where the ocean has undercut the lava and

drilled a hole through to the top. It's not super reliable, and if the surf is not high

NOT TO BE enough, it won't be erupting.

!

MISSED!

High tide is best. The lookout hangs below the parking lot with heavy railings to dissuade you from walking down to the blowhole itself. (Give yourself a pat on the back if you guessed that *liability* was the reason.) Of course, it's perfectly legal to boulder hop down to Halona Beach on your right and walk along the lava bench for a few minutes if you really want to visit the blowhole from below. If you do, be very cautious of the ocean, and never get between the ocean and the blowhole. Those who do and have been knocked in the hole are nearly always killed. Frankly, when we have visitors, we usually take them to see the blowhole from below. But we never do it when the ocean's raging, and we're always aware that our safety depends on the ocean being in a good mood. This is also where you park for the **Koko Crater Arch** hike.

Sandy Beach is your first good beach along this stretch. Strong waves and sunny conditions make this a nice beach to spend an afternoon, and there is almost always a food truck parked by the entrance. That giant lawn is where hang gliders and paragliders land after soaring the cliffs of Makapu'u. It's not uncommon to have a hang glider pilot come up to you and ask you to drive with him to the top of Makapu'u and return his car to Sandy Beach. (You can't drive up there on your own because permits are needed.) Sandy Beach is also where **ultralights** are launched. Some of the aerial photos in this book were taken from our ultralight launched from here. Although the air along the windward coast tends to be smooth, the mountain toward the east causes nasty turbulence right over Sandy Beach, and ultralight landings here tend to look pretty ugly. Those choppy conditions *do* allow for entertaining aerial displays from stunt kite flyers that frequent the grassy lawn.

As you round the easternmost part of the island, giant **Makapu'u Head** defines the eastern tip. There's a parking lot at the **Ka'iwi Scenic Shoreline Park.** A nicely paved road here snakes up to the 647-foot summit. (Can't drive it though.) At the top we noticed they have a wheelchair ramp leading to the lookout. (We're not sure if even Dwayne "The Rock" Johnson could push a wheelchair up 64 stories.) The road is hugely popular with locals who do their morning walks there. Sunrises are particularly nice from up top if you can motivate yourself to get up that early. During whale season the beasties tend to come pretty close to the point and are often visible from up there if there aren't too many whitecaps. If you're looking for a series of blowholes that puts Halona Blowhole to shame and you don't mind hiking, check out the **Dragon's Nostrils** write-up in *Activities* on page 196 as well as **Pele's Chair** at *Alan Davis Beach* on page 132.

Make sure you stop at the **Makapu'u Lookout** for expansive views up the coast (unless you already did the hike up Makapu'u, in which case you can skip it—the view is largely the same.) Then after you wrap around the corner, pull over again on the side of the road above **Makapu'u Beach** for a different angle. The vantage point is excellent. Although this beach is popular with locals who bodysurf here and at Sandy Beach, novice bodysurfers need to be leery since the shorebreak at these beaches tends to be pounding, which can drill you into the sand like a fencepost. Paragliders and model airplane enthusiasts take advantage of the updrafts here from

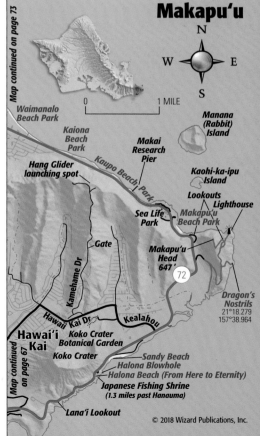

Makapu'u

N

W E

S

0   1 MILE

Map continued on page 73

Waimanalo Beach Park

Kaiona Beach Park

Hang Glider launching spot

Kaupo Beach Park

Makai Research Pier

Manana (Rabbit) Island

Kaohi-ka-ipu Island

Lookouts

Lighthouse

Sea Life Park

Makapu'u Beach Park

Gate

Makapu'u Head 647'

72

Kamehame Dr

Dragon's Nostrils
21°18.279
157°38.964

Hawai'i Kai Dr

Kealahou

Map continued on page 67

Hawai'i Kai

Koko Crater Botanical Garden

Koko Crater

Sandy Beach
Halona Blowhole
Halona Beach (From Here to Eternity)

Japanese Fishing Shrine
(1.3 miles past Hanauma)

Lana'i Lookout

© 2018 Wizard Publications, Inc.

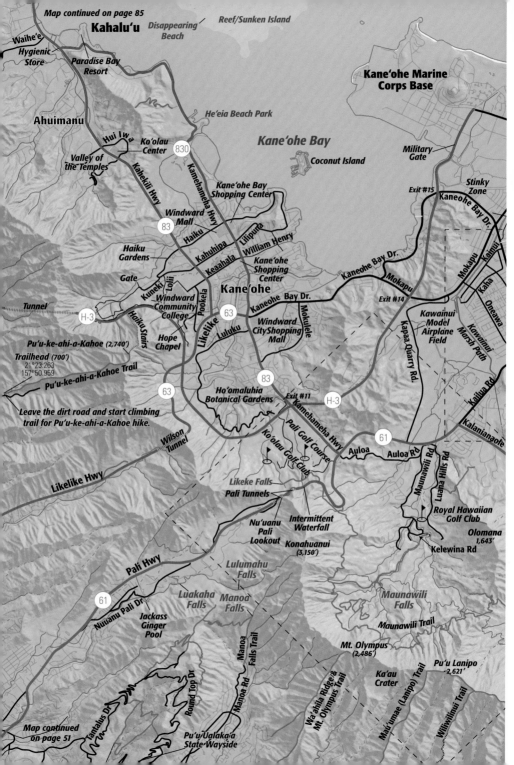

Map continued on page 85

Kahalu'u

Disappearing Beach

Reef/Sunken Island

Waihe'e
Hygienic Store

Paradise Bay Resort

Ko'olau Center

Hui Iwa

Ahuimanu

Valley of the Temples

He'eia Beach Park

Kane'ohe Bay

Coconut Island

Kane'ohe Marine Corps Base

Military Gate

Stinky Zone

Exit #15

Kaneohe Bay Dr.

Kahekili Hwy

830

Kamehameha Hwy

Kane'ohe Bay Shopping Center

Windward Mall

Haiku

Haiku Gardens

83

Kahuhipa

Lilipuna

William Henry

Kane'ohe Shopping Center

Mokapu

Mokapu

Kaha

Onaewa

Kainui

Gate

Keaahala

Kaneohe Bay Dr.

Exit #14

Kailua Rd

Kuneki

Lolii

Windward Community College

Pookela

Kane'ohe

Kaneohe Bay Dr.

Mokulele

Kapaa Quarry Rd.

Kawainui Model Airplane Field

Kawainui Marsh Path

Kalanianaole

Tunnel

H-3

Haiku Stairs

63

Likelike

Luluku

Windward City Shopping Mall

Pu'u-ke-ahi-a-Kahoe (2,740')

Hope Chapel

Trailhead (700')
21°23.263
157°50.959

Pu'u-ke-ahi-a-Kahoe Trail

63

Ho'omaluhia Botanical Gardens

83

Exit #11

H-3

61

Auloa

Auloa Rd

Maunawili Rd

Luana Hills Rd

Leave the dirt road and start climbing trail for Pu'u-ke-ahi-a-Kahoe hike.

Kamehameha Hwy

Ko'olau Golf Club

Pali Golf Course

Royal Hawaiian Golf Club

Olomana
1,643'

Wilson Tunnel

Likeke Falls

Pali Tunnels

Intermittent Waterfall

Kelewina Rd

Likelike Hwy

Nu'uanu Pali Lookout

Konahuanui
(3,150')

Maunawili Falls

Pali Hwy

61

Nuuanu Pali Dr

Jackass Ginger Pool

Lulumahu Falls

Luakaha Falls

Manoa Falls

Maunawili Trail

Mt. Olympus
(2,486')

Pu'u Lanipo
2,621'

Tantalus Dr

Round Top Dr

Manoa Rd

Manoa Falls Trail

Wa'ahila Ridge & Mt. Olympus Trail

Ka'au Crater

Mau'umae (Lanipo) Trail

Wiliwilinui Trail

Map continued on page 51

Pu'u/Ualaka'a State Wayside

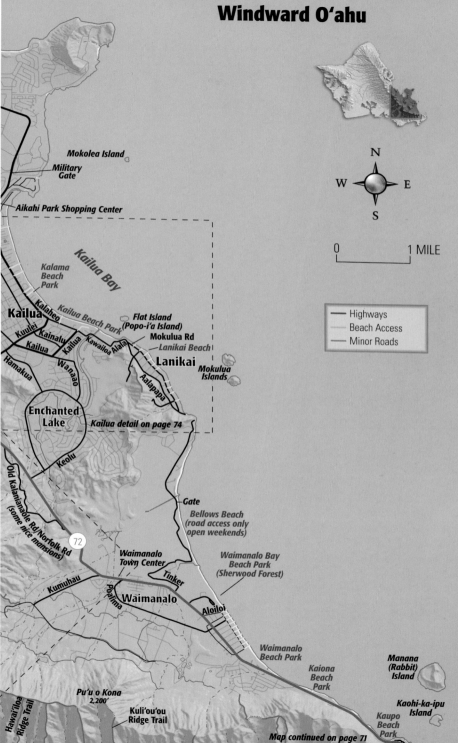

Mokolea Island

Military Gate

Aikahi Park Shopping Center

Kalama Beach Park

Kailua Bay

Kalaheo

Kailua Beach Park

Kailua

Kuulei

Kainalu

Kailua

Kailua

Kawaiioa Alala

Hamakua

Wanaao

Flat Island (Popo-i'a Island)

Mokulua Rd

Lanikai Beach

Lanikai

Aalapapa

Mokulua Islands

Enchanted Lake

Kailua detail on page 74

Keolu

Old Kalanianaole Rd/Norfolk Rd (some nice mansions)

72

Waimanalo Town Center

Tinker

Kumuhau

Poalima

Waimanalo

Aloiloi

Gate

Bellows Beach (road access only open weekends)

Waimanalo Bay Beach Park (Sherwood Forest)

Waimanalo Beach Park

Kaiona Beach Park

Pu'u o Kona 2,200'

Kuli'ou'ou Ridge Trail

Hawai'iloa Ridge Trail

Manana (Rabbit) Island

Kaohi-ka-ipu Island

Kaupo Beach Park

	Legend
Highways	
Beach Access	
Minor Roads	

N
W E
S

0 ———— 1 MILE

© 2018 Wizard Publications, Inc.

Map continued on page 71

Kailua

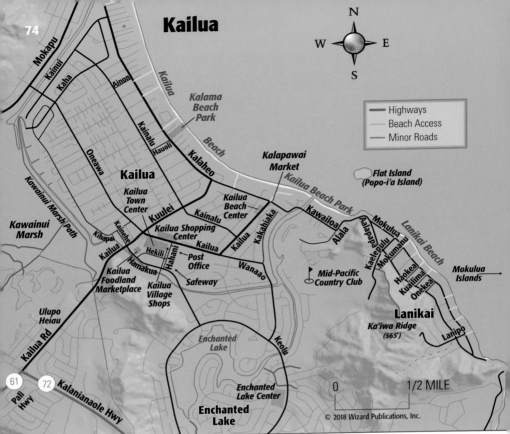

Kailua

Kailua Town Center

Kailua Shopping Center

Kailua Foodland Marketplace

Kailua Village Shops

Ulupo Heiau

Kawainui Marsh

Kalama Beach Park

Kalapawai Market

Kailua Beach Center

Kailua Post Office

Safeway

Flat Island (Popo-i'a Island)

Kailua Beach Park

Mid-Pacific Country Club

Mokulua Islands

Lanikai

Ka'iwa Ridge (565')

Enchanted Lake

Enchanted Lake Center

Enchanted Lake

Legend
- Highways
- Beach Access
- Minor Roads

0   1/2 MILE

© 2018 Wizard Publications, Inc.

the pullout. Behind Makapu'u is **Sea Life Park**, East O'ahu's version of Sea World. See *Attractions* on page 169 for more.

Those two islands you see off Makapu'u were probably where the last eruptions took place on the island. The shorter island, called **Kaohi-ka-ipu Island**, was made from a traditional lava flow when the ocean level was lower and the land there high and dry. It looks dark and burnt, a tribute to its relative youth. **Manana Island** behind it is a tuff cone like Diamond Head, made from a steam explosion. Locals usually refer to it as **Rabbit Island** because a local resident used to raise rabbits there in the 1880s. Today, thousands of seabirds make their home on the islands, and tiger sharks are known to frequent the area around it thanks to a healthy abundance of marine life.

Shortly after Makapu'u you'll come to the **Makai Research Pier** on the right. It's worth a quick stop. The pier is open to the public and you can walk out to the end for better views. The University of Hawai'i and NOAA use the pier to test underwater equipment, and for research missions. If the hangar door is open you might get to check out one of their Pisces-class submarines, which have an operating depth of more than 6,000 feet. If you feel like playing model, underneath the pier is popular with photographers.

Now you're driving through **Hawaiian Homelands** and the town of **Waimanalo**. In 1920 the government set aside over 200,000 acres of land to be used only by people of Hawaiian descent. Waimanalo is such a place. The town is lined by various species of pine trees in and out, but what you *won't* see are the numerous stables, ranches, and even the **Honolulu Polo Club**, all of which are dedicated to horsemanship in sleepy little Waimanalo.

The shoreline along here is almost uninterrupted sand beach consisting of Kaiona Beach, Waimanalo Beach, Bellows Beach and Waimanalo Bay Beach Park. The latter is backed by a thick forest of ironwood trees. To this day locals refer to this area as **Sherwood Forest.** That's because during the '60s the forest became a hot place to strip cars and rob beachgoers. The gang that was responsible called themselves Robin Hood and the Merry Men because they took from the rich and gave to...well, *themselves*, actually. Today, the Merry Men have been replaced by "longterm, unpermitted campers." The walk along Bellows is pleasant—and legal—but expect to have wary eyes trained on you from the Air Force personnel stationed behind the beach.

Though the leeward side's Wai'anae Range is taller, the **Ko'olau Mountain Range** on the windward side *looks* taller

A REAL GEM

and much more dramatic. The sheer, fluted cliffs carpeted with every shade of green are among the most wondrous sights on the island and never fail to impress. The tallest peaks of the Ko'olaus, just south (to the left) of the Pali tunnel and peaking at 3,150 and 3,105 feet, are called **Konahuanui**, literally translated as the *big, fat testicles.* Hey, we don't make up the legends, we just report 'em. (Perhaps they're named in honor of the first Hawaiian who had enough guts to climb them?)

As you look at the splendid cliffs of the Ko'olaus, consider how they went about burying the chief. In old Hawai'i, when a particularly beloved chief died, it was customary to sacrifice several of his trusted servants, as well. (And you thought *you* sacrificed a lot for your boss.) When the servant heard about his chief's death, he

Kailua town orbits Kailua Beach.
As it darned well should...

The Pali Lookout is one of the better reasons to take the Pali Highway to Kailua…

would kiss his wife and children goodbye and, without telling them why, leave to become a *moepuʻu*, or companion in death. He would then enter the hut where the chief's body was being kept and lie down between the dead man's legs. The only way his life could be spared was if one of the heirs to the kingdom so decided. If none of the dead chief's servants came forward to sacrifice themselves, one of his officers or relatives might be called upon to do so. This is why the chief's health was *always* a topic of interest to those closest to him. They had a vested interest in keeping him healthy.

When it came time to bury the chief, the funeral procession often hiked to the top of the Koʻolaus from the leeward side. The chief's bones, having been separated from the valueless flesh, were lowered by rope along with a digger. Once the digger gouged out a cavity in the cliffs, the bones were placed inside and the digger would tug on the rope. Then the men at the top cut the rope, and the digger plunged to his death,

taking with him the secret to where the chief's bones lay. In this way the sacred bones, which Hawaiians believed contained their *mana*, or spiritual power, could never be found and desecrated. And it was actually considered an *honor* to be the doomed digger.

KAILUA TOWN

Kailua is your classic beach town and, in our minds, one of the nicest places to stay if you're not going to stay in Waikiki, though it is no longer the sleepy town it was a decade or so ago. Though only 30 minutes from Honolulu via the Pali Highway, it's a world away from big city life. There are no resorts here, but vacation rentals and B&Bs are plentiful. Two of the finest beaches on the island bless this community, the kayaking in Kailua Bay to offshore islands is fantastic, and there are some excellent restaurants. If you're looking for a dreamy beach scene backed by offshore islands, **Lanikai Beach** is a must. If you want a long, delicious beach to stroll along or want to kayak these waters to a nearby island, you gotta check out **Kailua Beach**. While it's true that Kailua seems to be getting loved to death these days, there's a reason for the love. See *Beaches* for more on these.

In addition to the beaches, a couple things to keep an eye out for are scattered around Kailua.

On Hwy 61 (Kailua Road) between Hwy 72 and Hamakua Drive, unseen across from the Aloha Gas Station is the **Ulupo Heiau**, which now is little more than a pile of rocks. They have some signs describing the interesting geology of Kailua, taro beds and some nice views overlooking the mountains and valley. Across from the gas station turn onto Uluoa St. then right onto Manualoha St., then the next right onto Manuo'o St. and drive behind the YMCA to park in the lot next to the heiau.

At the end of Kainui Drive mauka (toward the mountain) of Kailua town is an access for a very nice regional park skirting the edge of the otherwise water-logged **Kawainui Marsh**. Though not a must-see, Kawainui Regional Park offers an extended walking path that carves through the wetlands. It isn't worth walking the whole length, but if you're looking for a chance to get away from people, this is the place to do it.

The Direct Highways to Kailua

There are three highways that drill through the Ko'olaus directly to the windward side, ending up in Kailua or Kane'ohe. Pali and Likelike are highways, not freeways, with traffic lights and intersections part of the way. H-3 is a classic elevated freeway.

Of all your non-coastal routes, H-3 is the most rewarding, especially going from Kailua to Honolulu. H-3 is an interstate highway. *Hey, wait a minute. Hawai'i's a bunch of islands. How can it be an interstate highway?* Simple. If we'd called it a *state* highway, *we'd* have to pay for it. I believe I speak for all Hawai'i

...and this is the reason to take H-3.

residents when I say thank you for your generous federal tax dollars.

Anyway, this 16-mile road cost almost $100 million *per mile* to build and took a mere *37 years* to complete. They spent *20 years* of that time doing environmental impact study after environmental impact study. But the results are incredible. If you saw it in a movie, you'd dismiss it out of hand as too beautiful to believe. Elevated high above the ground while cruising toward and next to the fluted cliffs of the Ko'olaus, this is the next best thing to taking a helicopter ride along the mountains.

You'll often notice that as you pass through the H-3 tunnel the weather might be different on each side. Weather on O'ahu is strongly affected by the mountains. Moist air from the northeast encounters the Ko'olau mountain range, rising and cooling. Cooler air can't hold as much moisture as warmer air, so the moisture condenses—in other words, forms a cloud. If it has more moisture than this now-cooler air can hold, it rains. With the air-deflecting mountain behind it, the traveling air sinks and gets warmer. Having already wrung out the moisture over the mountains, this drier air tends to be less prone to cloudiness. Hence, the leeward side's sunny days.

By the way, shortly before the H-3 tunnel (if you're coming from the windward side), look for a metal staircase on the side of the mountain on your left. It'll be winding its way up into the clouds. That's the **Haiku Stairs**, also called the **Stairway to Heaven**. We talk about it in detail in **Pu'u-ke-ahi-a-kahoe (Moanalua Valley to Haiku Stairs)** on page 248. Be careful here because the wide open freeway

The serene setting of the Byodo-In Temple exudes peacefulness.

limit sneakily switches to 45 long before the tunnel and police on motorcycles often literally *swarm* the stretch.

As an alternate to H-3, you can also take the **Pali Highway** (Hwy 61) from Honolulu. It heads straight into downtown Kailua. The Old Nu'uanu Pali Road on your right a few miles up makes a nice diversion from Pali Hwy. It's a short ride along yesteryear and there are a few hikes off this road. Until it was built, leeward residents who wanted to visit friends and relatives on the windward side had to take a winding trail up Nu'uanu Valley, where it terminated at a sheer cliff. From there a nerve-wracking portion slithered down the cliffs to the plains below. With the completion of the Nu'uanu Pali Road (later replaced by the Pali Highway), this place of fear became a place of wondrous beauty. Kane'ohe Bay, Mokapu Peninsula, the cliffs of Ko'olau and even Chinaman's Hat island off in the distance create a glorious expansive panorama at the **Pali Lookout**.

A REAL GEM

The last major Hawaiian battle took place here, and the results changed the political landscape. (See page 14 for more.) There are several short trails near here you can get to from the Pali Highway, including the **Pali Puka Trail, Lulumahu Falls, Judd Trail to Jackass Ginger Pool,** and **Likeke Falls.** See *Hiking* in *Activities* for details.

Bring the warmest clothes in your suitcase for the Pali Lookout. Yeah, sure, this is the tropics and the elevation is only 1,200 feet. But you're at a slit in a mountain that funnels the now-cooler trade winds piling up against the larger mountain, and you'll freeze your 'okole off here if you're not prepared. (Of course, maybe we're just wimps who have lived in Hawai'i too long.) To the right, the re-mains of the Old Pali Road are buried under a rockfall. It's $3 to park at the Pali Lookout.

Got any bacon with you? Local custom says that if you take the Pali Hwy with any pork in your car, bad things will happen to you. This is because this area was said to be the home of Kamapua'a, a demigod who was half man, half pig. If you have any pork with you, it's an in-your-face gesture that Kamapua'a will take offense with—and perhaps respond to.

The third highway poking through the mountain, **Likelike Hwy** (Hwy 63) is the least attractive of the trans-Ko'olau highways and should be your last choice. By the way, if someone asks, it's pronounced LEE-KAY-LEE-KAY, not LIKE-LIKE.

If you want to head back to Waikiki, take one of these highways. If you're gonna keep going to the North Shore, see the next chapter. We should probably have put Kane'ohe in the *North Shore Sights* chapter, but it felt…weird, because it's contiguous to Kailua.

KANE'OHE

If you're heading north, Kane'ohe is your next town. Orient yourself with the map on page 72. The most important landmark in Kane'ohe is the **Kane'ohe Marine Corps Base.** Forget your visions of row upon row of barracks with privates running around as sergeants bark out orders. This is a charming, self-contained city with all the comforts of home, sort of an island within an island. It has restaurants, a movie theater, gas stations, neighborhoods of beautiful houses, schools and school buses, car rental companies, stellar beaches and a very nice golf course called Klipper. Everything a growing marine and his/her family could want. The only thing you won't find here is…

you. It's an active marine base and access is restricted.

The prominent **Ulupau Head** at Kane'ohe Base is the result of steam explosions offshore that formed a separate island. The world was warmer then and the sea level higher. As the world cooled, the sea level dropped, connecting the land via a peninsula.

Ironically, Kane'ohe Base's destiny as an island apart from the rest of O'ahu is assured, both politically and geologically. It's *barely* attached to the main island by a nearly flooded plain. With naturally rising sea levels (which have risen 180 feet over the past 12,000 years), it almost certainly will be cut off from O'ahu within a hundred years or so without human intervention.

By the way, contrary to popular belief, Pearl Harbor was not the first place attacked on December 7, 1941. Kane'ohe was, since there was an airfield here that the Japanese wanted to neutralize before they went after the fleet on the other side of the island.

Driving along, if you've been lusting after the Ko'olau Mountains and want to drive a bit closer to them, you can take a detour to a free botanical garden that backs up to them. On Hwy 83 just north of its intersection with H-3 is Luluku Road. Up this road is the **Ho'omaluhia Park Botanical Garden** (808-233-7323). The drive through the gardens gets you more intimate with the mountains but walking around is less exciting due to a lack of maintenance. If you're interested in touring the gardens, see *Land Tours* on page 224.

The only thing more beautiful than the Ko'olaus on a clear morning is on those afternoons when the invisible trade winds cause the soft clouds to dance

What could be more magical than greeting a new day from Kailua Beach?

along the jagged summit in a scene that will surely cause you to think, *this must be what heaven looks like.*

If you take the Kahekili Highway (Hwy 83) through Kaneʻohe, north of Kaneʻohe town is the **Valley of the Temples**. This is simply a large cemetery. Well, maybe not so simple. It's $5 (cash only) per person to get in, and there are various temples scattered around the area. In the back is the greatest temple of them all. The **Byodo-In** is a grand replica of a 960-year-old Buddhist temple in Uji, Japan. Built in the 1960s to commemorate the 100th anniversary of the arrival of Japanese immigrant workers to Hawaiʻi, the temple is the absolute essence of serenity. It's like taking a mini-trip to Japan. Backed by the gorgeous Koʻolau mountain range and fronted by a large pond filled with koi fish and curious black swans, it's impossible to not feel peaceful here. (The only distraction is the seemingly constant sound of gas-powered weed whackers. Of course, it's those same personnel who keep the grounds so flawlessly sculpted.) This temple is still used today by worshippers. If you visit, it's customary to ring the richly toned, seven-ton bell, and let the resonance vibrate through you as a reminder that everything is transitory. Morning light is best here.

In Kaneʻohe Bay, **Moku-o-loʻe** (usually called **Coconut Island** was formerly owned by a Fleischmann's yeast heir. (Ironically enough, the island actually did "rise" while this yeast guy owned it. He doubled its size by dredging and planted the coconut trees.) Today the island is home to the University of Hawaiʻi's Institute of Marine Biology. Private tours are available weekdays for $80 per group, which includes a short boat ride over and a two-hour walking tour of the island. There's a touch tank and a cool hammerhead shark pen in the lagoon. Arrange in a month or two in advance by Googling HIMB or call 808-235-9302. The island is barely recognizable from its TV days in the '60s when it served as *Gilligan's Island* in the '60s.

Kaneʻohe Bay's reputation among long-time locals is less than pristine. For 25 years the military base and the local community discharged untreated sewage into the south part of the bay, and the bay became known as the *last* place you'd want to go into the water. Although the practice stopped in 1978 (treated water is piped to a trench *way* offshore where currents carry it away), many locals from the leeward side still connect Kaneʻohe Bay with bad water and avoid it, which pleases windward residents who get it all to themselves.

In fact, one of our favorite kayak trips on the island is in Kaneʻohe Bay. It visits a 1,000-acre sunken island and two beaches that appear and disappear twice each day. See *Kayaking* on page 218 for more.

After driving through the town of Kaneʻohe heading north, you're committed to the shoreline route that you'll be hugging for the next 40 miles.

EAST OʻAHU BEST BETS

Best Sunrise—From the top of Makapuʻu or Kaʻiwa Ridge in Kailua for the motivated

Best Beach Stroll—Kailua Beach

Best *Empty* Beach Stroll—Bellows Beach *During the Week*

Best Place to Get Drilled into the Sand—Bodysurfing at Sandy Beach or Makapuʻu Beach

Best Place to See Water Fly Out of a Cave— Spitting Cave of Portlock

Best Place to Lose Your Hat—Pali Lookout

Best Bodysurfing Waves—Kailua Beach

Yeah, now that's what we call a highway.

The North Shore is the prettiest drive on the entire island. Forget the big city and its multi-lane highways. This is a place with only a few traffic lights and a two-lane road that hugs the shoreline, embracing the Hawai'i of yesteryear. Along the way you'll find yourself constantly drooling over the beaches and mountain scenery.

We've marked the following maps in terms of miles and time (without stops or traffic) from Windward Mall in Kane'ohe. You'll usually know when you've gone from one town to the next.

This is a long chapter because once you've driven past Kane'ohe, you're committed to the drive to Hale'iwa. So, although part of windward O'ahu is on this tour, we're sticking with the term *North Shore Sights.* (*North Shore and the Northern part of Windward Shore Sights* wouldn't fit in the heading.)

KUALOA

As you approach the northern part of Kane'ohe Bay on Hwy 83, **Tropical Farms** is a mac nut farm with a very pretty garden area and gorgeous monkeypod trees providing shade. They're very generous with the flavored mac nut samples and coffee. (They can afford to be at these prices.) Though Tropical Farms offers *forgettable* guided tours of their farm, the variety of locally made soaps, oils, perfumes, honeys and sauces make their central shop a great place to spend an hour before heading farther north. Also on the property is a building dedicated to Hawaiian jewelry that features pearls and native koa wood in most of their designs. Watch out for the two hazards here: wasps flying around the sampling area and tour buses flying around the parking lot.

Kualoa Beach Park is at the very edge of Kane'ohe Bay. This gigantic beach park has an endless lawn, a long ribbon of sand fringing it and an *oh-so-tempting* offshore island called **Chinaman's Hat** (Hawaiian name Mokoli'i). This uninhabited island can be yours to rule. See *Adventures* on page 245. The road into Kualoa Park was an airstrip during WWII that extended *across* the highway (where the grass is today). When the P-38s (used here in WWII for photo recon) had to take off or land, they had someone stand at the highway to stop traffic. Instead of concrete, the entire 6,500-foot runway was paved with steel grates.

Past the park, **Kualoa Ranch** is a huge, breathtakingly beautiful windward ranch. It's also a giant visitor-processing machine that in some areas does a good job, but their prices ain't cheap. Some of their activities seem a bit over-hyped to us. For instance, on one of their tours, the "Secret Island Beach," they take you to is a sandbar that anyone can walk to from the adjacent Kualoa Beach. They also have horseback rides (nose-to-tail rides, but the mountain scenery is very pretty), ATV tours (same description), biking and ziplines. See *Activities* for more.

That old concrete chimney on the side of the road past Kualoa Park is all that remains of a short-lived, Civil War-era **sugar mill**. Shortly after it opened, the co-owner's young son was accidentally bumped into a vat of boiling sugar syrup and died. The mill closed five years later when they realized that the area didn't get enough rain.

Soon the highway starts cozying up to the ocean in a dramatic way. It's heavenly to drive along so close to the sand and the breakers. In the town of Ka'a'awa (pronounced as if you were coughing up a furball) you'll find **Uncle Bobo's**, which has good BBQ and cheap food across from Swanzy Beach Park next to the post office (before the 7-Eleven).

At the north end of town after mile marker 27 before the road curves into Kahana Bay is the **Crouching Lion**. Lava rocks on the mountain form the silhouette of a lion. Most people mistakenly look at the most obvious rocks near the road and think that's the lion. Look up higher, and there you'll find the little bugger with his mouth slightly open, facing somewhat away from you. By the way, don't believe any stories about a Hawaiian legend of a crouching lion around here. The ancient Hawaiians would have had as much familiarity with lions as they'd have had with chainsaws. Lions ain't native to Hawai'i.

KAHANA BAY

After the tongue-twisting Ka'a'awa is the easier-to-pronounce **Kahana Bay**. Although the bay's waters are never ultra-clear thanks to runoff from the Kahana River, the beach setting is picturesque, and it's rare to find more than a few people here during the week. One of the easier kayak trips is up the jungly-looking river. (See *Kayaking* on page 221 for more.) The state park behind the bay is the **Ahupua'a O Kahana State Park**.

By the way, your drive along the North Shore won't be exactly *filled* with dining options. Your best bet is to eat at one of the shrimp vendors ahead in Kahuku, wait until you get to the North Shore around Sunset Beach or Sharks Cove, or hit Hale'iwa, which has a good restaurant selection.

In the town of Hau'ula, **Sacred Falls Park** *was* one of the most popular waterfall hikes on the island. A fatal landslide on Mother's Day in 1999 and subsequent lawsuits prompted its closure. The state has since passed a law immunizing itself from future lawsuits (isn't it cool to be able to pass a law immunizing yourself?), but the falls and 1,300-acre park are still closed as bureaucrats ponder its future. The only thing they've been able to agree on is to change the name of this closed park to **Kaluanui State Park**. By the way, Kaluanui means *the big pit*. People find about about it on the internet and try to sneak in, but authorities are serious about enforcing the closure and will arrest anyone trying to trespass.

In this area after Kaluanui Beach (at a little street called Hula Hula), you pass over a very small bridge. It's over an intermittent stream, and this particular stream bed seems to be a dumping ground for the ocean to deposit sand. Vast amounts pile up on the mauna side of the bridge, and you will often see locals here filling canvas and plastic sandbags to keep the ocean at bay elsewhere. The source of sand seems endless here.

LA'IE

The biggest town along this part of the island is La'ie. In terms of driving time, there is probably no place on the island that takes longer to get to from Waikiki than La'ie. It's also light years away in terms of the culture. La'ie is a town heavily dominated by the Latter Day Saints (often called Mormon) Church. Their university, **Brigham Young University–Hawai'i**, has a campus and a beautiful temple here as well. (The temple is the first built outside of Utah. You are not allowed to go inside unless you are LDS, but they have a visitor center where they will enthusiastically share their

What's not to love about the northern end of Kane'ohe Bay and its uninhabited island, Chinaman's Hat?

faith.) The church is virtually everybody's landlord in this town where alcohol is not allowed to be sold. That's why there's a Tamura's Market in the adjacent town of Hau'ula, where nearby residents go for their liquid aloha. And the local Chinese restaurant only serves tea, if you ask for it.

One of the biggest attractions in all Hawai'i, the **Polynesian Cultural Center**, is in La'ie. This sprawling center was created to attract visitors, who help subsidize Brigham Young students from all over the Pacific. They do a particularly good job re-creating island life from around Polynesia. See *Attractions* on page 152 for more.

Take a right at the stoplight at Anemoku, then right on Naupaka. This leads to the not-to-be-missed **La'ie Point**. **NOT TO BE MISSED!** Oh, what a beautiful sight! This point is made up entirely of sandstone with several small islands offshore. The closest one is 432 feet offshore (looks closer, doesn't it?). It has a natural arch carved dead center that was created on April Fool's Day 1946 when a tsunami literally punched a hole through the island. To the right are more islands, along with a view of Windward O'ahu itself. The 360-degree vantage from this point is grand, and if the surf is up, the symphony of crashing waves is a delight to listen to.

Past the center of town, **La'ie Beach** is also known as **Hukilau Beach**. A hukilau is a fishing event where non-fishermen are able to catch fish. A net is laid out in a horseshoe shape with the open end toward the shore. While some people splash around, driving fish into the net, people on the shore slowly pull the net onto the land. After WWII, the LDS church performed a monthly hukilau here to help raise funds for the church. It got so popular

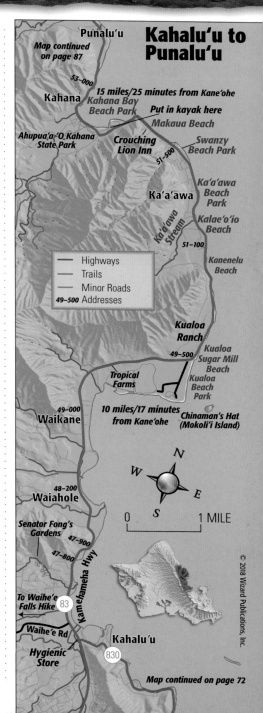

Kahalu'u to Punalu'u

Punalu'u

Map continued on page 87

53–000

Kahana

Kahana Bay Beach Park

15 miles/25 minutes from Kane'ohe

Put in kayak here

Makaua Beach

Ahupua'a 'O Kahana State Park

Crouching Lion Inn

51–500

Swanzy Beach Park

Ka'a'awa

Ka'a'awa Beach Park

Ka'a'awa Stream

Kalae'o'io Beach

51–100

Kanenelu Beach

— Highways
— Trails
— Minor Roads
49–500 Addresses

Kualoa Ranch

49–500

Kualoa Sugar Mill Beach

Tropical Farms

Kualoa Beach Park

49–000

Waikane

10 miles/17 minutes from Kane'ohe

Chinaman's Hat (Mokoli'i Island)

N
W E
S

48–200
Waiahole

Senator Fong's Gardens

47–900

47–800

Kamehameha Hwy

0   1 MILE

To Waihe'e Falls Hike 83

Waihe'e Rd

Hygienic Store

Kahalu'u

830

© 2018 Wizard Publications, Inc.

Map continued on page 72

Sometimes nature patiently chips away at things, and sometimes she's in a hurry. This sea arch off La'ie Point was created in one day when Mother Nature angrily put her fist through the island.

that a state agency, the Hawaii Visitor's Bureau, asked them to continue performing it and promoted it to visitors. So why doesn't the church still do hukilau there anymore? Because *another* state agency saw its popularity as a way to get money. The Hawai'i government decided it wanted to tax the event in 1970, so the Mormons simply stopped doing them. Incidentally, as with other things in La'ie, Hukilau Beach (or at least the access to it) is closed on Sundays.

After La'ie is a large state beach park called **Malaekahana State Recreation Area**. If you're looking for a beach that takes a bit more to get to than simply walking up and falling into the sand, **Moku'auia Island** (also called **Goat Island**) is 240 yards offshore from the park. You can usually wade to it, and those who put in the effort are rewarded with a picture-perfect crescent sand beach often deserted in the morning.

A REAL GEM

The notable thing about Malaekahana are the **cabins** for rent. They're old private beach houses that were taken over by the state when this area was converted into a park. Although pretty run down, they can be yours if you make arrangements in advance. See *Camping* on page 184 for more.

KAHUKU

After La'ie on Hwy 83, the town of Kahuku is famous for its shrimp trucks and shacks. Although shrimp is commercially grown nearby, some of the trucks get their shrimp from off-island sources. It's easy to look at businesses like these "sleepy little shrimp trucks" and assume that they're struggling little mom and pop enterprises. Sometimes they're much more. **Giovanni's Aloha Shrimp Truck** is a case in point.

The current owner bought the business for $120,000. Four years later, in 2001, the previous owner said she wanted it back. Apparently, she *really* wanted it back. According to prosecutors, she met with the owner and demanded he sell her the business back for the price he paid. He replied that it was now worth much more—$700,000, to be precise. (If you've ever seen the long lines at Giovanni's during lunch, that sounds reasonable.) When he refused to sign a contract for $120,000, two large gunmen walked in, threatened his family on the mainland, stuck a gun in his left eye and politely asked him to sign the contract (which he did). He later went to the police, and the woman was convicted of robbery, extortion and kidnapping. Sleepy little businesses, indeed.

You're nearing the northernmost part of the island. Past the shrimp vendors, there's a vast area on your right belonging to the **James Campbell Company**. Formerly an estate trust with 176 heirs worth *$2 billion*, it was broken up in 2007. Although they occasionally offer tours when it's not nesting season, don't bother. Except for the wild, windy shoreline (check out the desolate hike listed on page 209), the land you're not seeing is probably the ugliest part of the island. The land looks stressed, beaten up and tired. Every region has to have an ugly side, and this is O'ahu's, in our opinion. So don't be concerned that you're missing something special.

After Kahuku is a store on the ocean side called **Only Show in Town** (but the sign says **S. Tanaka Store Antique & Bottles**). This place sure lives up to its name. It's positively *packed* with very old bottles from early Hawaiian bottlers, endless Coca-Cola antiques, Japanese glass fishing floats and more. Worth stopping for if you like antiques and *if* they're open. Also take a peek at their neighbors, an art store that spe-

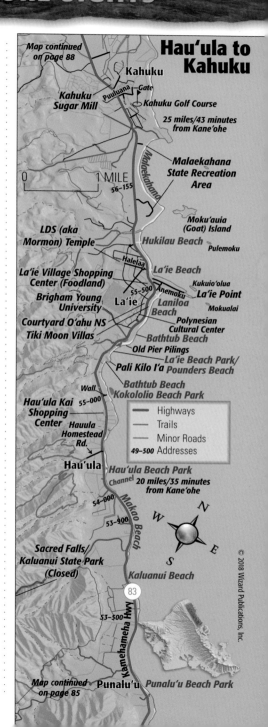

Hau'ula to Kahuku

Map continued on page 88

Kahuku

Kahuku Sugar Mill

Puuluana

Gate

Kahuku Golf Course

25 miles/43 minutes from Kane'ohe

Malaekahana State Recreation Area

0   1 MILE
56–155

Moku'auia (Goat) Island

LDS (aka Mormon) Temple

Hukilau Beach

Pulemoku

Halelaa

La'ie Beach

La'ie Village Shopping Center (Foodland)

Kukuio'olua

Brigham Young University

La'ie   55–500   Anemoku

La'ie Point

Laniloa Beach   Mokualai

Courtyard O'ahu NS

Polynesian Cultural Center

Tiki Moon Villas

Bathtub Beach

Old Pier Pilings

La'ie Beach Park/ Pounders Beach

Pali Kilo I'a

Bathtub Beach

Wall

Kokololio Beach Park

Hau'ula Kai   55–000

Shopping Center   Hauula Homestead Rd.

Highways
Trails
Minor Roads
49–500 Addresses

Hau'ula

Hau'ula Beach Park

Channel   20 miles/35 minutes from Kane'ohe

54–000

Makao Beach

53–900

N
W   E
S

Sacred Falls/ Kaluanui State Park (Closed)

Kaluanui Beach

83

53–500   Kamehameha Hwy

Map continued on page 85

Punalu'u   Punalu'u Beach Park

Turtle Bay to Waimea

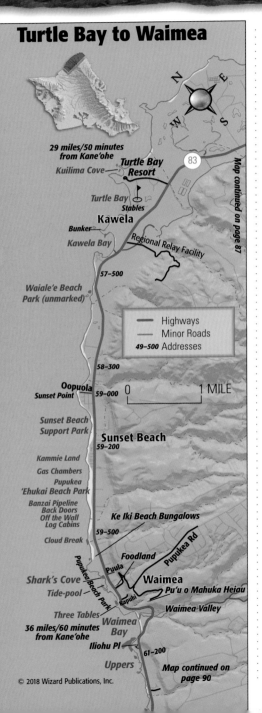

29 miles/50 minutes
from Kaneʻohe

Kuilima Cove

Turtle Bay Resort

83

Turtle Bay Stables

Kawela

Bunker

Kawela Bay

Regional Relay Facility

57–500

Waialeʻe Beach Park (unmarked)

Map continued on page 87

▬▬	Highways	
▬▬	Minor Roads	
49–500	Addresses	

58–300

Oopuola
Sunset Point

59–000

0 — — — 1 MILE

Sunset Beach Support Park

Sunset Beach

59–200

Kammie Land

Gas Chambers

Pupukea
ʻEhukai Beach Park

Banzai Pipeline
Back Doors
Off the Wall
Log Cabins

Ke Iki Beach Bungalows

59–500

Cloud Break

Foodland

Puula

Pupukea Rd

Sharks Cove

Tide-pool

Pupukea Beach Park

Kapuhi

Waimea

Puʻu o Mahuka Heiau

Waimea Valley

Three Tables

36 miles/60 minutes
from Kaneʻohe

Waimea Bay

Iliohu Pl

61–200

Uppers

Map continued on page 90

© 2018 Wizard Publications, Inc.

cializes in driftwood collected from the area. If you strike up a conversation with the shop owners, they may show you their collection of World War II metal fragments and pre-20th century blown glass pieces.

TURTLE BAY

Oʻahu has been amazingly successful at containing resorts in a single area. Outside Waikiki there are fewer than a dozen resorts. Turtle Bay is one of them.

As an aside, we always include aerial photos of all the resorts in the free *Where to Stay* section of our app. This resort and beach are always the hardest to photograph. Their location at the end of the Koʻolau Mountains is where different types of winds converge, and the air above this resort is almost always turbulent to the point of being violent. Trying to hold the camera steady and flying the pitching aircraft while screaming and crying for mama is a bit awkward, so if our aerial shots of this area are a bit blurry, you'll understand why. You'll also notice wind turbines along here and closer to Haleʻiwa. Between them there are 42 turbines cranking out 81 megawatts of power to feed Oʻahu's thirsty power grid.

THE NORTH SHORE

When surfers talk about the North Shore, they generally mean the 7 miles of surf breaks from Sunset Point to Puaʻena Point near Haleʻiwa town. Other islanders consider the North Shore to be everything from Sunset Point all the way out to the westernmost tip of the island at Kaʻena Point.

The population of the North Shore doubles during the winter surf season, and traffic often backs up near beaches visible from the road as rubbernecking drivers find wave-watching irresistible.

(Residents are the *worst* offenders.) During those times when the waves don't materialize during the winter, you'll see them *bumming hard core, brah.* The pulse rate of the North Shore slows considerably when the surfing season dies down in the spring. Laid back and casual become the order of the day.

Just before Sunset Beach you'll see **Ted's Bakery** on the left. You should know that their chocolate/haupia (made from coconut) pie is legendary on the island. Frankly, to us it tastes pretty unremarkable, but some island residents and many of our readers get downright teary-eyed over it. If you try it, please let us know if we're off the mark on this one.

The **Sunset Beach** area was known to ancient Hawaiians as Pau-malu. According to lore, there was once a local woman renowned for her ability to catch octopus. One day as she was preparing to go hunting here, an old man stopped her and told her to limit her catch to a certain number. She agreed but, while hunting, she got carried away and caught more than the allotment. Just then a giant shark came and bit off both her legs. Locals concluded that she had angered the shark god that watched over the reef and named the area Pau-malu, meaning *taken by surprise.*

Today Sunset Beach is a dreamy beach that brings fantastic waves in the winter and placid, warm waters in the summer. Unfortunately, beach erosion has been threatening some homes along here of late.

Imagine owning a beachfront house along here. Then imagine this: The stretch of shoreline from Sunset Point almost to Shark's Cove is all sandy beach. In 1919 a developer broke the entire 2 miles into individual parcels for beachfront homes. He sold them all in less than two months and pocketed—are you ready for this?—a whopping $46,000 *for all the parcels combined.* Today it would cost at least 50 times that amount for a *single* parcel.

Surf sites vary in their fame. But in all Hawai'i there is no more famous surf break than the **Banzai Pipeline**. During large (but not giant) surf, swells coming from the northwest form perfect barrels at this site. It's hard to find prettier waves anywhere in the world than on a good day

A REAL GEM

Despite the name,
you're more likely to see this...   *than this at Shark's Cove.*

Waimea to Hale'iwa

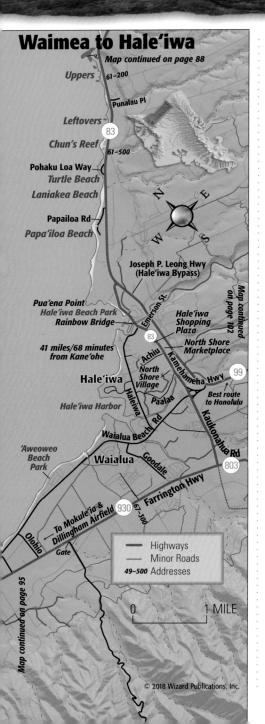

Map continued on page 88

Uppers 61–200

Punalau Pl

Leftovers
83
Chun's Reef
61–500

Pohaku Loa Way
Turtle Beach
Laniakea Beach

Papailoa Rd
Papa'iloa Beach

Joseph P. Leong Hwy
(Hale'iwa Bypass)

Map continued on page 102

Pua'ena Point
Hale'iwa Beach Park
Rainbow Bridge

Emerson St.

Hale'iwa
Shopping
Plaza

North Shore
Marketplace

83

Achiu

41 miles/68 minutes
from Kane'ohe

Kamehameha Hwy

99

Hale'iwa

North
Shore
Village

Haleiwa

Paalaa

Best route
to Honolulu

Hale'iwa Harbor

Waialua Beach Rd.

Kaukonahua Rd

'Aweoweo
Beach
Park

Waialua

Goodale

803

To Mokule'ia &
Dillingham Airfield

930

67–300

Farrington Hwy

Oloilo

Gate

Map continued on page 95

— Highways
— Minor Roads
49–500 Addresses

0   1 MILE

© 2018 Wizard Publications, Inc.

at the pipe. Yet there are no signs telling you where it is, and there's no beach named after it. So here's how to find it. The Banzai Pipeline is 100 yards to the left of **'Ehukai Beach Park** and 185 yards offshore. (The park—often missing a sign—is across the street from Sunset Beach Elementary School.) From the road you'll know if it's going off. Not because you can see the waves (which you can't), but because the small parking lot at 'Ehukai will be *filled* with local cars. (During calm summer months the amount of sand at the beach increases exponentially when truckloads of sand are transported here by the ocean.)

Past 'Ehukai is **Shark's Cove**. During summer months (May to September or October) this is one of the best places on the island to snorkel. Clear water, lots of fish and a fair number of turtles make this an inviting body of water. To the left of the cove is a giant tide pool that kids love splashing in. See *Beaches* on page 147 for more on Shark's Cove.

Just past Shark's Cove at the Foodland is Pupukea Road. About a half mile up this road, turn right and drive another 0.75 miles (over 11 speed bumps, which are well-scraped by drivers in a hurry) to come to the **Pu'u o Mahuka Heiau**. These remnants of a Hawaiian temple, perched 250 feet above Waimea Bay on a ridge, possess a peaceful and serene view from the top of Mt. Ka'ala all the way out to Ka'ena Point. It's worth the detour for the view alone. One of the plaques says they could communicate with Wailua on Kaua'i by fire, but that's probably a Hawaiian wives' tale since Wailua is 86 miles away. (It's doubtful even a monstrously large fire could be seen that far away, even in crystal clear conditions.) All that remains of this heiau

A REAL GEM

The jumping rock at Waimea Bay...and the sound of a belly-flop heard round the world.

is a lava stone foundation. While it's tempting to think of a temple as a spiritual place, this was a *luakini* heiau, where human sacrifices took place. Countless Hawaiians and possibly some westerners were murdered here to feed the hungry gods. When the Hawaiians overthrew their religious kapu system in 1819 (by their own hand and with no outside intervention or pressure—this was *before* any missionaries ever came to the island), few Hawaiians of that day shed a tear that this particular temple was being dismantled. Although the ali'i (chiefs) revered it, to the common man of that time *luakini* heiau were places of oppression and fear. Nearby residents sometimes come up and make offerings of fruits, fish, and other small foods. These are often well-received by local pigs, chickens and mongooses.

WAIMEA BAY

Highway 83 soon takes you to Waimea Bay, the place to be when the winter surf is *really* high—say 20-foot waves and higher. Surf of this height causes other surf sites to close out and simply look messy and frothy. (See page 238 to learn more about waves and what surfers look for.)

A REAL GEM

Most people observe big surf from the beach, but finding a parking spot at Waimea Bay Beach Park can be difficult. We prefer a spot from the left side of the bay. There's a dedicated public access from the end of Iliohu Place, though at press time locals

Who the Heck is Eddie…and Why Would He Go?

Drive around O'ahu and you'll see bumper stickers that say, "Eddie Would Go." The biggest big-wave surf contest in the world is the Quiksilver in Memory of Eddie Aikau contest (though a business dispute has put that name in jeopardy). It's held every few years—only when waves on the North Shore are 20 feet high or more. (A 20-foot wave, measured from the back as many Hawaiian surfers do, has a 40-foot face!

So who's this Eddie guy?

Eddie Aikau was a pure-blood Hawaiian big-wave surfer from O'ahu who, as a lifeguard at Waimea Bay, literally saved hundreds of lives by braving monster winter surf with waves three- to four-stories tall to rescue people who'd gotten into trouble. Often a helicopter would be called to raise the swimmer in a basket. Then Eddie would swim back through the surf to the shore.

In the '70s a voyaging canoe called the Hokule'a was built to prove that Polynesians had navigated to and from Hawai'i using only the stars. For the first trip to Tahiti, the crew brought along a navigator from Micronesia to teach them how to navigate using only the heavens. But tensions ran high and fistfights erupted. The Hawaiian crew resented the rules set by the science-minded white leaders, and the white leaders resented the Hawaiians who only seemed to want to smoke pakalolo (marijuana) and listen to their taped music.

In 1978 a second voyage to Tahiti was planned, and Eddie Aikau was accepted as a volunteer crewman. On March 16 a crowd of 10,000 gathered at Magic Island to see them off. Though the weather was turning foul, the great turnout created pressure to leave anyway. That night, after some hatches had been improperly shut, the hulls filled with water and the canoe capsized. Their radio was flooded, and their emergency beacon was lost. Eddie volunteered to take his surfboard through the 15-foot swells and 35 mph winds to Lana'i. The captain refused. Cold, wet and scared, the crew spent the dark night calling to each other to make sure no one had been washed away. The next day Eddie again asked to go. Although Lana'i was now 20 miles away through angry seas, the captain and his officers reluctantly agreed. "Eddie was godlike," one of his crew members said. If anybody could do it, it was Eddie.

The crew gathered around to say a prayer, and then Eddie started paddling his 12-foot surfboard. When he was 50 feet from the boat, he took off his life jacket (so he could paddle better) and continued. Eddie Aikau was never seen again. Later that evening the crew shot a flare into the air as the last inter-island flight flew by and, miraculously, the pilot saw it. The remaining crew members were rescued by a Coast Guard helicopter.

Today the name Eddie is synonymous in Hawai'i with trying, going for it, risking it all for your friends. Hey, brah, Eddie would go.

were parking at the end of Iliohu *Way* and taking a short trail through the brush. Either way it leads to a wicked vantage point. During the summer, the water is usually idyllic.

Behind Waimea Bay is the entrance to **Waimea Valley**. If you've read about **Waimea Falls Adventure Park** and are jonesin' for some of the adventure activities there, you're in for a disappointment. It's been converted to a low-key botanical garden and cultural center that also happens to have a waterfall you can swim to when it's flowing, and if you wear their *mandatory* life jacket. If you don't want to pay the cover charge, you can always relax in their outdoor seating and watch the meandering peacocks, free of charge. See *Land Tours* on page 223 for more.

In 1792 George Vancouver (as in Vancouver, Canada), was visiting the islands. He had been on Captain Cook's fatal voyage to Hawai'i 13 years earlier. Vancouver was exceptionally skilled at diplomacy and was well regarded by Hawaiian chiefs. While he was on Kaua'i, his sister ship stopped here at O'ahu's Waimea to secure water. The armed captain of that other ship and crew members were directed by the Hawaiians to travel farther up the stream (to avoid the saltier brackish water at the mouth). Then the Hawaiians further enticed the captain, the astronomer and two crewmen to come see some hogs and bananas they wanted to sell them. Once the men were away from their party, the Hawaiians stoned, then stabbed them to death (one crewman escaped) and took their arms. In the 1800s the renowned Hawaiian historian *Kamakau* interviewed one of the aging killers, who told him, "We killed the men to get the guns," and that chiefs had ordered that "if a ship came into the area,

The simple life on a North Shore beach...

[we] were to kill the foreigners and get the guns" (which had that magical power to kill a man from a distance).

Unfortunately, this would be only one example of Hawaiians killing westerners and vice versa in the early years of western contact. They could have learned a different approach from King Kamehameha on the Big Islands who, when he captured westerners, made them chiefs and gave them the accompanying benefits, creating loyal military advisers rather than adversaries.

Halfway between Waimea Bay and Hale'iwa town (and at the south end of a loop road called Pohaku Loa Way) is a small beach known locally as **Turtle Beach**. This is the only place in Hawai'i where the turtles are so gregarious, we've seen them actually swim after beachgoers who have gotten bored from so much turtle-watching. (We suspect that some nearby resident might be secretly feeding them to create this kind of behavior.) Anyway, they're not *always* there, but when they are, it's a joy to see turtles so close to the shore (sometimes *on* the shore) and so accepting of people nearby. Remember that it's illegal to touch or handle the honu (as they're

NOT TO BE MISSED!

known in Hawai'i), and beware that, right at the shoreline, waves might send them crashing into your shin. (Got the scar to prove it.) Against residents' wishes, the state erected a concrete barrier to make it less convenient to stop here. You'll have to find a place off the highway on either side of the barriers. (Don't park on Pohaku Loa Way.)

SURFING LIFE

There are two seasons on the North Shore—surfing season (during winter months) and the agonizing waiting season when the fickle waves pound the southern hemisphere. Winter waves usually start rolling in around November, and North Shore towns such as Hale'iwa and Waimea instantly transform from sleepy summer towns to jam-packed surfing meccas.

Strewn along this stretch of the island are numerous **surfing houses**, many with notorious names known to surfers throughout the country. Each night during surfing season, throngs of surfers and those attracted to the lifestyle gather in these houses where BBQs are smoking, someone is always lifting weights, beer is being consumed *at all times*, surfing videos or surfing video games are being

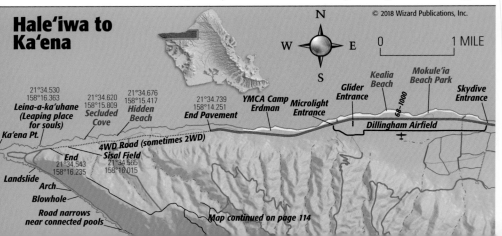

Hale'iwa to Ka'ena

© 2018 Wizard Publications, Inc.

N W E S

0   1 MILE

21°34.530 158°16.363
Leina-a-ka'uhane (Leaping place for souls)

Ka'ena Pt.

21°34.620 158°15.809
Secluded Cove

21°34.676 158°15.417
Hidden Beach

21°34.739 158°14.251
End Pavement

YMCA Camp Erdman

Microlight Entrance

Glider Entrance

Kealia Beach

Mokule'ia Beach Park

Skydive Entrance

Dillingham Airfield

4WD Road (sometimes 2WD)

End 21°34.543 158°16.235

Sisal Field 21°34.565 158°16.015

Landslide

Arch

Blowhole

Road narrows near connected pools

Map continued on page 114

Innocent swimmers were minding their own business when this rude turtle just cut them off. Some turtles at Turtle Beach simply don't have any manners.

played, and talk is about waves and those who ride them. Some have outside jobs, some don't. All share a passion for waves that non-surfers find baffling. You can listen to surfers talk for hours about how the waves are breaking and how they did or would respond. It's more than a lifestyle; it's closer to a religion.

Though O'ahu's North Shore is known around the world as home of the planet's best surfing, it's surprising to learn that until the 1950s nobody surfed any of the sites here. The waves were considered too big and too powerful, so Makaha in West O'ahu was the home to serious surfing. The first few hardy pioneers to

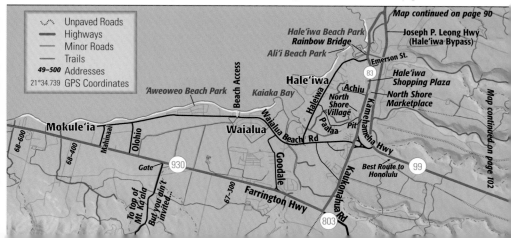

Map continued on page 90

Unpaved Roads
Highways
Minor Roads
Trails
49–500 Addresses
21°34.739 GPS Coordinates

Hale'iwa Beach Park
Rainbow Bridge
Ali'i Beach Park

Joseph P. Leong Hwy
(Hale'iwa Bypass)

Emerson St.

83

Hale'iwa Shopping Plaza

'Aweoweo Beach Park

Beach Access

Kaiaka Bay

Hale'iwa

Achiu
North Shore Village

North Shore Marketplace

Mokule'ia

Mahinaai

Olohio

Waialua

Waialua Beach Rd

Pa'ala'a

Pit

Kamehameha Hwy

68-600

68-400

Gate

930

Goodale

67-300

Farrington Hwy

Best Route to Honolulu

99

Kaukonahua Rd

803

To top of Mt. Ka'ala

But you ain't invited...

Map continued on page 102

surf the North Shore's waves got ground into dust by the breakers, but by the 1960s word got out, and the North Shore was "discovered" by the outside world. The big change occurred when the old heavy redwood boards were replaced by new, lightweight (and more maneuverable) balsa wood boards, and a radical invention allowed surfers to tackle taller waves that would have turned their boards sideways. The invention? The surfboard fin. Now surfers had a chance on big waves. By the time fiberglass boards came along, North Shore waves were being shredded by riders lured from all over the world.

HALE'IWA

Hale'iwa is the biggest town on the North Shore. It's a quaint town that centers around surfing in the winter. (There aren't any resorts up here, but B&Bs are easy to find online. Several good restaurants and some interesting shopping are available. If you're looking for a treat, consider the shave ice at San Lorenzo's or Matsumoto's on Kamehameha Highway. (The latter often has unjustifiably long lines, so don't hesitate to go to San Lorenzo's.) Hale'iwa Harbor is where you depart for your Swim with Sharks adventure on page 242.

If you're looking for a new profile pic, there's a hugely popular set of angel wings painted on the exterior of the green Volcom store. The wings are by an L.A. artist who painted dozens of them around the globe.

If you drive west on Highway 930 (Farrington Highway), there are stretches of sand beach after Mokule'ia Beach Park (see *Beaches* on page 150) that are usually deserted. Along the way, after passing Dillingham Airport, you'll come to YMCA Camp Erdman. If you're a fan of LOST,

pull over on the mauka (mountain) side of the road—the clump of yellow buildings will look eerily familiar. This is the compound where "The Others" lived. Unfortunately, the feeling of actually being there is not quite what it once was, since one of the buildings is now painted gray, which diminishes the effect. But there is still a Dharma Initiative sign marking the place and it's worth five minutes of your time. The show shot scenes all over the island, but most are indistinguishable jungle or beach locations. I'll always remember flying down the approach end of Runway 8 in 2004 and seeing the wreckage of Oceanic flight 815 scattered along the beach, which shocked the hell out of me because I didn't know they were filming a plane crash scene until coming upon it.

PAST THE PAVEMENT

Near the westernmost tip of the island the paved portion of the highway ends and turns into a dirt road, and there's a locked gate blocking you from going any further. Past the gate there are some wonderful natural treasures, but if you want to see them you'll likely have to walk (or try to catch a ride with some of the locals driving their lifted 4x4s) because the state has intentionally made it difficult for anyone who doesn't *own* their own 4WD vehicle to get a permit to drive the road. (And it's unlikely you brought yours from home with you.) Bring water since it's shadeless.

About 1.25 miles into the dirt road, 16 telephone poles past the metal gate, at a side road that *might* be marked with a sign saying C-1 at telephone pole #197, is a hidden beach. You can't really see it well from the dirt road. Imagine having a small, sandy cove to yourself. Might happen, might not. But you've got a

What could possibly motivate you to walk a 1.75 miles from your car?
How about Hidden Beach?

chance here. There's even a little snorkeling when the ocean's not pounding too hard.

At 1.75 miles into the dirt road (0.3 mile before the end of the dirt road) is a secluded cove that we're cleverly calling...secluded cove. (It has no actual name.) You can see it from the dirt road. The wind is almost always blowing in this area, and the seas are nearly always choppy. This cove is a wonderful exception. Except when the seas are very heavy, it's usually protected and calm with great swimming and a ruggedly beautiful, contoured shoreline patiently chiseled out of solid sandstone by the relentless sea.

The snorkeling is the best you'll find along the Mokule'ia shoreline. (Granted, this isn't an area renowned for its snorkeling—like being the best hockey player in all of Ecuador.) Though the visibility is a bit cloudy, there's a nice variety of little fish. (Shoreline fishermen tend to snag

their bigger family members.) Until around 2 p.m. on weekdays this area tends to be unoccupied. Late afternoons sometime bring 4WD-equipped fishermen. To the right of the cove is a small natural infinity pool, better than you'd find at a resort, great for swimming. When conditions cooperate and the tide is right, the pool is constantly refreshed by waves crashing over the natural rock wall, and the excess water flows back out over the lip. From inside, the pool looks boundless and mirror smooth, like it seamlessly blends with the ocean and sky. You can't see it—or its occupants—from the shoreline; you have to know it's there.

Now that you've gone 2.25 miles on the unpaved road, there's a rock barricade for vehicles. Past that you'll see a fence and gate, which means you've reached **Ka'ena Point** at the far western tip of O'ahu. The fence is there to protect nesting seabirds from predators. (You can go in, but leave your pet rat or mongoose

outside.) Less than a five-minute walk past the rock barricade (on the path to the right) is a layered sandstone rock on the ocean side of the path. This rock was absolutely sacred to the ancient Hawaiians. The word "sacred" can be overused, but in this case it can't be overstated. This area is called *Leina-a-*

ka'uhane—the leaping place for souls. The ancients believed that while you were on your deathbed, your soul left your body and wandered about. For those Hawaiians who lived on O'ahu, the soul eventually ended up here where it would climb this sandstone rock, face

A REAL GEM

In total, you've hiked a little more than 2.8 miles to get out here (it's 5.7 miles roundtrip) and your view to the left has been blocked most the way so you definitely don't want to miss this final surprise: walk far enough to peek around the corner of the mountain, and suddenly you can see the Wai'anae Mountains and the west coast stretching for miles and miles into the distance. The unexpectedly expansive view packs quite the wow factor.

The other way to get out here instead of starting from the north shore, is to hike starting from the west side of the island.

AIN'T TECHNOLOGY GRAND?

Above Ka'ena Point is a satellite tracking station. That title implies that it was built to track satellites, but space technology wasn't always so advanced. Throughout the '60s, until 1972, a super-secret "black" group called the *Corona Project* carried out one of America's most important reconnaissance tasks here.

Spy satellites launched about once a month took photographs of America's enemies during that part of the Cold War. But the images were just that—*photographs...on film*. The resolution of film was so much greater than beamable television cameras of that era that they had to take film-based snapshots. So how did they get the photos from the satellites to the spies who needed them? As strange as it sounds, canisters full of film were jettisoned from the satellites, small rockets guided the capsules to the appropriate drop zone 600 miles from O'ahu, and parachutes were deployed to slow the film's descent. Air Force cargo planes were guided to the parachutes from Ka'ena Point Tracking Station, and they snagged the parachutes *in mid-air*. The films were then taken back and analyzed.

the ocean and leap into the company of its ancestors—and at that exact moment, the person died. If a soul had no ancestors who cared enough to greet it, the soul fell into the *po pau 'ole o milu,* the endless night, or wandered about the island for eternity as a ghost, known in the islands as a night marcher.

Imagine how hard it would be to fly a bulky cargo plane just *barely* over the top of a rapidly sinking parachute and snag it with a loop dragged behind you. If the plane missed, the capsules landed in the ocean and were designed to float for one to three days before sinking. That's long enough for a U.S. ship to locate it, but not long enough to fall into the wrong hands if lost. They accomplished this time-critical float with a method that would make Betty Crocker proud—they simply drilled a hole in the capsule and plugged it with compacted brown sugar that would dissolve in the seawater at a known rate.

Of all the U.S. space programs, this one had by far, the highest failure rate. Of the first 25 satellites launched, *only three* returned usable photos. But they learned from their mistakes, ultimately launching 145 satellites and discovering that the dreaded '60s "missile gap" with the Soviet Union was a hollow bluff on the part of its leader, Nikita Khrushchev.

NORTH SHORE BEST BETS

Best Shoreline Drive—From Kualoa Beach Park to Hale'iwa

Best Place to Watch Turtles—Turtle Beach

Best Snorkeling—Shark's Cove (when it's calm)

Best Beach That You Can't Drive a Car to—Hidden Beach

Best Place to Stay Out of the Water—Anywhere on the North Shore when the surf's up

Best Photo Op of You Under a Waterfall—Waimea Valley

Best Surf Spot That's Not Marked—Banzai Pipeline

Best Use of a Cargo Plane—Snaring parachutes containing spy film

Commanding view from the platform above Ka'ena Point.

What a shame that few visitors will ever see some of the fantastic sights that Wai'anae has to offer, like Makua Beach.

Wai'anae in the west and Central O'ahu are the least visited parts of the island. Central O'ahu is dominated by vast fields of pineapple while Wai'anae is dominated by exceptionally clear water and a bad reputation among island residents.

If you're heading out to Wai'anae, skip to page 110.

CENTRAL O'AHU

This may be a little disorienting, but we're going to describe Central O'ahu from the north to the south. That's because we're assuming that most people will first see it *after* having driven around the North Shore, when they're on their way back toward Waikiki. Even if you bolted straight to the North Shore from Waikiki on a mission, this is how you'll tour it on the way back.

Taking Hwy 99 leaving Hale'iwa, you'll pass through the 155-acre **Waialua Estate Coffee & Chocolate Plantation** on the other side of Cook Island pine trees (used as a wind break). Coffee and chocolate have opposite harvest seasons, so workers can stay employed year-round, but they don't do tours.

Soon you'll notice that most of this area is dominated by one crop—**pineapple**. James Dole started planting the fruit here in 1900 and then bought the entire island of Lana'i in 1922, converting it to a gigantic pineapple farm. (They stopped growing it

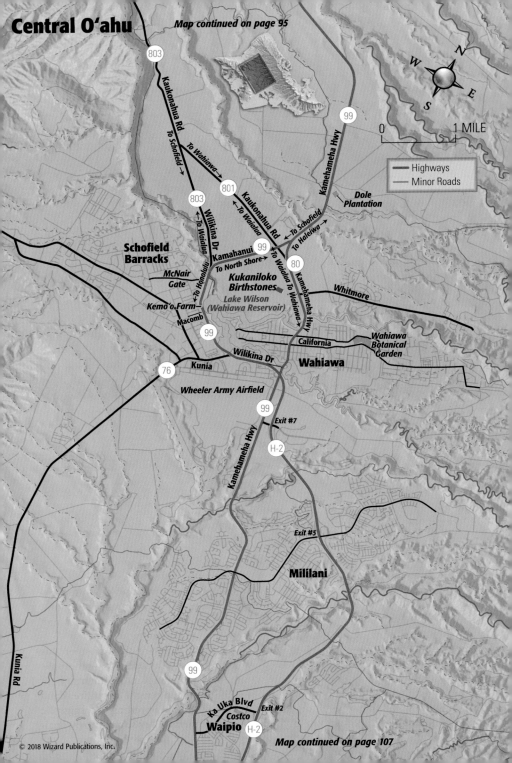

Central O'ahu

Map continued on page 95

803

Kaukonahua Rd

To Schofield →
To Wahiawa →

803

801

Kaukonahua Rd
← To Waialua

Wilikina Dr
← To Waialua

Schofield Barracks

Kamahanui
To North Shore →

McNair Gate

← To Honolulu
To Waialua To Wahiawa →

99

Kukaniloko Birthstones

Lake Wilson
(Wahiawa Reservoir)

Kemo'o Farm

Macomb

99

Wilikina Dr

76

Kunia

Wahiawa

California

Wahiawa Botanical Garden

Whitmore

80

Kamehameha Hwy

← To Schofield
To Haleiwa →

99

Kamehameha Hwy

Dole Plantation

N
W E
S

0   1 MILE

— Highways
— Minor Roads

Wheeler Army Airfield

99

Exit #7

H-2

Kamehameha Hwy

Exit #5

Mililani

Kunia Rd

99

Ka Uka Blvd

Costco

Waipio

Exit #2

H-2

Map continued on page 107

© 2018 Wizard Publications, Inc.

commercially on Lana'i in 1990 in favor of a more profitable crop—*visitors*.)

Pineapple likes to be warm during the day and cool at night. This plateau is at 1,000 feet and cooler than the shoreline. Dole Pineapple has 11,500 acres under cultivation. At 27,000–33,000 low-to-the-ground pineapple plants per acre (pineapples grow from the bottom on a stalk, not from trees), there could be as many as *350 million* plants out here. It takes 20 months for a new plant to mature. When they harvest the fruit, they twist the top off and replant it where it'll make more pineapples in a little more than a year.

The shape of the individual fields is no accident. They're laid out so that the arm of the harvesting machine can reach exactly halfway across the field while pineapple workers walk behind picking the fruit. It's tough, hot work, and walking through a pineapple field is a horrible affair. If you're curious to see what it's like, try practicing at home by walking through a giant pile of razor blades—same effect.

By the way, you'll hear lots of old wives' tales regarding how to check a pineapple for ripeness and sweetness. Pulling leaves from the crown, measuring the buds on the skin, looking for golden color, looking for smooth and flattened eyes—there are plenty of ways, and everyone seems to swear by their method. Living in Hawai'i and having purchased countless pineapples, we can say authoritatively that the secret to getting a sweet pineapple is...pure luck. None of these tricks seems to work for us. And despite Dole's contention that "they're all picked ripe," we've certainly gotten some pretty sour pineapples over the years. One thing that does seem to help is to put them in the fridge for a day upside down to let the sugar even out instead of pooling at the bottom. (Otherwise, the bottom's sweet and the top is sour.)

As an aside, excessive consumption of pineapple cores can cause "fiber balls" to form in your digestive tract. (You'll need instructions from your cat on how to cough them up.) And old-timers use pineapple juice to clean machetes and knife blades or will mix it with sand to clean boat decks.

On Hwy 99 just north of Hwy 80 and Wahiawa town is **Dole Plantation** (808-621-8408). While undeniably your classic "tourist trap," there are a couple of reasons some might want to stop here. They have a hedge maze that covers 137,000 square feet. According to the *Guinness Book of World Records*, it's the largest in the world. (They expanded it after they were beaten by the Irish a few years back.) The idea is to wander through the maze and locate eight hidden stations before exiting. It'll take up to an hour and costs $8. The hedge is 8 feet tall. (If you want to take a photo of it, the only way *we* could do it was to put the camera on a timer and hoist it up on a stick.) They also have a garden area that's $7 (and possibly overpriced at that unless you're a certified garden junkie) and a train ride tour for $11 ($9 for kids). A pineapple field is not exactly the most thrilling place to take a 20-minute tour, but kids seem to like riding the train. (Adults get antsy in about 5 minutes.) You'll learn everything you ever wanted to know about pineapple... but were afraid to ask.

Dole also has a gift shop with food in the form of locally grown coffee, hot dogs, chili and all things pineapple, including flavors of frozen Dole whip. (We'll boldly predict that "pineapple" will be featured as their "flavor of the day.") You can drop a lot of money quickly at Dole, but the gift shop's not bad. Also at Dole is a farmer's market with fresh local produce.

After Dole, heading south, you have a choice of taking Highway 99 through Schofield Barracks or Hwy 80 through Wahiawa, which has a mainland feel due to heavy presence of the military base here. Take Hwy 80. Just before Wahiawa on Hwy 80 you'll come upon a short dirt road on the right at the intersection of Hwy 80 and Whitmore. (A misleading sign says it's closed. What they *really* mean is it's closed to vehicles.) In the middle of a pineapple field, with the Waianae Mountains in the background, is one of O'ahu's less-visited yet oddly peaceful sites. The **Kukaniloko Birthing Stones** (shown on page 15) are where royalty of yesteryear came to give birth to future rulers. The rocks in this area are strangely weathered and look out of place, yet legend states that the patterns are natural, not manmade.

Royal birthing procedures were different from what commoners went through. When the time came, the woman would arrive at what was then a secret spot, and in the presence of 36 male chiefs she would position herself at certain stones and in certain ways to give birth while they watched. (Gee, *that* must have created quite the awkward moment...) Within minutes of birth the child was taken away, and the mother would not see her child again until it was grown. This was to ensure that the child would not be murdered. Infanticide in high-ranking families was common among rival chiefs.

The area wasn't always treated with such reverence though. The giant pineapple plantation in this area couldn't have cared less and grew pineapples all around, and *even amongst*, the stones, as evidenced by the tattered black plastic embedded in the dirt road leading from the highway. (The plastic sheeting was inserted into the ground to reduce the amount of water and pesticides used. Pretty ironic, isn't it? That plastic litter throughout the ground was *to protect the environment.*) Today, a protective ring of vegetation and stones is designed to dissuade you from walking amongst the stones.

In ancient Hawai'i, parenting was a much different affair than what we're used to. The rights of the grandparents superseded the rights of the parents. Parents could not raise their own child without the consent of the grandparents. First-born children were whisked away from the mother at birth and raised by the husband's relatives if it was a boy or the mother's relatives if it was a girl. And every boy, first-born or not, was taken from the woman's hut when old enough to be weaned and raised in the men's hut. Never again in his lifetime would the man be allowed to eat with women, even his mother *or his wife*. The punishment for any man caught eating with women was death.

Some children were designated at birth never to do any kind of physical labor for their entire lives. This extended to feeding themselves. Poi or fish would be dropped into their mouths and water poured directly into them. These people were required to sit around all day long on tapa mats being attended to, bringing laziness to a fine art. The 17th-century Hawaiian historian Kamakau referred to them as "human pets." (Today we simply call them *teenagers.*)

Youths raised by kahuna professionals, such as omen readers, deep sea fishermen, tapa cloth makers or star readers, were consecrated at birth, and everything associated with them was kapu—off limits to others. Their food calabash, their clothes, their houses—even their hair couldn't be touched or trimmed and

Get lost in the world's biggest maze at the Dole Plantation.

grew tangled and snarled. Only when their training was complete were the kapu lifted, and they could live a more normal and less sacred life.

WAHIAWA

In Wahiawa there's a garden called Wahiawa Botanical Garden off California Street. See *Land Tours* on page 225.

After Wahiawa or Schofield you'll take H-2 south to H-1.

Of course, there's more to this area than meets the eye. There are large military bases out here, which you can only glimpse from the road. What you *won't* see, however, can be more interesting. There are miles and miles of tunnels carved underground. There's also a massive underground complex called the Kunia Regional Signals Intelligence Operations Center buried near the pineapple fields. This is where intercepted messages from around the world are decrypted and analyzed and became famous when Edward Snowden stole and leaked classified material from here, revealing the extent to which the NSA monitors all of our phone and internet communications.

From here, you have several places you could head to besides going back to Waikiki.

MT. KA'ALA

Wai'anae and Central O'ahu are separated by the tallest mountain on the island. The top, called Mt. Ka'ala, is a flat plateau of swampy ground dominated by mosses and lichen. At 4,025 feet, it's usually cloud-covered, and trees at the top are stunted. Fully grown 'ohi'a trees—normally growing to over 20 feet tall—top out at only 2 to 3 feet, creating a natural bonsai garden. Unlike the similarly soggy summit of Wai'ale'ale on Kaua'i, which the Hawaiians considered sacred, Ka'ala was held in slightly less regard by

Pearl Harbor

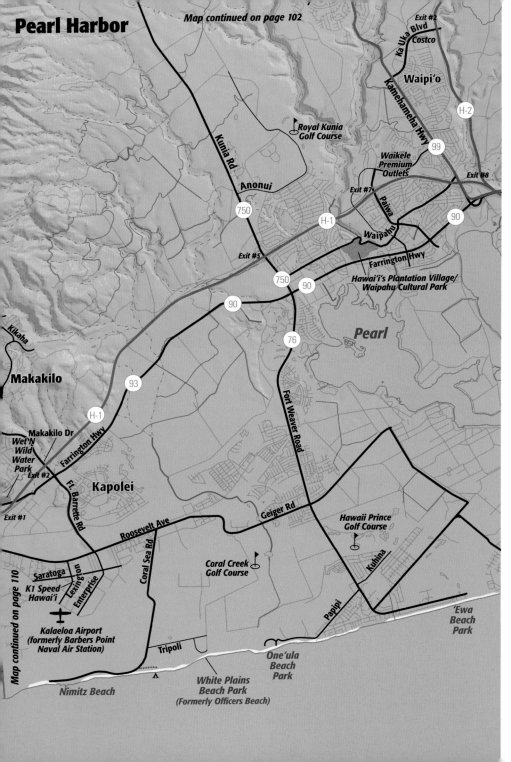

Map continued on page 102

Exit #2

Ka Uka Blvd
Costco

Waipi'o

Kamehameha Hwy

H-2

Royal Kunia
Golf Course

Kunia Rd

99

Waikele
Premium
Outlets

Exit #7

Exit #8

Anonui

Paiwa

H-1

90

750

Waipahu

Exit #5

Farrington Hwy

750

90

Hawai'i's Plantation Village/
Waipahu Cultural Park

90

Pearl

76

Kikaha

Makakilo

93

Fort Weaver Road

H-1

Makakilo Dr

Farrington Hwy

Wet'N
Wild
Water
Park

Exit #2

Ft. Barrette Rd

Kapolei

Geiger Rd

Hawaii Prince
Golf Course

Exit #1

Roosevelt Ave

Coral Sea Rd

Coral Creek
Golf Course

Kuhina

Saratoga

Lexington

Enterprise

K1 Speed
Hawai'i

Papipi

'Ewa
Beach
Park

Map continued on page 110

Kalaeloa Airport
(formerly Barbers Point
Naval Air Station)

Tripoli

One'ula
Beach
Park

Nimitz Beach

White Plains
Beach Park
(Formerly Officers Beach)

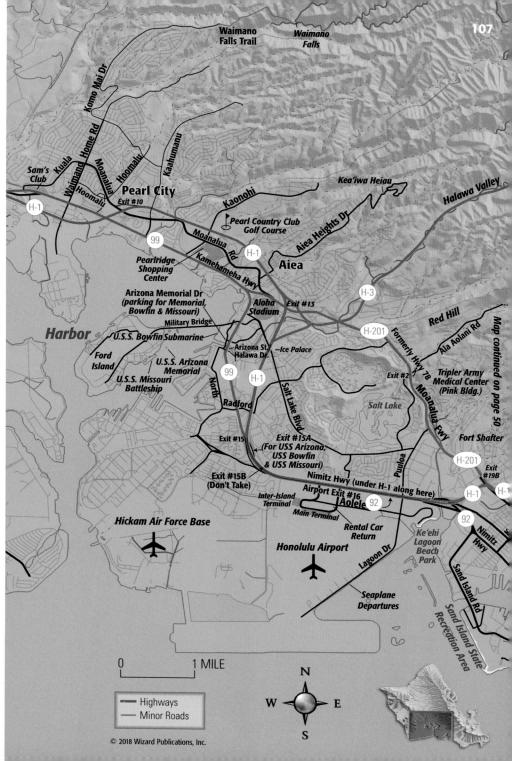

the Hawaiians of yesteryear. Nearly every recorded chant referring to Mt. Ka'ala seems to focus on the "cold dews of Ka'ala," and little affection for the place percolated down to the common man.

At the summit today are radar towers that your Hawai'i-bound pilot communicated with when you got within 200 miles of Hawai'i. Although there is a paved road to the top, it's gated and you're not very welcome up there. There's a separate trail to the top, but it's insanely difficult and not particularly rewarding in the views department. While not as tall, the top of the Ko'olau presents better views.

While it's tempting to assume the top of the mountain must have been the summit of the volcano that created the mountain, it's not. The actual summit was to the west. The peak of Mt. Ka'ala is simply the only remaining remnant of the original gently-sloping shield volcano that was once here. The rest has worn away from erosion, leaving this unusually hardened lava relic of the volcano's youth.

PEARL HARBOR

Pearl Harbor is named after the many pipi (Hawaiian oysters) that used to live here. Visiting ships from the late 1700s described abundant pearls from this harbor. A visitor in 1810 wrote that the king had discovered their value to the outside world and employed numerous divers to pluck the oysters from their shallow bed. By the end of the 1800s over-harvesting and runoff from nearby cattle operations had virtually eliminated the pearl oysters, but the name Pearl Harbor lives on, and its Hawaiian name, Pu'u-loa (long hill), is scarcely known, even among Hawaiians.

The deep harbor lagoon is separated into three lochs protected from the open ocean by a channel. Even those without any military knowledge can see the strategic importance of controlling such an awesome place to safely park countless large ships. The large island inside the harbor is called **Ford Island**. It houses some of the officers and crewmen stationed at Pearl Harbor.

In ancient times, Ford Island had an entirely different purpose. It was called Moku'ume'ume, meaning *island of the sexual game*. In those days, if a commoner

couple had trouble conceiving a child, they came here. Large groups gathered around a fire, couples sitting apart. A master of ceremonies would go up to a man, tap him with a maile wand, then tap a randomly selected woman, and together they went off into the darkness to share the night. If a child was conceived, it was regarded as the offspring of the husband, not the biological father. If no child was conceived, they'd head back to this island to give it a whirl again.

You can't do a driving tour of Pearl Harbor—it's still an active Navy base, and access is restricted. But the most popular visitor attractions on the island—the USS Arizona Memorial and the Battleship Missouri—are available for touring. See *Attractions* starting on page 156 for more.

'EWA

'Ewa is the area below H-1 on your way out to Wai'anae. This is where the

With the USS Arizona Memorial in the distance, symbolizing the day America was caught by surprise, sailors on the USS Nimitz aircraft carrier stand guard with machine guns ready, ensuring that a surprise won't happen again on their watch.

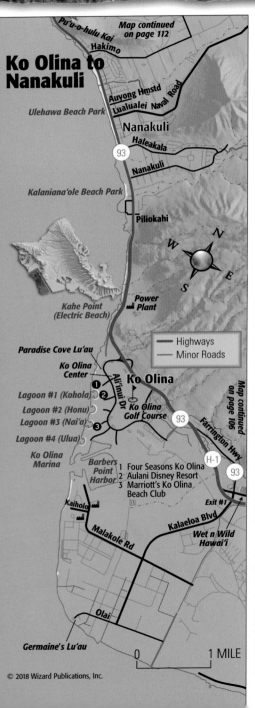

Ko Olina to Nanakuli

Map continued on page 112

Pu'u-o-hulu Kai
Hakimo
Auyong Hmstd
Ulehawa Beach Park
Lualualei Naval Road
Nanakuli
Haleakala
93
Nanakuli
Kalaniana'ole Beach Park
Piliokahi

N W E S

Kahe Point (Electric Beach)
Power Plant

Paradise Cove Lu'au
Ko Olina Center
Lagoon #1 (Kohola)
Lagoon #2 (Honu)
Lagoon #3 (Nai'a)
Lagoon #4 (Ulua)
Ko Olina Marina
Ali'inui Dr
Ko Olina
Ko Olina Golf Course
93
Barbers Point Harbor
Kaiholo
Malakole Rd
Olai
Germaine's Lu'au

— Highways
— Minor Roads

Map continued on page 106

Farrington Hwy
H-1
93
Exit #1
Kalaeloa Blvd
Wet n Wild Hawai'i

1 Four Seasons Ko Olina
2 Aulani Disney Resort
3 Marriott's Ko Olina Beach Club

0   1 MILE

© 2018 Wizard Publications, Inc.

county wants to direct future growth. It's hot, dry and not particularly pretty, so there's really not much for the visitor out here other than Hawai'i's Plantation Village, Hawaiian Railway Society and Wet 'n' Wild Hawai'i. See *Attractions* for more on these.

KALAELOA/BARBERS POINT

The Navy leased the land at Barbers Point in the early 1930s for their aircraft. Not planes, however. It was for *blimps*. (Yes, the Navy was a major blimp operator.) They later expanded the base for traditional aircraft and after the attack on Pearl Harbor, they converted the airfield to a massive pilot training area. At the end of the 20th century, the Navy handed the land to the state of Hawai'i, which now controls it. The area is very industrial, though there are a few decent beaches. See our Beaches chapter for more on beaches on the Wai'anae coast.

WAI'ANAE

Wai'anae is the name of a town, but it's also the name generally used to describe the western coastline leading all the way to Ka'ena Point. Wai'anae is one of the poorer sections of the island, and it has a reputation for being a rough place. In the '70s that was certainly true. A number of violent crimes against visitors created an image among island residents that persists to this day. *Don't go to Wai'anae*, they say. *You'll get beaten up.* Well, frankly, that's ridiculous, and those who espouse that attitude need to come out here more often. Because it's so dry, Wai'anae has some of the nicest ocean water on the island, and you shouldn't let its reputation dissuade you from partaking of its delights. We've gone to the police to confirm that today, violent crimes against visitors are extremely rare here. It's mainly petty theft—frankly, a lot of it. That means some dirtbag breaking into your car to steal your camera while you're at the beach, or even stealing your stuff right off your beach towel. In the past the beach parks here were often "taken over" by homeless encampments. Years ago authorities enforced the "No Camping" rules at all but one beach, creating nicer environments at most beach parks and a *dense* concentration of homeless farther north at Kea'au Beach Park. In 2012 they evicted the homeless even from this park.

When we're out in Wai'anae, we simply don't leave anything valuable in the car. (Frankly, we do that everywhere we go.) There's always a chance someone will break in anyway, but it has never happened to us anywhere in Hawai'i. (And we've left our car in a *lot* of places.) As for safety, common sense needs to be applied, no matter where you are. If you're at a beach park after dark, and the parking lot is filled with young toughs drinking copious amounts of beer, you don't need us to tell you that now is not the right time to go over and show them your fancy Rolex watch. The biggest problem we've found with Wai'anae isn't the people—it's the bad restaurants. There are a few decent places to eat and they are in our *Island Dining* chapter, but

An Oversight Leads to a Spared Gas Station— and Victory in WWII

Say what you want about the Japanese attack on Pearl Harbor: Militarily, the plan was brilliantly conceived and executed. The level of surprise was only matched by the level of destruction, and Japanese losses were minimal. Although U.S. aircraft carriers weren't in the harbor (by chance, not design), the Japanese nonetheless achieved their goals and didn't make any mistakes... except for one—a mistake so giant, so glaring and so important that it possibly ended up costing Japan the war.

When the Japanese warplanes were swarming around during the attack, their pilots were so single-mindedly focused on destroying ships and planes that they totally ignored row after row of conspicuous white fuel tanks above the ground. In them was the fuel that powered all of America's Pacific Fleet. If a single bomb had been dropped on just one of the tanks, it could have set them all ablaze. It would have taken a year to replace that fuel—a year that U.S. aircraft carriers would have sat idle without any gas. A year when the Japanese navy would have had free reign. A year that could have changed the outcome of WWII.

Having dodged that potentially fatal bullet, the Navy accelerated a plan that was already in the works—building giant gas tanks underground beneath Red Hill to hold the quarter billion gallons of fuel needed to power the Navy's Pacific Fleet. (Large naval ships can only travel a few feet per gallon.) To this day if you're near the H-3 and H-201 freeway intersection and look mauka (toward the mountain), you'll see Red Hill, the Pacific Fleet's gas station and the Navy's response to the Japanese's biggest blunder of the Pacific War.

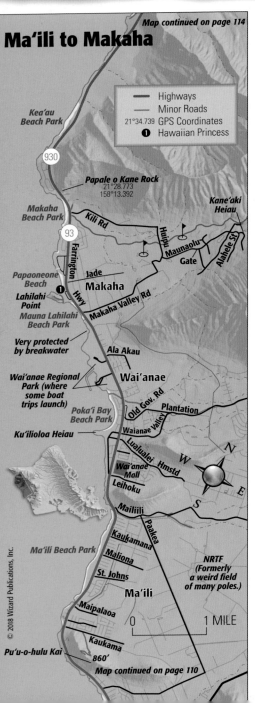

Ma'ili to Makaha

Map continued on page 114

Highways
Minor Roads
21°34.739 GPS Coordinates
❶ Hawaiian Princess

Kea'au
Beach Park

930

Papale o Kane Rock
21°28.773
158°13.392

Kane'aki
Heiau

Makaha
Beach Park

Kili Rd

Huipu

Maunaolu

Gate

Alahele St

93

Farrington Hwy

Papaoneone
Beach

Jade

Makaha

Lahilahi
Point

Makaha Valley Rd

Mauna Lahilahi
Beach Park

Very protected
by breakwater

Ala Akau

Wai'anae Regional
Park (where
some boat
trips launch)

Wai'anae

Old Gov. Rd

Plantation

Poka'i Bay
Beach Park

Waianae Valley

Ku'ilioloa Heiau

Lualualei Hmstd

Wai'anae
Mall

Leihoku

N

W   E

S

Mailiili

Paakea

Kaukamana

Ma'ili Beach Park

Maliona

St. Johns

NRTF
(Formerly
a weird field
of many poles.)

Ma'ili

Maipalaoa

0   1 MILE

Kaukama

Pu'u-o-hulu Kai
860'

© 2018 Wizard Publications, Inc.

Map continued on page 110

many people may prefer to stick with fast food out here. And like all beaches on the island, avoid them on weekends when they're crowded with local residents.

When H-1 ends, it becomes Hwy 93. Before the towns start rolling by, the resort area of **Ko Olina** is the main resort out here. Their four manmade lagoons offer super-protected swimming and some surprisingly good snorkeling in lagoon number 2 on occasion. By the way, the speed bumps at Ko Olina will *mess you up* if you don't respect 'em.

Past Ko Olina as you pass by the power plant, keep an eye out for **dolphins** here. You may get lucky. We've seen them more often here than just about any other place on the island.

The first town is **Nanakuli**. One explanation of how Nanakuli got its name is out of local embarrassment. In ancient times this was a dry, inhospitable place to grow food. Residents had little spare water or food. When travelers walked by, it was customary to give them nourishment. Residents here hid from approaching travelers, fearing shame if they had to refuse to be hospitable. When they couldn't avoid passing travelers, residents pretended to be deaf so they'd be able to feign a lack of understanding. When puzzled travelers moved on, they'd comment on the strange village full of nothing but deaf people who just stared at them. Nanakuli means to *look deaf.*

Just past Nanakuli you'll see an 860-foot hill called **Pu'u-o-hulu Kai**. If you're thinking, *I wonder what the view is like from up there,* see *Hiking* on page 212 for a description of the trail that works its way *relentlessly* up the side. The view is indeed majestic from atop and you'll probably be the only one up there. (Especially if your less-driven spouse stays in the air conditioned car.)

So Much More Than Just a Perimeter of Rocks

In the middle of Wai'anae town is Poka'i Bay Beach Park. At the south end of the park there's a point of land that juts out into the ocean. This is a remarkable place. More than 800 years ago the Hawaiians built a heiau (temple) then called Nene'u, now called the Ku'ilioloa Heiau, dedicated to teaching the art and science of celestial navigation. The ancient Polynesians were masters at transiting the Pacific ocean. They were able to navigate thousands of miles with incredible precision using techniques that far surpassed those of western man at the time. Then the worst thing that could happen to a culture of exploration occurred—they found everything in

their realm that could be found. They were so systematic and thorough, there was literally nothing in Polynesia left to discover. So sometime around 1350 AD, the Hawaiians stopped their 2,000-mile long journeys away from Hawai'i, and over time lost the ability to even know how to do it. Voyaging canoes evolved into inter-island canoes and the Hawaiians became isolated from the rest of the world.

Fast forward to the 20th century. In the 1930s the Army built a bunker and lighthouse on the point, nearly destroying what remained of the heiau, giving little consideration to what they considered a multi-platformed perimeter of rocks. They had no way of knowing that, according to legend, some of those rocks had been transported from Ra'iatea in what is now French Polynesia by a great navigator named Lonokaeho. In the late '70s federal funds were secured to right the wrong, and the local community, with the help of Bishop Museum, restored the heiau to what you see today.

If you visit the site, which would have had a structure on it back then, imagine how it must have been early in the second millennia, when children from the age of 2 would be groomed their whole lives to become master navigators. They would be trained to notice subtle things in the water that indicated the presence of an island far in the distance, memorize the movement of the stars, look for signs such as clouds that don't move (indicating the presence of an unseen island), actions of birds and countless other observations. They would develop such an extraordinary sense of place and situational awareness that at sea, surrounded by nothing but featureless water, they could accurately point to far off lands, taking dead reckoning navigation to heights that have never been repeated. The Polynesians truly were the greatest navigators the world had ever seen.

Makua to Kaʻena

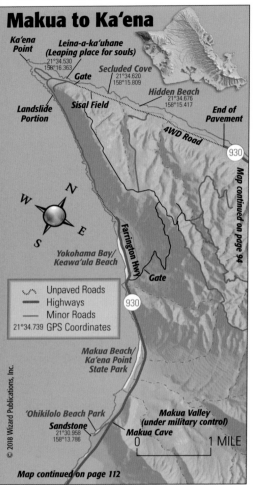

Kaʻena Point
21°34.530
158°16.363

Leina-a-kaʻuhane
(Leaping place for souls)

Gate

Secluded Cove
21°34.620
158°15.809

Hidden Beach
21°34.676
158°15.417

End of Pavement

Landslide Portion

Sisal Field

4WD Road

930

Map continued on page 94

Yokohama Bay/
Keawaʻula Beach

Farrington Hwy

Gate

Unpaved Roads
Highways
930
Minor Roads
21°34.739 GPS Coordinates

Makua Beach/
Kaʻena Point
State Park

ʻOhikilolo Beach Park
Sandstone
21°30.958
158°13.786

Makua Valley
(under military control)

Makua Cave

0   1 MILE

© 2018 Wizard Publications, Inc.

Map continued on page 112

Look mauka and you'll see NRTF Lualualei (the Naval Radio Transmitter Facility). Back in earlier editions we were mystified as to their purpose and simply referred to the area as a "weird field of many poles." Here's the real story: The two largest masts in this field are each 1,503 feet high, making them slightly taller than the twin Petronas Towers in Malaysia. The facility is one of five on the planet that communicates with *submerged* nuclear submarines using Very Low Frequency transmissions (3-30kHz). These radio waves can pass through solid rock and deep seas to send urgent messages to the subs while they're thousands of feet below the surface. In other words, if the order is given to commence global thermonuclear war, those joyous messages will pass through these massive antennas. Pretty wild stuff for sleepy Waiʻanae.

Next, the town of Waiʻanae is where some boat tours depart. The waters off the Waiʻanae Coast can be particularly blue due to lack of runoff and the steepness of the underwater terrain.

MAKAHA

Makaha is the last town along here. In talking about this part of the island and its rough reputation, you should realize that this is not a recent development. Even in ancient times Makaha—which means "savage" or "fierce"—was a place travelers feared. A notorious band of robbers and cutthroats lived up in the valley and ambushed groups passing by. These robbers were skillful at a type of fighting called lua (bone-breaking). They plucked all the hair from their bodies and smeared themselves with oil so they'd be hard to grab in a fight. At the north end of Makaha Valley on the *mauka* (mountain) side of the road across the street from Makaha Shores Apartments, you'll see a tall, upright rock. The top of that very rock, called Papale o Kane, was where the gang's lookout waited. When an approaching group was within striking range, the lookout would yell *low tide,* which signaled that the group was beatable. If he yelled *high tide,* it meant the group was too big or too well-armed to take advantage of, so the robbers would let them pass.

One of the least known resorts *on the entire island* is in Makaha. Hawaiian Princess has a heavenly location right on Papaoneone Beach, one of the lesser known beaches, and it's very reasonably priced for what you get. If you're not interested in staying in Waikiki, this resort has an incredible beachfront setting. (See our app for a review of this condo.)

THE END OF THE ROAD

The last 5 miles of shoreline is devoid of towns, and you'll be amazed at how little use beaches like Makua Beach and Yokohama Bay get during the week.

Makua Cave—also called Kaneana Cave—is an old sea cave gouged out by the ocean during a time when the world was warmer and the oceans higher. Now high and dry, it's on the mauka side of Hwy 93 just past mile marker 17. Park across the street. Legend says that nighttime visitors may come across the shapeshifting god Nanaue disguised as an old man roasting meat over a fire. Any travelers that join him will grow tired and Nanaue will transform back into his half-man, half-shark form before killing the visitors and eating them. This cave is now renowned as one of the most haunted sites in Hawai'i, but if you can brave the lore, it's also worth a stop—*in the daytime.* If you're looking for a secluded beach or a short hike to a tortured sandstone bench, see *'Ohikilolo Beach* on page 121 or the hike at *'Ohikilolo Point* on page 211.

Once at Yokohama Bay, the road ends. The western tip of the island at Ka'ena Point is almost 2.5 miles away. You can hike it; see *Activities* on page 212.

WAI'ANAE & CENTRAL O'AHU BEST BETS

Best Place to Impersonate a Rat in a Maze—Dole Plantation

Best Beach—Makua Beach

Best Forgotten Resort—Hawaiian Princess

Best Frequency to Send a Text Message to a Submerged Nuclear Submarine—3-30kHz or use the NRTF

Best Place to Observe the Speed Limit—Ko Olina

If you're driving to Wai'anae and want the perfect perch to soak in the sunset, you can climb 860-foot high Pu'u-o-hulu Kai to get a particularly grand view.

Yes, it still is possible to find uncrowded beaches, such as Kawela Bay, on O'ahu.

The biggest surprise about O'ahu is how many beautiful beaches there are and how often they're utterly uncrowded. Residents and visitors alike tend to congregate at the same popular beaches, leaving beautiful stretches of sand lightly touched. So we gave ourselves the difficult and thankless job of visiting every sand beach on the island to swim, snorkel and frolic. (See, and you thought all we did was *frivolous* stuff.)

No matter what kind of beach experience you're looking for, O'ahu has something for everyone. In trying to pick a beach, you should consider the island's geography. The **windward** side has some of the most underutilized and lovely beaches on the island, but it didn't get the name *windward* for nothing. If the trade winds are smoking along at 15–30 mph, these beaches tend to be windy. But if it's a 10–20 mph day, the cool breezes might be just right.

Wai'anae has lots of beaches that are protected from the wind thanks to the mountain behind them, and the waters tend to be clean and clear. But some of their beaches, especially near the Wai'anae towns, might be more crowded. Keep driving past the towns toward Ka'ena Point for the best two Wai'anae beaches.

North Shore beaches can be a wonderful playground in the summer with calm waters and beautiful vistas along with breezes that tend to be slightly *offshore* until you get to Hale'iwa, keeping nearshore waters smooth. But winter can bring monstrous waves that would rip you to pieces if you got careless.

And finally the leeward side with Waikiki, Ala Moana and Hanauma Bay tends to have calmer and safer water than the rest of the island, but you sure ain't gonna have 'em to yourself.

BEACH SAFETY

The biggest danger you will face at the beach is the surf. Though it is calmer on the leeward side of the island (where Waikiki is), that's a relative term. Most mainlanders are unprepared for the strength of Hawai'i's surf. We're out in the middle of the biggest ocean in the world, and the surf has lots of room to build up. We have our calm days when the water is like glass. We often have days when the surf is moderate, calling for respect and diligence on the part of the swimmer. And we have the high surf days, perfect for sitting on the beach with a picnic or a mai tai, watching the experienced and the audacious tempt the ocean's patience. Don't make the mistake of underestimating the ocean's power here. Hawai'i is the undisputed drowning capital of the United States, and we don't want you to join the statistics.

Other hazards include rip currents, which can form, cease and form again with no warning. Large "rogue waves" can come ashore with no warning. These usually occur when two or more waves fuse at sea, becoming a larger wave. Even calm seas are no guarantee of safety. Many people have been caught unaware by large waves during ostensibly "calm seas." We swam and snorkeled most of the beaches described in this book on at least two occasions (usually more than two). But beaches change. The underwater topography changes throughout the year. Storms can take a very safe beach and rearrange the sand, turning it into a dangerous beach. Just because we describe a beach as being in a certain condition does not mean it will be in that same condition when *you* visit it.

Consequently, you should take the beach descriptions as a snapshot in calm times. If seas aren't calm, you probably shouldn't go in the water. If you observe a rip current, you probably shouldn't go in the water. If you aren't a comfortable swimmer, you should probably never go in the water, except at those beaches that have lifeguards. There is no way we can tell you that a certain beach will be swimmable on a certain day, and we claim no such prescience. There is no substitution for your own observations and judgment.

A few standard safety tips: Never turn your back on the ocean (even when you're in it). Never swim alone. Never swim in the mouth of a river. Never swim in murky water. Never swim when the seas are not calm. Don't walk too close to the shorebreak; a large wave can come and knock you over and pull you in. Observe ocean conditions carefully. Don't let small children play in the water unsupervised. Fins give you far more power and speed and are a good safety device in addition to being more fun. If you're comfortable in a mask and snorkel, they provide considerable peace of mind, as well as opening up the underwater world. Lastly, don't let Hawai'i's idyllic environment cloud your judgment. Recognize the ocean for what it is—a powerful force that needs to be respected. Call 808-973-4383 for a surf report before choosing your beach for the day.

If you're going to spend any time at the shoreline or beach, water shoes are the best investment you'll ever make. These water-friendly wonders accompany us whenever we go to any beach. You can get them at lots of places, including the ubiquitous ABC Stores. Even on sandy beaches, rocks or sea life seem magnetically attracted to the bottoms of feet. With water shoes, you can frolic without the worry. (Though don't expect them to protect you from everything.)

The ocean here rarely smells fishy since the difference between high and low tide is so small. (In other words, it doesn't strand large amounts of smelly sea plants at low tide like other locations.)

Theft can be a problem when visiting beaches. Visitors like to lock their cars at all beaches, but piles of glass on the ground usually dissuade island residents from doing that at secluded beaches. We usually remove anything we can't bear to have stolen and leave the car with the windows rolled up but unlocked. (Though that may negate your rental car insurance.) That way, we're less likely to get our windows broken by a curious thief. Regardless, don't leave *anything* of value in your car. (Well… maybe the seats can stay.) While in the water, we use a waterproof pouch or box (which you can buy online) for our wallet and keys, and leave everything else on the beach. We don't take a camera to the beach unless we are willing to stay there on the sand and babysit it. This way, when we swim, snorkel or just walk, we don't have to constantly watch our things.

Use **sunscreen** early and often. Don't pay any attention to the claims from sunscreen makers that their product is waterproof, rubproof, sandblast proof, power-wash proof, etc. Reapply it every couple of hours and after you get out of the ocean. The ocean water will hide sunburn symptoms until after you're toast. Then you can look forward to agony for the rest of your trip. (And yes,

There's a reason why we say never turn your back on the ocean…

you *can* get burned while in the water.) Gel-based sunscreens work best in the water. Lotions work best on land.

People tend to get fatigued while walking in sand. The trick to making it easier is to walk with a very gentle, relaxed stride while lightly striking the sand almost flat-footed.

The Hawai'i Supreme Court ruled in 2006 that *all* beaches are public to "the upper reaches of the wash of the waves… at high tide during the season of the year in which the highest wash of the waves occurs." This means that you can park yourself on any stretch of shoreline sand you like. The trick, sometimes, can be access. You might have to cross private land to get to a public beach. We've pointed out a legal way to every beach on the island, and some of our maps have access routes in yellow to show you the way.

In general, **surf** is higher and stronger during the winter, calmer in the summer, but there are exceptions during all seasons. When we mention that a beach has facilities, it usually includes restrooms, showers, picnic tables and drinking water.

You might want to pick up a cheap-o beach chair at an ABC Store and donate it to your hotel when you leave the island.

Lastly, remember that just because *you* may be on vacation doesn't mean that residents are. Monday through Thursday is the best time to go to the beach. Local residents *love* their beaches, and they show their affection every weekend.

Beach conditions around the island are almost entirely determined by the direction they face, and the dividing lines around O'ahu are rather dramatic. From Makapu'u in the east to Kahuku in the north, you'll often find moderate, onshore winds and somewhat choppy seas year-round—being the *least* windy in the winter months— and wave sizes are rarely monstrous but

often respectable. From Kahuku in the north to Ka'ena Point in the west, giant surf in the winter and calm seas in the summer are often combined with light winds at the shore or winds coming from right to left, with windier conditions just offshore. (But onshore winds increase if the trade winds become more northerly.) From Ka'ena Point in the west to Barbers Point in the south, much of the winds are blocked by the mountains, and the surf tends to be big when there's a westerly swell, usually in the winter. The south-facing shoreline, including Waikiki and Hanauma Bay, tends to get small to flat surf in the winter and somewhat larger surf in the summer, but rarely gets the towering waves that the North Shore is famous for.

But remember, these are generalities. We've seen huge surf from the north in June, and we've seen the North Shore flat in February. Nothing can replace your own eyes and judgment. Ultimately, that's what'll keep you out of trouble.

We're going to start our beach descriptions from the westernmost tip of the island at Ka'ena Point on the left side of the fold-out back cover map and work our way around the island counter-clockwise. Beaches that are *supposed* to have **lifeguards** are highlighted with this ⊕ symbol.

The endangered **Hawaiian monk seal** (there are only 1,100 left in the world) occasionally come ashore for a snooze after a heavy meal or to avoid a predator. Many people assume the seals are sick or injured and attempt to coax them back into the water. If you are lucky enough to encounter one, please stay 150 feet away to avoid disturbing them. Beaching is perfectly normal. The fines for disturbing a monk seal can range as high as $25,000. Most seals dive as deep as 600 feet to feed and are considered the most primitive seals in the world with ancient social behavior. Unlike other seals, they don't come ashore in large numbers.

WAI'ANAE BEACHES

⊕ Yokohama Bay/Keawa'ula Beach

This is as far as you can drive in Wai'anae, and it's a worthy destination. This long, glorious beach is lightly used during the week because local residents will usually congregate at beaches closer to the Wai'anae towns and because visitors are usually told to avoid the Wai'anae Coast. (Which we consider bad advice.) The result is a heavenly stretch of sand with impossibly blue water, drop-dead gorgeous views and no weekday crowds. The offshore waters are clean and clear, and the beach is usually protected from strong winds by the mountain ridge behind you.

The beach tends to be wider in the summer and narrower in the winter, which can sometimes expose more sand-stone beachrock, but this is always a sandy beach, never stripped bare by big surf. Large waves can, however, create strong currents, so avoid the water when the ocean's angry. There's no shade, but there are full park facilities, such as restrooms and showers.

Yokohama is really a nickname that has stuck to the point so much that few islanders even recognize its real name, Keawa'ula Beach. Early Japanese immigrants used to come here in large numbers to fish, and other immigrant groups began referring to the area as Yokohama Bay.

If you're in the mood for a hike, check out the *Ka'ena Point Hike* on page 212.

❖ Makua Beach/ Ka'ena Point State Park

One of our favorite beaches on the island—and during the week it's *never* crowded. Here's the story. The U.S. military trains in the valley *behind* the beach, though they rarely visit the beach itself.

You can't drive any farther along the Wai'anae coast than Yokohama Bay. Then again, why would you want to?

Because of this, and the fact that it's several miles from the nearest town, local residents rarely come here in numbers. And even fewer visitors come here. The south end has a super-convenient access via a dirt road a half mile past Makua Cave (but before the tall observation tower on the mauka side of the road). This dirt road isn't easily noticeable, so most people drive right past it. This road might be gated during the week, though you are allowed to walk past the gate. Access to the northern end of the beach is from the pullout right next to the sand. Whether the ocean's calm or pounding, this beach stands apart as one of the most achingly beautiful on the island with clear blue waters, and it never fails to astonish us how lightly it's used during the week. Moderate to high surf can create currents and surge, so be cautious. No facilities, but there's some shade.

Makua is the second to last beach on Hwy 930 in Wai'anae several miles past the town of Makaha.

By the way, many residents refer to this beach as "pray for sex" beach in ref-

'Ohikilolo Beach is probably the least known beach in all of Wai'anae.

erence to the still-visible 1960s graffiti written on a rock at the south end of the beach.

❖ 'Ohikilolo Beach

Huh... where? Few locals and even fewer visitors have ever heard of this beach. It's a few miles from the end of the road in Wai'anae. Just before Makua Cave, a fence on the ocean side of the road causes most people to think the shoreline isn't accessible here. But many years ago the county set the shoreline aside as a beach park; they just never marked it or mentioned it. So although the land mauka of the beach is private, *the beach itself* is all yours. The lovely and secluded pocket of sand is mostly protected by a sandstone bench and is often deserted during the week. At high tide a large pool forms where fish and crab make a living.

There are plenty of turtles in the nearshore waters, but access to the open water is awkward and should only be attempted when the ocean's completely calm. Just past this beach is a peninsula composed of an intricate sandstone lattice. Check out *'Ohikilolo Point* on page 211 for more.

Access is via a 10-minute walk from your car. Park across from Makua Cave after mile marker 17 on Hwy 93 in Wai'anae. Take the trail at the left end of the lot down to the shoreline, then walk left along the shore. Don't leave anything valuable in your car here.

By the way, 'Ohiki-lolo is Hawaiian for either *prying out your brains* or *crazy sand crab*. (It's commonly translated both ways.) Don't know why, but either way someone was having a pretty bad hair day when they named it.

❖ Kea'au Beach Park

This is mainly a rocky coast backed by a very large lawn area with picnic tables, restrooms and showers. There is beach access to the far north end of the park. You'll see locals harvesting 'opihi (a shellfish eaten raw) and fishing here on weekends.

✛ Makaha Beach Park

A nice, wide beach that is rarely crowded during the week. Summer is the best time to visit because the wide sand is usually complemented by gentle water.

Sometimes small surf can make for some nice, long boogie board rides. If the surf's up, however, longshore currents converge in the center, then a rip current heads out to sea, so avoid if it's not calm. In the winter large waves create dangerous conditions, but that's also when you'll see some of the prettiest waves on this part of the coast. Local expert surfers *love* Makaha's winter waves. (And photographers without a $10,000 telephoto lens will *love* how close the surfers get to the shore.) Full facilities. Snorkeling is good when seas are right. Kick out to the closest mooring buoy, and follow the reef ledge to the farther buoy. If you were to keep kicking, you'd come to a good scuba site called Makaha Caverns a few hundred feet offshore, and boat companies often take divers here.

Located across the street from Kili Road and Hwy 93 in Makaha. See map on page 112.

❖ Papaoneone Beach

The beaches near the Wai'anae towns tend to be more heavily used, but this one is visited less than most because it's backed

A beachgoer battles the mid-week crowd at Makaha Beach Park.

You'd think with all those houses around that Papaoneone Beach would be crowded—yet it never is during the week.

by three resort buildings that seem to have the effect of discouraging non-residents (of the apartments) from coming here. We've never seen it crowded during the week. The beach is excellent, and the shorebreak is steeper than most beaches, so decent-sized waves rip up and down the beach, which can be a blast to ride if you're careful. Even bodysurfers will enjoy them if the waves are not too big and powerful. Just beware of undertow here, and don't try riding waves that are too big for you. Winter brings big surf; summer usually has flat waters and excellent snorkeling. Easy access from the pull-out across the street from Jade Street in Makaha, or take Moua Street and look for a *less* convenient public access next to 84-879 Moua St. No facilities and no shade except for the shadow of the apartments in the morning. Nearby locals sometimes call this beach **Turtle Beach**, not to be confused with a beach of the same name on the North Shore. If you take the

trail from the south end of the beach, it goes to the top of the point. The view from 231-foot-high Lahilahi Point is awesome. See map on page 112.

❖ Mauna Lahilahi Beach Park

Very pretty with Mauna Lahilahi hill standing guard at one end, picnic tables near the road and easy access. Water entry is awkward and difficult due to a rocky bench, so water activities here aren't much to speak of. The exception is a *very* protected portion at the south end across from Maiuu Street. Otherwise, park at Hwy 93 near Makaha Valley Road in Makaha.

○ Poka'i Bay Beach Park

This is one of the safest places to swim on the Wai'anae coast due to a protective breakwater. Even when the surf's high elsewhere, Poka'i may be relatively calm. For this reason, it's often packed, even during the week, with parents who bring their keiki to swim. Poka'i is also a popular canoe-launching location. Full facilities and some shade. One note—we've often seen reef sharks cruising inside the breakwater, though these animals, which rarely exceed 6 feet, are generally not considered dangerous to people.

In Wai'anae. Turn toward the ocean where Wai'anae Valley Road meets Hwy 93. See map on page 112.

Just to the south, out on the point, is the **Ku'ilioloa Heiau**, an ancient Place of Refuge where lawbreakers could elude punishment if they reached it and atoned with priests who where there. The lava remains are still in place.

● Ma'ili Beach Park

This beach is over a mile long with a nearly mile-long grassy lawn lined in parts with palm trees. Camping is permitted. Although the facilities aren't in tip-top shape, this beach is lightly used during the week, and it's a short walk from your car. The south end across from Maipalaoa Street has some protected swimming most of the time. During the winter some of Ma'ili's sand washes away, and high surf can bring strong rip currents.

In Ma'ili—can't miss it. See map on page 112.

❖ Ulehawa Beach Park

This one's also over a mile-long beach, but don't let that get you too excited. The beach park where Princess Kahanu Avenue meets the highway is the worst part of the beach. A sandstone bench makes the swimming poor. You're better

Who cares if they're man-made? The lagoons of Ko Olina have exceptionally good beaches.

off to the left (south) where the conditions are sandier, but overall, this isn't a great beach to spend some time. By the way, Ulehawa is Hawaiian for *filthy penis*, and was named in honor of a not-so-loved chief from the area.

⊕ Kalaniana'ole Beach Park

This is a small beach with a very steep shorebreak, which is lots of fun if you want to rake up and down the shoreline feeling the ocean's raw power. It's not so fun if the surf is too strong, or you're skittish about the ocean and don't want to feel the ocean's force unfiltered by more gently sloping shorelines elsewhere. High surf, especially in the winter, creates dangerous conditions. The right (north) end of the park has a lawn, ballfield and playground. At the extreme north end where the cyclone fence forms a 90

degree angle, you'll find a sandstone blowhole that snorts, gasps and spouts when the surf's up. On the south side, walk about 500 feet across the sandstone to find the **Mermaid Cave**.

Camping is allowed with a county permit but often occupied by... long term campers who may not have a permit. Located where Nanakuli Avenue meets the highway (Hwy 93) in Nanakuli. Full facilities.

❖ Electric Beach/Tracks/Kahe Point

Just before the impossible-to-miss power plant on Hwy 93 before Nanakuli is a tiny pocket of sand called Electric Beach. It's a popular scuba diving and snorkeling spot. Good snorkeling when calm, but visibility can be poor. The long beach just past the power plant is known by local surfers as **Tracks** (after the nearby, now-abandoned railroad tracks). The surf is often fairly gentle here, making the swimming good much of the time. Full facilities.

❖ Ko Olina Lagoons

A REAL GEM In the 1990s the developers of Ko Olina created four semi-circular lagoons mostly protected from the open ocean. The swimming is excellent and ultra-protected near the beach. Swim from the sandy shoreline to the open end where the snorkeling can be outstanding around the rocks. Watch for currents flushing in and out of the openings. These lagoons are extremely pretty, and sunsets from here are fantastic.

Lagoon number 4 has the most parking spaces—about 100. Lagoons 1, 2 and 3 have only 18 parking spaces (plus another 18 at parking lot 1B). Bottom line, whichever lagoon you choose, you should arrive before 10 a.m., or go in the late afternoon if you want to get a parking space. Otherwise, park at the Ko Olina Marina for $10 and take the short walk to the lagoons. A concrete path connects them. Signs say you can't bring temporary shade (umbrellas) or Frisbees, but beaches in Hawai'i belong to the public, so we don't understand how Ko Olina can enforce such rules. Cabanas *might* be available at Lagoons 2 and 3, first-come first-serve.

Take H-1 west until it becomes Hwy 93 (*after* exit number 1), and look for a road to Ko Olina on the *mauka* side of the highway. The roads to the lagoons are labeled. Open sunrise to sunset. See map on page 110.

'EWA & LEEWARD BEACHES

❖ Nimitz Beach

Lining the south end of Kalaeloa Airport, the water's better than 'Ewa Beach (below), and in winter the seas can get exceptionally calm, though swimming can be awkward due to reefs offshore. There's some shade, and it's not a bad place to stake your claim and stretch out on the sand. The beach park itself (with full facilities, called Kalaeloa Beach Park) has beachrock at its shoreline, but it's sandier at the eastern end. The best portion of the beach is near the campsites. Where Coral Sea Road veers right, there's a paved, then unpaved road called Eisenhower on the left. See map on page 106 and take Exit 5A.

❖ White Plains Beach Park

The best thing about this beach is the surfing break just offshore. Great novice surfing conditions—crumbling waves like Waikiki when conditions are right. But unless you bring your own board, you need a military ID to rent their surfboards. The beach is open to the public, but services are only available to the military. Swimming

isn't great due to lots of reef and rocks in the nearshore waters. Same directions as to Nimitz Beach, but turn left at Tripoli Road. Then go 0.5 miles and turn right on (possibly unmarked) White Plains Road. Weekends are crowded when local families enjoy the waters and the full facilities. Stick to weekdays.

❖ One'ula Beach Park

There's even less reason to come here than 'Ewa Beach. It's lined with beachrock that's hard on your feet and anything else that comes in contact with it. In past editions we said that "this is also where the area's... less-than-savory characters tend to hang out, from what we've observed." Well, we heard from one of them, who said, "That would be me and my friends, dedicated surfers who keep trim and healthy by a daily dose of paddling and surfing." Fair enough. Consider us properly chastised. Nonetheless, stink eye will possibly greet you if you visit.

❖ 'Ewa Beach

This beach doesn't really look very Hawaiian. If you were transported here, you might think you had ended up in Florida. With its long, yardstick-straight sand beach, a huge, well-kept lawn, basketball court and picnic tables behind it, the beach is appreciated by nearby residents but doesn't attract much attention from visitors spoiled by better offerings elsewhere. The water is always less than clear since so much of it originates in mucky Pearl Harbor and gets carried here by currents. And the surrounding 'Ewa Plain is just what the name implies—plain and featureless—except for the development. See map on page 106.

❖ Ke'ehi Lagoon Beach Park

Not much beach and not much lagoon,

for that matter. This park has tennis courts, a giant lawn and playgrounds adjacent to flat, calm water, though it's less than sparkly. Near the airport on Lagoon Drive; turn left onto Aolele. Mainly used to launch canoes.

❖ Sand Island

Sounds like a great place to go to the beach, until you consider it was known as Quarantine Island until the 20th century. The bottom half of the island is ringed with a beach park. The water can be cloudy, the shore drops to depth fairly quickly, and if you take a dip at the right time you'll catch a faint, trashy smell on the wind. The west end is actually kind of pretty, though. The southern portion that faces the open ocean has a nice sand beach and large lawn area, but it's backed by cranes and shipping derricks. The north end is lined by Coast Guard facilities and a view of downtown Honolulu, but if you stick to the east, you can catch a decent view of the larger ships (cruise ships and barges alike) pulling to the nearby piers.

The island does have a few historical points of interest. Back when it was known as Quarantine Island, it was the first (and sometimes main) stop for ships carrying contagious passengers. During WWII, beginning in December of 1941, the island began use as an internment camp for Japanese and Axis country expatriates. Its run ended in March 1943, at which point the interned citizens were sent to the mainland or to the nearby Honouliuli Interment Camp. Regardless, Sand Island isn't your scenic beach, and it doesn't carry the prettiest history.

❖ Kaka'ako Waterfront Park

This park makes a rotten first impression when you're driving up past an industrial area and a boat graveyard. But the park itself is actually a nice place to sit at the shoreline and watch the sunset because if there's any surf, it comes crashing into the lava rock wall. Watching it can be surprisingly relaxing. You'll join a group of almost all local residents—this place is unknown to most visitors—and sometimes the streets are lined with homeless people. Just west of Waikiki, take Ala Moana Boulevard to Ward Avenue to Ahui toward the ocean.

➕ Ala Moana Regional Park

These beaches are the main nearby alternatives to Waikiki beachgoing. If Waikiki feels a little small to you, Ala Moana is an ultra-wide beach with endless sand and shallow, very protected water. The southeast end can feel like a bathtub. Just be aware of where the sea-floor drops off to deeper water.

Behind Ala Moana is a gigantic lawn where locals bring their volleyballs, Frisbees, croquet and just about every other plaything you can imagine. The only shade on the beach is from the moving shadows of palm tree crowns. While visitors gravitate toward Waikiki, Honolulu residents tend to be the most frequent users of Ala Moana, and on weekends and holidays they pack the place.

Because it's so calm most of the time, it's popular with timid swimmers and families with kids. Of course, if the sound of screaming kids is what you're trying to get *away* from, you might want to go elsewhere. Full facilities. See map on page 51.

❖ Magic Island

This peninsula on the Diamond Head side of Ala Moana was created in 1964 and was slated to become a resort, but

Magic Island is close to Waikiki and has ultra-protected waters most of the time.

developers ran into money problems, so it was eventually turned into parkland. Even fairly large waves are usually diffused here and at Ala Moana, creating another bathtub backed by sand, lawn, palm trees, the city skyline and finally the Ko'olau Mountains.

This is classic Honolulu. The only areas you want to stay away from are the breaks in the wall that allow in ocean water. Water shoes are a good idea here because the bottom is not entirely sand-lined. No snorkeling—just swimming. From the south end you can watch small boats coming into Ala Wai Harbor.

Overall, we prefer Ala Moana over Magic Island due to its better water quality and sandier sea bottom, but it still qualifies as a *Gem* because of its other characteristics.

Waikiki Beach

Since this is the heart of where most people stay, we've put the description in the *Waikiki & Honolulu Sights* chapter. The beach areas from Kahanamoku to

Sans Souci are covered beginning on page 53.

❖ Kaluahole/Makalei Beach

Not too many people staying in Waikiki come to this small pocket beach because it's a quarter-mile walk from the nearest parking at Kapiolani Park. It's used mostly by residents whose houses line the shore. If you're up for a walk (or you have someone to drop you off), the swimming is good, and you're likely to be the only non-resident there. See map on page 66.

❖ Diamond Head Beach Park & Kuilei Cliffs Beach Park

These two parks are at the shoreline of Diamond Head, accessed by a road splintering off to the right at the southernmost part of Diamond Head Crater. There are only intermittent pockets of sand, and the surf is usually ridable here. Longshore currents heading toward Waikiki often form, meaning that surfers might not be able to effortlessly bob in place. Swimming and snorkeling aren't very good. Consider these beaches pretty to look at but not overly user-friendly for most water activities. Showers behind the beach. The sneaky little secret is to walk past the end of the road along the shoreline trail. Just around the corner is Kuilei Cliffs Beach Park, often used by nudists because of its remoteness. If you keep walking, you will come to Ka'alawai Beach.

❖ Ka'alawai Beach

One of the least-appreciated beaches near Waikiki. The section of sand closest to Black Point (the farther away, eastern end) has excellent swimming that's fairly protected most of the time, with good snorkeling opportunities. Lots of fish, though they seem unusually skittish, probably for the same reason as at Kahala Beach. The beach access is not well known, so it stays off the radar screen of most visitors. You get there either by walking along the shoreline from the easternmost Kuilei Cliffs lookout, or by taking Kahala Avenue to Papu Circle.

Turn right on Kulamanu Street, left on Kulamanu Place. No facilities. Some shade is available only in the summer due to the shifting sun. For what it's worth, it seems like we always see dogs on this beach. See map on page 66.

❖ Kahala Beach

Kahala is where the rich and not-so-famous live on O'ahu. Huge oceanfront mansions line parts of the shoreline here. Kahala Beach is the intermittent sandy strip on the far side of Diamond Head, from Black Point to Wai'alae Beach Park. You access it by driving from Waikiki until Kalakaua Avenue turns into Diamond Head Road, then Kahala Avenue. Continue and park near the intersection of Kahala and Elepaio streets where the curb isn't painted red, and take the first beach access you see.

The snorkeling here is different than places like Hanauma Bay. Forget big fish eyeballing you. Most of them have been

If you're looking for a quieter beach experience than Waikiki, Ka'alawai Beach is a short drive away, and the pace is waaay calmer.

Though this part of Wai'alae Beach is right next to The Kahala Hotel and Resort, it never seems crowded or frantic.

taken by resident fishermen. What's good about the snorkeling here are the small, intricate marine critters making a living over this flat, shallow reef. Most of the time you're swimming in only a couple feet of water, gliding just over the reef. Once away from the shore (and nearer the outer reef edge), the observant and patient snorkeler will notice tiny shrimp passing by, small blennies sticking their heads out of holes and a host of other small 1- to 2-inch fish going about their business. You'll want to wear a T-shirt to protect you when the water gets too shallow. Some cheap gloves wouldn't hurt either. The general flow of water is over the reef (it will resist your advances the closer you get to the edge), along the shore and out the channel at Hunakai Street. (So avoid the channel.) The closer to the reef edge, the more fish. (They're almost completely absent at the shoreline.) If the fish seem unusually skittish, re-

member: They've watched their bigger siblings get nabbed by critters that look *just like you.*

Near Black Point there's a small sand pocket where the point starts. As you approach it, you'll see lots of distortive perturbations in the water, and you'll notice rapid temperature changes. There are basal springs of brackish and fresh water percolating from the ground here. Fresh and saltwater don't like mixing, so you can literally see them rubbing against each other, and the lighter (and colder) freshwater tends to stay on top. Quickly push your flat hand through it, and you'll actually be able to *see* the normally invisible roiling turbulence you create as you pass through the water. Dig a hole in the sand just above the surf line and notice how it fills with water. The sand is saturated from the spring, and your feet sink faster in the sand here. If you've taken the beach access we suggested, you can swim to this pocket, then out toward the reef edge, let the current take you along toward (but stop before!) the channel, then take another beach access from the beach to Kahala Avenue and walk back to your car.

❖ Wai'alae Beach Park
Calm, protected waters most of the time make this a very good swimming beach, but snorkelers need not apply since the water isn't very clear. The best part of the beach is a few minutes' walk to the left, near The Kahala Hotel and its tiny offshore island. It's very pretty, and though that area is a resort beach, it's got a much more relaxed atmosphere than most resort beaches—plus they have beach toys for rent.

At the beach park itself, over the bridge to the right, the sandy shoreline is lightly used except by the beach house owners. (Remember, *you* own the beach, not the nearby homeowners.) Ironically, the worst part of the beach is the narrow, sandy stretch fronting the park itself due to stream runoff and the crumbling remains of an old sidewalk that occasionally poke through the sand. On Kahala Avenue near Kealaolu Avenue. Full facilities.

❖ Wailupe Beach Park
Very easy access off Hwy 72 near Aina Haina, but the uninviting water makes it a must-miss.

❖ Kawaiku'i Beach Park
A good place to launch a kayak or SUP if you just want to paddle the super-calm, protected turquoise water from here to Koko Head. The water quality for swimming is poor thanks to runoff from Hawai'i Kai. But it's pretty with lots of shade trees, picnic tables and facilities. At Hwy 72 and Puuikena Drive.

❖ Maunalua Bay Beach Park
At Hwy 72 and Keahole in Hawai'i Kai, this is the place to launch a boat, canoe, kayak, or other watercraft. Other than that, it offers a pretty sight while you eat lunch, and not much else.

❍ Hanauma Bay Nature Preserve

The snorkeling mecca of the island. We've described it in detail in the *East O'ahu Sights* chapter on page 67.

❖ Halona Cove

This is an idyllic Hawaiian sandy cove. So idyllic, in fact, that in 1953 it served as the site of the now-famous, roll-in-the-sand-while-kissing scene for the movie *From Here to Eternity*. When calm, the cove makes for great swimming. If there's a little surf, it provides good body-surfing. And when the surf is stronger, it becomes a washing machine that will clean your clothes by banging them into the side rocks—with you in them.

Park at the Halona Blowhole Lookout 1.4 miles past (east of) the entrance to Hanauma Bay on Hwy 72. Walk down the short, natural boulder stair-step path near the road. There's a bizarre sign *completely ignored by the masses* telling you not to go down to the beach from here. But we checked with the state and county, and they confirmed that you *are* allowed to go down to the beach.

❍ Sandy Beach
Pretty obvious name, huh? Like identifying a "wooden tree." For years local residents called it the "sand beach near the blowhole," and it was eventually shortened to Sandy Beach. Some call it Sandys. Anyway, this beach is ultra-popular with locals for its bodysurfing. Note that we said *locals*. That's because the sandy shoreline is steep, and the waves have a wickedly powerful shorebreak. Anyone who isn't very expe-

rienced is likely to (and often does) get pile-driven into the sand, resulting in some terrible neck injuries. (Barack Obama bodysurfs here when he's on island, but he's very experienced.) Unless you know what you're doing, consider bodysurfing elsewhere. We've often used the giant lawn next to the beach to launch our ultralight, and too many times we've seen ambulances here carting away injured bodysurfing visitors.

The park has full facilities, and that same lawn is popular with kite fliers, hang gliders (for landing—they *launch* off the cliff above Kaupo Beach Park) and other lawn sports. On Hwy 72 just before the road reaches its easternmost point.

❖ Alan Davis Beach

A small, secluded beach near Makapu'u point. This little gem of a beach is a great place to escape the Waikiki crowds and provides kids with a nice shallow water playground. It's a short hike to get here, which keeps some people away. On weekends it can get more crowded. There's a little shade under the trees to the right side. A rock feature nearby called Pele's Chair looks like a large lava La-Z-Boy. In front of the chair an old telephone pole wedged into the rocks extends over the ocean about 10 feet below. Use caution here. It can be dangerous to jump, so look before you leap. Swimming from the beach isn't really good for adults because the shallow water feels more like a wading pool. Go instead for a dip by the telephone pole away from the beach, though the water is pretty cloudy there—leave the snorkeling gear in the car. To get here, park at Ka'iwi Scenic Shoreline Park. (See the directions for *Makapu'u Hike to the Dragon's Nostrils* on page 196.) Walk uphill through the parking lot, then look to the

Experienced bodysurfers only need apply at Sandy Beach. All others will be pounded into oblivion by the shorebreak.

right at the gate, and you'll see a path going through the flat area toward the ocean. Follow it 0.75 miles. Once Pele's Chair comes into view, you're almost there. No facilities.

WINDWARD BEACHES

✪ Makapu'u Beach Park
This is the first beach on the windward side after you've rounded Makapu'u Head, and the boogie boarding and body-surfing can be excellent here. Conditions are similar to those at Sandy Beach—fantastic, but only for the experienced or the lucky, unless the ocean's pretty calm. During high surf the waves can wash up the entire beach. At times like that, the raging surf scratches and claws at the cliffs to the right, producing quite a sight. Even during smaller seas, the waves will feel pretty powerful for their size due to the shape of the nearshore seabed, making it fun to get tossed around as long as you're aware of the ocean's potential to rough you up.

The lookout above the beach is an excellent vantage point to see windward O'ahu, and on a sunny day the turquoise waters and black lava rock display an amazing opportunity for photos. There's convenient access at the bottom of the hill across from Sea Life Park. If you get the right angle, you should be able to snap a photo of you and your family with the offshore islands of Manana (AKA Rabbit Island) and Kaohi-ka-ipu in the background. Full facilities near the parking lot.

❖ Kaupo Beach Park
After Sea Life Park, across from the Oceanic Institute (where they farm shrimp), is a beach access and a small lawn that is used as a hang glider landing spot (hence the

Being crazy and irresponsible at Pele's Chair near Alan Davis Beach. It's a guy thing, right?

windsock). This is mainly a surfing beach since the shoreline is pretty rocky, but there's a nice tide-pool here. To the left of the nearby pier is where some introductory SCUBA dives take place, but frankly, the water conditions there are pretty poor, and you'd be wise to do your SCUBA diving somewhere else. Also known locally as Cockroach Bay.

❖ Kaiona Beach Park
Well known among residents as the home of the Waimano Canoe Club, this is, indeed, a good place to launch a canoe or kayak. A long reef offshore protects you from most of the ocean's force. Snorkeling can be good at times, but water visibility might be poor. Consider snorkeling about 700 feet off a house with a light green tile roof (which is far to the right of the

park entrance) for fairly good fish life and reef structure. Showers and restrooms available. Packed with local campers on weekends. If you drive past the park, a much less used part of the beach is easily accessible from the road just before it peels away from the shoreline. Just pull over and grab a spot. Gobs of nice sand, if not the clearest water.

❖ Waimanalo Beach Park

A long, very pretty strip of sand with great swimming much of the time. There are few beaches with pads of sand as thick as this one. The ocean's usually clearer than Kaiona, though snorkeling is still pretty poor. There are picnic tables, facilities and some ironwood trees for shade. Weekends are particularly crowded. Car breakins can be a problem here, so don't leave anything valuable in your car.

The nearby baseball field attracts lots of BBQers on weekends. Camping is allowed, but you may not feel very welcome. Easy to find on Hwy 72 after the highway leads away from the Ko'olau Mountains in Waimanalo near a ball park.

⊕ Waimanalo Bay Beach Park

Not to be confused with Waimanalo Beach Park, this confusingly named beach has a pretty thick pad of sand that drops to depth fairly quickly, making it fun to splash around in the water if you respect the fact that the waves will have a bit more force. Currents can form parallel to the shoreline (called longshore currents), but they're usually easy to get out of by swimming perpendicular to them back to shore. Full facilities. Very nice beach for a long walk. Heavily used on weekends. Located halfway between Kailua and Makapu'u (the easternmost point) off Hwy 72. Camping is allowed with county permit.

The forest behind the beach is know as Sherwood Forest because of a gang of robbers in the 1960s calling themselves Robin Hood that preyed on beachgoers here. The *Real Gem* designation refers to the super long beach walk available when you combine it with Bellows Beach.

⊕ Bellows Beach

This is an unusual beach because it's only open to the public from noon Fridays to midnight Sundays. (It's a county park that fronts a closed military base.) As a result of the weeklong pent-up demand, weekend use tends to be unusually high.

Here's the best part: Though access *from the road* is weekends only, Monday–Thursday you can usually walk from Waimanalo Beach Park north along the beach. Remember, all beaches are public, and they only seem to close the sand beach when they are doing military exercises. During the week, most of the southern end of Bellows is a deserted beach walk.

The waters offer pretty good swimming most of the time (though not good snorkeling), and the forest of ironwood trees behind the beach gives it an undeveloped feel. Camping is allowed on weekends with free county permit. Look for the entrance off Hwy 72 in Waimanalo town. There will be a military guard.

The beach has one historical high point. The first Japanese prisoner of war was taken here during WWII when a mini-submarine washed up on the reef, and the officer straggled ashore.

❖ Lanikai Beach

Lanikai has that dreamy, tropical look that postcards and paintings are made of. Beautiful, exceptionally soft sand, stunning blue water and two idyllic off-

A future developer gets his first lesson on how close to build to the shoreline.

shore islands combine to create the quintessential island atmosphere. Lanikai's no secret, and one thing that you need to know is that many of the descriptions you read about this beach are outdated.

The last 20 years haven't been kind to Lanikai. More than half of the beach that lives in the memory of residents—and those who created the paintings—is gone. It's ironic. House lots on the beach might sell for $6 million and up. These wealthy landowners built seawalls to protect their precious investments. According to many experts, seawalls cause the very kind of beach erosion that people try to prevent. The result? What was once a beach well over a mile long is now less than half a mile long. (The beach accesses south of Onekea lead to a sandless shoreline.) Much of the generous sand that once defined Lanikai has now shifted over to Kailua Beach, whose residents, no doubt, thank the Lanikai community for inadvertently donating their sand.

It may be smaller now, but Lanikai is still a feast for the eyes. And the snorkel-

ing along the stretch of water between Mokumanu Drive and Haokea Drive can be great, featuring a healthy community of coral and fish—mostly small fish, but lots of 'em. The only thing that keeps this area from having world-class snorkeling is a general cloudiness in the water. That shouldn't dissuade you; just don't expect it to be as crystal clear below the surface as it *appears* from above the surface.

By the way, the offshore islets are called Mokulua, and the name applies to both. This is fitting since Mokulua means *two islands*. They are also called "The Mokes."

There are beach accesses all along Lanikai, but parking is ridiculously limited. If you have a kayak to launch, go to the far end at Lanipo Drive. If you're looking for a larger patch of sand, the wide part starts at Kuailima Drive. The later in the day you get there, the harder it is to find a place to park. Mokulua Road is one way, and you're only allowed to park on the driver's side since there is a bike lane on the other side, where it is illegal to park. If you can't find a spot, check the side streets or walk from Kailua Beach. No facilities and no shade. In Kailua. See map on page 74.

Kailua Beach

This lovely 2.5-mile stretch of delicious sandy beach fits nearly everyone's profile of a beautiful tropical paradise. This is one of the best beaches on the island to simply stroll along as the waves splash your legs. Four different offshore islands beckon the adventurous. And Kailua rarely gets the monstrous 30-foot surf that pounds the North Shore (see *Banzai Pipeline* on page 147, if you're curious about what we mean).

The swimming, boogie boarding and bodysurfing at Kailua are phenomenal when conditions cooperate—which is most of the time. Snorkeling isn't worth your time, thanks to the runoff from Enchanted Lake and the Kawainui Canal.

The kayaking here is particularly good. See *Kayaking* on page 220.

This beach is your best opportunity to spot the elusive **mole crab**. These quarter-sized buggers live under the sand beneath the surf line and can only be pinpointed by subtle clusters of V-shaped water wakes as waves recede from their barely exposed eye-stalks. (They're different from the ghost crabs that live in holes above the surf line.) On those occasions that Portuguese man-o-wars drift in, mole crabs will snag a passing tentacle and pull it under the sand, munching away on it like spaghetti. Speaking of man-o-wars, they are, unfortunately, more common here, especially during summer months (April–October) than at most other beaches—one of the few dings to this otherwise great beach.

You can either park at Kailua Beach Park at Kalaheo and Kailua Road, or at Kalama Beach Park (less used) at Kalaheo and Hauoli, which gets you closer to the center of the beach. There are also several rights-of-way along Kalaheo, but parking might be a problem there. See map on page 74.

As an aside, during WWII, the island's police chief, for some reason, set a rule that "prostitutes can swim only at Kailua Beach." He also banned them "from all golf courses."

Kualoa Beach Park

A truly kickin' windward beach park. Straddling the point at the north end of Kane'ohe Bay, the park features endless lawn, plenty of facilities, camping, shade, picnic

If Lanikai Beach doesn't ring your wow meter, then you ain't got one.

tables and an uninterrupted sandy strip of shoreline with usually calm waters, a gorgeous mountain backdrop and a tempting and utterly picturesque island. **Chinaman's Hat** island is 614 yards offshore. About the only thing this park *doesn't* have is crystal clear waters. The ocean gets some runoff from nearby streams, so the water tends to be a bit cloudy. But the shoreline is usually so protected that swimming can be great here—just not the snorkeling.

If you walk along the beach to the right, the sand keeps going, leading to land fronted by **Kualoa Ranch**. Although they sell that as their "private beach," calling it a "secret island" that they'll take you to for $46, you can have it for free just by strolling onto it from Kualoa Beach. Remember, all Hawaiian beaches are *public*. Kualoa Ranch only owns the land *behind* the beach. (But don't tell that to any of the beachgoers who Kualoa charged to take them there—it'll just antagonize 'em.) Camping is allowed with a county permit.

❖ Kualoa Sugar Mill Beach/ Kanenelu Beach/Kalae'o'io Beach

As soon as you leave the entrance to Kualoa Beach Park heading north, the road starts hugging the shoreline, and sandy beaches present themselves. Although they're tantalizing (heck, we even used a photo of one to start the *North Shore Sights* chapter), they aren't the best beaches you'll find—they're just the *first* beaches lining the highway. Swimming is not bad but can be better elsewhere. Access is easy and obvious—just pull over when you want and dig in. These beaches tend to be fairly narrow.

❖ Ka'a'awa Beach Park

The sand is wider here than the beaches to the south, and the swimming's pretty good. Visibility is better, too, but often not good enough to encourage snorkeling. In Ka'a'awa. (We just love saying that word.) Access? Right next to the road.

❖ Swanzy Beach Park

This consists of a long, grassy lawn, basketball court, and covered picnic tables. Though the lawn is well-kept, the facilities are falling apart. Camping is allowed on weekends with free county permit, though there won't be much privacy at this roadside beach. There's hardly any sand, and while the waters are protected and reefy, the fish count is poor (probably overfished by local spearfishermen). A dozen miles north of Kane'ohe in Ka'a'awa.

❖ Makaua Beach

This is another park-your-car, fall-right-in sort of beach. It's between Ka'a'awa and Kahana Bay Beach Park (immediately after Swanzy Beach Park) heading towards the North Shore from Kane'ohe, but it doesn't offer much, except for a family-sized patch of sand. The nearshore waters are rocky and the area's pretty shallow, and during high tides or larger eastern swells, the sand is liable to disappear completely.

❖ Kahana Bay Beach Park

Kahana is a pretty arc of sand fronting Kahana Valley. The water is never pristine due to runoff from the Kahana Stream, but if you don't care about snorkeling, it's a nice place. There are trees for shade and picnic tables, and there's rarely more than a handful of people during the week. And if you want to kayak, the river feeding the bay makes for a very enjoyable Kayak trip. See *Kayaking* on page 221. Can't miss it in south Kahana 15 miles north of Kane'ohe on Hwy 83.

❖ Punalu'u Beach Park

Here's the perfect beach for the lazy beachgoer. You drive up and… well, that's it. The beach literally touches the road. No muss, no fuss. And what a beauty it is. Long, inviting stretch of sand, lots of shade, full facilities, partial protection from an offshore reef and surprisingly few visitors during the week. Unfortunately, the surrounding area has seen better days, so while the ocean is beautiful, what's around it is lacking. In the winter the beach narrows during periods of high surf, but overall, this is an under appreciated windward beach. The snorkeling isn't world class, but the swimming much of the time is over a sandy bottom. Just stay away from the channel to the left (north) where currents can form. North of the facilities (and a bridge where the channel is) the beach gets even better and less used. In Punalu'u on Hwy 83; can't miss it. See map on page 87.

❖ Kaluanui Beach

Ya see the sign, ya pull over. Walk 50 feet and jump onto the sand. It's that easy, and it's usually empty during the week. Lots of sand here and thickly padded offshore. But don't venture too far out since channel currents can get strong.

❖ Makao Beach

Another ridiculously easy-to-access

Kahana Beach doesn't have the clearest water on the island thanks to the nearby river, but if you're looking for delicious scenery or good kayaking, you've found your destination for the day.

beach. It's right next to the road, so find a place, pull over, and enjoy the sun. The sand here is narrow and will likely be almost gone at high tide, but the water is highly protected due to an offshore reef. The only current is at the far north end, right where the water exits through the channel. Snorkeling can be good in the summer, but during the winter you may see some general cloudiness. Unfortunately, during both seasons the area appears to be overfished. On Hwy 83 just south of Hauʻula.

❖ Hauʻula Beach Park
The good news is that access is easy and convenient, and the park has full facilities. Camping is allowed with county permit. The bad news is that the water tends to be cloudy and it's overfished. Overall, not a must-see beach. On Hwy 83 in Hauʻula across from 7-Eleven.

❖ Kokololio Beach Park
There are a few beach estates just north of the park. In case you're wondering what kind of people can afford an estate

Instructions for Punaluʻu Beach: Drive up, open door, fall out onto the sand…repeat if necessary.

on a lovely beach like this, here's one example: The estate just south of the stream near Pali Kilo Iʻa is owned by the local electric company and used as a perk for its executives. (Apparently, we lowly ratepayers aren't invited.) Anyway, the beach is very pretty and has full facilities.

There's a small area with good snorkeling some of the time for adventurous snorkelers. If you follow the large wall that bisects the park to where it *would have* touched the water, and enter slightly to the right and paddle out a short way, longshore currents will carry you to the left along a short, reefy wall that sometimes has an impressive number of fish. It's like being on a conveyer belt. Then in a hundred feet or so, swim perpendicular to the current (toward the shore), and walk back to where you started. (This is the typical current—we imagine that stronger currents could prove problematic if the surf's raging.) Sometimes,

inexplicably, we've seen the fish almost completely absent. Other times they're everywhere. The far north end has a protected area sometimes called Bathtub Beach. (Not to be confused with La'ie Beach Park Pounders, which also goes by the nickname Bathtub Beach.)

Camping is allowed here, but you may be happier elsewhere. See map on page 87.

❖ La'ie Beach Park/Pounders

In La'ie, 1 mile past (north of) Hau'ula Kai Shopping Center, is the parking lot

A REAL GEM

for La'ie Beach Park. (It's also known locally as Pounders.) This is an attractive beach with a sandstone cliff defining the right (south) end. It's the waves at that end that inspired the name *Pounders*. When the surf's decent, the pounding waves can make for some good bodysurfing. But if you're not careful, they can also pound the living daylights out of you. Better and safer swimming is at the north end near the old pier pilings.

If you walk to the left along the beach for a few minutes, past the old pier pilings and around the corner, a wonderful treat awaits. Except during high tide and high surf, a wonderfully protected set of ponds creates bathtub-smooth water, hence its nickname— **Bathtub Beach** (not the same spot as the identically named Bathtub Beach at Kokololio Beach). This is a fantastic place to splash about in the ocean while still feeling protected. (Of course, you're still in the ocean, so anything can happen, and high surf means that all bets are off, so you might not even be able to reach it by walking along the shoreline.) And the mountain views from here are *da kine*.

❖ Laniloa Beach

In La'ie town there's an easy-to-miss public access 0.2 miles past McDonald's (toward Kahuku), just before the

Over the river and through the woods, to Kokololio Beach we go.

It's not hard to see why this hidden stretch of shoreline, which you can't see from the road or from nearby La'ie Beach Park, is affectionately called Bathtub Beach.

road curves left. We usually park on the other side of the street. The 60-second path takes you to a lovely ribbon of sand that overlooks impressive La'ie Point. Though the waters have a mostly rocky bottom, the swimming is usually safe due to a protective reef farther out. There is a sandy patch in the water to the left of the shoreline access point. That, along with its mostly forgotten status, makes this a great beach to spend an afternoon. A few trees provide shade. See map on page 87.

❖ Hukilau Beach/La'ie Beach

If you go to a lu'au or listen to anyone play Hawaiian music for very long, you'll hear this song: *Oh, we're going / to a huk-ilau / a huki huki huki huki hukilau...* This refers to the age-old practice of circling a portion of the ocean with a net and driving the fish in. Then a group of people hauls out the fish-laden net. That's what used to happen at this beach, and it was quite a sight to see—until the taxman heard about it. After that, the practice of **Hukilau** stopped altogether. See page 85 for more.

Still, Hukilau Beach is yet another beautiful windward beach with fantastic views of Goat Island to the left, Pulemoku Rock directly offshore and La'ie Point on the right. There's not much shade here. The right side of the beach is partially protected by reef and is often safe to swim. The south end is also called La'ie Beach, which has its own beach access at the end of Halelaa Street, but the no parking sign usually convinces people to park at Hukilau Park. If you feel like walking, you could stroll 0.7 miles along the beach to the point nearest Goat Island, then wade to its offshore beach. Or park closer—see *Malaekahana Beach* on page 142. Most of the beach users here are students from nearby Brigham Young University. Showers available. Closed Sundays.

❖ Goat Island/Moku'auia Island

Goat island sits 720 feet off Malaekahana State Park. It has two beaches of its own, and the one to the left is fantastic. It's a classic, curving sandy beach with awesome swimming most of the time, thanks to the protection offered from the two points and an offshore reef. And since you need to swim to it (really, wade to it up to your chest unless the ocean's raging—you'll need water shoes since the bottom's uneven and sharp), it's never crowded. What a *great* getaway. Sometimes, especially in winter, waves can wrap around Goat Island and slap each other right where you'll be wading. You may get bumped around a bit if that's happening. Huge surf means you don't go.

In the mid-1800s, this small island was the home of a Hawaiian lawyer who kept two mistresses here. When the king of Hawai'i learned of this, he ordered the lawyer arrested. You know what they say… never mess with a lawyer, even if you're a king. The attorney did some research and found out that his offshore island wasn't recorded on any of the king's maps. So he declared that it wasn't part of Hawai'i, and that he was now king of his own island. (Even in the 1800s, lawyers would be lawyers.) The ploy worked, and the Hawaiian king left him alone.

❖ **Malaekahana Beach**
One of the less-appreciated beach parks near the northern tip of the island. The beach is a mile long and has pretty good swimming if you wear water shoes (since the nearshore waters are rocky). Near the northern (left) end there are several beach cabins. They're old private beach houses that the state took over when this area was converted into a park. Though they're pretty run down, they can be yours if you make arrangements far enough in advance. See *Camping* on page 184. Malaekahana seems to be one of those beaches that stays unknown to most visitors, so odds are you'll be sharing it with mostly residents. Offshore is Goat Island/Moku'auia Island with its exclusive beach that you need to wade to.

Between the towns of La'ie and Kahuku on Hwy 83. There are two en-

What makes the beach on Goat Island so special? 'Cause ya gotta earn it, brah…

trances. The first (southern) one is closest to Goat Island and has more facilities. The second one leads to the cabins. See map on page 87.

❖ Kahuku Golf Course Beach

Think of it as a rose with thorns: Look, but don't touch. More specifically, don't swim. That's because there's a pretty impressive rip current that's usually present here. But the good news is that the beach is often empty and exhibits a certain wildness. Sand and sandstone beachrock are the ingredients topped off by ever-present wind. You can walk along the shoreline for miles here—so much so that we've detailed it as a hike on page 209 since access to it is a bit awkward. At the northern tip of the island.

❖ Kuilima Cove

The snorkeling off the middle/right behind the semi-protective reef can be exceptional, even Hanauma Bay-like in terms of fish count, although this bay is much smaller and not as protected, so

You don't have to be staying at the nearby Turtle Bay Resort to enjoy the semi-protected waters of Kuilima Cove.

the snorkeling isn't as reliable. (Sometimes nothing but sea urchins.) Stay away from the channel at the right end where the reef ends, and avoid the left side where the bay empties into the open ocean. Visibility won't be stellar—it's often somewhat cloudy. But the fish life can be extraordinary at times.

To get here, drive past the northern tip of the island and Kahuku and pull into the impossible-to-miss Turtle Bay Resort. Fight your way to a parking spot and take the path to the right of the hotel. Often crowded. See map on page 88.

❖ Turtle Bay

Past the Turtle Bay Resort, the western part is lightly used and beautiful. There's even an island to wade to when it's super-calm (which sometimes happens during summer months). The snorkeling around that island can be good, but currents can be a problem here, so be cautious. Much

It may be next to Turtle Bay, but we see more monk seals in this area than anything else.

of the beach is fronted by beachrock, so swimming is often awkward. Winter waves make swimming impossible.

The name Turtle Bay comes from years ago when green sea turtles used to lay eggs on the beach. They don't do that anymore, and the bay is not necessarily more turtle-infested than any other beach. (Just so you don't get your hopes up.) Don't confuse Turtle Bay with *Turtle Beach/Laniakea Beach* described on page 150.

❖ Kawela Bay

A REAL GEM There aren't many places like this on O'ahu: a beach so little known that it's essentially a secret. If you don't live nearby, you probably don't know about this one. One end of the beach has a few houses on it, but it's a gated community—can't go there. From Hwy 83 it's not visible. The trailhead is 1 mile past (toward Hale'iwa) the prominent Turtle Bay Resort entrance near the northern tip of the island. See map on page 88. (Another trailhead is farther down at a small bridge.) Park at the end of a long chain-link fence, where you may see a produce stand across the street.

Walk around the fence (it's legal—you are *not* trespassing), and when you get to some *incredible* banyan trees, go straight to the beach and head to the right along the sand. Kawela Bay rarely, especially during the week, has more than a handful of people on it.

The middle/right portion has the best swimming with its sandy patches. (Bring polarized sunglasses to see through the surface better.) The left (west) end, where the houses are, has some weak basal springs that gurgle out of the sand above the ocean line. But it's the far *right* end that you want. It has your best snorkeling, though overall, the bay isn't a great snorkeling spot due to some sediment that comes out of the river. That side also has calm, lapping waves, abundant shade and striking beauty, along with a serenity that you'll remember for years. In the winter, big rains often cloud the water for days at a time, but it never keeps this beach from being lovely.

❖ Waiale'e Beach Park

Unmarked at press time, this pretty little park has a small island 153 feet offshore. (Standing at the point, you'd *swear* it was closer.) When it's calm (and *only* when it's calm), the snorkeling to the right of the island can be exceptional. Lots of big and small fish and even occasional barracuda and octopus swim around this tiny area. If it's flat calm, consider swimming around the back side of **Kukaimanini Island**, which is intricate and lattice-like and looks very different than the front of the island. See if you can find the basal spring barely percolating from the beach sand area closest to the island. Located on Hwy 83 almost 2 miles southwest (toward Hale'iwa) of the entrance to Turtle Bay Resort (but northeast of Sunset Beach). See map on page 88.

NORTH SHORE BEACHES

These beaches are quintessential dual-personality beaches. During the winter (October–April) they can produce staggering waves that keep all but expert surfers out of the water—classic *look, but don't touch* beaches. During the rest of the year, seas are *usually* small to calm.

⊕ Sunset Beach Support Park/ Pau-malu

During the summer months (May–September or October) this is an exquisitely beautiful beach that is irresistibly inviting. You won't find a better-looking beach to frolic on than Sunset on a calm day. Though mostly sand-bottomed, there are some reef areas near the lifeguard station and on the right (north) side that can offer downright kickin' snorkeling, very clear water and lots of fish. Otherwise, just wade in the crystalline water till you're waterlogged. The sand drops quickly, so

Do I really need to say why this is called Sunset Beach Park?

During calm days (usually from May to October) Shark's Cove can offer insanely good snorkeling opportunities.

you can be in chest-high water only a few feet from shore. Check with the lifeguard for conditions. Restrooms across the street, as well as showers (which are unusually cold—we wonder if the pipes are ensconced in a chilly basal spring).

This steepness, along with fairly coarse sand, creates good conditions for Monastery Tag (named after a beach in California where we accidentally invented it one day after a scuba dive). Now bear with us—it'll sound a bit strange—but we've shown this to others and they *love* it. The three ingredients you need are unchecked waves, a steep beach and a padded (sandy) bottom. Basically, you lie in the water at the surf's edge, and zip up and down the beach up to 30 feet each way on a thin cushion of water, digging feet and hands into the sand to control your ascent and descent. Like a low-to-the-ground sports car, the sensation of speed is greater. Here, you're only inches above the sand, and the trick is to go as far up the shore as possible without get-

ting stranded. To people on the beach it looks like you're mindlessly scraping along the sand, but actually you're unscathed as you orient the shape of your body for maximum efficiency. A mask and snorkel make it much easier. As with all *worthwhile* and important endeavors, it takes years of practice and dedication. On your back, front, head first, feet first—it's important to master them all. You really feel the power of the ocean this way. Obviously, you can't do this when the ocean's flat, and you'd be crazy to do it when the ocean's raging. Only during those in-between times.

🔆 'Ehukai Beach Park

Few locals refer to this beach by this name, but that's what's on the sign out front. During summer months the ocean transports mountains of sand here, making the beach wide and thick with good swimming.

But it's the winter when this spot occupies its special place in the world of surfing. Because 'Ehukai is the home of the most famous surf site in all Hawai'i—the **Banzai Pipeline**. Classic tube-shaped waves roll ashore from the surf break to the left of the beach park, and experienced surfers and boogie boarders ride them with undisguised glee. If you're looking for a great surfing photo while the area is getting a west/northwest swell, Pipeline is the place to be. Just sit on the beach and watch da buggahs shred 'em.

Between Sunset Beach Park and Waimea Bay on Hwy 83 across the street from Sunset Beach Elementary School. See map on page 88.

❖ Pupukea Beach Park

This park is divided into two main areas: Shark's Cove and Three Tables.

❖ Shark's Cove

First of all, it ain't overly sharky. It was so named by divers years ago because it sounded more exciting than "the area to the right of the tide-pool at Pupukea."

A REAL GEM

This tiny cove offers fantastic snorkeling and SCUBA much of the time during the summer (May–September). Yeah, it's popular and sometimes crowded with people. But it's also crowded with fish since this area is a preserve. You may find gobs of fish and the occasional turtle, hard-to-find octopus and even bait balls at times. Entry can be awkward over the slippery rocks. Most people enter from the left side, so if you want some wiggle room, consider entering from the right side of the cove. Snorkelers should stay inside the cove.

SCUBA divers will love the shallow but interesting diving inside the cove. It's very relaxing since you don't need to kick far too see good stuff. Just slowly meander

This lovely part of Pupukea Beach Park, called Three Tables, is named after the offshore reefs.

around the clear water, looking under rock shelves. Good for underwater photos. The more adventurous will wander out of the cove, staying to the right where walls, small caves and chasms await. Even inside the cove, experienced divers will enjoy the relief of big ol' boulders, overhangs and sandy patches. And since it's so shallow (less than 30 feet), even heavy breathers will have staying power. Consider getting 63s instead of 80s to make it easier. One caveat: The cove is not at all tolerant of swells. Even a 2-foot swell, if aimed straight into the cove, can stir up the shallow water and make conditions annoyingly cloudy and surgy.

During high tide the tide-pool to the left gets deep enough to become a giant swimming pool when seas are calm. Visitors mistakenly think *this* is where they're supposed to snorkel. Granted, it looks interesting from the shore. But there are relatively few fish in there. Stick with the cove unless you hate the thought of venturing into deeper water. Big surf makes this tide-pool area dangerous and, of course, ruins the cove itself for swimming.

The rock defining the left side of the cove is often used as a place to jump into the water. Remember to look before you leap.

Across from an old gas station next to Puula Road. Snorkel gear can be rented across the street near Foodland. See map on page 88.

Waimea Bay in the summer when the swimming is peaceful.

Waimea Bay in the winter, when the swimming is a tad more challenging.

❖ Three Tables

A REAL GEM

Good snorkeling when calm around the little table islands (there are more than three at low tide). It can be a little surgy, and you'll want to avoid this place when the surf's up. SCUBA intros take place here. It's shallow (35 feet max) but has interesting underwater terrain with lots of overhangs, crevices and boulders off to the left, though divers are still better off over at Shark's Cove. Overall, a nice sandy beach with no facilities or lifeguard. Unmarked, it's where tiny Kapuhi Street meets Kamehameha Highway (Hwy 83) just north of Waimea Bay.

⊕ Waimea Bay Beach Park

A REAL GEM

Say the words "Waimea Bay" to surfers, and their eyes will light up. This is the most famous big wave surf site in the world. In the winter, waves 20–40 feet high are not uncommon. Visitors and lo-

cals alike delight in coming here during these swells, lining the shoreline and road, and watching the best surfers in the world take their chances sliding down these four-story walls of water. A collapsing wave can snap boards, snap people, or hold 'em underwater for minutes at a time. If you're on Oʻahu in the winter and the surf is giant, *this* is where you want to go. (Other surf sites close out with big surf. See *Waves 101* on page 238.) Needless to say, you don't want to get anywhere near the water during big winter surf. You'll die… period… no kidding.

What a shock to come here in the summer and find placid, lake-like water. The area around the southern end (left side) of the bay offers utterly magnificent snorkeling when calm. The entire area leading to the offshore islets is studded with fish, interesting terrain and turtles. In fact, turtles are plentiful from here all the way to Turtle Beach, but the water gets cloudy after you leave the bay—

from Uppers to Chun's Reef—due to intruding basal springs. Stay in Waimea Bay and around the islands for the best snorkeling during calm seas.

The giant rock near the left end of the beach is a popular cliff-diving spot. People often climb up from the shore-facing side and leap off the back/right end. It's a pretty far drop, and you're on your own in evaluating it. Jumpers have to walk past the No Jumping sign to get to the top.

Waimea Bay Beach Park has full facilities. It's 5 miles north of Hale'iwa or 36 miles from Kane'ohe on Hwy 83. Open 5 a.m.–10 p.m.

❖ Chun's Reef

Most people drive right by this park without noticing it. This is a decent place for beginner surfers when the surf is light because the ideally shaped reef creates waves in nearly any size swell. If you don't care about surfing waves, park here and walk to the right along the sand to rarely visited **Kawailoa Beach**, AKA **Leftovers**. Although there are houses on it, you'll rarely see many visitors here. Chun's Reef Park is near the 61-500 address across from Ashley Road between Waimea Beach Park and Hale'iwa.

❖ Turtle Beach/Laniakea Beach

This beach is famous. Not among people, but apparently in the turtle community. Because the honu (Hawaiian for turtle) sometimes congregate here in impressive numbers and seem so tolerant of people that we've seen swimmers get bored and swim away, only to have the turtle swim after them. This is the only place we've ever seen in Hawai'i where the turtles do this. (We suspect that some nearby resident might be feeding them to

get this result.) Naturally, the honu aren't *always* here (turtles *hate* to get into a predictable rut), but they're here *most* of the time. And when they are, it's great.

Water visibility here is often poor. On Hwy 83 between Waimea Bay and Hale'iwa, at the south (toward Hale'iwa) end of a loop road called Pohaku Loa Way. Residents request that you do not drive on their quiet street but instead park on the mauka side of the highway. The state erected concrete barriers to force you to walk a little farther to get here. Don't let them dissuade you—it's worth the short walk.

Although the beach keeps going south, the swimming is not very good due to currents and the beachrock that lines much of the nearshore waters. Go for the turtles, not for the swimming. South of here is **Papa'iloa Beach**.

By the way, Turtle Beach is a modern name. It sure beats the ancient Hawaiian name for this beach, which was Kukae'ohiki meaning *excrement of the ghost crabs*. (Just doesn't have the same ring to it, does it?)

➊ Hale'iwa Beach Park

Nice big lawn and usually a calm, protected shoreline, but the proximity to the river and harbor creates less than pristine water. It's popular with the local community. On Kamehameha Highway (83) in the heart of Hale'iwa.

❖ Mokule'ia Beach Park/ Kealia Beach

Across from Dillingham Airfield near the northwestern tip of the island, this is a great place for kite surfing (or watching it). Near-constant winds and a sandy shoreline create excellent conditions. Mokule'ia stretches for miles in both directions.

Just past (west of) the beach park you'll find a series of usually deserted beaches. Even when other North Shore beaches are packed, you may be shocked to find these beaches completely empty. Sure, it tends to be windy here, and the swimming is dicey in winter due to longshore currents, though it can be a bit better in calmer seas. But if the idea of an empty, sandy beach is appealing, you have a good shot here, and access is a snap. These are O'ahu's forgotten beaches, which is ironic since you can drive right up to them. Some of the stretches have sandy nearshore waters; others have waters lined with sandstone beachrock. Biggest downside here is that litter from local weekend use seems to occur more often than at most beaches. Porta-Potties available.

❖ Hidden Beach

A REAL GEM

How fitting that we end the *Beaches* chapter with this beach. Few people on the island even know about it. It's past the end of the pavement on Farrington Highway (930) on the North Shore, about 1.25 miles into a gated, but walkable, 4WD dirt road. It's a good place to stop on your way out to Ka'ena Point. At a side road that *might* be marked with a sign saying C-1 at telephone pole #197 is quite the prize: a hidden beach with a dry, mountainous backdrop. You may even have this small, sandy cove to yourself. Snorkeling is possible when the ocean's not too pounding. Otherwise, just enjoy the remoteness, our reason for giving it a *Gem*.

Although locals drive their 4WDs to it on weekends and afternoons, Hidden Beach is often deserted during weekday mornings.

The Polynesian Cultural Center has shows and demonstrations throughout the day.

Attractions are about specific destinations. You gotta drive there or take a bus there, and it's the only reason you're in that area. This chapter excludes lu'au (covered at the end of the *Island Dining* chapter), but includes the attractions the island is famous for.

CULTURAL & EDUCATIONAL ATTRACTIONS

Polynesian Cultural Center

55-370 Kamehameha Hwy, Laie • (808) 293-3333

It's as far from Waikiki on O'ahu as you can get—both literally and figuratively. Near the far northern tip of the island in La'ie, the Polynesian Cultural Center is a laid-back re-creation of various island villages from across Polynesia. In addition to Hawai'i, you can explore Tahiti, Tonga, Fiji, Aotearoa (New Zealand), Samoa and Rapa Nui (which you probably know better by the name Easter Island). They don't pretend to be completely authentic—power outlets, plywood, electric lights and cell phones are ever-present—but it's definitely *not* a Hawaiian Disneyland with rides and dolphins leaping out of the water. What they've attempted to do here is to create a non-frantic environment where you can wander around at your leisure and learn about all things Polynesian. You'll see various styles of huts, cultural demonstrations, lots of dancing, spear-throwing and more. Coconuts trees, palm fronds and a meandering, cement-lined lagoon create an island atmosphere that's certainly closer to reality than anything you'll find in Waikiki.

The Church of Latter-Day Saints (LDS, or Mormon) created and runs this place in association with Brigham Young University-Hawai'i. Your entrance fee helps subsidize students from all around the Pacific. In exchange, those students work here at the PCC, so it's likely you'll come in contact with many young people from the very countries represented in the faux villages. Hearing them sing in their various languages is a real treat.

Start by taking a canoe trip to the other side of the PCC and walk your way back, stopping along the way whenever something strikes your fancy. You may find yourself playing drums in Tonga or getting a fake tattoo in the Marquesas Islands. You definitely don't want to miss the 2:30 p.m. canoe pageant (get in place early to grab a good seat). And you might want to wear a wide-brimmed hat since even on windy days there are areas where the winds are blocked, and it can get hot.

The PCC is worth the time if you have any interest at all in learning about the Polynesian way of life. And although it's extremely popular with visitors, the PCC has managed to keep a good and friendly attitude. It doesn't feel like a mob scene, and the staff is top-notch. You can tell they feel honored to be working here, showing you their way of life.

Prices are pretty steep. It's $65 for admission only ($52 for kids 4–11), or you can add a *lu'au* package for an additional charge, which also includes an excellent evening show called *Ha: Breath of Life*. There are far too many dining options to go into detail, so see their website to customize your experience, which includes discounts for booking 10 days or more in advance. It's an extra $25 for bus transportation to and from designated drop off points in Waikiki (a 60–90-minute drive away). Or for $35 they will pick you up at your hotel in a small shuttle bus. The PCC is open from noon–6 p.m. There's too much to see in one day, but if you're so inclined, you can come back within three days for free. Closed Sundays.

Chinatown

This isn't a manufactured, made-for-tourists Chinatown. This is the real deal. And for me, having once worked in China for a few years, going to the markets here is like going back to the Far East. Stroll through the crowded aisles, and you'll find raw chicken feet, freshly caught fish (some still swimming in tanks), whole pig heads, more fruits and vegetables than you even knew existed, Asian orange soda (which is ubiquitous in China), salted duck eggs and more—all with the sound of Cantonese in the background and the ever-present haggling: *How much? Figh dalla!*

That person you just bumped into might be the star chef at the fancy Waikiki restaurant where you ate last night. Chinatown is where many of the island's chefs get their fresh seafood and veggies. This is also where much of the Kahuku shrimp from the North Shore ends up—still live and wiggling in the early morning.

The real fun is in the Kekaulike Market (between King and N. Hotel on Kekaulike

Street) and the Maunakea Marketplace. You'll want to arrive in Chinatown by 10 a.m., before it gets too hot and when the merchants are still hungry for a sale.

The area has always been a bit unsavory, owing to its close proximity to Honolulu Harbor. From the early 1800s all the way up until WWII, Chinatown is where sailors came to spend their money like... well, drunken sailors, and it gained a well-deserved reputation as Honolulu's red-light district. (In the post-war tourism boom, most of that seedy activity moved to Waikiki for a time, but there's still a giant glowing neon Club Hubba Hubba sign on Hotel Street that remains as a relic of Chinatown's heyday.) Today Chinatown is sorely dilapidated, but the area is on the upswing as fine-dining restaurants keep rushing in to take advantage of the relatively cheap rent. This is where you'll find some of the best restaurants on O'ahu. (See *Island Dining* for recommendations.) But you'll also find rampant homelessness, and if you get away from the main drags at night, you'll see homeless people sleeping in nearly every doorway.

Bishop Museum
1525 Bernice St, Honolulu • (808) 847-3511

The most comprehensive museum in the state is *filled* with thousands of historically and culturally significant artifacts, including the feathered cape worn by King Kamehameha the Great. There's also a *real lava* demonstration two times a day in the science center.

The museum was established by the husband of Bernice Pauahi Bishop, the last descendent of King Kamehameha the Great, to preserve and perpetuate the legacy of the Hawaiian monarchy, so there's a noticeable bent to the way some of the

Bustling Chinatown is the place to buy foods you won't find at Walmart.

history is described. But overall, the collection does a good job of showcasing the state's heritage. Priceless royal heirlooms sit side by side with more common items like lava poi pounders and bone fishhooks. (No indication if any of the fishhooks were made from human bone, as was often done at that time.) Other items on display include carved wooden tikis and a feathered representation of the war god Kuka'ilimoku, as well as a real grass hut, shark's tooth-studded weapons that were used to disembowel unsuspecting enemies, jewelry, a 55-foot sperm whale skeleton, and a conch shell that's more than 600 years old and worn from generations of Hawaiians who rubbed it while blowing through it like a bugle.

The regal Kahili room is dedicated to the royal lineage, but the third floor of the Hawaiian Hall is better if you're looking to understand the history of the Hawaiian Kingdom and annexation period.

They also have a separate Science Adventure Center geared toward kids with lots of things to poke, pull and push. Their "erupting volcano" that simply spits orange

Bishop Museum has the best collection of historical artifacts in the state.

water is lame, but downstairs they heat volcanic cinders at 2,500 degrees for two hours in a brass furnace, and when it's molten, they pour out lava. (Demonstrations at noon and 2:30 p.m.) Even if you've seen lava up close before on The Big Island, this display is riveting.

There are multiple planetarium shows throughout the day. You'll learn a little bit about how Hawai'i's night sky is different than what you might see at home, and they also have a program that focuses on how Polynesian explorers navigated by the stars.

Anyone with an interest in history or the Hawaiian culture will want to devote at least a couple of hours to this museum. $25 per person, $17 for kids 4–12 and $22 for seniors. In Honolulu at 1525 Bernice Ave. From Waikiki get on H-1 West, take exit 20B, go right on Houghtailing and take an immediate left on Bernice Street. Open 9 a.m.–5 p.m. $5 parking.

Hawai'i State Art Museum
250 S Hotel St, Honolulu • (808) 586-0900

On Richards at Hotel Street. It has art from Hawai'i artists, as well as others from around the world. Entrance is free. If you're an art buff, it's worth your time. Others may not be so impressed. Closed Sunday and Monday. Their café is popular but unimpressive.

Doris Duke's Shangri La
4055 Papu Circle, Honolulu • (866) 385-3849

It's the 1930s, and one of the richest women in the world, the sole heir to a tobacco empire, buys a scrumptious oceanside piece of property at Black Point. She has an obsession with Islamic art and architecture. This is a time before oil becomes synonymous with the Middle East. A time when someone, with enough money, could travel to Iran, Iraq and neighboring countries and buy what are now priceless art and architectural pieces for a relative pittance. And that's what Doris Duke did. Today, her 5-acre palace is what results when you mix 150 workmen, 50 years of effort, limitless money and a reverence for antiquities.

Three times a day, two groups of 12 people are guided through Doris Duke's estate for $25, and it's nearly always sold out a week or more in advance. You'll meet at the Honolulu Museum of Art at the corner of Beretania and Ward Avenue and be driven to the estate. It'll take 2.5 hours (1.5 hours at the house). There's no A/C in the house, so try to get an early tour. No children under 8 allowed. Open Wednesday through Saturday.

We didn't expect to be so impressed. Though touted as Islamic, there are plenty of non-Islamic pieces, some as old as 1,000 years. And we're not talking about paintings on the walls, but rather a sensory overload of Middle Eastern history that is simply astounding. Forget what's happening in the world right now. These pieces predate the tensions that define our relationship with that part of the world today. The tour visits the Syrian Room—an overwhelming experience for the eyes that'll make your heart beat faster.

You board the van at the **Honolulu Museum of Art** (900 S Beretania St, Honolulu • 808-532-8701). If you visit the museum, for a $20 admission, you'll find a healthy mix of interesting 2,000-year-old artifacts and self-indulgent abstract junk that only an artist's mother can love. Kids 18 and under are free. (You just have to promise not to return them…) Closed Mondays.

HISTORICAL ATTRACTIONS

Pearl Harbor
(WWII Valor in the Pacific)
319 Lexington Blvd, Honolulu • (808) 422-3399

There are three historic Navy vessels all moored near each other in Pearl Harbor. And, frankly, all three are worth your time. The sunken U.S.S. Arizona is the most somber of the three, the USS Missouri the most impressive in its scale, and the Bowfin the most interesting for observing what it must have been like to live in a submerged vessel. The Pacific Aviation Museum has restored vintage aircraft from the war over the Pacific. Consider purchasing the Passport to Pearl Harbor Pass in advance. For $65 you get admission to the U.S.S. Bowfin & Museum, the Mighty Mo Tour on the U.S.S Missouri, admission to the Pacific Aviation Museum, and the audio tour for the U.S.S. Arizona Memorial. If you purchase the passport from **www.recreation.gov** *in advance*, it also includes the boat and movie ticket for the Arizona Memorial for the day and time of your

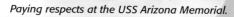

Paying respects at the USS Arizona Memorial.

choosing. If you return within seven days with your ticket, for $10 extra you can see what you missed the first time.

Directions to all are the same: From Waikiki, get on H-1 West. Take exit #15A (*not 15B*), which says "Arizona Mem./Stadium" and stay on Kamehameha Highway (99) West, past Radford, past Arizona/Halawa Road, then left on Arizona Memorial Place/Kalaloa. (If you get to the stadium, you went too far.) You'll see signs. See map on page 107.

If you're coming from the *other* way, take exit 10 off H-1 toward Pearlridge (right fork), then merge onto Moanalua Road. First right on Kaahumanu Street, then left on Kamehameha Highway and right on Arizona Memorial Place. (Those Hawaiian words will get hideously butchered by your GPS.)

Parking can be difficult at peak times. If you don't see a spot, keep driving. There's often an opening or two in a parking lot on your right, next to a pool before the overpass.

Because of security (this is an active Navy base), you're not allowed to bring bags of any kind. If you don't want to leave things in your car, there's a building to the right of the main entrance where they'll store them for $4 per bag. Swimwear is not allowed.

The **USS Arizona Memorial** (808-422-3300) is the single most popular visitor attraction on Oʻahu. When on Dec. 7, 1941, the Japanese attacked Pearl Harbor, 21 vessels were damaged or sunk. But it was the sinking of the USS Arizona that caused the most deaths—1,177 young, promising lives were cut short when an armor-piercing bomb dropped from a Japanese plane drilled through her top deck and ignited the battleship's own ordnance. The vessel sank in 9 minutes, and only 337 were able to escape. In all, over 2,400 people were killed during the sneak attack here, a figure that would stand as an unwelcome record for six decades. It seemed like the kind of event that could only happen in the distant past, until a modern generation experienced its own sneak attack. And like Sept. 11, 2001, America rode a roller coaster of emotion after Pearl Harbor—from shock to anger to resolve. For Pearl Harbor it took an empire's entire military might—a whole fleet of ships and subs, including six aircraft carriers, 353 planes and thousands of soldiers. September 11th required four planes and 19 men with boxcutters. But, whatever

Woe to any enemy that ever saw the business end of these USS Missouri guns, which could hurl a 2,700-pound projectile 23 miles.

the source, it awakened a nation that had previously felt safe and insulated from the harshness of the world.

Visiting the memorial is one of those must-dos on O'ahu, and for good reason. Since there are so few WWII vets left, it makes WWII real for the rest of us. *We know how WWII ended because we've lived our lives after the attack.* But those men still entombed under your feet at the memorial only knew the shock and awe of how they died. And it's not until you're standing on the memorial, perched over the sunken ship, that the echo of their lives can be heard. And when you see the massive marble wall with their names engraved, only then does the beginning of WWII turn from an event that happened as part of our history to an assault that stole the lives of people like you and me and galvanized a nation.

There are still some 500,000 gallons of fuel stored in tanks onboard the ship, and if the water is calm, you'll see a rainbow sheen on the surface from small drops of oil still leaking to the surface, eight decades after it was sunk.

The free memorial visit includes an excellent 23-minute film, a short boat ride and 15 minutes at the memorial. (Sit on the starboard—right—side going out, port side coming back for the best photos.) It'll take 75 minutes total. They hand out 1,300 tickets daily, and the earlier you get your tickets, the more likely you are to get the time you want. Get there too late, and you'll have to take what ever time they have left. Or you can wait in the standby line, and they fill empty seats as they are available. A much better and lesser-known way is to book in advance at a government website called **www.recreation.gov** for $7.50, which includes the audio portion of the tour. You should know, however, that even when that site says tickets are sold out, extra tickets are often available directly at the box office. The 3-hour tour will take you through the renovated $56 million visitor center, into the two museum galleries and then into the movie and onto

Closed Summer '19 15 min. tour of Battle ship Row instead

the boat and memorial. Then the tour picks back up at the visitor center, pointing out some interesting sights and artifacts around the grounds, and telling the stories behind them that you would otherwise overlook. If you don't want the audio tour, see one of the other attractions mentioned below, or go have lunch.

The **USS Missouri Battleship** (63 Cowpens St, Honolulu • 877-644-4896) is a short distance from the sunken Arizona. When the Navy was looking for the final resting place for this proud warship, the symbolism of this location wasn't lost on them: placing the floating ship that ended WWII next to the sunken ship where the war began. Because it was on the Missouri's deck that the Japanese signed the surrender agreement, bringing the bloody fighting in the Pacific to a close.

The "Mighty Mo" was launched in 1944, near the end of the war. It was the last battleship ever built, and after only 11 years in service it was considered obsolete and mothballed in 1955. It seems hard to imagine how a state-of-the-art battleship—the toughest and most visually menacing ship ever built with guns that could fire a 2,700-pound projectile *23 miles*—could be considered obsolete. In essence it comes down to this: It's more effective to *drop* things on the enemy than to *throw* things at 'em. Once ship-based aircraft had matured, aircraft carriers were far more efficient at projecting power than the greatest battleship could ever be. Even though the ship was brought back to service in the mid-'80s for a short time and armed with Tomahawk missiles, the usefulness of battleships had long since passed, even for a giant that's 887 feet long and weighs over *100 million* pounds.

It costs $29 for the Mighty Mo Pass, $13 for kids 4–12. (If the security alert is high, they will ask for a photo I.D. to get on the ship.) You have some options with this pass. You can take the 35-minute guided tour, a self-guided audio tour, or you can do the guide-to-go iPod touch tour, which is loaded with 3 different audio and visual tours around the ship. The $65 all-encompassing *Passport to Pearl Harbor* gives you the Mighty Mo tour, but for $25 extra *strongly consider* the Heart of the Missouri tour. It takes you into the firing rooms, engine room and other nuts and bolts areas not available on self tours. Ironically, at least half the ship is off limits, even to guided trips. The reason? It's dirty. And although conditions were good enough for sailors who were there on the ship's final tour, it's not clean enough for the epa to sign off.

However you tour it, it's a real treat to peer into this symbol of America's might during the mid-20th century. The sheer scale of this vessel can only be appreciated in person. It's amazing to stand on its giant teak deck, under the massive guns capable of such destruction, and try to imagine the dread that must have been felt by any enemy who watched this warship coming at them in anger.

Just in front of the entrance to the Missouri is the **USS Oklahoma Memorial**. In all, 429 officers, sailors and marines were lost on the Oklahoma, second only to the Arizona. The men were recovered, the hull was patched and the ship was sold as scrap to a company in San Francisco. As it was being towed across the Pacific, a storm caused her to sink again, this time forever, just 540 miles east of Hawai'i.

The almost forgotten attraction here is the **USS Bowfin** (11 Arizona Memorial Dr, Honolulu • 808-423-1341). Launched in 1942 (and nicknamed the Pearl Harbor Avenger), this submarine sank 44 enemy ships and now is available for self-guided tours for $15 ($7 for kids 4–12). The latest you can start the tour is 4 p.m., and it'll take about 30 minutes. They'll give you a narrative audio recorded by the ship's last WWII captain. (Strangely, they refuse to give you the audio *if it's raining* outside… even though the submarine is enclosed. All the other attractions, which are *not* enclosed, will let you use audio in the rain. Just sayin'….) Anyway, it's great to walk through this sub and see the instruments and experience how the sailors lived and fought. From the turrets to the torpedoes to the toilets—you'll see it all. When you're done, the nearby **Submarine Museum** (808-423-1341) is *excellent*— much better than the Arizona's museum. Kids under 4 are not allowed on the sub, but they can go into the museum.

Pearl Harbor is not just about boats. The historic hangars at Ford Island

For only $15 you'll get to see the USS Bowfin submarine the way her crew saw her—without the two-year stint.

house the **Pacific Aviation Museum** (808-441-1000). It has a small but growing collection of vintage aircraft. You can follow the timeline of the attack on Pearl Harbor highlighted by a fully restored Japanese Zero and a private plane that was in the air and attacked by the first wave of fighters.

The jewel of Hangar 37 is actually a rusty pile of steel found in a pasture on the island of Ni'ihau. On December 7, 1941, a Japanese Zero was hit with anti-aircraft fire and made an emergency landing on an island he had been told was uninhabited—Ni'ihau. Airman 1st Class Shigenori Nishikaichi had been instructed to wait for a submarine, but found the island was very much inhabited, mostly by Hawaiians. He quickly befriended the three people on the island who were of Japanese ancestry and escaped from his Hawaiian guards with their help. His freedom didn't last long as he was eventually overpowered and literally crushed by a local Hawaiian who had been shot *three times* by Nishikaichi. Over time the crashed Zero weathered

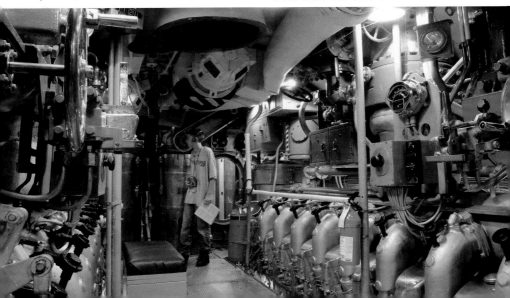

away and was stripped by local farmers of its steel skin. But what remains is still an incredible physical piece of history.

Admission is $25 and $35 for a guided tour. Check out the flight simulators for $10 extra. It'll take about 25 minutes during which you shoot down as many enemy planes as you can and then land your plane on the runway. The technology isn't state of the art, but it's fun. There are also displays about Midway, Guadalcanal, Doolittle's raid, and a Stearman biplane that President George H.W. Bush flew as a pilot-in-training.

Punchbowl Cemetery

2177 Puowaina Dr, Honolulu • (808) 532-3720

The National Memorial Cemetery of the Pacific at Punchbowl is an immensely moving place. The Hawaiian name for this crater is Puowaina—hill of human sacrifices. It's eerily fitting that it is now a cemetery for those in the military who sacrificed their lives in the Pacific.

Driving into the crater is an experience that is guaranteed to put a lump in your throat. At the far end is a giant statue of Columbia holding a laurel branch. Be-

Using howitzers, soldiers fire off a 21-gun salute during a ceremony at Punchbowl.

tween you and her are the graves of more than 45,000 men and women, including unidentified sailors killed during the attack on Pearl Harbor. No large tombstones—just simple slabs marking the final resting places. In addition to these graves, you'll find more than 28,000 names carved into the walls. During the wars of the mid-20th century, young men died in such vast numbers and so rapidly that there wasn't always time to keep track of them. These names are of those "whose earthly resting place is known only to God." Under the sculpture of Columbia is a quote from Abraham Lincoln when he wrote to the mother of five sons lost in the Civil War: "The solemn pride that must be yours to have laid so costly a sacrifice on the altar of freedom."

There are some interesting displays of the various battles that claimed these lives. Look at them from the left side to the right. The cemetery is open from from 8 a.m.–6 p.m. Entrance is free.

Before leaving, be sure to visit the scenic lookout (which is easy to miss if you don't know it's there). From the cemetery entrance, follow the road to the far left side of the crater and park by the restrooms, then take the short walk up a paved path. From up here you're looking over downtown Honolulu, and you can see all the way from Diamond Head to the east past Pearl Harbor to the west.

The simplest way to get to Punchbowl from Waikiki is to take Ala Wai Boulevard., right on Kalakaua, left onto Beretania, then right onto Alakea, which becomes Queen Emma. After you cross a bridge over H-1, continue straight through the intersection. Take Puowaina Drive on the right, going uphill. There should be a sign here directing you. Take a look at your odometer. At 0.7 miles, slow down because Puowaina Drive makes a 90-degree turn. (The road does continue over a bridge, but the name changes to Tantalus Drive.) Stay on Puowaina all the way to Punchbowl Cemetery. (It executes easier than it reads.)

'Iolani Palace & Downtown Historic Buildings

The best reason to venture downtown is to check out Honolulu's collection of historic buildings. They are clustered around 'Iolani Palace, so start there and use it as a reference point to find the others. See map on page 50.

'Iolani Palace

364 S King St, Honolulu • (808) 522-0822

The United States has been a republic since it broke from England, so we don't really have any examples of royal palaces—except for 'Iolani. These islands were a kingdom from 1795 until 1893, and in 1879 Hawai'i's last king, David Kalakaua, ordered this palace to be built to show all the world that Hawai'i had a monarchy

just as grand as any other. There are many historic buildings downtown, but 'Iolani Palace is the finest of them all.

The palace, which was completed in 1882, features a number of innovations, including indoor plumbing, an early telephone, and it even had electric lights. (This was before the White House had electricity.) There's a grand staircase, a throne room that was used for throwing fancy balls, an elegant dining room, music room, and the king's personal study. But the story of the structure itself is less consequential than the story of the king who built it.

Kalakaua was the first king not directly related to the Kamehameha line. He was actually elected by the Legislature, in a contentious race against the dowager Queen Emma (widow of Kamehameha IV). To win that race, Kalakaua aligned himself with business interests, and pledged to stick to the current system that many natives already viewed as giving too much power to foreigners. He won by an overwhelming margin of 39–6, but the results led to riots, and Kalakaua had to ask American and British forces to help quell the violence.

As king, Kalakaua made several trips abroad. He became the first reigning monarch to visit Washington, D.C. when he went to negotiate a reciprocity treaty (basically a free-trade agreement) that gave the U.S. military use of Pearl Harbor in exchange for allowing Hawaiian sugar to be sold to the U.S. without tariffs. The sugar industry boomed as a result; exports grew by more than 10 times, giving ever greater influence to the plantation owners. He later became the first monarch to circumnavigate the globe, on a trip that aimed to secure more immigrant labor and cultivate alliances. (Kalakaua had a vision of creating a pan-Pacific confederation, a united oceanic empire, under the protection of Japan.) It was on this trip that he met Thomas Edison in his lab and received a demonstration of his technologies. But for all of Kalakaua's efforts to modernize and strengthen the kingdom, The Merrie Monarch, as he was known, also spent lavishly. He was enthralled with the opulent wealth of the European monarchs who he tried to emulate, and he got caught up in corruption scandals as a result. His power was significantly diminished toward the end of his reign when he was pressured into signing a new constitution as economic problems grew.

'Iolani Palace is as much a testament to the desire to restore it as it is to the king who built it. It was only used as a royal palace for 11 years. For the next 75 years a series of governments used it as a Capitol building and, frankly, let it deteriorate to the point that some wanted to bulldoze the building in the late '60s. Most of its artifacts were auctioned off over the years, but once bureaucrats got a new Capitol building next door, local volunteers worked for years to retrieve many of the artifacts and restore the palace to the glorious condition you see today. (Although, the palace today is still much sparser inside than it would have been then, but with a little imagination you can picture people living here and servants bustling about.) The beautiful woodwork, the grandness of design and the great info conveyed along the way make it a worthwhile diversion.

You can wander around the grounds outside for free or pay for a tour of the inside. 'Iolani is open Monday–Saturday 9 a.m.–4 p.m. Reserve in advance since only 20 people are allowed per guided tour ($22 per person; not suitable for kids under 5). It's $15 for a pretty good self-guided audio tour. Do yourself a favor and wear socks, since they will make you take off your shoes and wear gross dust mops on your feet to protect the wood floor.

Don't miss the crown jewels in the throne room, and be sure to check out the basement. It's filled with historical pictures than help put events in context. (And it's fascinating to see members of the royal court in European dress, festooned with medals and sashes and cords.) The medals (also on display) were given to Kalakaua by foreign heads of state trying to curry his favor in order to gain access to Hawai'i's strategic ports—a subtle reminder that the history of monarchies everywhere, even in Hawai'i, is the story of powerful ruling families vying with other powerful ruling families to maintain their power.

Kamehameha the Great Statue
417 S King St, Honolulu

Directly across the street from 'Iolani Palace there's a statue of Kamehameha the Great. In 1810 he became the first chief to rule over all the Hawaiian Islands. This is the most famous of four nearly identical statues. The original was cast in Paris in 1880, but it was lost en route to Hawai'i when the ship carrying it sank near the Falkland Islands in the South Atlantic. (This was still decades before the construction of the Panama Canal.) Not to worry, it was insured and they used the claim to order another one. Shortly after commissioning the replacement statue, the *original lost statue* showed up at Honolulu Harbor. Turns out that the captain of another ship had stopped in the Falklands to take on fresh water, and spotted the original "lost" statue while strolling through town. Someone had salvaged it from the ocean floor. The captain bought the statue and shipped it, this time successfully, to Hawai'i (where he flipped it for a quick

King Kamehameha the Great was the first Hawaiian to rule all of the islands.

profit.) The damaged original was then repaired and sent to the Big Island where it now stands near Kamehameha's birthplace in north Kohala. After Hawaiʻi became a state, a third statue was cast from a mold of the one in Honolulu and placed in the U.S. Capitol in Washington, D.C. The fourth (similar-looking but larger) statue was originally intended for Kauaʻi, but whoever thought that idea up didn't know his history. You see, Kamehameha never succeeded in his attempts to militarily conquer that island, so the idea of putting up a statue to honor his failed attempts didn't go down well with the Kauaʻi folks. So it was sent to Hilo on the Big Island instead. On Kamehameha Day (June 11), these statues are draped with hundreds of flower lei.

So it's statue number two that stands in Honolulu in front of the Judicial Building today.

Judicial Building
417 S King St, Honolulu

The Judicial Building today is where the state Supreme Court meets. The reason it looks so ornate is because it was originally designed as a palace (before the construction of ʻIolani), but the need for government offices became more important, so the building's intended purpose changed before it was finished. It was completed in 1874, and for the next 22 years it served as the central government building. And in January 1893, it was the scene of the overthrow of the Hawaiian Kingdom.

This is how it came about. When King Kalakaua died without any children, his sister Liliʻuokalani ascended to the throne. She'd previously ruled as regent during his overseas voyages. Frustrated by limits on her power, the queen announced her intention to abolish the 1887 "Bayonet Constitution" that had been forced on her brother several years before, hoping to rule as an absolute monarch. (The 1887 Constitution gave most of the power to the Legislature and made the monarch a figurehead.) But the queen overplayed her hand, giving those who opposed her an excuse to act. A group of mainly western, pro-American businessmen quickly formed the "Committee of Safety" to protect the constitution, and they declared the queen to be in illegal rebellion against the lawful government. Tensions were high as members of the foreign-born community and royalists prepared for a confrontation.

It was here, in front of this building, on Jan. 16, 1893, that a contingent of American marines and sailors positioned themselves after landing at Honolulu Harbor, ostensibly to protect American lives and property. Lili'uokalani realized she was at a disadvantage, and, wanting to prevent bloodshed, she yielded. On Jan. 17 the committee declared a new provisional government and flew the American flag over the government building. The Republic of Hawai'i was born.

The United States recognized it as an independent country in 1894. It was annexed by the U.S. in 1898 and became an official territory in 1900.

Now walk along the street in the direction of the one-way traffic.

Kawaiaha'o Church
957 Punchbowl St, Honolulu • (808) 469-3000

Kawaiaha'o Church (at the intersection of King and Punchbowl) is the oldest Christian church on O'ahu. The church walls are made from 1,000-pound chunks of coral chiseled from reefs 10–20 feet deep. Think of this place as Hawai'i's Westminster Abbey, the place where generations of royalty worshiped. Christianity flourished in the islands thanks to the support and protection of the monarchy. At the same time, the monarchy relied on the early missionaries to learn Western ways. (Native Hawaiians had already got-

ten rid of their own religion *before* the first missionaries arrived in the islands, in part because of widespread dissatisfaction with the restrictive kapu system that prevented, among other things, men and women from eating together under penalty of death.) On the grounds there is a tomb containing the remains of a lesser-known king, Lunalilo, who wanted to be buried next to his people rather than in the royal mausoleum.

The building across the street with the red-tile roof is the **Honolulu City Hall**.

Mission Houses
553 S King St, Honolulu • (808) 447-3910

Past the church you'll find the Mission Houses. These are some of the earliest living quarters built by missionaries upon their arrival in 1820. The 45-minute tours are a bit pricey at $10. Think of it as more of a lesson on early missionary life and their efforts to create a written Hawaiian language. The whole experience is educational, if a bit dry. Closed Sunday and Monday.

Queen Lili'uokalani Statue

Between 'Iolani Palace and the Capitol building (on the backside of the palace), there's a statue of Queen Lili'uokalani, Hawai'i's last monarch.

State Capitol Building
415 South Beretania St, Honolulu

Hawaii became the 50th state in 1959, and the State Capitol building was completed ten years later. ('Iolani served as the Capitol before that.) The style is more architecturally dissimilar than any other state Capitol we can think of. Instead of a rotunda with a dome, it's open-air, and the building is bracketed by shallow reflecting pools that make it look like an island. You probably won't get a

Getting up close and personal at the Waikiki Aquarium.

chance to go inside the actual House or Senate chambers, since Hawai'i has a part-time legislature, and lawmakers are generally limited to 60 session days per year. (During that time they will find ways spend *every tax dollar* they can find—and then some.) The best view is from the front side, on Beretania Street.

Washington Place
320 S Beretania St, Honolulu • (808) 586-0248

The large, white house across the street from the Capitol, at Beretania and Richards Street, is Washington Place. This was Queen Lili'uokalanai's personal residence. In 1895, two years after the overthrow removed her from power, a stockpile of weapons was found buried in the garden, and the queen was arrested for aiding a counter-rebellion that attempted to restore the monarchy. (She denied having any involvement.) The queen was tried for treason and imprisoned in 'Iolani Palace, and eventually released eight months later when she agreed to formally abdicate the throne in exchange for a pardon for herself, and to spare the lives of royalist conspirators who had been sentenced to death. Today, the house is used for political functions, and there's a separate residence in back where Hawai'i's governor lives.

Depending on how much you're into history and whether you take the palace tour, you can spend a half day or more exploring the downtown area. But if all you want to do is wander the palace grounds, take a picture of the Kamehameha statue and maybe see the Capitol building, you can easily knock that out in under an hour. If you're hungry afterward, **Chinatown** a few blocks over has some great restaurants. See *Island Dining*.

Directions: Head into downtown Honolulu. The palace is at South King and Richards Street. Pay close attention to the signs and what time they start towing (they open up a lane for rush hour traffic) or you'll be taking an Uber on a detour to the impound lot on Sand Island. See the foldout map on page 50.

Hawai'i's Plantation Village
94-695 Waipahu St, Waipahu • (808) 677-0110

We've lived in Hawai'i for quite awhile, but we got more of a feel for the essence of plantation life during this 1.5-hour tour than in all the time we've lived here.

In the 1990s the county took this parkland and attempted to re-create a typical sugar plantation camp, and they did a pretty good job. Historically, each plantation camp represented a single ethnic group. Here they've created regions of camps representing Chinese, Portuguese, Puerto Rican, Japanese, Filipino, Okinawan and Korean camps. Don't hesitate to engage your guide because that's what makes the experience so cool—at least for us it was. It's $15. The last tour starts at 2 p.m.

Located at the west end of Pearl Harbor. Take H-1 to exit 7, left on Paiwa toward the ocean, right on Waipahu. Look for it eventually on your left. Closed Sundays.

Hawaiian Railway Society
91-1001 Renton Rd, Ewa Beach • (808) 681-5461

For train junkies and those with kids, this is a sugar plantation railroad car and paraphernalia collection dating from 1888 to 1947. Their prized possession is a fully restored private parlor car used by Benjamin Dillingham to entertain royalty and foreign diplomats. On weekends they have a 90-minute train ride through 'Ewa. ($15 for adults, $10 for kids or $30 for a ride in the private parlor car available for rides on the second Sunday of each month.) Keiki might love the air horn and track rumble, but you'll be struggling to stay awake. They don't take reservations except for the private parlor car.

JUST-FOR-FUN ATTRACTIONS

Waikiki Aquarium
2777 Kalakaua Ave, Honolulu • (808) 923-9741

Not to be mean, but just about any aquarium built on the mainland in the past few decades outshines the tiny Waikiki Aquarium. There are no giant tanks with SCUBA divers feeding the fish, no big sharks, no touch tanks, just a series of smaller tanks with colorful fish and coral (from around the Pacific, not just Hawai'i) and an outdoor seal enclosure with two very bored monk seals with medical issues that prevent them from surviving in the wild. Smaller kids react with excitement, but adults expecting the same kind of *ooh-*

It's hard to say who's mugging for the camera— the dolphin or the boy.

The dolphin show at Sea Life Park is their most popular attraction.

ah value you'd get a bigger aquarium will likely be disappointed.

In fairness, the $12 entrance fee ($5 for kids 4–12) certainly doesn't imply extravagance, and it's fun to be able to identify fish you saw if you've already been snorkeling. Two hours of parking included free with admission, but you can walk here from most Waikiki hotels. In Kapiolani Park on Kalakaua Avenue.

Swimming With Dolphins

Although it's not exactly a nail-biting event, we could call *hanging with dolphins* an attraction or an adventure. And although it's marketed toward kids, when we've been there, the majority of customers have been adults.

Two companies offer this—**Dolphin Quest** and **Sea Life Park**—creating two radically different experiences. We brought along our 15-year-old nephew as a "consultant," and the verdict from all of us was unanimous—Dolphin Quest is a *far* better experience.

Dolphin Quest (5000 Kahala Ave, Honolulu • 808-739-8918) is an up-close-and-personal dolphin experience. You'll even don masks to watch underwater as they swim by you. And you'll touch them to your heart's content. The only thing you won't do is get pulled through the water by them (our nephew's only complaint with Dolphin Quest since they do that at Sea Life Park). The trainers' love and affection for these animals is obvious. Dolphin Quest's dolphins live in a much nicer world than they do at Sea Life Park. For $225, you'll spend about 25 minutes in the water with these mammals. For $310 you get the 35 minutes of water time plus 25 minutes on the dock learning more about them. Kids 5–9 years old have a 1.5-hour program for $199—20 minutes with the dolphins in the water and the rest at the beach, with some stingrays and other educational experiences. Dolphin Quest is located at The Kahala Hotel and Resort, 15 minutes east of Waikiki. The same outfit does this on the Big Island and Bermuda, and for most of the year it's a good idea to make a reservation a month in advance.

Sea Life Park (808-259-2500) has three programs—a $140 short program where dolphin interaction is minimal, a $200 program where you'll get pulled through the water by them, and for $260 you get all of the above *and* will have two dolphins push you around by your feet. For what it's worth, the dolphins didn't seem as healthy or happy here. (Granted, that's a super-subjective observation and only our admittedly untrained opinion.) And the swimming pool-like enclosures were smaller. The experience didn't feel as intimate as it did at Dolphin Quest—more like being processed. Park admission is included with the prices.

Sea Life Park
41-202 Kalanianaole Hwy, Waimanalo
(808) 259-2500

This is O'ahu's version of Sea World, though it's *far* smaller than most mainland aquarium parks. And that's probably the thing you'll notice most. Even the tanks that the dolphins live in seem small. It costs $40 to get in ($25 for kids 3–12), plus $5 to park (cash only), but you can see this whole park in a couple of hours. Things included with admission include a so-so dolphin show at 12:30 p.m., a pretty good sea lion show and several feedings. (Though you pay extra if you want to be the one feeding them.) You'll notice *many* opportunities here to spend more money on additional attractions such as snorkeling with sting rays for an additional $30 or participate in their dolphin programs for an extra $90 to $215 on top of admission. (Though we prefer the **Dolphin Quest** program described above.) When you go to their activity booth to sign up for these things, it seems like they're usually pushing "specials" to make it cheaper.

Sea Life Park isn't usually too crowded and seems to be a hit with kids. More than half of their customers are Japanese tour groups, and some of the narrations are first in Japanese. You can drop a lot of money fast here, but it's not a bad attraction. They've also got something you won't see anywhere else: a wholphin. That's a half Atlantic bottlenose dolphin, half false killer whale hybrid.

Near the easternmost tip of the island on Highway 72 near Waimanalo.

Wet 'n' Wild Hawai'i
400 Farrington Hwy, Kapolei • (808) 674-9283

It's all about waterslides and other ways to get wet. This place is usually packed on weekends but often uncrowded Monday–Friday. It's on the small side, but the rides

Your water playground at Wet 'n' Wild.

Stop doggin' me, man...

are well-chosen to appeal to people of all ages, and it's an easy place to spend half a day or more sliding into various pools and getting hammered in the wave pool or simply floating along in the current-driven whirlpool. If it's sunny, you will really appreciate this tip: Wear water shoes. Most people wear flip-flops and leave them at the bottom of the rides, then fry their feet on the endless ramps and steps.

Also, you'll need a lanyard for your glasses. And if you don't want to eat park food, they're good about letting you go in and out of the park.

It's $50 to get in, which includes most of the attractions. Kids under 42 inches tall are $38. (Tots are free.) They have pay lockers to store your junk, and a few attractions, such as *Da Flowrider* (a static, rideable wave), cost extra. Closed some days in non-summer periods, and expect them to close and rotate rides when it's slow. They also have a **lu'au** here.

Honolulu Zoo
151 Kapahulu Ave, Waikiki • (808) 971-7171

There is a sign near the entrance declaring it the best zoo to be found for 2,300 miles in any direction. That may be true, but only because the mainland is farther away than that. It's like being declared the best bartender in the town of La'ie.

(You'll have to look at *North Shore Sights* to realize why that's not much of a boast.)

Unfortunately, the Honolulu Zoo is merely so-so. It's 42 acres of cages, and that's the problem. The habitats are poorly designed with too few vantage points, and the mesh they use on some of the cages makes it difficult to see the animals. Too much metal, too little openings. This is especially a problem with the numerous bird exhibits. The inability to get a good look is annoying, because the zoo actually has quite a few big animals, including tigers, elephants, rhinos, giraffes, zebras, lions, chimpanzees, and a hippo. The African section is the best, as the warm climate here is well-suited for these animals. Bottom line—adults without kids may not find it incredibly compelling. With kids? Hey, it's a place with animals; they'll be entertained for a few hours. The animals are most active in the morning; avoid at midday due to heat. Cost is $19; kids 3–12 are $11. Open 9 a.m.–5:30 p.m. daily. On the east side of Waikiki. Oh, and there's a pretty good ropes playground for kids if they want to pretend to be spider monkeys.

K1 Speed Hawai'i
91-1085 Lexington St, Kapolei • (808) 682-7223

It's tempting to think electric go-kart racing is a kid's attraction. But I assure you—adults will walk out with a kid-like grin on their face. You and up to a dozen other drivers rip along an indoor track, squealing around corners, trying to beat everyone's time. I was surprised at how intense the racing felt. Spectators get to stand right next to the track. Food is restricted to vending machines between races, or you can bring your own food. Avoid this place *like the plague* on weekends—super busy. All in all, a fun way to blow $30–$100 (all prices include $8 membership). Located in Ewa near Kalaeloa Airport at 91-1085 Lexington St.

Coral Crater Adventure Park
91-1780 Midway St, Kapolei
(808) 626-5773

What would you do if you owned a 35-acre hole in the ground, the result of an abandoned military quarry that's overgrown with trees and generally unloved? Turn 10 acres of it into an adventure park and team-building location, of course.

Coral Crater Adventure Park has a toe-tingling 60-foot high adventure tower that you traverse in various ways trying not to fall off (you're tied in, of course), a **freefall** stopped by harness and magnetic brake, **giant swing**, a **climbing wall**, a tiny **ATV course**, **ziplines** and their renowned **zombie apocalypse**. (We've reviewed their ziplines and ATVs in the *Activities* chapter.)

The zombie tour is like an escape room on steroids. You have to make your way through a makeshift military outpost, search for keys and door passcodes, find an antidote and rescue someone, all while killing zombies with a laser M4 (that actually recoils) and then zipline your way back to safety—*in the dark*. These are real zombies (well, during work hours—we don't know what they do when they're off the clock—they reportedly used *Boy Scouts* in the early days because they didn't have enough employees), and when you see (and hear) them come out of the forest at night, it'll creep you out.

This attracts people of all ages and backgrounds (kids as young as 6 can go,

The adventure tower at Coral Crater is not the place to be if you're afraid of heights.

ATTRACTIONS

but it's best for 13 and up). To win, your group must complete the objectives and get to the zipline in 25 minutes, so make friends with the group before the action starts to improve your chances. (Far fewer groups are successful than you'd think.) Park management seems to be always experimenting, always tinkering, so we won't give away the specifics of the tour. (It's better to be surprised/terrified anyway, right?) But we like their attitude and their overall attempt to be fun without taking themselves too seriously. $120 for a tour you'll be sure to tell your friends about.

In Kapolei in the dry southwestern part of the island.

Kualoa Ranch
49-560 Kamehameha Hwy, Kahaluu
(800) 231-7321

Kualoa Ranch is a working cattle ranch where the seventh generation owners supplement their income by offering visitor activities and renting out the valley

From ATVs to ziplines with a bit of horseback riding and biking is what Kualoa Ranch is all about.

for TV and film production. (In fact, it's likely that cattle are now a small part of their business, considering how big their other two industries are.)

This 4,000-acre valley just north of Kane'ohe on your way north from Kailua is *very* picturesque. Films such as *Jurassic Park, Jurassic World, Pearl Harbor, Godzilla, Tears of the Sun* and *50 First Dates,* along with TV shows such as the new *Hawaii Five-O, Magnum P.I.* and *LOST* have all been filmed here. (Don't worry about trying to remember all of those. They will certainly remind you during your tour.)

Activities such as **zipline** and **ATVs, biking** and **horseback riding** (reviewed in the *Activities* chapter) along with movie tours, boat tours and more are all available. Overall, they do a good job on most of the tours and guides seem well trained and friendly. But their "Secret Island Beach" is pretty lame. To access that beach for free, all you have to do is walk along the shoreline from Kualoa Beach Park, remembering that all beaches are public land to the highest washes of the highest waves during the highest season, according to a Hawai'i Supreme Court ruling in 2006.

In a sudden burst of clarity, the boogie boarder realized that the guy at the rental counter was only kidding when he suggested that the Banzai Pipeline would be the perfect place to ride his first wave.

If you want more from your Hawaiian vacation than a suntan, O'ahu offers a multitude of activities that will keep you happy and busy. Among the more popular activities are glider rides, ocean tours, golfing, hiking, scuba diving and kayaking.

We've listed the activities here in alphabetical order. Beware of false claims on brochures. We've seen many fake scenes in brochure racks. Computers allow photo manipulation to create realities that don't exist (which, by the way, we don't do).

Activities can be booked directly with the companies themselves. Ask them if they have any coupons floating around in the free publications, or if there is a discount for booking direct. You can also book through **activity brokers and booths**, which are numerous and usually have signs such as *free maps* or *island information*. Allow me to translate: The word free usually means *I want to sell you something*.

What we're about to tell you has gotten our other books pulled from some shops and badmouthed in some circles, but the truth's the truth. The objective at activity booths, as is the case with many concierges, is to sell you activities for a commission. *Occasionally,* you can get better deals through activity booths or your concierge, but not often, because 25–35 percent of what you're paying is their commission (which they call a "deposit") for making the phone call. That's why calling direct can sometimes save money. Companies are so happy they don't have to give away one-quarter to one-third of their fee to activity booths, they'll sometimes give you a discount.

Here's an example: A friend of ours was coming to the island, and before he even arrived, the concierge from his hotel called him *on the mainland* to ask if there was anything they could do before his arrival to make things better. Specifically, "Are there any activities you'll want to do, such as scuba or helicopters we can book before you get here? The good ones tend to fill up early." My friend was impressed at their thoughtfulness, but declined, saying he knew the person who wrote this guidebook and would use that. The concierge proceeded to badmouth the book and strongly suggested he use the concierge's advice.

Telling our friend Peter what had *really* happened was like telling a kid that there's no Santa Claus. "Peter, they weren't calling you as a *courtesy* before your trip. They were salespeople, pushing activities on you and directing you *not* to the best companies, but to the ones who give them the *highest commission*. They were hoping to collect 35 percent or more from everything you did on the island." By the way, our explanation is also why the concierge didn't like our books. They'd rather be perceived as helpful than as salespeople. The reality is they're a bit of both.

Selling activities is a *big* business on O'ahu, and it's important to know *why* they're pitching a certain company. If an activity booth or desk steers you to XYZ snorkel cruise and assures you that it's the best, that's fine, but consider the source. That's usually the company that the booth gets the *biggest commission* from. We frequently check up on these booths. Some are reputable and honest, and some are outrageous liars. Few activity sellers have ever done any of the activities unless they got it *free* and the company *knew*

who they were. On the other hand, we *pay* for everything we do and review activities *anonymously*. We have no stake in *any* company we recommend, and we receive *no* commission. We just want to steer you in the best direction we can. If you know who you want to go with (because you read our reviews and decided for yourself), call them directly first.

A warning: Many of the companies listed have a 24-hour (or more) cancellation policy. Even if the weather causes you (not them) to cancel the morning of your activity, *you will be charged.* Some credit card companies will back you in a dispute if the 24-hour policy is posted, some won't. Fair? Maybe not. But that's the way it is.

If you've read many travel books, you're familiar with the grumpy and pretentious travel writer, the kind who's impressed by very little because he's so much more advanced than peons like you and me. Well, we pride ourselves in not being like that. We're all here to have fun! But having written our neighbor island books before *Oahu Revealed*, we've noticed that, relative to the outer islands, there's a complacency that permeates many of the Waikiki activity providers. A constant influx of potential customers has bred a less-than-hungry attitude. That doesn't mean you won't get good service—it's just that you might need to look harder for it.

AIR TOURS

To see O'ahu from the sky is to explore areas you can't reach by land. But the kind of experience you have depends on the kind of vehicle you want to take. You can be aloft in a helicopter, airplane, powered hang glider or glider. These are radically different experiences, and we've covered them all.

If you opt for a helicopter flight, get one that showcases more than just Waikiki. The Koʻolau Mountain range, which starts here, is the star of any aerial tour.

So you'll know my perspective, I'm a pilot myself and fly traditional fixed-wing planes, seaplanes and microlights. I don't have a helicopter rating, but have flown in the choppers (anonymously reviewing them).

We've been unabashedly enthusiastic in our recommendation of helicopter tours of Kauaʻi and the Big Island and lukewarm about them on Maui. Consider us lukewarm about these tours on Oʻahu as well. Compared to the other Hawaiian islands, Oʻahu helicopter tours are a bit less compelling. Kauaʻi, the Big Island and even Maui all have more nooks and crannies to explore than Oʻahu due to the physical structure of the mountain ranges here. Although the Koʻolaus are beautifully sculpted and corrugated, they don't lend themselves to aerial exploration as well—they just don't *feel* as mysterious from the air—at least the way companies do tours here. They're incredibly beautiful, but a drive along H-3 from Kailua to Honolulu can give you a view that rivals some of what you'll get from a helicopter. For the money, it's hard to recommend a helicopter flight on Oʻahu.

That said, if you want one anyway, the company we prefer is **Paradise Helicopters** (808-969-7392). They use four-seater MD 500s and leave from the Turtle Bay Resort on the North Shore. They're *totally* flexible and will pretty much fly where passengers want. Call in advance since they need three people to book the 60-minute Magnum Experience flight (which is $349) or the 40-minute Valley and Waterfall Explorer (which is $269). Unlike others, they'll visit the Waiʻanae Coast. You can also arrange a charter for $1,604 an hour, which can be split four ways. (They charge $50 extra *per person* to take the doors off on any tour.) By the way, despite incorrect media stories, doors off flights are still allowed as long as restraints that can be removed quickly are used, which they are here.

Makani Kai (808-834-5813) leaves from Honolulu Airport. They use six-passenger

Rock your world by flying along the coast in a powered hang glider.

A-Stars for their 60-minute tours for $343–$397, plus some shorter flights. They sound like a great trip on paper, yet are horrible in their execution. Their manager wrote to us because he disagreed with our review. He also questioned whether I had ever flown with them because they couldn't find my name in their records. (Inside scoop to readers—I rarely use my real name when reviewing because I don't want to be treated differently.) The safety video says you have a mic to talk to the pilot, but onboard, we were told that they had been "banned over a decade ago because they could be used as a weapon." (Even the FAA laughed when we fact-checked *that* one.) And although the pilot's narration was pretty accurate, it was so hideously boring that he might as well have been reading from a map. This was the first tour in all the years I have been doing reviews that I saw a passenger *doze off* multiple times.

Blue Hawaiian (808-831-8800) is the biggest helicopter company in Hawai'i with *very* nice Eco-Star birds and is preferable over Makani Kai.

AIRPLANES

If helicopters aren't your thing, a surprisingly good air tour is **Island Seaplane** (808-836-6273). They have a float plane—a de Havilland Beaver, which holds 6 passengers as well as a Cessna 206. You don't choose the plane; they do. Although some of their facts are a bit shaky, the pilot does a pretty good job on the narration. They try to fly their route so that both sides get good views, but overall, the left side is the best due to the counter-clockwise direction of the tour. They have a 30-minute flight for $179 and a pretty good 60-minute flight for $299. (We just wish they'd fly along the Wai'anae coast, too, since central O'ahu is uninteresting.) Co-pilot seat available upon request. Earlier flights are usually smoother. Most of the time the pilot stays at about 1,500 feet.

POWERED HANG GLIDERS

First, I need to get something out of the way. Flying a powered hang glider (known as a trike) is different than any other type of aircraft. When I was growing up, I used to have a recurring dream that I could flap my arms and fly like a bird. My father flew little Cessnas, which, though fun, felt more to me like a car in the air than flying like a bird. I had forgotten my flying dreams until I reviewed a company on Kaua'i that gave lessons in this odd little craft. As soon as my instructor and I took off, I realized that a person *really could* fly like a bird. *This* was what the flying bug felt like! I was so smitten with the craft that I eventually hired the instructor on Kaua'i to teach me, and now I fly trikes myself. So although I have no personal interest in any company teaching trikes in Hawai'i, my perspective isn't as remote as it is for most activities. After all, it's not possible to anonymously review some companies, like Paradise Air, because I know the pilots. (We're all members of the small aviation community.)

With that explanation, powered hang gliding is an activity I recommend. Don't confuse this with hang gliding. This craft has an engine, it's bigger and more stable, and some even have a powered parachute attached to the craft...just in case (a safety feature boasted by only a small number of pricey traditional airplanes). Trikes take off and land on regular runways, and the ease and grace of the craft are glorious. (Rent the movie *Fly Away Home* if you want to see what they're like.) It's as close to flying like a bird as any form of flight I know. I have over a thousand hours in trikes and, in my opinion, they are incredibly safe in properly trained hands. (For the record, there have been fatal accidents in Hawai'i—just as there have been fatal helicopter flights—though only one trike fatality involved a quality pilot, in my opinion.) I grin like a fool every time I fly and have never reviewed an activity that generates more enthusiastic responses from other participants. It seems that whenever I see people coming off a trike, its passengers are frothing at the mouth with excitement, proclaiming that it's the best thing they've ever done on vacation. (Unless they're on their honeymoon, of course; then it's the *second* best thing.)

We've seen a number of companies start and stop here, but only one that we'd recommend. The local company is **Paradise Air** (808-497-6033) out of Dillingham Airfield on the North Shore. The pilots are very methodical in their approach to giving lessons in their high-end aircraft and maximizing your time in the air. With three trikes operating, couples can fly at the same time. They charge $180 per half-hour, $230 for 45 minutes, $280 per hour. They have cameras mounted on the aircraft (still and video) to get shots of you that no one back home will believe, and they can burn DVDs of your flight on the spot. (Pretty cool.) They primarily fly mornings when conditions are best, and it's best to book in advance. Ages 12 and up.

GLIDERS

Gliders, sailplanes, skysurfing—whatever you call it, these engine-less aircraft offer a fun way to see the western tip of the island. You get towed up by airplane, then during typical trade winds, ridge lift from the nearby mountains provides the buoyancy necessary to keep you aloft. Most people assume that glider rides are nearly silent. Sorry to burst your bubble, but most of these are 35-year-old gliders, and the wind noise can be so loud that it might be hard to hear some of the things your pilot is saying to you. (Newer, quiet three-passenger gliders are obscenely expensive, and companies are hesitant to invest in them.) One thing we strongly suggest is that you spend the extra $20–$50 to sit in front and take control if you want. (Don't worry, the pilot can control it from the back seat, too.) Although some are three-person crafts, the back bench is crowded with two people unless you're *real* small. If there are two of you, consider tacking on another $40 and taking separate rides. For instance, if it's $170 for two passengers at once for 15 minutes, it would cost $210 to do two separate rides.

Three companies are out at Dillingham Airfield on the North Shore. **Original Glider Rides**, AKA **Honolulu Soaring** (808-637-0207) and **Hawaii Glider & Sailplane Academy** (808-222-4235) provide similar rides for $100–$115 per person, plus the extras listed above, and you're in the air for about 15–20 minutes. (If these prices seem especially fluid, it's because both companies *seem* to charge different prices depending on how they feel. Frankly, we're not sure *what* you'll pay.) They want you there long before your flight (assuming you'll be late). Ask them what time you'll *actually be flying*. It's not an aerobatic ride (that's extra, too), but it's lots of fun and it's gentle. Generally, the earlier in the day you go, the smoother the air. By the way, neither company requires a credit card for a reservation.

The third company at Dillingham is **Acroflight International** (808-221-4480). They use a motorglider. It's no exaggeration to say that they literally scared us out of the sky, on multiple levels, and we absolutely, positively wouldn't recommend them for any reason. We'd love to say more, but let's leave it at that.

These are those four-wheeled things that look like Tonka Toys on steroids with knobby tires. They're pretty fun to ride, though at press time there was only one company giving tours on these.

Kualoa Ranch (808-237-7321) on the windward side north of Kane'ohe has rides on their ranch. Though the ranch is pretty, they use relatively small 400cc bikes and take up to 16 riders per group, keeping them lined up single file. It's $85 for a one-hour tour, $130 for two hours. You must be at least 16 years old.

Coral Crater Adventure Park (808-626-5773) is a cool place, but their ATV tour is simply one or two laps around their mile-long track and simply can't compete with

Soaring in a glider is fun, but it's not as quiet as most people think.

what you get at Kualoa Ranch. Consider this along with one of their other activities, such as their adventure tower or zipline. $120. In Kapolei in the southwestern part of O'ahu.

If you're staying in Waikiki, you can't help but notice the numerous bike racks with the same type of bikes attached. **Biki** (aka **Bikeshare Hawai'i**) has single-speed bikes strewn around Waikiki and Honolulu. Since this a pretty flat area, riding is pretty easy and convenient. No worrying about parking. No waiting for buses. The drawback is if you have stuff to carry, you'll need a backpack since their "luggage carrier" is pretty small. Plus, you might take a bike to a location one way, only to find there's no bike available for your return trip. But overall, this feels like a good fit for Waikiki and is a great way to stretch your biking legs. They have lots of pricing structures, from a single ride for $3.50, $15 for unlimited 30-minute rides for a month, and others.

If you want a guided tour, **Bike Hawai'i** (808-734-4214) does a pretty good job. They have a 4-hour single track tour for $145 that is meant for more serious mountain bike riders rather than those used to dirt roads. They have nice Kona Bikes with good components, and the guides show you how to ride them properly. This tour is strenuous in the Maunawili Trail area, but you make lots of stops for natural and cultural interpretation. They also have a downhill trip down Tantalus Drive that includes a hike to a waterfall for $115. Overall, a good outfit.

Pedal Power Bike Tours (206-795-0920) takes tours of up to six riders around Waikiki or Honolulu. Good if you are

nervous about striking out or your own. Otherwise, you're better off grabbing a Biki bike and doing it much more cheaply. $50 for the 2-hour Waikiki tour, $70 for 3 hours of Honolulu.

Kualoa Ranch (808-237-7321) has 90-minute (which includes the briefing) tours of a small portion of their beautiful windward ranch for $100. You ride ebikes, which are power-assisted. Don't think moped; think helping hand when going uphill. You will be on an unpaved road, and the pedaling is pretty easy. For Waikiki pickup, add $15.

What's not to love about spending the day on the water? The ocean off the leeward side of the island (meaning near Waikiki) tends to be fairly calm and somewhat protected. Whether you want to do a snorkel tour, whale watch or a sunset cocktail or dinner cruise, there are lots of boating opportunities off O'ahu.

Ocean tours off Waikiki tend to be on giant boats. (It's simple economics—getting a boat slip in Kewalo Basin is so valuable that anyone with a permit tends to use it for a big boat.) The exceptions are some of the boats that come right ashore at Waikiki.

FROM WAIKIKI BEACH

Let's start with the most convenient ocean tours. Some boats slide right onto the beach at Waikiki.

The best one we've seen by far is the **Spirit of Aloha** (808-234-7245) that leaves from the Hilton Hawaiian Village pier. It's $129 for 2.5 hours and includes lunch (deli only), snorkel and sail. For $109 you can go out in the afternoon minus the lunch but with two free alcoholic drinks (unlimited soft drinks). They provide full snorkel gear (including fins), but they make you wear an inflatable snorkel vest (which you don't have to inflate), even if you're an Olympic swimmer. The crew does a good job teaching people how to use the snorkeling gear, though the speech in the beginning is well-rehearsed and delivered without much enthusiasm. They'll motor out and sail back from Diamond Head. This cruise is a little more subdued compared to some of their competitors. You'll get two free drink coupons, but we predict that if you want more, you'll hear, *I'm buying,* from one of the crew. The sunset cruise is $89 and includes bar snacks. Another option is the Friday night fireworks cruise for $149, which includes a hot buffet pupu-style.

If the Spirit of Aloha is full, our next choice is the **Maita'i** (808-922-5665). It's a 44-foot catamaran, and for $39 you can take a no-frills 90-minute sailing tour. No food, no snorkeling, and beverages are extra. The 90-minute sunset trip is $49 and includes all beverages. They also offer a 90-minute moonlight sail on Fridays to enjoy the fireworks with an open bar for $49. The crew is very friendly and accommodating. They'll let you go sit on the nets out front, but only when the boat isn't in motion. They pull ashore between the Sheraton Waikiki and the Halekulani.

Our least favorite Waikiki snorkel boat is **Holokai Catamaran** (808-922-2210). (Winds permitting, they won't just motorsail. They'll kill the engines and sail in quiet.) The 2.5-hour snorkel trips are $60. They open the bar after snorkeling, but it's a cash bar. They provide masks and snorkels but no fins—you'll have to bring your own. The snorkel spot is the same as most other boats, which is fairly nice. (We won't ruin the surprise.)

Our biggest gripe is how we've seen them handle wildlife. On multiple occasions during the snorkel tour we've seen them pull an octopus from its hole and proceed to wear it like a hat to amuse passengers. Then they passed the poor creature around the boat for everyone to handle until it was so exhausted it couldn't swim once finally returned to the water. Though that's not illegal, it leaves a bad taste in our mouths.

They have a 90-minute sailing tour without snorkeling for $35. The sunset trips are $55 for 90 minutes and include a free open bar and sometimes a slightly more raucous atmosphere. It's a hoot to ride the net (one of their forward trampolines), though you might get wet. On Fridays there's an hour-long fireworks cruise for $50 plus cash bar. They can hold up to 49 passengers but usually go with fewer, and they land in front of the Outrigger Reef Hotel.

The **Manu Kai** (808-386-7422) has 2-hour snorkel sails for $50 aboard their big yellow catamaran. The sunset cruise is 90 minutes for $35. A no-muss, no-fuss way of getting on the water, meeting people and taking advantage of the open bar (three drinks included). The drinks are strong, and they want you to have a good time. Their sister boat, **Na Hoku II** (808-554-5990) is very similar except it's $40 for a 90-minute sail. Same three-drink bar included. Just show up at the boat in front of the Outrigger Waikiki on the Beach hotel, and if they have room, they'll take you.

Near the Manu Kai is a similar $25 walk-up, hour-long trip on the **Kepoikai II** (808-224-7688). They'll usually cut the motor and sail awhile offshore. Kids 6–11 are $15; those under 5 years old ride free. Popular with large Japanese groups. Beer and mai tais available but extra. Often a more subdued boat experience.

It's hard to believe that a boat trip so close to Waikiki can still transport you to another world.

The **Mana Kai** (844-626-2524) is a walk-up sailing catamaran that beaches in front of the Duke Kahanamoku Statue. This laid-back cruise is good if you want to avoid the heavy drinking that goes on with some of the other cruises (although they do allow you to bring your own booze). $25 or $30 for a 1-hour daytime tour, or $35 for the sunset cruise.

OUTRIGGER CANOE RIDES OFF WAIKIKI

Outrigger canoe rides have been a Waikiki staple for over a century. **Aloha Beach Services** (808-922-3111, ext. 42341) has rides for $20 (you get to ride two waves—they have a four-person minimum), or you can charter the whole eight-passenger outrigger canoe (includes two captains, extra paddlers are $50 per hour) for $300 per hour. Directly next door **Waikiki Beach Services** (808-388-1510) rides two waves in a private canoe for $25 per person, four people minimum.

Near the Duke statue, **Star Beach Boys** (808-699-3750) will give you three waves for $20 in a *slightly* bigger canoe.

FROM KEWALO BASIN

If you're looking to sail, **Makani Catamaran** (808-591-9000) is a great choice, but snorkelers might want to look elsewhere. Makani literally means *wind*, which is appropriate for this ultra fast, top-of-the-line 64-foot sailing cat. No expense was spared on this catamaran. They claim that the carbon fiber mast alone cost $400,000. The boat's sleek design lets it rip through the waves faster and steadier than any other cat we've seen.

There are two heads (bathrooms) on board, as well as trampolines at the bow to relax on (though you might get wet). The 2-hour afternoon sail ($99) comes with one drink. The 2-hour sunset cruise ($109) brings one drink and a hot buffet. No one pressures you to dance or sing on this sail. Just kick back and enjoy the ride. The morning snorkel sail ($119) comes with a strange rule. You are allowed to swim without a life vest *as long as you don't wear a mask and snorkel.* Snorkelers gotta wear it. Overall, the crew is nice, and the drinks are potent, but choose another boat if snorkeling is important.

For Kewalo Basin trips, bring quarters for the parking meter—50¢ per hour—or park across the street at Ward Warehouse.

FROM WAI'ANAE

If you don't mind driving out to **Ko Olina** (35–45 minutes west of Waikiki *barring traffic*), the waters off the Wai'anae Coast can be delightful during summer months (April–October).

The **Ko Nau Lani** (808-234-7245) at Hawai'i Nautical is an impressive 65-foot catamaran. (Though it's a sailing cat, they'll mostly motorsail.) They feed you well, and the crew is laid back and friendly. We weren't impressed with their snorkel spot and were disappointed that, even if you're an Olympic swimmer, they *insist* that you wear a flotation device, though you don't have to inflate it. Three-hour morning trips are $129 (plus $30 if you need transportation from Waikiki) and include light breakfast and build-your-own-sandwich for lunch with hot shredded pork. You also get two alcoholic beverages. If you still need more, they're dirt cheap. They leave from Wai'anae boat harbor.

Ko Olina Ocean Adventures (808-396-2068) does 3.5-hour trips from their sailing catamaran for $144. SNUBA is also available for $75. For that you get to linger

A boat cruise off Waikiki can feel so relaxing, you'll think somebody has stolen your bones.

underwater for 30 minutes with a regulator on a 20-foot hose. They feed you pretty well after the second snorkel stop. They also have a 44-foot rigid hull inflatable boat that they use to find dolphins, get way in front of them and then put you in the water to watch quietly as the dolphins swim by. This can be an incredible experience if the dolphins cooperate, which they usually do. Just stay calm so you don't spook them. $139 for 3.5 hours.

Ocean Joy Cruises (808-677-1277) has a nice 61-foot power cat that isn't too crowded with the maximum 49 passengers. Their snorkel instruction on the boat may be thorough, but they fail to help the aqua-phobic masses into the water. Instead they point to the ocean and say, "Go for it." The lack of help causes a traffic jam every time. They also require you to wear flotation devices whether you want to or not. Even if you're an Ironman swimmer, you can't escape that rule. The buffet's just OK, and the mai tais are worse. It's hardly worth $149, plus the $10 to park at the marina.

Wai'anae Regional Park in Wai'anae is a farther drive from Waikiki, but **Wild Side Specialty Tours** (808-306-7273) has a 42-foot and a 32-foot catamaran. The larger cat takes a maximum of 10 people, and the tour is $175 for 3 hours. The smaller boat runs $195 with a maximum of 6 people for 3.5 hours.

Dolphin Excursions (808-239-5579) is a 32-foot rigid hull inflatable. 22 people max. No shade, no toilet. Their goal is to locate dolphins, then let you slip into the water with them, and they claim a 90 percent success rate. (We've also seen them claim 70 percent success, so you decide.) $130, which includes lunch at a café afterward. Snorkeling also when surf permits. You'll save 10 percent if you provide your own transportation to Wai'anae.

Dolphin Star (888-373-1646) is a 65-foot double decker that holds 149 passengers and is the only snorkel tour that goes all the way to Yokohama Bay and back. The area on the bow is great for photographers, and you get a fun ride if the boat is heading into a swell. The service is super friendly, and kids will enjoy it. Their gourmet burger buffet is impressive. One drink included, then break out your wallet. Their instructional snorkel speech is long, and they make you wear an inflatable vest, but you don't have to inflate it. The snorkel spot is different every time because they drop anchor at the best spot they find. You're kept on a pretty short leash once in the water, but overall, it's a very good tour. Cost is $83 ($50 for kids) for the 2-hour dolphin watch or $111 for the 3-hour tour that includes snorkeling. Leaves from the Wai'anae Boat Harbor.

FROM HALE'IWA

North Shore Catamaran (808-351-9371) does summer (meaning May–September) 4-hour snorkel trips for $95 in their 40-foot sailing cat (includes lunch). It's $80 in the afternoon with no lunch. Nonalchoholic beverages are included or BYOB. They do a sunset cruise all year round for $60.

IN KANE'OHE BAY

All Hawai'i Cruises (808-942-5077)— aka Captain Bob—uses a 42-foot power catamaran for a four-hour excursion that includes a burger lunch at an offshore sunken island (really a sand bar). $128, which includes pickup from Waikiki. The sand bar is a cool place to hang out, and there's some (mediocre) snorkeling available. Overall, a reasonably good deal.

DINNER CRUISES

See *Island Dining* starting on page 307.

Boogie Boarding

Boogie boarding (riders are derisively referred to as *spongers* by surfers) is where you ride a wave on what is essentially a sawed-off surfboard. It can be a real blast. You need short, stubby fins to catch bigger waves (which break in deeper water), but you can snare small waves by simply standing in shallow water and lurching forward as the wave is breaking. If you've never done it before, stay away from big waves; they can drill you. Smooth-bottom boards work best. If you're not going to boogie board with boogie fins (which some consider difficult to learn), then you should boogie board with water shoes or some other kind of water footwear. This allows you to scramble around in the water without fear of tearing up your feet on a rock or sea urchin. Shirts or rashguards are very important, especially for men. (Women already have this problem covered.) Sand and the board itself can rub you so raw your *da kines* will glow in the dark.

Boards can be rented just about anywhere for $10–$25 per day. See the *Beaches* chapter for descriptions of specific beaches. Popular boogie boarding spots for visitors include the **Kapahulu Groin** in Waikiki and **Ala Moana Regional Park**. Those with experience should check out **Makapu'u Beach Park** and sometimes **Sandy Beach**. Many of the **Wai'anae** beaches offer great boogie boarding when the ocean's cooperating. **Kailua Beach** on the windward side is good, and you can rent boards from **Hawaiian Watersports** (808-262-5483) and **Kailua Beach Adventures** (808-262-2555).

CAMPING

O'ahu is a great place to camp with 18 different areas—four state camping areas and 14 county campsites. Unfortunately, camping is no longer free.

County sites require a $32–$52 county permit from the **Division of Parks & Recreation, Permit Section** (808-768-2267). You can also get permits online. It's $32 for a three-day weekend stretch

Catching a wave isn't the biggest challenge. The hardest part is holding onto the board and your pants at the same time.

Maleakahana State Rec. Area
Kaiaka Bay Beach Park
Kokololio Beach Park
Hau'ula Beach Park
Ahupua'a O Kahana State Park
Swanzy Beach Park (weekends only)
Kualoa Beach Park
Kea'au Beach Park
Ho'omaluhia Botanical Gardens (weekends only)
Lualualei Beach Park
Kea'iwa Heiau State Rec. Area
Ma'ili Beach Park (weekends only)
Bellows Field Beach Park (weekends only)
Waimanalo Bay Beach Park
Nanakuli Beach Park
Waimanalo Beach Park
Kalaeloa Beach Park (weekends only)
Sand Island State Rec. Area

(even if you only camp one day) and $52 for a five-day weekday stretch.

At all campsites you can only camp Friday through Tuesday (unless otherwise noted on map above).

For state camping sites the rules are more complicated and the system more rigid. (We fell asleep halfway through the process description.) Apply in person at the **Division of State Parks** (808-587-0300) or apply online. You cannot apply more than 30 days in advance. It's $18 per night per campsite for up to six persons ($3 per night for each additional person over 2 years of age).

The cheapest place to buy your camping gear and supplies is the **Walmart/Sam's Club Superblock** (808-954-9481) just outside of Waikiki on Keeaumoku and Makaloa.

One of the more interesting camping opportunities is the **Malaekahana Beach Campground** (808-674-7715) near the northern tip of the island in La'ie. These were private beach "cabins" run by a church as a substance abuse location until the mid '90s. They are highly sought after, so call as far in advance as possible. Rates range from $59–$118 per night (more for big groups), depending on the hut or cabin you choose. Ask for one near the beach. At press time they were wrangling with the state for a lease and didn't appear to be putting much, if any, money into the dwellings, so expect to rough it.

Escape Rooms

Escape Rooms aren't unique to Hawai'i, but if you've ever wanted to live out a full-scale, interactive puzzle, then you'll probably love this. Each Escape Room has a theme (we've seen them range from wizard adventures to jewel heists), and the good ones do an excellent job of immersing you in the story with detailed sets. Most Escape Rooms on O'ahu are smaller than what you'd see on the mainland. (We've always been told that size doesn't matter, but if you're claustrophobic, you may want to pass.) Most games are limited to an hour, though there are some exceptions. Most companies also list success rates and difficulty levels for each game on their websites, if you want to know how others have done.

Breakout Waikiki (808-926-1418) puts on a good show. They have six rooms that can hold groups of two to eight at once (though some of their bigger puzzles require at least four people). Their sets have less fluff than some of the other rooms we've seen, which makes them a little easier and a lot less convincing. Located in Waikiki at the King's Village Shops; entrance is on Prince Edward Street. $42 per person. If you aren't keen on sharing your adventure, consider booking a private room.

Hawaii Escape Challenge (808-379-0952) in Aiea was by far our favorite experience. Their rooms are filled with props (most that you won't use) that offer a compelling and convincing story. The games here are also more challenging than most other places, so if you find a theme you like, you're in for a treat. Games can accommodate from three to 12 people. Our preferred location is at the Pearlridge Center in Aiea and offers four games. Their other location is at Windward Mall in Kaneʻohe with only one game. $28 per person, and all rooms are private.

Scaventour (808-373-6869) is unlike other games. These take place all across Waikiki with guides and involve finding locked cases and bags, as well as jumping from location to location before the time runs out. The games are done in groups of four to 12 and are almost entirely outdoors, though they have some team and corporate games that can accommodate anywhere from 12 to 500 people. (They also can convert corporate facilities into escape rooms for team-building events.) $29 for adults, $24 for children. They do *not* have a physical address, instead meeting their patrons at the game's starting point.

Deep sea fishing is synonymous with Hawaiʻi. Reeling in a massive marlin, tuna or tough-fighting ono is a dream for many fishermen. When there's a strike, the adren-aline level of everyone on board shoots through the roof. Most talked about are the marlin (very hard fighters known for multiple runs). These goliaths can tip the scales at over 1,000 pounds. Also in abundance are ono, also called wahoo (one of the fastest fish in the ocean and indescribably delicious), mahimahi (vigorous fighters—excellent on light tackle), ahi (tasty yellowfin tuna) and billfish.

Most boats troll nonstop since the lure darting out of the water simulates a panicky bait fish—the favored meal for large game fish. On some boats, each person is assigned a certain reel. Experienced anglers usually vie for the corner poles with the assumption that strikes coming from the sides are more likely to hit corners first.

You should know in advance that in Hawaiʻi, the fish belongs to the boat. What happens to the fish is entirely up to the captain, and he usually keeps it. You could catch a 1,000-pound marlin and be told that you can't have as much as a steak from it. If this bothers you, you're out of luck. If the ono or other small fish are striking a lot and there is a glut of them, or if your fish is under 100 pounds, you might be allowed to keep part of it. You *may* be able to make arrangements in advance to the contrary.

By the way, you'll never please the captain if you bring bananas on a boat. They are forbidden by tradition on fishing boats. The superstition dates back to when cargo was unloaded by hand. Bananas often carried deadly spiders, so workers had good reason to consider them unlucky.

Most charters leave Kewalo Basin near Waikiki with some departing from Waiʻanae and Haleʻiwa on the North Shore in the summer. Most have 4-, 6- and 8-hour charters. Mornings offer best conditions. Prices are about $155–$200 per person for a shared charter. 8-hour private charters go for $650–$1,100 or more for the big boats. Usually, the bigger the boat, the higher the price since most are licensed to take only 6 passengers. Individual boat rates can change often depending on the season, fishing conditions and whims of the owners. Consequently, we'll forgo listing some of the individual boat rates since this information is so perishable and instead list a few companies that we recommend. Call them directly to get current rates. If you have 4 or more people, make it private so you can exercise more control.

If you're easy-queasy, take an anti-seasickness medication. There are people who never get sick regardless of conditions, and those who turn green just watching *A Perfect Storm* on Netflix. Nothing can ruin an ocean outing faster than being hunched over the stern feeding the fish. Scopolamine patches prescribed by doctors can have side effects including (occasionally) blurred vision that can last a week. Dramamine II or Bonine taken the night before and the morning of a trip also seem to work well for many, though some drowsiness may occur. Ginger is a mild preventative. Try powdered ginger, ginger pills or even *real* ginger ale—can't hurt, right?

Tipping: 15–20 percent split between the captain and deck hand is customary if you are pleased with their performance. If the captain is a jerk and the deck hand throws up on you, you're not obligated to give 'em diddly.

Because boat slips are so hard to get near Waikiki (Kewalo Basin), companies share boats or swap customers constantly. (They like you to charter the whole boat.) **Maggie Joe** (808-591-8888) has three nice boats. Also consider **Wild Bunch** (808-596-4709) and **Magic Sport Fishing** (808-596-2998).

Sashimi Fun Fishing (808-955-3474) has several boats at Kewalo Basin. They do some exclusive charters and some shared. They use two *less-than-pristine* 65-foot Deltas, and they do shark hunts at night. Nearby **Blue Nun Sport Fishing** (808-596-2443) has a rusty boat and a salty crew. Even when nothing's biting, they'll keep going, and going, and going…

Out of Wai'anae Small Boat Harbor there's **Boom Boom** (808-306-4162) and their 50-foot Sportfisher.

In Hale'iwa **Chupu Sportfishing Fleet** (808-637-3474) has five boats ranging from 27- to 47-footers. **Go Fishing Hawaii** (808-637-9737) uses a 30-foot "banana boat," but it's cheaper if you've only got four people. **North Shore Sportfishing** (808-450-7601) has a nice 47-foot Hatteras 6-pack that does half-day charters for $950.

GOLFING

With its balmy trade winds, sunny skies and rich soil, O'ahu is an absolutely ideal place to build a golf course. And we're not the only ones who think so. More than *three dozen* courses carpet this tropical island. No matter what kind of golfing animal you are, O'ahu surely has a course that'll fulfill your dreams.

The one area where O'ahu courses come up short compared to their neighbor island brethren is with oceanside courses. There are only four: one's a military course, one's a private club, the third—Turtle Bay—inexplicably lets a thick grove of trees block your view most of the time. Only at a crusty nine-hole municipal course—Kahuku—does the promise of playing near the ocean come true. But don't fret. With *so* many courses on such a beautiful island, golfing on Oʻahu will keep you smiling.

It's impossible to review all the courses—hey, we've only got so much space here. So below are some of the more notable choices. See the golfing table for prices and specs. If you want to read in depth reviews of these courses, our smartphone app *Hawaii Revealed* goes into much more detail.

There is only one near Waikiki, the **Ala Wai Municipal Course**, and it's avoidable due to overcrowded conditions and dull play. You can do better than this.

Over in the Kailua area, three courses stand out. **Royal Hawaiian Golf Club** is one of the most beautiful courses in the whole state. Set in the center of Maunawili Valley behind Olomana Peak near Kailua, the back *ten* (yes, they have a real 19th hole, and it ain't a bar) in particular are draped in such a verdant setting that its nickname of *Jurassic Park* seems totally appropriate. But it is humiliatingly hard, so bring your lucky clubs. **Koʻolau Golf Club** is almost as beautiful and almost as hard. Next door the **Pali Golf Course** is a much cheaper municipal course with mangy fairways but nice views.

Near the northern tip of the island you have a couple of ocean-side courses. **Turtle Bay Golf Course** gives you two choices and both are usually uncrowded during the week. The **Palmer Course** is the better of the two. It's well marked, pretty wide open and not a wickedly challenging links-style course. The **Fazio Course** seems to get less respect—and seemingly less maintenance. Play this one only after you've played Palmer. It's extremely open and pretty easy on the ego. As mentioned above, both courses, inexplicably, take very little advantage of their close proximity to the ocean. Trees will block your view almost the entire time, so it doesn't really *feel* like oceanfront golf. If that's what you're gunning for, the nearby **Kahuku Municipal Golf Course** is for you. The good news about this one is it's dirt cheap, right on the ocean and sparsely played during the week. The bad news is crummy fairways (no sprinklers here) and unimaginative play on this nine-hole course.

Out in the southwestern part of the island, **Ko Olina Golf Club** has a beautiful layout and is very well maintained. Fairways are wide open and they make good

Golf Course	Phone	Par	Yards	Rating	Fees
Ala Wai Municipal Course	(808) 733-7387	70	5861	66.8	$66
Coral Creek Golf Course	(808) 441-4653	72	6347	71.5	$140*
Kahuku Municipal Course	(808) 293-5842	70	5398	65.2	$22
Koʻolau Golf Club	(808) 236-4653	72	6406	73.7	$155*
Ko Olina Golf Club	(808) 676-5300	72	6815	73.3	$225*
Pali Golf Course	(808) 266-7612	72	6524	70.4	$66
Pearl Country Club	(808) 487-3802	72	6787	72.7	$150*
Royal Hawaiian Golf Club	(808) 262-2139	72	5541	67.7	$160*
Turtle Bay/Fazio Course	(808) 293-8574	72	6828	73.8	$125*
Turtle Bay/Palmer Course	(808) 293-8574	72	6795	73.2	$195*

indicates carts are included and mandatory.
Yards and ratings are from the blue tees.

O'ahu may have fewer oceanfront courses than the neighbor islands, but the beauty of the tropics is never far away.

use of man-made waterfalls. Similarly appealing a slight cheaper is **Coral Creek Golf Course** halfway between Ko Olina and Pearl Harbor.

Lastly, in central O'ahu there is **Pearl Country Club**. Mature trees and rolling hills keep it interesting, but we've seen the fairways deteriorate at times so we're not sure what you'll experience. Used more by residents than visitors.

Gun Clubs

Depending on where you're from, shooting is either a fact of life or an impossibility. Waikiki is the only part of Hawaii where handguns and exotic hardware is accessible.

Waikiki Gun Club (808-922-6442) offers packages ranging from $79 (36 shots from .22, .38 and 9mm guns) to $500 (for 55 blasts from .50 caliber semi-automatics). It doesn't take long to burn through your ammo, especially for those with an itchy trigger finger. Depending on your instructor and how busy they are, two people *might* be allowed to purchase a low-end package *and* a high-end package and swap shooters. (Non-shooters are relegated to watching a monitor in the lobby.) The downside of switching is that lobbing projectiles from a Beowulf or Desert Eagle make the .22s seem like spitballs.

Hawaii Gun Club (808-922-6442) offers the same product as Waikiki Gun Club, only at a different location.

Because O'ahu has such a large and active population, hikers will find the island *filled* with good hiking trails. This presented a problem for us. Which ones do we include? What we ended up doing was including a few of the more popular trails (Diamond Head and Manoa Falls, for example) along with some lightly used trails, some of them never before seen in any book. If you're an ultra-serious hiker who wants more options than our hiking section allows, there are a number of hiking books for O'ahu. Probably the best one is *The Hiker's Guide to O'ahu*.

Shameless plug here: If you're planning to go hiking, you might want to download our Hawaii Revealed app from the iTunes store or Google Play. We've GPSed the trails so you can see where you are on the map and know you're going in the right direction. The best part is that you don't need a cell signal for the GPS function to work.

HIKING NEAR HONOLULU

Diamond Head (2 Miles Round Trip)

Diamond Head is that iconic volcano crater that defines the Honolulu skyline. And just like the Statue of Liberty in New York, the St. Louis Arch and San Francisco's Golden Gate Bridge, you're practically *required* to visit it.

The first thing you'll notice after entering the crater (through a long tunnel bored through the side) is that you are in an open field surrounded by high cliff walls, nearly perfectly circular and more than 3,500 feet in diameter, as if you're at the bottom of a massive, fluted bowl. That's because Diamond Head is a tuff cone. It formed in the waning days of O'ahu's growing phase, about 100,000 years ago, as the island moved away from the hot spot due to plate tectonics, and sea water seeped into the magma chamber. Ocean water flashed from liquid to gas, and the resulting pressure buildup caused a violent explosion of steam and ash. That's why it looks more like an impact crater on the moon than a traditional volcanic cinder cone—the rim is where cemented ash fell back to earth. Scientists think the crater rim is higher on one side because that's

the direction the wind was blowing during the eruption.

The government bought Diamond Head in 1904 so the military could build a bunker up top. From there, a few eagle-eyed spotters could target enemy battleships by triangulating their position against Mt. Tantalus, and then direct artillery fire from the mortar batteries down below. The guns were never fired in war; by WWII the advent of the aircraft carrier made these kinds of coastal defenses obsolete. But the switchback trail up the interior of the crater remains.

On the trail you'll gain 560 feet over about a mile, and it takes most people about 1.5 hours. That's 30 to 40 minutes to go up, 20 minutes at the top, then the return. On this trail you'll see everyone from Ironman triathletes to people literally using walkers (though they probably won't be hiking the same speed, and the walker users may not go all the

way to the top). The trail has sections of unevenness, so wear shoes instead of flip-flops. Short marching steps work best along the constant incline. Near the end, you'll climb 74 stairs followed by a tunnel, then 99 very steep stairs, plus a spiral staircase, followed by a few more steps. (Ignore advice to bring a flashlight—the interior portions are lit.) If stairs aren't your thing, there's a less steep (but longer) paved path to the left after exiting the tunnel.

It's crowded at the top—it wasn't designed to accommodate more than 3,000 hikers per day—so you may have to wait your turn. But once you're at the 761-foot summit, it's all worth it. Waikiki looks beautiful from up here. With line-of-sight stretching from Barbers Point almost 20 miles west to Koko Crater 9 miles behind you, it's easy to see why the military bought this landmark—it's the perfect place to watch over all of leeward O'ahu.

Most buildings inside the crater are for civil defense, and they're off limits. (In 2018 a state employee working in one of those buildings sent a false alert warning of an incoming ballistic missile attack to everyone's phones, causing a statewide panic among residents and visitors who thought they might only have minutes to live.) For decades the FAA also housed its air traffic controllers for Honolulu Center here. (Doesn't it seem odd that the government agency in charge of the sky would choose to put its main office in a hole?)

There are two great reasons to do this hike early—to avoid the heat and assure yourself of a parking space. It's $5 per car, or $1 per person if you're walking in, cash only. If the parking lot is full, another option is to park in the small lot on the left, just before the tunnel, and walk the short distance into the crater. Otherwise, you'll have to park outside at Kapiolani Community College and

From the top of Diamond Head, Waikiki and Honolulu take on a whole new perspective.

walk an additional 1.25 uninteresting miles up the road. Bus riders will also have to make that additional hike.

Sunrise is not worth it, unless your idea of a good vacation is getting up early just to wait in a long line that snakes

- -

It's only a mile walk to Manoa Falls—long enough to dissuade casual visitors, but close enough for almost any hiker to visit. Sometimes it flows a lot, sometimes it's a trickle.

almost all the way to the top. And they close before sunset, which is a shame. (If you're looking for a good sunrise hike, try the *Koko Crater Railway Trail* on page 199, *Makapu'u Hike to the Dragon's Nostrils* on page 196, or the *Ka'iwa Ridge Hike/ Lanikai Pillbox Trail* on page 207.)

To get here, take Kalakaua down to Monsarrat, then head up that street for over a mile to the entrance on the right. (Monsarrat changes to Diamond Head Road.) Water and restrooms are available at the visitor center by the parking area, but there are none on the trail.

Manoa Falls Trail
(2 Miles Round Trip)

This is generally considered the second most popular hike on the island (after Diamond Head), but we haven't seen nearly as many people on it as its reputation suggests. It's popular for good reason. The trail is close to Honolulu, but the isolated jungle valley is a world away from the city noise. The surrounding forest is staggeringly beautiful. It's only a mile each way (though you gain 800 feet in the process), and it rewards you with a very pretty 160-foot-high waterfall.

Right from the get-go, it's obvious that this is an impossibly lush area. Giant trees with luxuriant clinging vines, elephant-eared ape (pronounced ah-pay) plants and every shade of green you could want along with a soundtrack of tropical birds create an Eden-like atmosphere. The stream is always nearby, and the verdant growth is ever present. Once at the falls, there's a bench to sit on and listen to the hissing water. All in all, a very rewarding hike for relatively little effort.

To get there, either take McCully out of Waikiki, past H-1 and onto Metcalf, then left on University Avenue, or if you're on H-1, take the University Avenue exit (24B) and head mauka (toward the mountains). University Avenue will become O'ahu Avenue. Then take the right fork—not the right *turn*—at a confusing five-way intersection onto Manoa Road and drive until you see a paid parking lot ($5). Bring mosquito repellent. The trail is mostly well maintained and much of it is lined with gravel, but expect muddiness—possibly *a lot* of muddiness—if it's been raining lately. (Which it probably has—that's why it's so lush here.) Rarely, the falls dry up to a disappointing trickle.

By the way—that hulking gray building by the parking lot used to be an aviary at a once-popular exotic bird park (a real tourist trap that also had an amphitheater where trained cockatoos would ride a bicycle across a tightrope). Today, the grounds of the defunct attraction are largely overgrown, similar to the days when Hawaii-born singer-songwriter Bruno Mars lived in a shack on the abandoned grounds when he was a kid.

Judd Trail to Jackass Ginger Pool
(0.5 Miles Round Trip)

Super short, super sweet and probably super crowded. It's a very small falls and a large pool near the Pali Highway. You may see people jumping from a small ledge, but it's pretty shallow. There's even a small part of the rock that acts like a natural water slide where you can slide down the rock and into the pool below.

To get to there from Waikiki, get on H-1 west and take exit 21B to the Pali Highway heading north. Take Nuuanu Pali Drive on the right for exactly 1 mile. Park on the side of the road near the bridge, and you'll see the Judd trailhead. Start on the trail and cross the stream. You may be able to boulder hop here and get across without getting wet. If the water is flowing too high to cross, don't attempt it—the pool won't be worth swimming in anyway. Immediately after crossing the stream, you'll see a well-worn trail going through a bamboo forest on the right side of the main trail. Take this trail which parallels the stream. *Do not* follow the main trail, which does *not* follow the stream. The path can be muddy, and some exposed roots make it slippery in a few places, but it's very short. Follow the stream through this lush valley and enjoy the scenery. Within 10 minutes, you'll pop out at a small waterfall and a large pool.

Lulumahu Falls (1.8 Miles Round Trip)

Here's a jungle waterfall that's easy to get to (it's only about a 20-minute drive outside Waikiki) but is still nicely secluded. It's in the Nu'uanu Valley off the Pali Highway (near the **Pali Lookout**). The unmaintained trail goes through a bamboo forest, past a reservoir with wide-open views of lush green mountains, then along a valley stream to a waterfall you can shower under.

To get there from Waikiki, get on H-1 west and take exit 21B to the Pali Highway (Hwy 61). Then take the exit for Nuuanu Pali Drive and follow that road all the way until the end, where it will reconnect with the Pali Highway. Where it does, you'll see a dirt parking lot to your right. (Or just make it easy on yourself and put "4459 Pali Highway, Honolulu" into your map app.)

The land you are going to be hiking on is government property (it's the Honolulu Watershed), and you're supposed to get a permit to print out and leave on your dash and another copy to carry with you while hiking. Most people don't seem to bother doing that, but you never know when they might issue tickets. You can get the permit online at **https://trails.ehawaii.gov** for $2.50 per person.

Going through the bamboo forest, you're almost immediately presented with a choice: Go left or go straight. We prefer going left along the highway because you get a better view when you come out. You'll soon come to a small grass hill that leads up to an elevated dirt road with sweeping views of the reservoir. Look across the reservoir to the gap in the mountains. That's **Pali Puka** on the ridge to the left, and Pali Notches on the ridge to the right, with the Pali Lookout nestled between the gap. It was in this area that Kamehameha's forces drove the last hold-outs of the O'ahu army up this valley, until he finally forced them over the edge at the cliff between those ridges.

Follow the dirt road past the reservoir and then go up the concrete stairs. You'll come to a fenced-in area to your right; go through it, and continue to follow

Lulumahu Falls is less than a mile from your car but a nice place to rinse off.

the path. Now you're following the stream. There are many paths running along, which can be a little confusing, but try to keep as close to the stream as you can, and you won't get lost. You're going to have to cross the stream a few times from one side to the other on slippery boulders when you've got mud on your shoes. On a weekday, you may have this trail mostly to yourself, but weekend use is high enough to smooth the bark off the fallen trees (from all the people sliding their butts over it before you).

When you get to the end, the reward is a twisting waterfall with a final drop of about 50 feet. No pool to swim in, but here's the really nice thing: The final drop is angled, and the water hugs the rock on the way down, so you can stand under it without getting pummeled by a direct flow, making it one of the best waterfalls for taking a shower. (That said, remember that rocks or other hard, heavy objects can still come down at any time.) For a rather quick hike, it's nicely secluded in the jungle and feels adventurous. It's about 35 minutes one way with about 400 feet of elevation gain, which you won't really notice until the last bit where you have to scramble a little as you approach the falls.

TOP OF THE WORLD HIKING

The Ko'olau Range is the long mountain that stretches 36 miles, effectively defining the windward side. (See foldout back cover map to orient you.) From its meandering summit you'll find some of the best views on the island. Look one way, and most of the windward side stretches before you. Turn around, and the leeward side from Honolulu to Makapu'u Point is all yours.

The leeward side of this range gently slopes toward the sea, so that's where all the trails to the summit are. (The windward side of the ridge is cliffy.) Erosion has created a repeating pattern of ridges and valleys. What does this mean for the hiker lusting after the views up there? It means you'll be walking up one of the many ridges until you get to the summit.

Weather is the big question mark—more specifically, cloud cover, which would turn your grand, expansive view at the summit into a whiteout. Mornings are usually your best chance for cloud-free conditions, but sometimes it's best in the afternoon. Bottom line: You need to look to the summit before you go and, if it's clear, cross your fingers and hope that it'll stay that way.

Knowing that you don't have the time or desire to hike all the trails to the summit, we've expended considerable effort viewing the windward side from all the summit trails. Some, such as the Hawai'iloa Ridge Trail, have access issues. Fortunately, one of the best, **Kuli'ou'ou Ridge Trail**, is accessible and offers great views. That's because it's far enough north to get the wicked views of the windward side without being so far north that your sweeping vistas begin to get clipped by a peak called Konahuanui.

Kuli'ou'ou Ridge Trail
(4 Miles Round Trip)

Unlike most ridge trails that service the Ko'olau Range, this one begins at the bottom of a valley. Despite its low beginnings, the trail climbs 1,800 feet to the top in only 2 miles. Most other trails in the Ko'olau Range climb more than 2,000 feet and can be almost twice as long. Because of the summit's lower elevation, you're more likely to see the view at the top of this regularly cloudy vista. If it's a really clear day, you'll be able to see Moloka'i, Lana'i and Maui.

Heading east of Honolulu, H-1 ends and becomes Kalanianaole Highway (Hwy 72), adding streetlights and pedestrians to the eight lanes of automobiles. A little over 4 miles after this, look for Kuliʻouʻou Road on your left. Follow this street into the valley as it jogs left at a stop sign, then right again at the next intersection. From the highway, it's exactly 1 mile to your final right turn on Kalaʻau Place. Park your car near the cul de sac at the end of this road. The trailhead is down the access road blocked by a gate. This is a heavily used trailhead, so there are plenty of signs marking the way.

You'll begin on the Kuliʻouʻou Valley Trail. It intersects with the ridge trail after 0.2 miles. Turn right. See map below.

A dozen or so switchbacks will carry you up 800 feet without getting seriously steep compared to what's ahead. Take your time and save your energy. Once on top of the ridge, you'll have entered the Kuliʻouʻou Forest Reserve. This area might make you forget that you're in the tropics. The ironwood trees and Cook Island pines are so thick that you'll see very few other trees. It reminds us of a Rocky Mountain pine forest. This is a good area to stop and smell the pinesap.

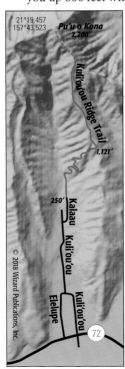

Shortly after reaching the ridge, you'll find a pair of covered picnic tables. Not only is this a great place to take a break, it's also the halfway point. From here, the trail gets steep and unrelenting. Exposed roots make the climb slippery in many places. At times the trail will disappear under the carpet of pines needles. Just keep marching upward, and the trail will show its face again.

When you leave the forest, you'll get your first views from high up on the ridge. Once on top, your view goes from Kailua, Waimanalo Beach and Rabbit Island on the windward side to Koko Crater and Diamond Head on the leeward side. It can be really windy up here, making it chilly after a sweaty hike. If you plan on staying up top for a while, you might want to bring some long sleeves.

The view from here is nice, but it could be better. To the left of the summit is a higher peak called Puʻu o Kona. Only advanced hikers and people with no fear of death should attempt this. Going left from the summit, you would traverse the Koʻolau Ridge Trail along the narrow edge of these mountains. Take your time maneuvering around rocks and climbing up fixed ropes, as it would be difficult to recover from a fall up here. You'll know when you've reached Puʻu o Kona when you get a clear view of the entire windward side from Chinaman's Hat to Rabbit Island. On a clear day, add Molokaʻi, Lanaʻi and Maui to that view for one of the best vistas the island has to offer.

EASTERN OʻAHU HIKES

Makapuʻu Hike to the Dragon's Nostrils
(2.5 Miles Round Trip)

There's a smooth, nicely paved road (called **Kaʻiwi**) that heads to the top of Makapuʻu Head, the easternmost point of the island. (You can't drive it, though.) Over 1.25 miles it gains 520 feet at a reasonably constant pace. This is a very pop-

ular hike with locals and visitors alike due to the sweeping views from up top and good whale watching. What's less known is what lies at the foot of Makapu'u Head.

It gets hot by late morning here, so start this hike early. We like to walk up for the sunrise with flashlights, though it might be hard to motivate yourself to get up *that* early. (The vehicle gate doesn't open until 7 a.m., so the walk is slightly longer.) Take McCully out of Waikiki, then right on Kapiolani and up to H-1 east. Drive till you're past mile marker 9 on Hwy 72, east of Waikiki. Drive past the gate to the parking lot. The road ascends the back side of the hill first, then slithers around to the windward side halfway up. Stop at an information plaque about whales and look for the buggers below if it's whale season (December– April). Remember that plaque on your way down.

Near the top, a lookout presents an unexpectedly dreamy view of Manana (AKA Rabbit Island) and Kaohi-ka-ipu islands and Waimanalo beyond. *Wow!* The vista is fantastic. All around you are reminders of the military significance of this hill during WWII. Old bunkers and gun emplacements lie all over this mountain. Wild cactus dot the mountaintop. The Makapu'u Lighthouse is below you on a bluff, but it's off limits.

The actual summit is another 10-minute hike past old bunkers and up the ridge. Walking away from the lookout, a short-lived stretch of blacktop heads toward the summit and quickly becomes a trail. Follow this up to the ridge and past the highest pillbox. From here, 647 feet above sea level, you can add Diamond Head and Koko Head to your view.

Now here's the surprise. On your way back down toward your car, before you get to that whale plaque we talked about, keep an eye out to the left below you. There's a lava bench that's only partially visible in spots. Do you see any mist? How about water shooting into the air? Maybe, maybe not. The hill blocks most of the view of it. But from the whale plaque, a faint trail works its way down the mountain to the lava bench below. And there you will find, *some* of the

The Dragon's Nostrils aren't as reliable as the Halona Blowhole, but when they're going off, they're far more interesting.

time (though not *all* the time), a cluster of blowholes.

We've seen lots of blowholes in the islands. But these stand out as the most numerous in one spot, and they successfully convey a feeling of barely contained violence. It's as if there is a giant, furious beast pounding at his confines to get out. Sit a while, and you'll realize that there may be as many as seven blowholes down here on a good day. Some go off only occasionally. The snorting twin nostrils sound frightening and dangerous, and you can feel the ocean several feet below the lava shelf you're standing on, pounding away at the lava. This great beast will escape someday; you can feel the inevitability in the air. Take your time here, but never take your eye off the violent ocean. Unlike many blowholes around Hawai'i, the opening is probably too small for an adult to fall into, meaning it's OK to get into the splash zone. One of the twin nostrils separates the spray on the way out, creating three eruptions.

There's a good chance that the ocean may be too calm for the blowholes to work. Probably 60 percent of the time

they're *not* going off. East swells and long period swells work best, but it'll be hard for you to know if that's what's hitting the island. Low tide seems to *diminish* the blowholes, but that's when the waves may smash against the shoreline the most dramatically, creating explosions of water shooting well over 100 feet into the air when the surf is really high. What we're saying is you won't really know what to expect until you start going down the trail. If the ocean's calm, there *is* a nice consolation prize. Some deep tide-pools make wonderful bathing. But only use the tide-pools if the ocean's calm. Pounding seas make them hazardous.

The trail can be a little slippery going down and faint going back up—try to make a mental note of it. Also, don't tempt fate by getting too chummy with the ocean down here. Keep your distance unless you're *sure* you're in a safe place. Bring water for that climb back up to the 400-foot level. And wear closed-toed shoes.

Koko Crater Arch (0.5 Miles Round Trip)

This one is so short it barely counts as a hike, but it leads to a cool rock arch on the side of Koko Crater, and you'll gain 300 feet of elevation along the way. From the Halona Blowhole parking lot, cross the street and walk left, then follow the guardrail until it ends just past mile marker 15. Scramble up the rocks here, which is awkward and the worst part of the hike, or if that looks too intimidating, there is an easier way up about another 400 feet farther up the road. Either way, watch out for traffic zipping around the narrow corner. The well-worn path leads to the base of the arch. (If you have a good eye, you can see the arch slightly to the right of the trail for almost the entire hike as soon as you get onto the ridge. It's harder to spot during dry times when the vegetation is brown.)

The trail gets progressively steeper the closer you get, but the 45-degree angle really doesn't look that bad until you get higher onto the saddle, and then the increasingly intimidating incline (and the tug of gravity) keeps most sane people from going up and over the arch. It is possible, but the transition is tricky, and if you fall here, you probably won't be able to stop yourself. (The **Koko Crater Railway Trail,** below, is a better way to get to the very top, if that's what you want to do.) Explore underneath the arch instead. The easiest way to get under it is on the left side of the arch. The view from up here is stunning, and you can make it up and back in less than an hour.

Koko Crater Railway Trail
(1.5 Miles Round Trip)

This is one hike where it's impossible to get lost—it's just straight up. The trail follows an inclined tramway the military built during WWII to easily get men and supplies to a radar station at the top of 1,208-foot-tall Koko Crater. The installation is gone now, but a concrete pillbox and some structural debris remain.

The trail is almost always crowded with area residents who use it for exercise.

Soaking up the shade under the Koko Crater Arch.

It's easy to spot the people who climb this trail everyday—they're the ones with ripped quads and calf muscles, and disproportionately teeny upper bodies. In 2015 while still serving in office, President Obama surprised a bunch of hikers by powering his way up the trail, surrounded by a protective detail of Secret Service agents. (Regardless of your political views, you've got to feel sympathy for the poor aide who had to lug the nuclear football to the top.)

You'll hear people say there are 1,048 stairs or some such number. Hard to say for sure—we always lose count. And calling them stairs is misleading—these are slanted, irregularly spaced rail ties, some of them missing or replaced with paving stones, and you'll have to take steps between them. Just over halfway, there's a bridge over a ravine with nothing between the ties and the ground below, so if you're leery about crossing it, crawl, or look for the trail through the brush on the right to go around. After this, the rails are at their steepest until you reach the top. The entire trail is only 0.75 miles, but it can take anywhere from less than 20 minutes (for the super fit) to more than 1.5 hours. Bring water, pace yourself, take breaks when you need them, and—this is important—move aside for faster hikers and those who are descending. If you plan on going for sunrise, bring flashlights and a jacket. The breeze up top is cold early morning.

Once you make it to the end of the tracks, don't stop—go a little farther to find the very top. From there you've got a commanding 360-degree view. You can see down into the crater itself, and, looking back the way you came, Hanuama Bay and Koko Marina. You can even see Diamond Head and part of Waikiki in the distance. Follow the ocean-side of the rim as far as you like (the path is narrow but not too difficult) for some different perspectives and then return.

Koko Crater is the most prominent landmark on the southeastern corner of the island, and you can almost find your way there on visual navigation alone. From Waikiki, take the H1 east until it turns into Kalanianole Highway (Hwy 72). See

Try not to get lost on the Koko Crater Railway Trail.

You'll be huffing and puffing when you first get to the Pali Puka Lookout, so put down your pack and suck up some water. You deserve it.

map on page 71. Turn left onto Lunalilo Home Road in Hawai'i Kai, then right on Anapalau Street. It ends at the entrance to Koko Head District Park. Drive to the back and park in the farthest lot. Behind and above the baseball field there's a paved road that heads toward the beginning of the tracks. The trail connecting the two is just opposite a rock wall. On weekends, it sounds like a war zone from the constant sound of gunfire from a nearby gun range. Avoid midday heat.

HIKES AROUND KAILUA

Pali Puka Trail (0.5 Miles Round Trip)

Half mile round trip. Piece of cake, right? Absolutely—if you're immune to gravity. For the rest of us mere mortals, it's a puffer, because you climb 50 stories in 0.75 miles. But it's worth it for the amazing views. Basically you're climbing the ridge that starts at the Pali Lookout on Pali Highway. This ridge separates the two sides of the Ko'olau Mountains, so it's a scenic feast for the eyes the whole way.

On your way up, there's a particularly narrow portion that requires walking along the edge of a precipitous drop, but if that makes you nervous, you're not the only one—other survival-minded hikers have forged a path through the vegetation, away from the edge, to bypass that part. Once you get to a large rock spire, the path comes to an end. (You could go past it, but it's way too hairy and involves dubious ropes.) Scramble about 5 feet down the path to the left, and you'll see the puka (hole) in the rock to peer through at windward O'ahu. The cool wind rushes through the hole, providing a nice place to rest after huffing and puffing to get up here. Take a rest and enjoy the breathtaking view—you've earned it.

To get to the trailhead, follow the driving directions to the *Pali Lookout* on page 79 and park. Instead of following the crowds to the official lookout, walk across to the left of the parking lot where vans and buses park. Where the right-most bus would park, it would point to some missing rocks in the wall near a metal pole. The trail starts here. (There's a sign saying don't go, but we're confused by that because we see people hiking it all the time, and we've even seen state officials, in uniform, allowing hikers to head up the trail.) The path splits in the beginning, but you can go either way. We prefer the path on the right because there are more roots to grab onto. Avoid when windy or wet.

Meet Likeke Falls, your achievable goal for today.

Likeke Falls Hike
(Less than 1 Mile Round Trip)

This falls has always been a side trip from the Pali Trail. But some rocks fell on that trail, and the state closed it while they were trying to figure out what to do about them. (*Moving* the rocks does not appear to have occurred to them yet.) And since reliable waterfalls are hard to come by on O'ahu, we wanted to include this shorter, alternative way to get to them. It's less than half a mile, and you gain less than 200 feet of altitude. What we like best about Likeke is that even during dry times it flows.

You start in the back of the parking lot of the Ko'olau Golf Course in Kane'ohe. There might be a vehicle chain across the entrance. You'll take the trail until it combines with a trail off Auloa-Ki'ona'ole Road. Forget what Mama said about looking both ways if you cross this street. It's been closed since 1994. So much illegal activity occurred along the hidden bends of this road that the county had to block it off.

The trail goes up and eventually reaches an old stone road. You're only going up that road for a few minutes when

O'ahu has fewer waterfalls than Kaua'i and Maui, Maunawili Falls is occasionally deserted for short stretches, but it's normally a popular place to frolic in the water.

you come to a Y intersection, and you'll angle back right where the trail takes you to Likeke Falls. It's about 30 feet high with two *small* pools below. You can take a cold shower if you climb above the high pool to a ledge under the main stream. If you were to continue down this trail (Likeke Trail), you'd eventually end up near the Likelike Highway (Hwy 63), just before the Wilson Tunnel. (You don't want to do that today.)

To get here from the intersection of the Pali Highway (61) and Kamehameha (83) in Kailua, take Kamehameha a short ways until it goes under H-3. Then look for Kionaole Road in the left side and take it to the golf course parking lot.

Maunawili Falls Hike
(2.5 Miles Round Trip)

This is a small but pretty and user-friendly waterfall on the windward side, and the hiking is straightforward. It's 1.3 miles each way and will involve 500 feet of climb round-trip. Most people will take 40–60 minutes each way, but if it's muddy (which can be pretty often), it'll take longer. You'll have to cross the

Maunawili Stream once, though during normal flow you'll *probably* be able to boulder-hop and keep your feet dry.

The trailhead starts at the intersection of Maunawili Road and Kelewina Road in Kailua. From the Pali Highway (Hwy 61) turn onto the *second* Auloa Road (the one that's *not* across from Kamehameha Highway), and stay on the left fork to veer onto Maunawili Road. Take that to the end to Kelewina Road, and park around the corner on Lola Place.

The trail is beautiful, jungly and fairly easy to follow because it's heavily used, though muddy. (Proof is in the form of the large number of orphaned flip-flops and shoes along the way.) Bring bug spray. It's a fairly constant incline upward for the first mile. You'll see ginger, heliconia and banana sprinkled along the way. Some of the trees have exotic vines all over them. Wretched coffee addicts (like me) will appreciate the wild coffee trees lining the trail in several spots. They have dark, slightly wrinkled leaves and small white blossoms at times. On the Big Island, where coffee is grown commercially, the blossoms are so nu-

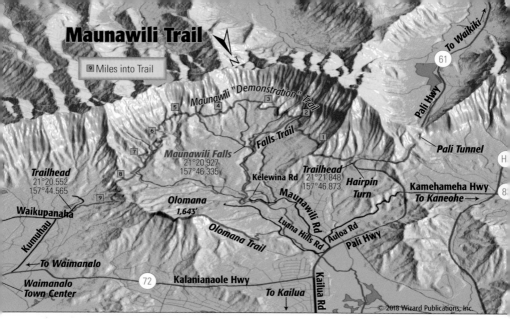

Maunawili "Demonstration" Trail

To Waikiki

61

Pali Hwy

Falls Trail

Pali Tunnel

H

Maunawili Falls
21°20.927
157°46.335

Kelewina Rd

Trailhead
21°21.848
157°46.873

Hairpin
Turn

Kamehameha Hwy
To Kaneohe →

8

Trailhead
21°20.552
157°44.565

Maunawili Rd

Olomana
1,643'

Luana Hills Rd

Auloa Rd

Pali Hwy

Waikupanaha

Kumuhau

Olomana Trail

← To Waimanalo

Waimanalo
Town Center

72

Kalanianaole Hwy

To Kailua
↓

Kailua Rd

© 2018 Wizard Publications, Inc.

merous when blooming it's sometimes called Kona snow.

Just before the stream crossing you'll see a small concrete channel. This was built long ago to harness spring water from Api Spring, which you'll see coming out of the mountain.

About 400 feet after the spring, you'll cross the stream. Follow the trail to the left that parallels the stream. Soon you'll come to a bench and a set of stairs leading 110 feet down to the stream below. At the bottom the main trail leads back into the jungle. *Don't* follow the main trail here. Follow the faint trail to the right of the stream stream another 500 feet, and you'll be there. Time to claim your prize—a waterfall that you can wade under. Since there aren't a huge number of accessible waterfalls on O'ahu, you probably *won't* have it to yourself. We've seen it empty for 20 minutes at a stretch *at most*, and we've seen it packed with locals on weekends. There's a trail on the far side of the falls that leads up to a platform that locals jump off, but it's steep and treacherous, and we don't recommend it. If you do it

anyway, check where you'll be jumping *before* you leap.

Maunawili Demonstration Trail
(9.3 Miles One Way)

There's a bowl-shaped valley called Maunawili tucked into the Ko'olau Mountain range that's mauka (toward the mountains) of Kailua town. The northeastern tip of this valley is defined by Olomana Peak. The northwestern tip is what the Pali Highway punches through. In between is a wonderland containing one of O'ahu's finest hikes.

Now there are several ways to skin this cat. The best way, *by far*, is as a shuttle hike—starting from the west and ending in the east. Now, we realize that renting a separate cheap-o car for the day and leaving it at the other end is a burden that many won't bear. Fair enough. We'll describe it from one end to the other and, if you only use one car, you can hike it one way until you're halfway to satisfied, then turn around and go back. But consider springing for the extra car or hail an Uber or a taxi; this one's worth it.

You may read elsewhere that this hike only climbs a few hundred feet. Don't you believe it. That false notion is obtained by casually looking at topographic maps, noting that the trail starts at 600 feet, tops out at 1,000 or so (it's actually 1,120), never deviates from the contour lines *too much*, and guessing. Sounds good. But when we used a GPS with a built-in altimeter to keep track of all the "little hills and dales," we got very different results. You may only climb a hundred or so feet with each wiggle on a map—which barely shows up on a topo. But do that 25 times or so, and together those little climbs add up to 2,460 feet of climbing over 9.5 miles. And that's *without* the side trip to the falls. It's not until the second half of the trail that those climbs start to get tiring.

Read these two paragraphs slowly—there's a lot of meat in them. The hike starts at the long, hairpin-turn pullout on the Kailua side of the Pali Tunnel.

From H-1 near Waikiki, you'll go 7 miles up the Pali Hwy, through the second tunnel, and pull over at the marked lookout after the runaway truck ramp. The trailhead starts here toward the right of the pullout.

If you're leaving a car at the other end, take the Kalanianaole Highway (72) to Waimanalo. Go mauka (toward the mountain) at Kumuhau Street, right when it ends at Waikupanaha, then go 0.25 miles until you see a turnout on the right side at the trailhead. Driving back with your *other* car to that hairpin turn from here, you'll get back on the Pali Highway going mauka, drive past the hairpin (which you can't turn into from that side) through the tunnels, eventually turn right at the exit for the wayside park, back up the mountain, around through the wayside,

A pack-laden hiker marvels at the fluted walls of Maunawili Valley.

back onto the highway going toward Kailua, and back through the tunnels again to the hairpin turn. (Phew!) See map on page 204.

Now you begin this memorable hike. After a couple minutes on the trail you'll continue straight at the intersection of the Pali Trail. As you start to leave the traffic noise behind, the trail begins to wind through lush forest, and the views change rapidly. In one moment you're overlooking Kailua and the coast, then turn a corner and you're looking at a wild and lush valley. Around another corner is a mountain carpeted with lush ferns, and around another you're overlooking a pretty banana farm. Many hikes on O'ahu require a long climb, culminating in a grand view at the top. This hike rewards you incrementally along the way. You never have to go too long without a treat.

About 2 miles into the trail, you'll come to an intersection… and a decision. Up until now you've had it fairly easy in the elevation department—somewhat gradual climbs. About 0.8 miles down that optional ridge is **Maunawili Falls** (see page 203), a small but pleasant falls to spend some time. (Parts of this trail can be a bit overgrown.) But it means giving up (and then reclaiming) 500 feet of elevation quickly. If you're doing an out-and-back hike, it's worth a stop. If you're going all the way to Waimanalo, you may not have the time or juice to go to the falls. Either way, at least go down the trail about 5 minutes, then turn around. The perspective of the fluted cliffs of Ko'olau is mind-boggling.

Staying on the Maunawili "Demonstration" Trail (as it's called), you'll find the variety of plants amazing. Ti plants, tree ferns, kukui trees, wild orchids, 'ohi'a

You won't be alone on the Ka'iwa Ridge Hike, so you'll have to share the awesome views of the Moku-lua Islands.

trees, koa trees—such a nice mixture in this valley. And the birds are more numerous than at almost any other place on the island. Especially delightful are the shamas, with their beautifully complex song. In places the bird chatter and music is intense enough, depending on the time of day, to drown out conversation.

Mile after mile, the views and forest just keep getting better and better. About halfway in, you've now left behind nearly all traces of civilization. The trail zigzags over and over again into Eden-like lushness. You may even come across a small waterfall or two along the way, if it's been raining recently.

After 8 miles or so the visions of beauty might start getting supplanted by visions of cold beer. At least they did with us. You'll arrive at an intersection underneath powerlines. Go to the right here and at the other two intersections ahead, and you'll eventually reach your car—and soon those cold beers.

This 9.3-mile trail is on the side of a mountain much of the time, giving opportunities to take a tumble if you are particularly clumsy. Also, keep track of the time it's taking. You want to leave early enough to take your time and to ensure you're not on the trail in the dark. Hiking shoes are best as several areas may be muddy, especially the second half. But overall, this is a well-cared-for and easy-to-follow trail.

Ka'iwa Ridge Hike/Lanikai Pillbox Trail
(1 Mile Round Trip)

It's super popular, and it's short—only about a half mile each way. Over that distance you'll gain almost 500 feet, so expect to puff and pant and wheeze and whine. But the views of the Mokulua Islands 1.25 miles away and dreamy **Lanikai Beach** below make it worth the sweat. Best times are either sunrise (if you're so motivated) or late afternoon when the sun is behind you. (The water actually looks the most blue at midday, but you don't want to hike this trail in the heat—there's not enough air in all Kailua to fill your lungs. Plus, that's probably when you want to be in the water anyway.)

In Kailua, drive as if you're going to Lanikai Beach, then take a right on Kaelepulu Drive. Just before it ends at a private gate, look to the left for a cyclone fence. The trail is at the top of that unnamed road along the fence. At the top are a couple of WWII military pillboxes (concrete, dug-in bunkers) used for observation. The view is best from the second one. Parking can be a challenge, so you'll likely have to park farther away and walk to the trailhead. See map on page 74.

Kawainui Marsh Path
(3 Miles Round Trip)

This is a 1.4-mile (each way) dead flat cemented path through the Kawainui Marsh—sort of Hawai'i's version of the Everglades on a tinier scale. It's not much of an exaggeration to say that once you've seen the first 60 seconds or so, you've seen it all. Swamps are not exactly a hotbed of variety when it comes to scenery. Nonetheless, it's popular with walkers and joggers, and the views of the distant mountains are pleasing in the morning or afternoon. There are two places to park. The north end is the better of the two. In Kailua, take Oneawa to Kaha. The path hooks from the right side.

Pu'u Ma'eli'eli Trail/
Kane'ohe Bay Pillbox
(2.4 Miles Round Trip)

This hike has one of the best ratios of payoff-to-effort-expended of any trail in Hawai'i. A roughly 45-minute hike

Kane'ohe Bay finally reveals itself from atop Pu'u Ma'eli'eli.

(less on the way back) leads to an elevated, panoramic view of Kane'ohe Bay on O'ahu's east side. It's the closest thing you can get to an aerial perspective without paying for a helicopter tour.

You gain about 600 feet, but it's not quite as hard as it sounds. The trail starts with a long dirt hill that turns extremely muddy and slippery if it's been raining recently, and there's one steep part with a rope (which you probably won't need, but it's nice that it's there). But aside from the heart-pounding beginning on the long-dirt hill, it's mostly a gentle incline, and the trail is well-defined. (There are several narrow side trails connecting to this one, but it's usually obvious which is the main trail. If you get confused, just remember to always stick to the path that leads up.)

The trail starts directly across from the **Valley of the Temples**. Take the Kahekili Highway (Hwy 83) north through Kaneohe and find a spot to park on Hui Iwa Street. After parking, walk back to the highway and turn left (south, as if heading toward Kailua). The entrance is on the left (ocean) side of the road, just before the end of the long guardrail. It's mostly a shaded walk through the woods.

When you reach the top of the big hill (you'll know it when you hit it), be careful to avoid falling into the first WWII pillbox—it's buried, and you'll walk right over an open hole in the roof. Almost immediately after you'll come to the second bunker and the end of the trail. What a view! From here, you can see the Kualoa Mountains and Chinaman's Hat to the left, the 1,000-acre sunken island in the middle of the bay, and Marine Corps Base Hawai'i and Coconut Island to the right. Sit and enjoy it. If someone ever builds a zipline from up here down to the ocean, they'll be a hero. But until then, you'll have to return the way you came.

Waihe'e Falls Hike (3 Miles Round Trip)

This moderately easy, 1.5-mile hike on a dirt, road gains 750 feet and takes you through lush rainforest before placing you at the base of the 30-foot Waihe'e Falls. To get to the trailhead, drive north of Kane'ohe where Hwy 830 merges into

Hwy 83. Take your first left *after* the Hygienic Store onto Waiheʻe Road, and follow it until it ends at a gate. Parking near the gate is tight, so leave your car by the street curb. See map on page 85.

The sign on the gate reads "Keep Out," but that's apparently outdated since we *confirmed* from the state and the Board of Water Supply that you're now allowed to hike into Waiheʻe Valley. After passing through the gap in the fence on the left, a gravel road stretches into the forest. This will take you all the way to the falls with a few interesting stops along the way. This hike is a nice one to do if you don't want to get too dirty, and after all, it's not too often you can gain access to a nice waterfall on Oʻahu, let alone have a gravel road to walk right to it.

After a half mile (15 minutes) you'll reach a popular swimming hole in the stream on the left. We've seen kids jumping off the spillway, but check the depth of the pool first and then decide if you're comfortable with it. Just after this, there will be a small clearing backed by an ominous concrete façade with a locked metal door at its base. This is one of only a few *dike tunnels* on the island. It's like a horizontal well cut into the water table of the mountain. (Notice the water flowing from under the door.) The Board of Water Supply used to give tours here until 9/11 caused them to heighten security. Now they only schedule tours for elementary school kids.

From here the road is less maintained, and it gets much steeper. Look for openings in the trees along the road for views of the valley walls. This stretch is a banyan tree forest, and you'll see many of these interesting giants growing off the sides of the road. You're getting close when you come to a colossal banyan on the right hand side, partially growing in the road. The road goes about 20 feet farther, and you can see the falls through the trees straight ahead. Follow the path on the end of the road, and you'll pop out at the base. There is no pool to swim in, but you can easily take a refreshing shower under these cascading waters.

NORTH SHORE HIKING

Northern Tip Empty Beach Walk
(Mileage Varies)

Although the beaches on Oʻahu are rarely deserted, here's an exception. The northern tip from the Kahuku Golf Course almost to the Turtle Bay Resort (about 5 miles) is beach and beachrock (sandstone). And since there's no convenient access (except for a club that has the keys to the landowner's locks), it's nearly always deserted during the week. Though not technically a public access, for years locals (mainly surfers) have been parking at the public golf course at the end of Puuluana Road and discreetly walking to the left of the parking lot along a dirt road to the shoreline. See map on page 87. And although the county has their typical "No Trespassing" signs at the golf course, the wink-and-nod system seems to be in effect, from what we've observed. (Theft can be a problem here, so don't leave anything valuable in your car.) Although the land *behind* the beach is private, all beaches are public in Hawaiʻi, so stay at the shoreline to stay in a public area.

Winds are virtually always blowing along here, and the frothing whitecaps, smell of the sea spray and the empty shoreline all combine to make a memorable walk. Remember the trick to walking in sand—gentle, relaxed strides while lightly striking the sand almost flat-footed. You probably won't want to swim

The wild, windy beach near the northern tip of the island makes an ideal secluded beach walk.

here since rip currents are common. One downside is that this location seems to attract lots of flotsam and jetsam. It also occasionally attracts… non-permitted long-term campers who don't exactly exude aloha.

CENTRAL O'AHU HIKING

Waimano Falls (3 Miles Round Trip)

Waterfalls are difficult to find on Oahu, and these two are gems. It's popular with residents, so you probably won't have this place to yourself. It's fairly short but steep and well worth the effort to get here. Most of the hike *to* the falls is

downhill. The way back is what gets your heart pumping. With all the undulations, you're gonna climb 1,200 feet.

You start on the Manana trail, north of Pearl City. Park your car in the residential neighborhood, and walk through the gate at the end of the cul-de-sac. The first half mile is paved to a water tank. Once unpaved, the trail can be slippery on the exposed roots. There are some nice lookouts on either side of the trail near the power lines; take your time here to enjoy the sweeping views. Soon you will be going downhill under cover of the forest. Just under a mile into the hike the trail splits. To the right, the trail ascends a hill, and to the left it descends, traversing the valley. We recommend that you go right, up the hill on the way to the falls, and take the other trail on the way out. Once you get to the top of the hill, the rest of the way to the falls is entirely downhill. Starting with what's locally known as "cardiac hill," this steep hill is a couple hundred feet long and is covered with exposed roots, and if it's wet, can be quite muddy.

Once at the bottom, the trail becomes narrow and windy, and there are a lot more rocks to trip over. Soon you'll find yourself on a very narrow trail surrounded by thick strawberry guava trees. It feels like you're in a tunnel of trees. When the trail splits (at 1.3 miles), go left for the more direct, easier to follow route. Soon the trail turns sharply downhill and you arrive at the first pool. The falls at this pool aren't very tall, but the pool is fairly deep, and you may see people jumping off the rocks or from the rope swing into the water. Use your judgment as to whether and how you enter the water. If you look to the right of the falls, you will see a faint, very steep trail going up to the top of the falls. Follow this path, and you'll come to a shallow pool with a very picturesque and much taller (perhaps 25 feet) waterfall. The pool at the bottom isn't as deep, but it is nice for wading. There is also a trail on the right side of the falls that goes up to a bird's-eye view of both falls and pools. Soak up the wild beauty of this place and have a snack. You're gonna need it.

Remember Cardiac Hill? Well, it didn't get that name coming down. But we have a trick for you that will help. Stay to the left side while going up, and keep an eye out for a path skirting the edge of the valley. If you take this trail, you'll emerge at the very first fork you came to on your way in, and you will have saved yourself some cardio.

To get to the trailhead, take H-1 west and stay right to merge onto H-201. Then stay right to rejoin H-1 and take exit 10 to Moanalua Road. At the third traffic light go right onto Waimano Home Road, then three more traffic lights and take a left onto Komo Mai Drive. The trailhead is at the end of this dead-end road. Park on the side of the road away from the no parking signs. Please be respectful of the neighbors here so this trail can continue to be available to the public.

WAI'ANAE HIKING

'Ohikilolo Point (0.7 Miles Round Trip)

This is a short hike—only 10–15 minutes out to it. But it leads to one of the most interesting lattice-like sandstone benches we've seen in Hawai'i. Once you get to the stony peninsula, walk out as far as the ocean safely allows toward the water. This is all lithified sand, and the ocean is dissolving this former sand dune, creating sharp, awkward footing. Think of it as a large rocky bench that's been bathed in acid. Many of the places at the outer edge have holes and tiny arches eaten into the sandstone.

Farther back you'll see lots of salt in the depressions. During the winter, giant surf sometimes washes over the entire bench. If that's the case when you're visiting, there won't be much to see here (other than your own demise if you're foolish enough to walk out onto the bench when it's being pounded). Those large boulders that lined the trail on your way out were tossed there during such periods, which gives you an idea how strong the surf can be at times.

To get here, drive to Wai'anae to near the end of the road. After mile marker

Bring water and sunscreen, because you'll be climbing 860 feet in the cruel sun to get to the top of Pu'u-o-hulu Kai.

17 is Makua Cave on the right. Park across the street from the cave, and take the trail on the left toward the shoreline, then walk left along the shore. The point is just after 'Ohikilolo Beach. Don't leave anything valuable in your car here.

Pu'u-o-hulu Kai/Pink Pillbox Trail
(2 Miles Round Trip)

Just past Nanakuli on the west side, there's an 860-foot hill called Pu'u-o-hulu Kai with a trail winding its way up the side that leads to five WWII pillbox bunkers. The most prominent of these (you can see it from the road) is painted bright pink. (Pretty much every old pillbox on O'ahu is covered in graffiti, but the people who painted this one did it to support a friend fighting breast cancer.)

The trail is worth hiking as part of a day of activities on the west side, or if you're staying in the Ko Olina resort area, but it isn't something you'd drive from Waikiki to do. From up top, Ma'ili Beach and the Wai'anae mountains unfold before you, making it worth the sweat

that has poured out of you. Since this is on the west side, it's a fantastic place to watch the sunset, but that means hiking up in the late afternoon when it's hot (there's no shade on the trail) and hiking back down in the dark. You also don't *ever* want to leave valuables in your car on this side of the island.

To get here, hang a right after the hill onto Kaukama Road and drive 0.25 miles until you see the unmarked trail (it starts by light post #10) on the right side of the road. It's less than a mile to the top, but bring water and a hat. Also, the loose rocks and desert-like plants will make you glad you wore closed-toe shoes.

Ka'ena Point (4.8 Miles Round Trip)

There are two ways to hike out to the westernmost tip of the island at Ka'ena Point—from the west side of the island heading north, or from the north shore heading west. Starting on the west side is the shorter way to go (and the way described here). Drive along Hwy 93/930 until it ends at Yokohama Bay. Nearly every map out there shows a 4WD road wrapping around Ka'ena Point. And nearly every map is wrong. The "road" soon becomes a trail, and it's not possible—nor would it be legal—to drive all the way. See map on page 114.

Almost immediately into the hike there are opportunities via short paths from the road to amble over to the shoreline, which is dominated by sandstone lovingly sculpted by nature into a series of chasms, arches and holes. It's fun to look down into them as the ocean snakes its way through the maze.

Be aware that, although the wind may be calm here, you're in what pilots call a rotor from the mountain behind you, and wind gusts can strike from any direction at any time. (That's why pilots *hate* rotors.) Look up and you'll probably see clouds racing by in the *opposite* direction from the wind that's blowing on you.

In several areas the road exposes itself for what it really is—a former railroad track—and some of the trestles are still visible. In the old days this was how sugar cane was transported from Hale'iwa to Honolulu.

At 0.7 miles from your car, after a rare wide spot in the road, look for a series of interconnected tidepools below, one suitable for swimming if the ocean isn't raging. (Vague directions, we know, but there's little to reference along here.) It's an interesting place to watch the way the ocean exchanges water into various pools.

Be alert to opportunities to walk along the shoreline or along one of the many trail segments that are on the berm next to the road. It'll take longer, but it's more interesting, and you can always take the faster dirt road on the way back.

At 1.2 miles from your car, just below some old railroad ties hanging over the edge of the trail, you may hear a sharp-pitched, gasping sound. Throughout Hawai'i, blowholes are relatively common, where the ocean undercuts the lava bench, shooting water and sometimes loud air though a hole. Though this one is man-made (probably drilled by the railroad), it produces the loudest horn we've ever heard when the ocean's cooperating. There's also a nice sea arch just past the blowhole.

Ka'ena Point is as far west as you can go.

From here on, a couple of narrow stretches convert the road to a trail. Riding a mountain bike here can be fun. After 2 miles you'll come to a gap where a 2006 landslide took out part of the trail, but there's an easy and obvious path around it above the landslide.

As you approach the point, things start to change. During normal trade wind weather you and the nearby ocean have been protected from the wind by the mountain next to you. Near Ka'ena Point a line of demarcation in the form of a distinct wind line abruptly transports you from a protected world to a windy one. Look for the transition line offshore. The ocean is often a white-capped, frothy mess, and you'll feel instantly cool.

The Ka'ena Point Natural Area Reserve is fenced off to protect against predators because this is where many of the island's albatrosses live. They burrow holes in the sand here. Go through the gate and then stay on the trails so you don't disturb them if it's nesting season. At Ka'ena Point itself there's a rock offshore which marks the westernmost point on O'ahu. This is called *Pohaku o Kaua'i*. According to legend, a demigod named Maui tried to bring together O'ahu and Kaua'i. Casting his magical hook across the channel, he snagged Kaua'i and gave a huge tug. Unfortunately, the hook came loose (landing inland and creating Ka'au Crater), and only a huge boulder from Kaua'i was pulled ashore here—the rock that you see in front of you. Hawaiians so believed in their legends that the channel to this day is called the Ka'ie'ie Waho Channel, named after the towline made from the 'ie'ie root that Maui used in his attempt.

This is a great place to be if the island is getting big surf from both the north and the south. The rocks at this point are getting slammed from northern swells

that may have originated in Alaska. The south side of the rocks may be assaulted by New Zealand-born swells. There's also a good chance you'll see some endangered Hawaiian monk seals. (Keep your distance.)

You're 2.4 miles from your car back at Yokohama Bay, and you get to enjoy terrific views of the Waianae Mountains on the return hike because of the way the coastline curves on this part of the island. If you'd rather do this hike starting on the north shore, you can. It's windier on that side, and almost a mile longer, but there are some wonderful natural treasures along the way, including a hidden beach and a natural infinity pool. See the description in the "Past the Pavement" section of the **North Shore Sights** chapter for more details on page 96.

Mount Ka'ala Summit
(8 Miles Round Trip)

If you're the type who likes to bag summits, this is your hike. The highest peak on the island is Mt. Ka'ala at 4,025 feet. While it's true that there is a beautiful, smooth paved road leading to the top, it's *not* for riffraff like you and me. It's gated and only available to government personnel who work on the radar up here. *They* drove up from the North Shore. *You'll* be hiking from Wai'anae on the west side.

First, this hike is *not* for beginners. It's a moderately dangerous trail of a little less than 8 miles round trip that takes 7–8 hours to hike, so be sure to start early. Bring a long-sleeved shirt for the top where it gets chilly. The trail is well maintained and is marked with purple spots on trees, bushes and rocks.

The trail begins at the end of Waianae Valley Road. (Try to ignore the broken down cars and garbage on the opposite

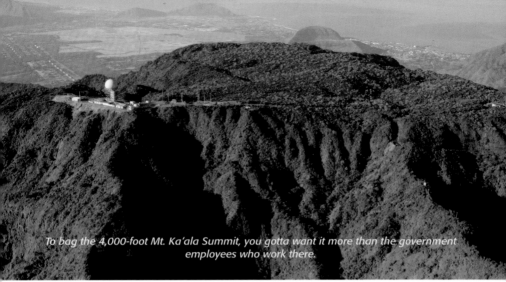
To bag the 4,000-foot Mt. Ka'ala Summit, you gotta want it more than the government employees who work there.

side of the parking lot.) Walk around the metal gate, then start ascending steeply up a paved road, first passing a water tank on the left, then Waianae Water Well 1 on the right. You'll also see hunters' trails on the right. Don't be surprised if you run into a large pack of dogs and their local owners.

The pavement ends at Water Well 2. Continue up the steep dirt road. Close to the top of the dirt road will be a covered picnic table. Take the trail on the right by some large boulders and purple trail markers. As you get to a ridge, bear right around the rocks and turn left down into a gully and cross a small stream. Out of the gully, following the trail, you will come to a partially open ridge (stop to soak in the great views) surrounded by strawberry guava. If you're lucky, you'll find a few bunches. (The ripe ones are deep red and very sweet. The light red kind are a bit tart but still edible.)

Continuing up the path, you'll come to a huge boulder with a rope to ease your passage. In fact, from here it's all a steep incline using ropes with some extremely narrow footpaths. Eventually at the top is a sign for Ka'ala Nature Preser-vation. After all the rope sections you will come to the ridge top, which is a bog with trees covered in thick moss. The trail becomes a boardwalk for a time until it ends and you climb the last ropes to the top—the end of the trail at Mount Ka'ala Summit.

Up there is a radio tower with an ac-cess road called Mt. Ka'ala (which is gated because it's only for government personnel). For the best views turn right at the road, come to the gate of the radio tower entrance and make a left. Walk around the gate with a swing door to a second door, and you'll be in the back of the tower facing a incredible view of Honolulu.

HORSEBACK RIDING

When people envision riding a horse in Hawai'i, they often picture themselves riding along a beach. On O'ahu, **Hawai'i Polo Trail Rides** (808-220-5153) comes closest to allowing you to experience that fantasy. Close, because most of the trail is on private land behind the beach, not actually down where the surf meets the sand. (Still scenic though.) They offer

a 75-minute afternoon ride for $88 and a sunset tour is $98. It's $128 for private and advanced rides. The private rides (minimum two people) are the same route and times. The advanced rides include an advanced trot and cantering in the field in addition to the trail ride. Closed some Sundays. On the far west side of the island's north shore.

Turtle Bay (808-293-6000) is a nose-to-tail experience. You won't be galloping along with sand and salt flying everywhere. But some portions parallel the fabulous North Shore at Turtle Bay, and there's something inexplicably charming about that scene. It's $85 for a 45-minute ride, $115 for a 75-minute version in the late afternoon. Near the northern tip of the island at Turtle Bay Resort on Hwy 83. They can be bad about returning phone calls.

Kualoa Ranch (808-237-7321) has 1-hour rides for $85; 2 hours for $130. It's totally nose-to-tail walking-only, but the mountain scenery is *gorgeous*. On the windward side 10 miles north of Kane'ohe on Hwy 83. Good for novices, but Kualoa is sort of a visitor-processing machine.

Happy Trails (808-638-7433) has hour-long rides in the hills above Waimea Bay on the North Shore for $95 for 90 minutes. ($115 gets you 2 hours on the same trail with more stops.) The ride itself is entirely nose-to-tail with no passing permitted because the horses are inherently competitive, and you could cause an unintended race. The trail is in a forest almost the whole time with limited views. Bring bug spray.

It's our observation that those with little to no experience and maybe a bit skittish will enjoy Kualoa the most. Riders with the most experience will probably like Hawai'i Polo the most. The rest will likely fall somewhere in between. If you've never (or rarely) ridden horses, remember that horses respect strength. They can smell fear a mile away. Be confident. And if you're not confident…fake it. Don't ever let them feel that they're in charge.

Call them Jet Skis or Wave Runners (which are brand names), these motorcycles of the sea can be rented at several locations around the island. Sometimes you'll be restricted to a small area usually set off by buoys. But if want to hover above the ocean, then turn those nozzles down for a more thrilling ride.

Early morning is usually the most smooth. Late afternoons can be choppy from the wind. Late morning seems to offer a good balance of smooth water seasoned by a little texture. Most people get tuckered out after 30–45 minutes, especially if you're like me and you drive it like it's stolen.

Companies like to encourage riders to double up, claiming it's "more fun." Hardly. Of course, having two people on one jet ski brings more revenue to the company while only using one machine. (Hmm, pretty cynical, aren't we?) Regardless, doubling up increases the chance of someone falling off, from what we've observed.

One thing you might want to consider is wearing goggles. Frankly, riding jet skis without them can be annoying if there's any wind. Companies that won't provide goggles should be avoided.

The best one is **Watercraft Connection** (808-637-8006) in Hale'iwa on the North Shore. They rent them for $100 per 45 minutes, and you can ride them in the open ocean, not on a circular track like the other two. Goggles available for $3. You must be at least 16 years of age to drive the jetski.

Aloha Jet Ski (808-721-1754) operates out of Ke'ehi Lagoon, a very sheltered body of water near the airport. Cheapo goggles available for $5. (You're better off bringing your own.) $89 (one person) or $134 for two people for 45 minutes on a circular track.

H2O Sports Hawai'i (808-396-0100) is at Maunalua Bay near Hawai'i Kai, 20 minutes east of Waikiki. They charge $80 for only 30 minutes on a circular track. No goggles available. $110 for two people per jetski. Not available weekends or holidays.

ROCKETMAN

Not really a jet ski—technically an *ultra-modified* jet ski—but we didn't know where else to put it. This is where a picture is worth a thousand words. Imagine

One of these activities is very cool. But the other is epic.

a couple of fire hoses shooting you up into the air, powered by a jet ski engine. There are two ways to do this.

Jetlev is like a backpack. You do the steering with guidance from your instructor, courtesy of a speaker in your helmet. They only thing they control on your first "flight" is the throttle via a remote control. After some instruction, they strap you tightly to this jet pack and start you out slowly as you drag yourself through the water. If you take to it well, you'll eventually find yourself 10–15 feet above the water, steering slow circles next to a fixed water platform that holds your instructor and any witness (for an extra $30) you want to watch your first jet pack flight. You'll get about 15 minutes, and it will zip by faster than you wish. All this can be yours for a mere *$199*. Expensive? Definitely, so look for discounts. And if you don't catch on, you'll merely flop around in the ocean like an idiot with everyone on the water platform watching. (But you'll do fine. I have faith.) Either way, this is one unique ride, and as soon as I was done, I wanted to do it again. These $100,000 contraptions—called **Jetlev**—ain't exactly common, and chances like this don't come around often. **H2O Sports Hawai'i** (808-396-0100) does this offshore Hawai'i Kai in Maunalua Bay. Photos and video are extra, and when you're done with the jet pack, you gotta wait for them to take you back to shore when they are good and ready. Not available weekends or holidays.

X-treme Watersports (808-670-1362) has a flyboard, which they market as **Flyboarding Hawai'i**. You meet at Kewalo Basin before heading out to Sand Island. They aren't very organized, and sometimes you'll end up with very long waits despite when you were told you would

be doing this. It's $28 extra if you want to have someone ride along and take pictures of you.

Now for the experience. It's absolutely epic! We found it easier to learn than we expected with waterjets attached to your fixed boots. It feels similar to a snowboard. Turning takes some practice, and if you are proficient enough they might let you do dives like a dolphin. Keep a constant eye on the jet ski. You are pulling it (and the instructor who controls your throttle) around, and if you get too close, they'll kill your jets to keep you from smacking into it. Is it worth $399 for an hour? (Half that for half the time.) Let's reverse engineer that. If you can stand parting with $400, this is an *awesome* place to blow it. And it's way better (and cheaper if judged by the minute) than Jetlev.

Ocean kayaking O'ahu's nearshore waters can be heavenly. There's something unmistakably exotic about watching your kayak's shadow slide over coral reef systems on your way to an offshore island.

The two best places to kayak are **Kane'ohe Bay** and **Kailua Bay**. Although many of the resorts rent kayaks for use off Waikiki, this is a relatively dull paddle. Do it for the novelty of kayaking, but not for the sights.

KANE'OHE BAY

One of the most dramatic kayak trips you can take—and the one with the smoothest waters—is one that almost no one does for a simple reason—it's to a sunken island of over 1,000 acres that you can't see from shore. It's Hawai'i's version of Atlantis.

One of our favorite kayak destinations is the 1,000-acre sunken island in Kane'ohe Bay, lightly used during the week but enjoyed by locals on weekends, like the day this photo was shot.

The central part of Kane'ohe Bay has a *huge* barrier-type reef. (Technically, it's not a true barrier reef, but it has the same effect.) Unlike most reefs around Hawai'i, however, this one is nearly as broad as it is wide and is covered in most areas by sand. During the ice age 12,000 years ago this area was part of O'ahu, 180 feet above sea level. When the earth warmed and the seas rose, it became separated from O'ahu as an island, then vanished, transforming itself into the fringing reef we know today. At low tide part of it is still exposed as a football field-sized beach rising from the sea. At its farthest edge, a stranded sandstone island, the "summit" of this Atlantis forms the only visible remnant, towering a mere 14 feet above sea level.

See Kailua Bay (below) for details about **renting a Kayak** (except on Sundays). There's also a company at Kane'ohe Bay next to He'eia State Park called **Holokai Kayak & Snorkel** (808-781-4773) for similar prices. (See map on page 72.) Convenient location. They contacted us and implied that they were the only game in town for kayak rentals because "the State

no longer allows kayaks to launch at the pier." Uh, with all due respect, that's not exactly correct. You don't have to rent from them. You just can't use the boat ramp. It's far easier anyway to launch from the beach to the left of the pier in front of the Kane'ohe Canoe Club. Another option is to launch from the shore to the right side of the boat ramp. The water is shallow, and there is grass and gravel to gear up on instead of slippery concrete. Either option is legal (we checked with the state and the canoe club), and both are more comfortable options anyway.

When you launch, look behind you at the mountain peak with a powerline pole on it—that's what you'll be paddling toward when you return. The edge of the reef is just over a mile to the north. Look for Ka-papa Island—the only part of this Atlantis you can see—and paddle toward it. The waters are almost always smooth here. You may have a headwind going out—which should increase later and help you coming back. Almost immediately you'll go over shallow coral and fish. It's like snorkeling without the mask. Polarized sunglasses help you see through the glare.

Approaching the sunken island is otherworldly. Suddenly there's a sand beach 2–3 feet beneath your kayak, and you seem magically suspended above it as you glide along. To the left, if the tide is cooperating, a short paddle will bring you to the disappearing beach. On weekends locals bring their boats and their BBQs out and make a day of it. Weekdays you may have it to yourself. Even if the island is submerged, get out and walk along the shallows of this "beach." It's a surreal experience. Then look toward Kapapa Island. If you want to visit, head straight toward it from the south.

As you approach Kapapa, a strange phenomenon occurs. East shore surf, if it's up, is pounding at the outer edge of the shoal, but Kapapa Island is protecting you from it, creating a corridor of calmness except for the wraparound swells that are literally colliding with each other right under your kayak as you get nearer. Stay in the center to stay in the corridor. Once near Kapapa, the colliding wraparounds may start to become annoying, and you may want to hop out in the shallow water and walk your kayak ashore. (Water shoes are necessary as the ground is reefy here.)

The sandstone island is a good place to have your lunch under the shade of trees and gaze back at O'ahu and the shoal you just passed over. You're now 2.4 miles from where you launched your kayak. Exploring the island reveals lots of sandstone overhangs. Unfortunately, it might also reveal litter left by thoughtless fishermen who are too lazy to haul out what they hauled in. Return the way you came.

KAILUA BAY

A second ocean kayak trip is inside Kailua Bay, kayaking to **Flat Island** or one of the **Mokulua Islands** off Lanikai

Beach. (Only the left of these twin islands is landable—the other is a bird sanctuary.) Waters are usually fairly protected (but not nearly as protected as Kane'ohe Bay), and these offshore islands, while popular with other kayakers, still make a great destination. The northern Mokulua Island has a beach to sprawl onto. And Flat Island, or Popo'ia, has lots of pukas (holes) along its outer edge. Rental kayaks are not allowed on either island on Sundays, only privately owned.

If you want a shorter paddle to the Mokulua and are transporting your kayak, start from the far end of Lanikai Beach less than a mile from the islands.

For Kailua paddling, you'll have to rent from a company away from the beach and haul it to the beach. Expect to pay $45–$59 for a single, $55–$69 for a double for a *half* day. The following companies are all located in Kailua, and you'll have to strap it to the top of your car except for **Kailua Beach Adventures** (808-262-2555), which is close enough to put it on a cart and wheel it over: **Hawaiian Watersports** (808-262-5483), **Twogood Kayaks** (808-262-5656) rents and will deliver to a private residence, or put the kayak on your car. **Windward Watersports** (808-261-7873) will put the kayaks on your car, or they will deliver to a private residence.

An alternative is **Hawai'i Beach Time** (808-585-1474), which will deliver to vacation rentals, and their prices are better than the traditional kayak players.

OTHER KAYAKING DESTINATIONS

The **North Shore** has winds that are usually a kayaker's best friend—along the shore from north to south. If you can handle a shuttle paddle (kayak one way, and one of you takes the bus back to your car), put in at Waimea Bay and take out at

If the ocean's not your thing, the Kahana River makes a short but sweet jungle paddle.

Haleʻiwa for a nice wind-at-your-back-most-days, 5-mile tour of some of the island's prettiest beaches. Only paddle here when the ocean is calm, usually during the summer months (May–September).

The waters off **Hawaiʻi Kai** tend to be pretty placid most of the time, so paddling is less challenging, but water quality and views aren't as impressive.

The kayaking along the **Waiʻanae Coast**, especially toward the end of the highway near Yokohama Bay can be good. You probably won't have the same favorable following winds as the North Shore paddle, but the water tends to be wickedly clear.

KAHANA RIVER

This is the only river on the island that's worth kayaking, and it's super-relaxing. (Some would point to ʻAnahulu Stream as well, but it's not as compelling.) Kahana is a mile each way down a tropical, dripping-with-life river with pretty mountain views in the distance and trees overhanging the banks for shade.

You put in at Kahana Bay—look for the easy-to-miss Huilua Fishpond access road at the east end of the bay where you can literally drive right to the river mouth. This bay is 15 miles (25 minutes) north of Kaneʻohe on Hwy 83. Then paddle up the river under the highway bridge (on weekends, locals fishing off it might not appreciate your presence—we prefer to do this on weekdays). Since it's only 2 miles round-trip, don't dig in and paddle too furiously—it'll be over too quickly. Instead, paddle and glide and soak in the environment for a relaxing 1.5–2 hour cruise. In 2011 they filmed a tv show here called *The River* because it had good scenery. Make sure you bring lunch and repellent for mosquitoes. (If you forget the latter, then you thoughtfully brought *their* lunch.) When you're done, you can also paddle around normally protected Kahana Bay. Though the bay is reported to be a spawning area for hammerhead sharks, they ain't interested in you in your kayak.

RENTING A KAYAK

For renting *outside of Waikiki or Kailua Beach*, the biggest (and the most knowledgeable) kayak shop on the island is **Go Bananas** (808-737-9514) just outside of Waikiki. They'll strap the kayak(s) to your car, and you're off. They're cheaper than the Kailua companies. They also have a great selection of waterproof items. $30 per full day for a single, $45 for a double, add $10 for a 24-hour rental (which most of the other companies do as well).

In Hale'iwa on the North Shore, **Surf N' Sea** (808-637-9887) rents kayaks by the hour. Convenient for the area, but pricier than Go Bananas.

Also called kitesurfing. Imagine a modified wakeboard with fins at both ends. Then let a special, controllable four-line kite drag you along. As with windsurfing, you don't have to go the direction the wind takes you—you have control. Despite what some instructors tell you when they want to sign you up, it's harder to get up on the board than windsurfing and will take lots of lessons. But *oh*, what fun it is! More fun than windsurfing once you're comfortable on the board. One way you can prepare before you get here is to buy a two-string kite and master it so that you can instinctively maneuver the kite. It's not that hard, but it helps if you can steer the kite without thinking.

Lessons are *expensive* and seem to change with the whims of the company. **Windward Watersports** (808-261-7873) charge $179 for 3-hour group lessons, private for $279, or a course they call *chump to champ* that's 9 hours long. (They should probably call it chump to champ to *whooped…*) It costs

$479 for a two-person semi-private, or $699 for private.

Hawaiian Watersports (808-262-5483) gives lessons at Kailua Beach for $240 ($299 for private) for 3 hours per person. Call for more options and prices. Transportation to and from Waikiki available.

Honolulu Kite School (808-292-7022) has lessons at shallow flats in the water at a "secret location" that's accessible only by boat, instead of the beach. (I'm terrible with secrets—it's Kane'ohe Bay.) They also use an escort boat to coach you along the way. They offer 4-hour blocks for $399 and discounts for two people. Call for details.

The learning curve is steep. First you need to learn how to operate the kite (which is a hoot). Next comes body dragging. Though it sounds like something they do to you if your credit card is declined, it's actually when you let the kite drag you through the ocean while you manipulate it. Then comes the good part—*riding the board*—which may or may not happen during your first lesson.

SEGWAY TOURS

Remember Segway scooters? Those odd, upright transporters that were gonna revolutionize the world and the way cities were built, but instead just became an expensive way for security to patrol airports and such? There are a couple of companies doing tours on these, and if you've never ridden one, it's a cool novelty the first time.

We much prefer **Hele Huli Adventure Rentals** (808-293-6024). Their off-road versions allow you to cruise on trails, partially along the north shore Kahuku shoreline, through a somewhat beat-up forest and along a golf course. The "tour" part is not especially compelling—we wish they'd do less talking and more scootering—but overall, it's a fairly cool way to spend 90 minutes for $125. During the stopping time you'll find yourself always in motion, wiggling and leaning and twitching the scooter constantly because...well, *'cause you can.*

In Waikiki there's **Segway of Hawai'i** (808-941-3151). You'll feel much more restricted on this tour because of the urban environment. But they're cheaper, starting at $75 for a half-hour tour up to $170 for a 2-hour trip. **Segway of Hawai'i Kailua** (808-262-5511) does Segway tours in Kailua town starting at $90.

GARDEN TOURS

There are several gardens on the island, and they are by no means equal. The best are the Waimea Valley and Koko Crater.

Longtime visitors will be puzzled to see **Waimea Valley** (808-638-7766) listed under gardens. It used to be called **Waimea Falls Adventure Park** with lots of adventure activities. After years of legal wrangling, the Office of Hawaiian Affairs now controls the valley with a mindset of preservation plus the notion of cultural education. Think of it as a botanical garden with a waterfall. Someone must have gotten scared by a lawyer here, because you are *required* to wear a lifejacket if you swim near the waterfall.

The giant garden itself (1,875 acres) is beautiful, and the setting on the Waimea River is tranquil. Take the opportunities to veer from the main road and walk along the river. (If you don't bring mosquito repellent down near the river trail, you'll donate more blood than you ever

Waimea Valley, once a well-known adventure park, is now the island's prettiest botanical garden.

knew you had.) Most people make a bee-line to the falls 0.75 miles away (and slightly uphill) and take their time coming back. There are changing rooms at the falls if you brought your suit. The 40-foot-high falls dries up at times, especially in the summer. $16 to get in, $8 for kids 4–12. A golf cart shuttle to the waterfall is $6. At the mouth of Waimea Bay north of Hale'iwa on Hwy 83. You'll probably spend about 1.5 hours here. Tours are self-guided only.

Koko Crater Botanical Garden (808-522-7060) has a large plumeria grove filled with every color and scent of plumeria imaginable, though it only flowers in the spring months. There is a 2-mile loop trail that circles the basin of the entire crater. It's an extremely dry environment that lends itself nicely to support a pretty impressive collection of massive Dr. Seuss-looking cacti, dry land plants and palm trees along the way. The plants and cacti are nicely labeled, and you can grab a free brochure from the parking lot for a self tour of the 60-acre park. The price is right—it's free—and we've rarely seen more than a few people on our visits. See map on page 67.

Owned by the University of Hawai'i, **Lyon Arboretum** (808-988-0456) is located just minutes from Honolulu, but worlds away from the hustle and bustle of the city. With 194 acres of jungle and even an intermittent small waterfall, this is a nice place to get away for a couple of hours and explore a real rain forest environment. There are even wild cockatoos that echo through the forest, providing an exotic air to the wilderness. The trails are lined with unusual gingers, palms and a myriad of exotic flowers from around the world. The main trail is an old, uneven lava stone path; the side paths are narrow and can be very slippery. Bring bug spray and

hiking shoes. Admission and parking are free, but they gladly accept donations. To get there, click on the map feature or follow the directions to *Manoa Falls* on page 192. Once you see the paid parking lot for Manoa Falls, go past the lot and turn right onto what looks like a paved golf cart path (the road is very narrow). Drive past the gate on the narrow, moss-covered road, and it will dead end at the arboretum parking lot. Check in at the office/gift shop, and they will give you a map of the grounds.

Foster Botanical Garden (808-522-7066) is small—only 13.5 acres. But it's pretty, has some of the largest trees we've seen in Hawai'i—one with a diameter of 10 feet—and their hybrid orchid collection is particularly nice. It's $5 to get in, $1 for kids 6–12. At 50 N. Vineyard Blvd. From Waikiki, take McCully out, left on Beretania, right on Nuuanu, left on Vineyard.

Another option is the **Ho'omaluhia Park Botanical Garden** (808-233-7323) in Kane'ohe on Luluku Road. It's off Hwy 83 (Kamehameha Hwy) just north of H-3. This 400-acre garden (built by the U.S. Army Corps of Engineers as a flood protection tool to protect Kane'ohe) backs up against the Ko'olau Mountains, which are simply gorgeous in the morning light, and even has a 32-acre lake. It's run by the county, and admission is free. You don't need to do a lot of walking here since you can drive to the many parking lots, each of which is devoted to areas featuring plants from different parts of the world. Even if gardens aren't your thing, it might be worth a quick drive along the main road to get a vantage point of the mountains that is hard to achieve otherwise, and the health of the plants in this area is impressive. They used to allow you to bring your own *horse*, but stopped that practice. So if you were thinking about bringing your stallion from home, might as well nix that idea. Open 9 a.m. to 4 p.m.

In Central Oʻahu is the **Wahiawa Botanical Garden** (808-621-5463). Most of the 27 acres are in a ravine with marked plants along a primitive trail. The best part is the upper terrace near the entrance. It's more of a lush park with small, landscaped gardens throughout. Open areas are covered in groomed lawns, surrounded by stained concrete paths, ornate lampposts and benches. The garden started as an arboretum experiment in the 1950s, and they put more effort into maintaining the upper level than the ravine. Open 9 a.m. to 4 p.m., free admission. See map on page 102.

These last two gardens are must-misses. In Kahaluʻu is **Senator Fong's Plantation & Gardens** (808-239-6775). The tour seems more geared toward Japanese tour groups and at $15 isn't worth it. Closed Saturdays. The almost useless **Liliʻuokalani Botanical Garden** (808-522-7066) in Honolulu is a pretty poor excuse for a garden, and normally we'd steer you away from it. But it has one thing going for it—a small waterfall. (Of the four major Hawaiian islands, Oʻahu is the poorest when it comes to accessible waterfalls, so beggars can't be choosers.) Visit the falls and then leave—there ain't much else here for you. Admission is free, as it should be.

Parasailing is where you become a human kite, attached to a parachute and pulled by a boat via a long line. It's an 8-minute ride, though, which includes reeling in and reeling out. It's been our experience that parasailing *looks* more fun and thrilling than it really is and doesn't seem worth the money. Think of it as a $60 amusement ride. (People afraid of heights, however, will no doubt be properly terrified.)

One tip (*especially* for guys): Don't wear any slippery shorts, or you may cinch forward in your harness resulting in…the *longest* 8 minutes of your life.

The companies (except H2O) operate out of Kewalo Basin a few minutes west of Waikiki.

X-treme Watersports (808-670-1362) has traditionally been your best bet. They have four trips—$75 for 5 minutes on a 500-foot line, $80 for 7 minutes at 700 feet, $83 for 9 minutes on 850-foot line, or $90, and they'll reel out almost a quarter mile—1,000 feet—for 11 minutes.

Hawaiian Parasail (808-591-1280) has five options. $50 for 3 minutes on a 300-foot line, $60 for 6 minutes on a 600-foot line, $72 for 8 minutes on an 800-foot line or $85 for 10 minutes on a 1000-foot line—though they want 1–2 hours of your time from start to finish.

H2O Sports Hawaiʻi (808-396-0100) is out of Maunalua Bay 20 minutes east of Waikiki. It's $60 for 6 minutes on a 600-foot line, $75 for 8 minutes on an 800-foot leash.

You'd think that the most populous island in Hawaiʻi would have marginal SCUBA diving, but you'd be wrong. The diving here is incredible, and this is the shipwreck capital of Hawaiʻi.

WHERE TO DIVE

Although diving takes place all over the island, there are five main areas that most dive companies use. **Waiʻanae** in the west, the wrecks off **Waikiki**, **Hanauma Bay**, near **Hawaiʻi Kai** and the **North Shore** in the summer.

A convention of surgeonfish.

Overall, **Wai'anae** offers the best dive conditions. It's calm most of the year, and visibility is often 100 feet or more. We don't recommend late afternoon dives there since you'll be fighting traffic the whole way. (Morning trips there go *against* the traffic.) One of the more interesting Wai'anae dives is the **Mahi**. You'll get an idea of what happens to a ship that has been underwater since 1982 after two hurricanes and an embarrassing incident involving a Navy anchor. The ship has broken in half, but it's a fun dive, and it's often accompanied by patrols of spotted eagle rays flying in formation.

The wrecks off **Waikiki Beach** are probably our second choice, because divers *love* shipwrecks, even if it's a simple sunken fishing trawler, and the visibility once you're away from the shoreline tends to be 100-foot plus with diverse fish life. Waikiki dives are super convenient since the boats leave from Kewalo Basin a few minutes away on Ala Moana Boulevard. Describing the individual Waikiki companies seems pointless since there are only a half dozen or so big boats and about 50 companies that charter space on them. (You probably won't have any say as to which boat you're on.) In general, dive operators off Waikiki are diver processing machines, and we found little difference between them. Get 'em in; get 'em out. You'll probably dive one of the three wrecks offshore for one dive, and a shallow dive the second. The Waikiki shipwrecks are the **Sea Tiger, YO-257** and the **San Pedro** right next to it. At these latter two wrecks you might see the Atlantis Submarine ambling about. Wave at 'em—some of their customers are probably wishing they were you.

Hanauma Bay Nature Preserve (see page 67) is a shore dive, and though shallow (mostly 35 feet or less), it tends to be protected and calm and, though visibility isn't as good as other parts of the island, the fish life is excellent. Hauling heavy scuba gear to the shore (even using the trolley service to the bottom) is a bit daunting, so guided trips are recommended. **Living Ocean** (808-436-3483) does guided shore dives here, introductory dives. $120 (which is pricey for a one-tank dive).

Although the **Hawai'i Kai** area has some good dives (including an old Corsair airplane), it comes in fourth for us because the visibility tends to be less, and the terrain of most of their sites is a bit less interesting. (Though some of the sites are fantastic, we're playing the odds here.)

IF YOU'VE NEVER DIVED BEFORE

Nearly every diver starts their diving life with a supervised intro dive. And, like us, you might be motivated to continue diving and become certified. You'll get instructions on land, then your instructor will take you and a few others down and should stay with you the whole time. Some companies do intro dives off boats, but we recommend shore dives for your first time. It'll seem less rushed, and new divers can get intimidated jumping into water over their heads from a boat. Introductory dives cost $100–$140. Some companies, like **Hawaiian Diving Adventures** (808-232-3193), will take you on their two-tank boat dives for $130, and while the certified divers are sucking their first tank, you'll be learning the basics on the boat, then hopping into the water, but you still get a two-tank dive. Not a bad plan if you don't mind having your first dive off a boat.

For shore dives you'll have to travel away from Waikiki (because shore diving there is poor). **Surf N' Sea** (808-637-9887) in Hale'iwa does intro shore dives during summer months at Shark's Cove and in the winter they're usually at Electric Beach/Tracks/Kahe Point in Wai'anae. One tank is $95; two tanks is $120.

THE COMPANIES

Most of the dive outfits feed you little if anything between dives. (Note to dive companies: The quickest way to a diver's heart is to have simple cookies between dives. Over the years we've been reviewing dive companies around the state, it's *amazing* how an $8 bucket of cookies from Costco can turn a boat full of hungry divers into raving fans.)

There are *tons* of SCUBA operators on O'ahu, and compared to the neighbor island SCUBA companies, they don't seem to put as much effort into differentiating themselves from each other, especially the Waikiki operators. Disappointing company after disappointing company. The best one we've found is **Hawaiian Diving Adventures** (808-232-3193) out of Kewalo Basin. They use a six-pack instead of a cattle boat. The rental gear is in good condition and well maintained. Good pre-dive briefing, and they don't keep you on a tight leash underwater. When you surface from your first dive, they will have crackers, soda and water, as well as a fresh cut pineapple waiting on deck. It's $130 for a two-tank dive with gear rental, plus $15 if you want a computer. **Waikiki Diving Center** (808-922-2121) is an adequate second choice for $125 for two tanks. You can go cheaper—**Island Divers** (808-423-8222) will take you for $99. But we would never, *ever* recommend them.

Prices are higher in Waikiki, cheaper in Wai'anae and Hawai'i Kai, so it'll range from $99–$159 for a two-tank boat dive depending on where you dive.

In Wai'anae there's **Hawai'i Nautical** (808-234-7245). Their boat, the Sea Breeze II, leaves from Wai'anae Harbor and takes up to 10 divers. The staff is friendly, and they do a good job briefing before the dive. There's plenty of water and granola bars on board between dives. The rental gear is well-maintained, but they don't offer you computers, and they only have three-quarter wet suits. They keep you on a pretty tight leash and dive

Hawaiian Reefs—*Why is it that...?*

What is that crackling sound, like bacon frying, I always hear while snorkeling or diving? For years this baffled people. In the early days of submarines, the sound interfered with sonar operations. Finally we know the answer. It's hidden snapping shrimp defining their territory. One variety is even responsible for all the dark cracks and channels you see in smooth lobe coral. A pair creates the channels, then "farms" the algae inside.

Why are there so few shellfish in Hawai'i? It's too warm for some of the more familiar shellfish (which tend to be filter-feeders, and Hawai'i waters don't have as much stuff to filter). But Hawai'i has more shellfish than most people are aware of. They hide well under rocks and in sand. Also, people tend to collect shells (which is illegal), and that depletes the numbers.

Why do coral cuts take so long to heal? Coral contains a live animal. When you scrape coral, it leaves proteinaceous matter in your body, which takes much longer for your body to dispatch.

Why do some of the reefs appear dead? Much of the "coral" you see around O'ahu isn't the kind of coral you're used to. It's called coralline algae, which secretes calcium carbonate. It's not dead; it's *supposed* to look like that.

What do turtles eat? Dolphins. (Just teasing.) They primarily eat plants growing on rocks, as well as jellyfish when they are lucky enough to encounter them. Unfortunately for turtles and lucky for us, jellyfish aren't numerous here.

Is it harmful when people play with an octopus? Yes, if the octopus gets harmed while trying to get it out of its hole. Best to leave them alone.

Why does the ocean rarely smell fishy here in Hawai'i? Two reasons. We have relatively small tide changes, so the ocean doesn't strand large amounts of smelly seaweed at low tide. Also, the water is fairly sterile compared to mainland water, which owes much of its smell to algae and seaweed that thrives in the bacteria-rich runoff from industrial sources.

Why is the water so clear here? Because relatively little junk is poured into our water compared to the mainland. Also, natural currents tend to flush the water with a continuous supply of fresh, clean ocean water.

Why do my ears hurt when I dive deep, and how are SCUBA divers able to get over it? Because the increasing weight of the ocean is pressing on your ears the farther down you go. Divers alleviate this by equalizing their ears. Sounds high tech, but that simply means holding your nose while trying to blow out of it. This forces air into the eustachian tubes, creating equal pressures with the outside ocean. (It doesn't work if your sinuses are clogged.) Anything with air between it gets compressed. So if you know someone who gets a headache whenever he goes under water...well, he must be an airhead.

as a group, so if someone is low on air, everyone will have to come up. Kinda pricey at $159 for a one-tank intro dive or a two-tank certified dive, but the choices are few in Wa'ianae.

If you prefer six-pack vessels, **Aaron's Dive Shop** (808-262-2333) out of Kailua leases various six-pack boats operating from multiple locations around the island, including Wai'anae. Although their shop personnel seem to slide into that arrogant dive shop attitude pretty easily, we've had good luck with their boat crews. Water *only* on board and some granola bars. Our biggest complaint is that rental gear doesn't include computers (and they don't have any), so the dive profiles will be set by the divemaster, not your actual dive. If you have your own, bring it along and tell them you'll follow your own profile. $130 for two tanks gear included.

Shopping

If you're looking for gifts to bring back home for family and friends (or maybe something for yourself), you came to the right island. Daytime in Waikiki is all about the beach and water activities; nighttime is all about the food and shopping. Opportunities to spend money are *everywhere*, but don't be surprised if the retail clerks at the more upscale places largely ignore you—they know from experience that most vacationers from the mainland are just browsing. The salespeople prefer to instead focus their attention on the overseas tourists, many of whom come here specifically to shop. (Believe it or not, Hawai'i's outrageously high prices are *a steal* compared to Tokyo). It's not practical to list and evaluate every store, so here's some general guidance on *where* on O'ahu you'll want to shop.

The obvious place to start your shopping spree is Kalakaua Avenue (the main drag running through Waikiki.) Tons of high-end stores line the street (although for the most part, they are the same kinds of stores you'd find in any major metro area of nearly a million people.) The nearby **Ala Moana Center**, just outside the boundaries of Waikiki, is the largest mall in the state.

The **King's Village** (on Kaiulani Avenue at Koa, one block inland from the Waikiki Beach Center) is where you can find stereotypical Hawai'i souvenirs like carved wooden tikis and hula girls to wiggle on your dashboard, that sort of thing. If you're willing to venture outside the protective Waikiki cocoon, one of the best souvenir stores on the island is Na Makena. It's hidden inside a large gray building by the Manoa Falls trailhead. They sell some of the same cheap trinkets you can find anywhere, but they also have a large variety of high-quality souvenirs, including unique items such as authentic hula accessories and weaponry made with shark teeth.

The other main shopping area is the town of Hale'iwa on O'ahu's **North Shore**. The main road through town is lined with art galleries, surf shops, and boutique clothing shops, most clumped in close enough proximity to each other that you can park and then walk. Also on the North Shore, up near the northeastern tip of the island at Laie, there's a collection of gift shops outside of the **Polynesian Cultural Center** that you can browse without paying admission.

In **Central O'ahu**, there's a gift shop at the **Dole Plantation** but you guessed it... most of the items are pineapple themed. There's also a big gift shop at Pearl Harbor with *lots* of historic and military themed items.

If you're running short on time and still have a long list of people to buy gifts for, there are ABC convenience stores on nearly every corner of Waikiki where you can buy boxes of chocolate-covered macadamia nuts.

Skydiving is available on the North Shore at Dillingham Airport. You don't need us to tell you whether you should try this or not. It's either *Yeah, cool, where do I sign?* or *Yeah, right. Are you out of your mind?* Either way, it's around $170 (they may quote higher, but most discount or direct you to coupons) for one of the most scenic tandem jumps available in the United States.

I put off doing this activity for the first couple editions. I had done a solo jump on a static line some years previously (where an attached rope pulls your chute for you) but was a bit chicken to do it at Dillingham and said so in the write-up. Once I gave in and took the plunge (so to speak), I kicked myself for waiting so long. Jumping out 2 miles above the ocean over the North Shore was absolutely incredible. (One tip—*don't* wear a collared shirt or your one-minute free fall will feel like a non-stop bee sting on your neck.) The trade winds push you back onshore during your time under the canopy. You'll have the option of buying photos or video of your dive and will probably look at them more often in the years to come than most of the other shots from your trip.

It takes about 90 minutes for the whole process (half of that time is signing an endless string of waivers). You'll be strapped to an instructor, and both of you will be dropped from 8,000–14,000 feet, free-falling for up to a minute. Both companies have a 240 pound weight limit, and they charge extra for every pound you weigh past 200, so it's coffee and a bran muffin for you this morning. There are two main players, and we

A first time—and last time—skydiver gets her much coveted bragging rights.

prefer **Pacific Skydiving Center** (808-637-7472). Their regular jump is from 8,000 to 10,000 feet for $149 but we'd suggest the 14,000 foot jump for $179. (Is a few extra seconds of pleasure worth $30? Probably…) **Skydive Hawai'i** (808-637-9700) doesn't seem to like using their phone and wants you to do everything online. The operation feels more like a processing machine. Prices are similar and they tout their HALO jump from 20K for $1K. Arrange in advance.

If you've ever gazed into an aquarium and wondered what it was like to see colorful fish in their *natural* environment, complete with coral and strange ocean creatures, you've come to the right place. Hawai'i features a dazzling variety of fish. Over 600 species are found in our waters. We can't conceive of a trip to Hawai'i without snorkeling at least once. We got the reef, we got the water, and we got the fish. What more do you need?

We'll admit that we're snorkeling junkies and never tire of experiencing the water here. If you snorkel often, you can go right to our list below of recommended areas. But if you're completely or relatively inexperienced, you should read on.

For identifying ocean critters, the best books we've seen are *Shore Fishes of Hawai'i* by John Randall and *Hawaiian Reef Fish* by Casey Mahaney. They're what we use. You should see plenty of butterflyfish, wrasse, convict tang, achilles tang, parrotfish, angelfish, damselfish, Moorish idol, pufferfish, trumpetfish, moray eel, and humuhumunukunukuapua'a or Picasso triggerfish—a beautiful but very skittish fish. (It's as if they somehow *know* how good they look in aquariums.)

We know people who have a fear of putting on a mask and snorkel. Gives 'em the willies. For them, we recommend boogie boards with clear windows on them to observe the life below.

A FEW TIPS

- Feeding the fish is generally not recommended since it introduces unnatural behavior to the reef, and it actually causes the variety of fish to dwindle since bolder species do well and soon crowd out meeker species. It has been officially banned at Hanauma Bay.
- Use *Sea Drops* or another brand of anti-fog goop.
- Spread it *thinly* on the inside of a dry mask, then do a quick rinse.
- Most damage to coral comes when people grab it or stand on it. Even touching the coral lightly can transfer your oils to the polyps, killing them. If your mask starts to leak or you get water in your snorkel, be careful not to stand on the coral to clear them. Find a spot where you won't damage coral or drift into it. Fish, future snorkelers and the coral will thank you.
- Don't use your arms much, or you will spook the fish—just gentle fin motion. Any rapid motion can cause the little critters to scatter.
- If you have a mustache and have trouble with a leaking mask, try a little Vaseline. Don't get any on the glass—it can get *really* ugly.
- We prefer using divers' fins (the kind that slip over water shoes) so that we can walk easily into and out of the water without tearing up our feet. (If you wear socks or nylons under the shoes, they'll keep you from rubbing the tops of your toes raw.)
- Try to snorkel in calm areas. If you're in rougher water and a large wave

Snorkeling at Shark's Cove offers some of the best conditions on the island— when the surf's calm.

comes and churns up the water with bubbles, put your arms in front of you to protect your head. You won't sense motion, and may get slammed into a rock before you know it.

WHERE TO SNORKEL

The *Beaches* chapter describes the snorkeling potential of the various beaches around the island. Pay special attention to these:

North Shore

During summer months meaning April–September):

Shark's Cove—Outstanding snorkeling during calm seas but can be crowded.

Three Tables—Not as good as Shark's Cove but nice around the separate reef areas.

Waimea Bay—The south end (the end closest to Hale'iwa) is *fantastic* when calm and lightly snorkeled.

Kuilima Cove—Protected most of the time and often has an excellent fish count. Next to Turtle Bay near the northern tip of the island.

Sunset Beach—One small stretch can be nice when calm.

Turtle Beach—Usually cloudy water but often lives up to its name and has the friendliest turtles we've seen anywhere in the state—somebody *must* be feeding 'em.

Leeward Side

From Waikiki—which has lousy near-shore snorkeling—to the eastern tip:

Ka'alawai Beach—The nearest place to Waikiki where you can snorkel decent waters.

Hanauma Bay—Legendary. See page 67 for details.

Kahala Beach—Not as dramatic but nice life on a small scale.

Wai'anae Coast

Papaoneone Beach—During calm (usually summer) months, turtles are often plentiful.

Ko Olina—Protected man-made lagoons have good snorkeling near the openings to the open ocean.

SNORKEL GEAR

As for snorkeling gear, it can be rented just about anywhere. If you're going to snorkel more than once, it's nice to rent it for the week and keep it in your car so you can head to the water any time your little heart desires. If you want to buy your own, the cheapest prices will be at the **Walmart/Sam's Club Superblock** outside of Waikiki on Keeaumoku. Also consider **Costco** if you're a member.

SNORKEL BOAT TOURS

These can be fun, though many of the boats moor close enough to Waikiki Beach to be influenced by its poor visibility. See *Boat Tours* on page 179 for more.

If you're in need of some pampering, O'ahu has more than their fair share of spas. But be forewarned—prices here are much higher than what you'd expect on the mainland. And tack mandatory 20 percent service charges on any prices you see. (It's voluntary at the Laniwai.)

Probably our favorite is not even in Waikiki. It's 23,000 sq. ft. of heaven on the west side, in Ko Olina at **Laniwai Spa** (808-674-6300) at the Aulani, A Disney Resort & Spa. The staff is top notch and very professional and the 5,000 sq. ft. tropical hydrotherapy garden with 6 rain-style showers is very relaxing. Allow enough time to linger. They seem to sweat the small details here and you are constantly getting spoiled with amenities. One of their signature treatments is the Kilikili (fine, gentle rain) which includes a full body exfoliation with a lomilomi massage under streaming jets of warm water. An amazing experience, but beware that the room will become very steamy toward the end. Treatments start at $165 and go up and up.

On the other hand the **Mandara Spa** (808-945-7721) at the Hilton Hawaiian Village has great facilities—they claim the biggest in Waikiki but we couldn't get the square footage. You can spend hours enjoying the grounds, but they suffer from inconsistent results from the massage therapists. They remind us of a restaurant that has a great view and fails to execute on the food. They have a beautiful outdoor pool area with hot tub and a staggering 25 treatment rooms. But then they give you thin, well-worn robes and have men and women share an elevator and waiting room, creating awkward moments. (Fortunately the relaxation areas are not co-ed.) In all, gobs of potential but execution needs attention. Prices start at $155.

We like the **Moana Lani Spa** (808-237-2535) at the Moana Surfrider Westin. It's 18,000 sq. ft. with beautiful beach views (unfortunately with busy beach noises). Staff is very helpful and professional. Water and fruit are provided in relaxation area and the decor in main areas is plain because the focus is on Waikiki Beach. Treatments are consistently good, with Swedish being their signature, tailored to your needs. Their hot tub is really hot—bring along some pasta to cook next to you. Overall, they run a tight ship here, easy to recommend. Prices start at $135.

submarine

You won't *Run Silent, Run Deep*. You won't hear the sound of sonar pinging

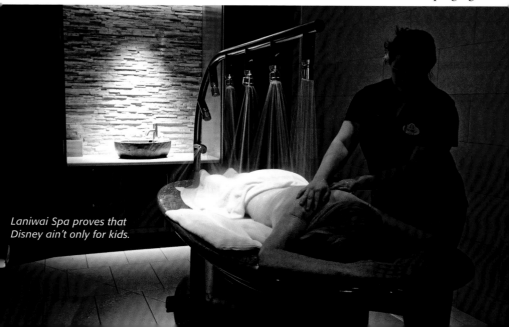

Laniwai Spa proves that Disney ain't only for kids.

Now that's a window view!

away in the background. And it's rare that anyone shoots torpedoes at you. But if you want to see the undersea world and *refuse* to get wet, *dis is da buggah.* **Atlantis Submarine** (808-973-9811) operates two subs offshore, leaving by boat from the pier at the Hilton Hawaiian Village. Although they also have subs on Maui and the Big Island, we think their Oʻahu tour is the best because it visits sunken ships, a plane and some artificial reefs. In fact, their dive site, which goes deeper than 100 feet, is a popular scuba site, so if you go in the morning, you might see SCUBA divers out your porthole, climbing over the shipwrecks.

This is the opposite of an aquarium—this world belongs to the fish, and *you* are the oddity. It's $125 for the 64-passenger sub (slightly larger windows and

seats), $115 for the 48-passenger sub. Avoid the 10 a.m. 64-passenger tour unless you want your narration in Japanese. This 40-minute ride is a kick. Kids like it, adults like it, and even certified divers like us enjoy it. Claustrophobics will probably be too busy staring through the windows to be nervous. Photographers will want to turn *off* the flash and consider manual focus as cameras seem to have a hard time on auto. Wear a bright red shirt, and watch what happens to its color on the way down. Also, you have to descend (and later ascend) a ladder with a line of people behind you to get into the sub. Why am I mentioning this? Let's just say that ladies may want to leave their skirts back at the hotel.

Make *sure* you validate your parking slip, or the parking fee might be nearly as much as the sub ride.

What your first wave feels like...   ...what it looks like.

SURFING

O'ahu is the center of surfing in the islands, some say the world. And that's as it should be. This is where it was invented, this is where it was exported from, this is where so many great surf sites are, this is where the surfing culture thrives, and this is where you'll find one of the easiest beginner surf sites the planet has to offer—right where you're staying in Waikiki. That's no exaggeration. Having lived on all the major Hawaiian islands, we can tell you that no other beach has the ideal combination of ingredients like Waikiki. Perfectly shaped and sloped, waves at Waikiki crumble and push, spending their energy slowly. (Experts like breaking waves that curl and spend their energy faster, but those would kick your 'okole in the beginning.) Concessionaires give lessons right from the Waikiki Beach Center. It's about $60 for an hour lesson—five people max per group. You'll usually be allowed to keep the board an extra hour, but first-timers are usually so exhausted from paddling short distances (it's more tiring than it looks) that you'll probably pass on that extra hour—for now. Private lessons aren't as desirable as you may think for one reason: You'll be grateful for the rest as your fellow shredders take their turns.

Despite your preconceptions, odds are you *will* be able to ride a wave during your very first—and probably only necessary—lesson. Instructors come and go at these concessionaires, and although some of them can be pushy jerks, most are fine and it's incidental to your objective—riding your first wave. And oh, what a water god you'll feel like when you snag that first ride. The beginner boards are big and floaty, not like the small sticks you see the experts using.

Simply head to the **Waikiki Beach Center** in the heart of Waikiki and sign up. You do not need reservations, and classes are usually given on the hour. They also give lessons off the Hilton Hawaiian Village at a break called Kaisers, but beware that its waves aren't as reliable as the smaller swells off Waikiki Beach Center.

Although Waikiki is the optimal choice, if the south shore is too flat (or too big) during your stay, you can also try these companies that teach elsewhere:

Sunset Suratt (808-783-8657), locally known as Uncle Bryan, does a good job up on the North Shore. Their 2-hour lessons for $80 are a great way to learn outside of Waikiki. In Hale'iwa.

Located in Kailua, **Hawaiian Watersports** (808-262-5483) rents all kinds of water toys, such as surfboards, boogie boards and kayaks. They also give kite-boarding and surfing lessons.

Surf HNL (808-371-8917) used to be called **Girls Who Surf** which was an intriguing name—especially if you envision a bikini-clad hottie teaching you to surf. The bad news is that we got a guy instructor. The good news is he did a great job for $139.

Once you've had a lesson, you might want to return and rent a board to practice. Waves will seem a bit harder to catch because you don't have an instructor placing you in the perfect location and giving you a shove. Spend a few minutes on shore looking at the surf, and choose the location that seems to be breaking the way you want. As for not getting that shove off from the instructor, you'll simply have to paddle harder when you want to catch a wave. Stick with big, floaty boards. One way to cheat is to buy a pair of webbed gloves. (You might want to buy them on the internet before you arrive as they're hard to find on island. With these, you don't need to paddle as many strokes because each stroke is so much more powerful. It might look a bit weird, but it'll give you an edge, and it's much less tiring. Also make *sure* you wear a rash guard or simple T-shirt, or you'll get rubbed raw from the board in two spots you *don't* want rubbed raw.

And be aware of the territorial feelings residents have about their precious surf sites on O'ahu. Respect gets respect. If you don't feel welcome at a surf site, then you're not. Be nice and find another spot.

Stand Up Paddling, or **SUP**, is very popular in Hawai'i. The hardest part about learning to surf is standing up on the board while it's moving. This sport has made things easier by giving you a board big enough to dance on. (When talking visiting

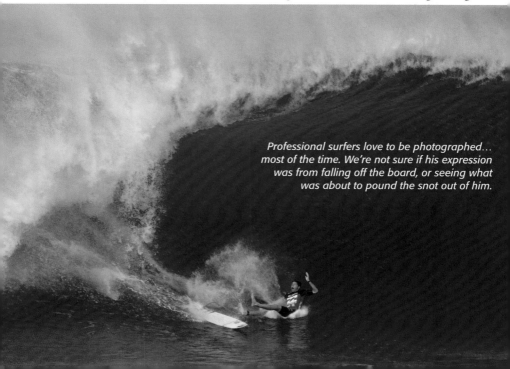

Professional surfers love to be photographed... most of the time. We're not sure if his expression was from falling off the board, or seeing what was about to pound the snot out of him.

Waves 101

Waves are mesmerizing to watch, and people can spend countless hours gazing at them. But most people don't realize that what they are seeing is the shock wave of an event that occurred far over the horizon.

Ocean swells are created by winds—usually hundreds or even thousands of miles away from us—that blow in the same direction long and hard enough to push the surface of the water away from what's beneath, forming ripples, then chop, then swells. These swells can travel quite efficiently over vast distances, carrying the spent energy of those localized winds with them. Think of the swell as a type of rolling battery, having been charged by winds from another part of the globe. South swells usually come from New Zealand storms; north or west swells often come from Alaska or Japan.

Near the shoreline, an ocean swell becomes a wave when it starts to feel the bottom, slowing it down. The surface water slows later than the deeper water, and the swell essentially gets ahead of itself, forming a wave. What kind of wave it will be depends on many factors, the most important being the slope of the ocean bottom. Gradually sloping bottoms like those at Waikiki form spilling waves that crumble—perfect for beginner surfers. Nearly all the energy is used up horizontally, pushing you forward. Ground that becomes shallow suddenly, like a reef ledge, form breaking waves called tubes or barrels—much lusted after by the big boys and girls. Lots of energy is directed downward in addition to the horizontal push.

The angle of the reef ledge relative to the swell is also important. If the swell hits the ledge head-on, the wave breaks everywhere at once, all across the shore—beautiful, but ultimately useless to surfers who prefer to ride more parallel to the shoreline, or down the line of a wave that's breaking over a longer period of time.

Now it might be tempting to think that the bigger the swells, the better the wave will look, but that's not the case. Each surf site has its optimal swell size. If it gets too big, the waves either break everywhere at once or break in large, irregular sections, becoming an unsurfable mess. Strong wind, either sideshore or onshore, also can close out a surf site by making it too bumpy. That's why surfers, when deciding where to surf, care about the swell direction, size and the winds. If they're hoping to surf at a prized site such as the Banzai Pipeline, the size of the swell might be perfect and winds might be light, but the direction it's coming from might be perpendicular to the ledge there, making it break all at once rather than at an angle. If the swell gets bigger, it might trigger the break at Waimea Bay (with its deeper ledge), but will close out Pipeline.

So when you see surfers gazing upon the ocean, they're looking at it from a perspective of beauty, physics and a little geometry. If you get a chance, look for an excellent locally made movie called Fiberglass and Megapixels about big wave surfing and the incredible process of filming them in the water.

relatives into trying it, I liken them to small garage doors.) SUP boards are wider, thicker and longer than the biggest longboards people commonly learn to surf on. SUP instruction focuses on keeping your balance while using a tall paddle to move you into the waves. (This provides an excellent central core workout, with your feet—of all things—hurting the worst.) The sight of people standing and dipping long paddles in the water has earned SUP surfers the subversive title "janitors" or "moppers" from traditional surfers. The size of the board, as well as the fact that you are already standing up, gives you an advantage in catching waves early. You don't have to drop in exactly where the wave is breaking. Moppers can catch waves behind the lineup, but all surfing rules apply once you've caught the wave. Traditional surfers will be more inclined to drop in on your wave since they'll feel that you didn't work as hard to get it as they did.

Prices and lessons are similar to regular surfing. Go with one of the surfing guys listed above.

You can waterski in the ultra-protected waters of Hawai'i Kai. You should know in advance that the water there often has *lots* of moon jellyfish, but they don't seem to be a problem as far as we've observed. **Hawai'i Water Sports Center** (808-395-3773) does waterskiing for $59 for 20 minutes. They also have other things, such as wakeboards, they can drag you on behind the boat. (If you've never waterskied before, it's more tiring than it looks). Ride-a-longs are $30 extra. They can be pretty rude at times.

Whale Watching

Though they're not the only whales here, **humpbacks** are the stars of whale watching. They work in Alaska during the summer, building up fat, then vacation here from December to March or April when the females bear their young and the males sing the blues. More than 1,000 whales come to the islands each year, and the mothers and calves stay close to shore. Only the males sing, and they all sing the same song, usually with their heads pointed down. No air bubbles come out while singing, and scientists aren't sure how they do it. Humpbacks don't eat while they're here and may lose one-third of their body weight during their stay in Hawai'i. (I doubt that very many *human* visitors can make that claim.)

There's no question that the whale watching varies from year to year. Some years the humpbacks are boisterous and raising hell, constantly breaching, blowing and generally having a good time. Other years they seem strangely subdued, as if hung over from their Alaska trip. What's really going on is that some years O'ahu's whales visit other Hawaiian islands. Perhaps whales, too, want to avoid getting into a rut.

Few industries in Hawai'i bring as much shameless, phony advertising as whale watching. Computers allow fake scenes with relative ease. (For the record, we don't use computers to doctor our photos.) Some show whales leaping so close to boats you think they're going to get swamped. Just so you know, boats are forbidden by federal law from getting closer than 100 yards. The fine for violating a whale's personal space is obscene. The whales themselves are allowed to initiate closer contact (and they're rarely fined), but in general, count on staying a football field away. That's ok, because these over-sized buggahs are so big that at that distance they're still incredibly impressive.

See *Boat Tours* on page 179 for a description of the different boats. In addition, **North Shore Catamaran** (808-351-9371) has 2.5 to 3 hour trips for $67 in their 40-foot sailing cat from December–April. (They motor sail unless they have stiff winds.) Leave from Hale'iwa. Beverages only; bring your own food. This is probably your best bet. *However*, winter is the time of big swells on the North Shore, so if you're a cookie-tosser, you may want to avoid these guys.

Star of Honolulu (808-983-7827) is more like a ship than a boat. Dec.–April they do 2.5-hour whale watching tours for $71 with buffet lunch, $53 without lunch. A vessel this big won't be the most responsive to whale sightings, but they'll generally go where they see the action, and their super-high deck lets you see more action.

In general, we've been less impressed with whale knowledge and facts from O'ahu companies than on other islands, especially Maui where there's more professionalism. However on O'ahu, especially off Waikiki, whale watching seems more like an afterthought for many companies.

If you're looking for the opportunity to skim the treetops or see beautiful valley views from a new perspective, then this is the way to spend your afternoon. The idea is easy—strap into a harness and literally hang out while zipping from platform to platform. O'ahu is the last major island in Hawai'i to start building ziplines, and your choices here are all very different experiences.

The most intense zipline course is **Climbworks Keana Farms** (808-200-7906) in Kahuku. They *only* do ziplines—unlike the other two companies, which offer several activities—and they have the

Zipping through Kualoa Ranch.

longest and fastest zips on all of Oʻahu. While up there you'll fly across eight tandem lines that zigzag through lush forests and red dirt farmland. Their *uncles* will take you on ATVs to the top, and they're prepared to teach you all about what growing up on the island was like for them. They start you off with 400 feet of line and quickly ramp it up until you reach zips five and six. Zip five is the fastest at 41 mph, whereas zip six is the longest with 2,270 feet of cable (even though they'll tell you it's a half mile). The remaining lines are almost disappointing, but you may still be coming down from the adrenaline rush. Unlike the other two, Keana Farms isn't afraid of letting you flip upside down in your harness, and their additional rappelling, rope bridges, and rope hoists sprinkled throughout the course will help keep you entertained during 3-hour tour. Biggest dings are long waits between zips, and their guides aren't as friendly as the other companies. No riders under 7. Maximum weight is 270 pounds (and if you're under 85 pounds, you may ride strapped to a guide). $169 per person, plus $30 if you need transportation from Waikiki.

Amidst their many other activities and tours, **Kualoa Ranch** (808-237-7321) offers a spectacular view of Kualoa Valley. It's a place where parts from many dozens of films have been shot, including many well-known scenes from the *Jurassic Park* franchise, parts of *Pearl Harbor*, and the café scene from *50 First Dates* and TV shows such as *Lost* and *Hawaiʻi 5-0*. They aren't afraid to boast about this either, which is good because the 20-minute drive to the course would otherwise be dull, leaving you to focus on the uncomfortable journey. Seriously, on these quaint buses with worn out seats you'll feel *every bump* in the road. After the ride, you're left to the seven tan-

dem lines in a 2.5 hour course. Zip four is the longest, with just shy of a quarter mile (1,320 feet) of line to fly along. You'll hit the course's top speeds of 34 mph here as well. These guys do a much better job of keeping you entertained, and you'll spend less time waiting for groups ahead. Instead, your non-ziplining time is spent learning about the plants in the area, the history of Hawaiʻi and some of the best eats from the people that live here (they even managed to tell *us* about a new restaurant). Gotta weigh between 70 and 280 pounds, with a permitted height between 4'8" and 6'9". Other requirements are available on their website (they have *thigh* size requirements as well, which is unusual). $160 per person, plus $15 if you need transportation from Waikiki.

Finally, you have **Coral Crater Adventure Park** (808-626-5773). As far as ziplines go, this is like splashing in a puddle instead of swimming in the ocean, but that doesn't mean you should gloss over this place, because there's a twist. Their longest line is 580 feet long, has a top speed of 24 mph, and ends up being used twice throughout their six zips (there are only five unique lines; zips three and six are the same cable). The area also lacks the upper-valley beauty the other two offer, as this is in an old limestone crater. Here's where they differ: They zip you *through* the tree branches (and they maintain them daily to ensure safety), something that no other zips can offer. And even cooler, you can zip *at night* if you want. $140. We don't recommend a straight zipline during the day. But if you do it at night or combine it with some of the more interesting things thay have going there (such as their high ropes tower or the zombie apocalypse— see *Attractions* on page 171) it's more compelling. Located in Kapolei in the southwestern part of the island.

ADVENTURES

Don't bother bringing bait on this fishing trip—you're the bait.

Some of the activities described below are for the serious adventurer. They can be experiences of a lifetime. We are assuming that if you consider any of them, that you are a person of sound judgment, capable of assessing risks. All adventures carry risks of one kind or another. Our descriptions below do not attempt to convey all risks associated with an activity. These activities are not for everyone. Good preparation is essential. In the end, it comes down to your own good judgment.

SWIM WITH SHARKS

There are two kinds of people—those who pay to stay clear of sharks and those who pay to get up close and personal with the scary critters.

From a Cage

If swimming with dolphins is a little too tame for you (after all, how many people ever get eaten by mere mammals?), how about swimming with sharks? This is where you hop into a cage protruding just above the surface of the ocean. For 15 minutes you watch as sandbar sharks and possibly some Galapagos sharks circle your cage menacingly. Two, three, 10, maybe 15 sharks. Watching these predators just inches from you is fantastic. They're amazingly graceful and stealthy. We've SCUBA dived for years, but it wasn't until we did this simple *snorkel* trip that we were able to spend this much quality time with these animals. The cage keeps them out, and the biggest openings are covered with Plexiglas, which you'll appreciate when the big sharks bang into it. All in all, it's an incredible adventure.

It all started decades ago with crab fishermen 3 miles off the coast of Hale'iwa. They'd pull their traps from the sandy bottom 400 feet below and throw the remaining bait overboard. Sharks became accustomed to this buffet and started hanging around, and companies started offering shark tours in the early part of this century (you know, it *still* feels kind of funny saying that).

The boat ride is short, and there's no food onboard, unless you like chum—think of it as sushi without the craftsmanship. (Companies are not supposed to chum anymore, but we've seen it happen on the sly.)

Some people say shark cage tours are a bad idea, that it unnaturally brings sharks closer to shore. Others say it's harmless and that these types of sharks don't come near the shore and never attack beachgoers. We aren't smart enough to know which is correct; we'll just tell you what it's like, and let you decide for yourself.

Consider wearing a tucked-in shirt to help keep you warmer in the water, especially in the winter, and take Dramamine or the equivalent if you're prone to seasickness, since the boat will be bobbing the whole time. It can take two hours from the time you show up at the Hale'iwa Boat Harbor to being on your way to lunch after your adventure. Companies go out year-round, only dissuaded if North Shore surf is big enough to close Hale'iwa Harbor. (Earlier tours are better, since the ocean is usually calmer and the sharks are more active.) They claim that shark no-shows are very rare. Snorkel gear provided. And remember, this brings new meaning to the phrase, "Keep your arms and legs inside the cage at all times."

Of the two shark cage companies, **North Shore Shark Adventures** (808-228-5900) seems more reliable. They carry 24 people per boat, eight in the cage at a time. They also offer the luxury of more spacious cages. (The jury's still out on whether or not sharks prefer sardines, but you'll appreciate the extra space.) It's $120 per person, $60 for kids 3–12. Ride-alongs are $70.

Hawai'i Shark Encounters (808-351-9373) will take 12 people max, split into groups of six at at time in the cage. The experience is generally comparable to taking a tour with North Shore Shark Adventures, but we've noticed they tend to go out in rougher seas, on days when the other guys cancel. And the first time we went out with this outfit, someone stole our GoPro, along with all the cool images on it. It *might* have been another passenger, but the crew didn't seem overly concerned about it, and frankly, we're still miffed. It's $116 per person, $83 for kids under 12, and $94 for ride-alongs. They've got hot water to rinse off afterward.

We Don't Need No Stinking Cages

For those who think that cages are for *posers*, you can also swim freely with the beasties. Two companies do this, both out of Hale'iwa—**One Ocean** (808-649-0018) and **Islandview Hawai'i** (808-354-0626), and each charges $150.

A couple of things you should know. You might want to bring your own mask and snorkel since they will likely only have one size, which may not fit all. Depending on conditions, you might simply be floating in place while looking at the sharks, but there's also a chance you'll be kicking hard the entire time to keep up with the current.

It's thrilling to see the sharks so close, but some may find it unnerving when the sharks become numerous and you can't keep track of them. Though their behavior may not be aggressive, it's likely that some people might find the notion of a shark charging right at them aggressive. They

will come right up next to you. And when they come from behind and whisk right by your mask? Yeah, that's a bit intense. Others will love every part of it.

Expect to spend about an hour in the water. We've observed Island View going out in conditions One Ocean will cancel for. If you have a camera, put it on a 3-foot selfie stick. It may be required, and, at the very least, it somehow feels like a weapon in your hands.

NIGHT SNORKELING

There you are, swimming in the ocean under an inky black sky full of stars. The only source of light is your water-proof flashlight slicing through the ocean like a light saber from *Star Wars*. Your beam cuts across a school of needlefish attracted to your light, then rests on a parrotfish snoozing in its nightly made cocoon. While it's true that snorkeling wouldn't normally be considered an ad-venture, doing it at night is an entirely different matter.

Make sure you read the *Snorkeling* section on page 231 and about box jellies in *Hazards* on page 31.

On the leeward side we like Ala Moana Regional Park because it's relatively safe for the novice night snorkeler and offers better snorkeling than people would ex-pect. This is a heavily used beach park during the day, and beachgoers certainly tend to scare the fish away. But when the sun goes down, some of those fish return. Visibility won't be good—and the swim out to the reef can be spooky through the suspended particles in the water. But at the reef's edge a hundred yards or so from the shoreline you'll see lots of shrimp, small fish and crabs, and if you're observant, octopus. (They are hard to see at night, even when you're looking right at them.) Park at the part closest to Waikiki, paddle out to the reef, and work your way to the right, slowly, along the inside of the reef. Make a mental note of your position when you start so you can return to the same place. And don't leave anything valuable in your car for any dirtbags to grab. The park is open until 10 p.m.

On the North Shore, your best and safest bet is often Kuilima Cove at the Turtle Bay Resort near the northern tip of the island. (See *Beaches* on page 143.) The bay is usually fairly well protected. During the day it's not the best snorkeling you'll find, but we like it for night snorkeling because as long as you stay on the right side of the cove, you don't run the risk of getting pounded by the ocean unless seas are raging. And that's super important when you don't have daylight to keep you oriented.

RULE YOUR OWN ISLAND

If you ever wanted to be the master of your own island kingdom, you can either start a revolution here in Hawai'i (hey, if you plan to lower our state taxes, we may join you), or you can simply do it this way: There's an island called Mokoli'i (aka Chinaman's Hat) that's 614 yards offshore from Kualoa Beach Park near Kane'ohe. (We were in a particularly precise mood that day, so we measured it with a golfing rangefinder—*definitely* a par 5.) Anyway, this island can be yours—just bring your mask, fins, and make sure you eat your Wheaties that day.

During the swim over, we've never experienced any particularly strong currents, though we don't fully understand the tidal mechanics at this part of the bay, so it's possible it could happen. Your trip over should be *partially* protected by an offshore reef. If the seas are calm, there's a small sandy beach on the back side of the island around the left (north) point. Otherwise, just come ashore at the nearest point and scramble up the rocks.

Once on your island you can wander around the bottom portion along faint trails. You'll need shoes; either water shoes, or you can stuff your regular shoes in a garbage bag and hope it doesn't leak. If you want to climb to the top, the best "trail" (such as it is) begins at the shoreline going up at the part of the island closest to O'ahu, to the right of a bare dirt spot. The second part of the climb is ridiculously steep—scramble to the peak at 206 feet

The current rulers of Mokoli'i Island (Chinaman's Hat) meet to discuss important matters of the kingdom. And try to figure out how they will get back down.

Leaping off the rarely seen back side of Mokulua Nui Island.

while holding on for dear life. Otherwise, just hang around near the lower levels and pass new laws or whatever it is that new rulers do. Your kingdom may be invaded by kayakers. (But remember, only those who swam here can truly be rulers.)

As a fallback, if your conquest of Chinaman's Hat isn't possible, Goat Island. (See *Beaches* on page 141.) is a worthy candidate for occupation.

PADDLE, HIKE & JUMP

The first two aren't particularly adventurous, but the last one is. You'll need to get a kayak (see *Kayaking* on page 218) at Kailua Bay and make a beeline to Mokulua Nui Island. (It's the island to the left off Lanikai Beach. (See map on page 74.)

Once at the beach, you'll need to hike to the left along the shoreline for about 10 minutes. The footing is a bit awkward, and you'll want to wear water shoes (like water socks). You'll come to what looks like a channel that cuts off a large piece of the island. If you're a jumper and want to

try your luck, there's a lava pedestal overlooking a pool at the back of the channel. People sometimes jump into the surgy water below and climb back out to repeat the feat. Don't try it if the ocean is too strong, and certainly don't consider this if you're not a confident swimmer. You could hit a rock, drown, get swept out or get eaten by a shark. (Hey, just trying to convey that *this* part of it is the adventure.) Note (in our photo above) where the person is jumping from. We've seen YouTube videos of people jumping from higher up, but that concept *utterly* terrifies us, and we certainly don't recommend it.

NIGHT SHIPWRECK DIVE

Perhaps simple SCUBA dives seem too tame for your adventurous blood. Fair enough. How about diving a shipwreck—at night? It's hard to describe the feeling of discovery that you experience when the top of a ship—even one sunk just for divers—suddenly falls across your flashlight beam cutting through the darkness. There are several wrecks dotting the island (see *SCUBA* on page 225 for more). The biggest problem you'll have is arranging your dive. **Hawaiian Diving Adventures** (808-232-3193) does this two times a month or, if you have 4 or more people, they'll make a special trip for your group. They dive the Sea Tiger wreck. **Aaron's Dive Shop** (808-262-2333) does this once a month or with a minimum of six but are inclined to dive the Corsair (an airplane). The dive lights they use are usually not the best. We prefer bright LED lights. If they won't provide you with a good light, consider splurging and buying one to enhance the experience.

MERMAID CAVE

On the Wai'anae coast there's a stretch of shoreline where an ancient coral reef has been stranded above the water. Scientists differ as to whether this was caused by higher sea levels dropping to where

they are today (regardless of current trends, seas have been higher in the distant past than they are now) or due to uplifting. (Visualize a heavier person next to you sinking into a bean bag and raising you up. In this case, the displacer is the massive Big Island of Hawai'i.) Regardless of its cause, it's a very rare thing in Hawai'i. And as this ancient, stranded coral table is pummeled by the relentless ocean, it has a tendency to be undercut, forming caves. Such is the case with Mermaid Cave (aka **The Tunnels**).

As you walk out to the openings, take the time to look at your footing. You'll see tiny pukas created by coral polyps along with the occasional ancient shell embedded into the coral. Once you get to the entrance holes in the reef, don't be in a rush. Take your time to evaluate the ocean conditions. Watch what is happening from the various openings, and visualize what could happen to you if a

He don't look like no mermaid I ever saw...

rogue set of large waves came ashore while you're down there. Because it can happen. These caves are not the place to be if the ocean is raging. Waves smash into the reef, shoving water inland. The caves allow you to get *under* the surface, but you're vulnerable to getting squeezed or jammed against the top of the cave, smashing your head or possibly drowning. We've been inside during big waves at high tide, just to see what it was like—and we don't advise it. Consider this only when the ocean is cooperating.

Also, if you have the ability to *dunk a basketball*, you can ignore this part. If you're like me and can't, then your biggest challenge will be getting out of the cave. Because to access it, you have to drop into a 6-foot opening onto coral rubble and will have to use your strength to get back out. *Do not* underestimate how hard that will be. We like to bring a 3-step ladder, drop it into the cave, and use it to enter and exit. Now, the odds are reasonably good that you probably *didn't* pack one of those in your luggage, but

they *do* sell them at the Home Depot in Kapolei at H1 and Kalaeloa Boulevard.

To get here, take H1 past Ko Olina. About 1.4 miles past the power plant, look for Laumania Street on the left. Drive to the end and park. (See map on page 110.) You're at the south end of Kalaniana'ole Beach Park. (I'm not even going to *pretend* you can pronounce that one.) Walk to the shoreline, and the caves are 300 feet to your left. Enter and exit only from the most inland entrance. And say hey for us to any mermaids you see….

PU'U-KE-AHI-A-KAHOE (MOANALUA VALLEY TO HAIKU STAIRS)

One of the coolest places on O'ahu is the Haiku Stairs. Wooden ladders were originally strung up the ridge of Haiku Valley during WWII to facilitate the creation of a tower anchoring part of a *mile-long* ultra-powerful radio antenna stretching across the valley. The military would use this antenna to communicate with their ships throughout the Pacific and

When you get to the radar dish (at left) you're treated to the ultra-grand view of the windward coast, as well as the forbidden Haiku Stairs below you.

supposedly into the Indian Ocean. (Their goal was to have a transmitter so powerful that it could transmit to *submerged submarines in Tokyo Bay*.) Those access ladders were replaced by wooden stairs and finally a metal staircase. The 3,922 stairs climbing 2,200 feet became one of the coolest hikes on the island until vandals damaged part of the staircase in 1987. The local government was all set to reopen these stairs in 2005, going so far as spending almost $1 million to fix them up for hikers. But then intra-government squabbles and intransigence took hold, and today there is a *guard* posted at the base of the stairs to keep out hikers while the politicians point fingers at each other. (Sorry to sound so preachy, but it *really* is a crying shame.)

So if you can't climb 'em, how do you get to 'em? Well, there just so happens to be a beautiful hike up the ridge from the *Honolulu* side. It's state land, and hikers are permitted to cross. There's a pass-through at the start of the 3-mile dirt road.

The trail is in Moanalua Valley, one of Oahu's best-kept secrets. This area is home to many endangered species of plants, birds and snails, and contains historic sites from ancient Hawaiians and the Damon family (who sold this land to the state in 2007). It culminates at the top of the Ko'olaus with the Haiku Stairs draped down the other side of the mountain.

The views from the top and along the way are amazing. Expect to see Pearl Harbor and the entire Wai'anae Range during the climb and a towering view of Kane'ohe Bay from the summit. The trail has two parts, a 3-mile road walk that hardly climbs, and a 2-mile ridge trail that's as hard to find as it is to hike. Be sure to bring a lunch and lots of water.

To get there (see map on page 107), take H-1 west from Waikiki and take exit 19B (a two-lane, left exit) onto H-201. This is the shortcut that bypasses the airport. Next take Exit 2 and follow the signs for Moanalua Valley, taking a quick right to the off-ramp. Stay on Ala Aolani Road until it ends at Moanalua Valley Park. You'll want to start this hike *early* for two reasons: The 10-mile round trip trail will take at least 7 to 8 hours to complete, and the Moanalua Valley Park closes its gate at 7 p.m. (they open at 7 a.m. if you want to race the clock), locking your vehicle inside if you don't make it back in time. We like to park *on the street* just before the gate. That way you can return late and still drive home.

Only hike during dry conditions. As you ascend the razorbacks, you'll find that the rain has carved channels in the trail, and during a shower they begin to look eerily like water slides that go *right over the edge* of the mountains. Also, it's easy to get lost at the beginning. We've had users report getting lost the first time using our book, but they found success using our GPS-enabled app.

The trail begins on the dirt road in the back of the park and rises to a gate. Go past the gate and stay on the road until you see a sign warning about rodent control systems. The sign is close to where the ridge trail begins. Immediately you'll notice how lush this valley is. Along the road, ginger and ferns are abundant. There are markers by the side of road that point out some of the important sites in the area. At difficult-to-find marker 3, a trail leads into the woods past a gigantic monkeypod tree to one of the Damon homesteads. It's now merely a stone staircase and a foundation, but it's a striking contrast to the encroaching jungle.

Back on the road, this is where things get complicated. To find the trail that climbs the *correct* ridge, you have to count how many times you cross the (usually dry) stream. The road crosses the stream seven times on seven stone bridges. After the final bridge, at marker 10, a large boulder covered with petroglyphs sits under a mango tree. Next you'll cross the stream 10 more times (no bridges, but there are remnants of stone bridges, and some crossings are overgrown). Not all crossings are paved, so try to pay close attention. After the tenth crossing, as the road bends right, you'll see another rodent control sign and a trail sign for the Kulana'ahane Trail. Do *not* take this trail. Fifty feet *beyond* the sign, a shallow drainage ditch pours from the road into the stream. This is your trail. It *may* be marked with orange tape. Follow it across the stream and up the other side.

Right away, you ascend steeply up the middle ridge of Moanalua Valley. The next 2 miles are straightforward: climb, climb, then climb some more. There are some ropes on the steepest parts—some of these are good climbing ropes and others are shoelaces lashed to shrubs, so use at your own discretion. (This is the *Adventures* section, after all, and we ain't vouching for anything.) The trail is overgrown in places and non-existent in others. The ridge gets narrower and more exposed as you near the summit. Staring down at the trail, your peripheral vision looks down a thousand feet in both directions. When it seems like you're on a razor's edge, take your time and concentrate. There's no rush—you parked your car on the street, right?

Be sure to turn around for the views of Honolulu and Pearl Harbor. Eventually, you can see the entire Wai'anae range to your left. Nearing the summit, the trail levels out, allowing it to hold more water. Expect to march through ankle-deep mud and channels similar to those described earlier, and don't be surprised to see or hear feral pigs roaming around—you're on their turf now. From the top, the view sweeps from across Kane'ohe Bay, and the Mokulua islands off Lanikai to Waimanalo. In all, you've gained 2,500 feet in elevation from the trailhead. That's 500 feet in 3 miles on the road and 2,000 feet in 2 miles on the ridge. (Yeah, it's steep.)

Muddy trails diverge in every direction from the top of Pu'u-ke-ahi-a-Kahoe. The 10-minute path on the left (nearest the leftmost USGS benchmark) will take you to the concrete structure with the large dish antennas on top, the terminus of the closed Haiku Stairs. You now have a perfectly legal way to see the stairs from the top. Starting super early maximizes your chances of not having clouds obscure your hard-won summit quest.

WA'AHILA RIDGE TO MT. OLYMPUS

Why put another ridge hike in the Adventures section? Simple. It's fairly tough (2,600 feet of climbing and 5.75 miles round trip), there are steep areas where you can slip, and there are numerous places where a wrong step could be fatal. Yup, that'll do it. But it also rewards you with a dramatic view of the windward side—from Coconut Island in Kane'ohe Bay to Bellows Beach south of Kailua—if the clouds are cooperating.

You'll start at an elevation of 1,030 feet, and your objective is at 2,486 feet. Therefore, you'll read in other places that there's about 1,500 feet of climbing. Yeah, you wish! What people seem to forget is that when a climbing-type trail undulates up and down, every downhill section on the way up to your goal means you have to gain that elevation three times. Once initially, once to regain it after a downhill, and again climbing *up* that downhill on the way back.

Though your legs may still be shaking, stop on your way down from Mt. Olympus to admire the view of Honolulu.

Right after the trailhead the trail splits—you'll take the left fork. The trail is hot and windless in the beginning, and vegetation blocks all views. You'll start climbing right away, then promptly lose much of the elevation you just sweated for. Get used to it. There will be some super steep sections followed by infuriating descents.

Keep an eye out on the left for some awesome views behind you of Honolulu. If you're afraid of heights, you'll hate some of the stretches where a narrow ridge trail straddles a horrible fall on both sides. You'll probably also dislike some of the rockface scrambles. A couple of side trails merely lead to power poles.

Unfortunately, you can't often see the summit you're striving for, so you'll start to silently threaten it. *Those clouds better not be surrounding that summit, grumble, grumble...*

The intersection of the Kolowalo Trail (which goes left; you'll go right) has a warning sign saying the trail is unmaintained from this point. But on our last hike, the trail appeared to be well used and was not a problem. Some steep climbing stretches make having a rope a good idea (for the return). You can loop it around a tree to help you down, then pull on one side at the bottom. The last part is especially steep, slippery, and there's not much to grab except for the spider web of ropes sprawling across the red clay. If it's raining, you may be screwed—simple as that. Either way you may choose to slide back down on your 'okole during your return. Long pants aren't a bad idea as they'll also protect your legs from the ferns that sometimes scratch at you during the second half of the trail.

Once at the top you'll have a truly Olympian view. Keep heading to your right along the ridge for a better opening. Then ponder whether you want to scramble that last little saddle to the actual summit, or simply drink in the view from this part of the Ko'olaus while remembering all those downhill sections (which are now *uphill* sections) that now await.

From the top, if you walk a little farther down the trail, you will be able to see three cinder cones. The third cinder cone doesn't look like the other two. Look down and to the left and you'll see what appears to be a circular-shaped meadow. It's actually a swamp, a sight few people ever see—Ka'au Crater. It's hard to imagine that at one point there was hot lava shooting hundreds of feet into the air from this now-swampy jungle.

It'll take most people at least 6 hours to complete this trip. To get to the trailhead from H-1 going east, take the King Street exit (25A), turn left under the highway onto Waialae Avenue, then turn left onto St. Louis Drive. After lots of winding, just before St. Louis ends, turn right onto Peter Street, then turn left onto Ruth Place and head into the Wa'ahila Ridge State Recreation Area. Park in the lot and look for the trailhead. See map on page 66. If you're coming from Waikiki, take McCully out of Waikiki, right on Kapiolani, which becomes Waialae, left on St. Louis and follow the directions above.

DAY TRIP TO MOLOKA'I'S LEPROSY SETTLEMENT

Moloka'i is a long, skinny, green island 26 miles southeast of O'ahu. The island owes its shape to a cataclysmic event that occurred hundreds of thousands of years ago, when much of the volcano that makes up East Moloka'i suddenly broke off and fell into the ocean. The landslide generated tsunami waves as tall as skyscrapers and sent *half-mile-sized* chunks of rock rolling 100 miles across the ocean floor. The collapse also left behind staggeringly tall sea cliffs up to 3,000 feet high—the highest in

the world. Much later, an eruption at the base of these cliffs created land that is adjacent to, but utterly apart from, the rest of the island: a flat, isolated peninsula, with only a narrow, manmade trail gouged into the side of the cliff to allow land access. A perfect natural prison. This is where people with leprosy were sent to die. Today, the formerly notorious leprosy settlement is a national historic park that you can visit as a day trip from O'ahu.

Starting in 1866, more than 8,000 people afflicted with the disease (now called Hansen's Disease) were banished from society and sent here to the Kalaupapa peninsula. It was a hideous and vile place in those days, completely neglected by a Hawaiian government that only wanted to forget it existed. In 1873, a 33-year-old priest from Belgium named Father Damien arrived to tend to the unfortunates, giving no thought to his own safety. Although there is no way he could have known it at the time, 95 percent of the human population is naturally immune to the disease, which means 19 out of 20 priests sent to Kalaupapa could never have gotten contracted it. Unfortunately for Damien, he was among the 5 percent who could. He eventually contracted the disease and died there in 1889.

Despite spending 16 years of his life in selfless dedication to the most reviled people and working to turn Kalaupapa into a real settlement—a place to live rather than just a place to die—Damien was tormented on his deathbed with the fear that he was unworthy of heaven. The Catholic Church felt otherwise, and in 2009 he was officially declared a saint. Kalaupapa has a second saint declared in 2012—Mother Marianne Cope, who arrived in 1888 to care for the ailing Father Damien and who died of natural causes there in 1918. Today there are still about a half-dozen elderly, now-cured patients who continue to voluntarily live at Kalaupapa, even though the forced quarantine was lifted in 1969.

The most popular way to visit is via the Kalaupapa Guided Mule Tour (808-567-6088), which takes you down the trail on the 1,700-foot cliff to the settlement below. The ride down may be the most epic thing you'll do in Hawai'i, especially if you're not used to riding. The mules that visitors ride have great temperaments and make the trek down and up the mountain nearly every day. Trusting your mule is key to enjoying the whole experience. (There's a 250-pound weight limit.) Book in advance. It's $209, which includes lunch and the tour of the peninsula below. The views are spectacular. If you're already on Moloka'i, you can hike the trail yourself, but you still need to get a permit from Damien Tours (808-567-

6171) to enter the settlement. No one younger than 16 allowed.

Once at the bottom, Damien Tours takes you on a historic four-hour bus tour of the settlement. It's $60 (cash or check only). The tour does not include your transportation to Kalaupapa or lunch, so bring your own food along with plenty of water. (If you're flying over from O'ahu, you don't have to go through the normal TSA security, so you can bring your water on the plane.) Supplies here are hard to come by; they only get barge service *once a year*.

Flights to the main airport on Molokai (MKK), on the other hand, are easy to come by from Makani Kai Air (808-567-6088), though flying directly into Kalaupapa (LUP) is less reliable, so call the airline. Or better, Kalaupapa Guided Mule Tours and Damien Tours will both arrange your flight details for you. Tickets run about $50 each way.

Yeah, you'll have to ride a mule down this trail. Any questions?

A Place to Eat 270
Alan Wong's 270
Aloha Salads 286
Ama'ama 297
Arancino 267
Assaggio 274
Atlantis Seafood &
 Steak 259
Auntie Pasto's 275
Azteca 283
Banzai Sushi 294
Barefoot Bar 261
Beach House 294
Benihana of Tokyo 268
Bic Tacos 298
Big City Diner 286
Big Wave Shrimp 295
Bob's Pizzeria 286
Bogart's Café 283
Boots & Kimo's Homestyle
 Kitchen 286
Boston Style Pizza 275
Boston's North End
 Pizza 286
Breakers Restaurant &
 Bar 295
Brick Fire Tavern 279
Bubbies Ice Cream 283
Buho Cocina 269
Buzz's Original
 Steakhouse 286
Café Hale'iwa 295
Champa Thai 287
Chart House 259
Cheeseburger
 Beachwalk 259
Cheeseburger in
 Paradise 259
Cheeseburger Waikiki 259
Chef Mavro 274
Cholo's Homestyle
 Kitchen 295
Chuck's Cellar 259
Cinnamon's 287
Coquito's 300
Cream Pot 260
Crêpes No Ka 'Oi 287
Cuckoo Coconuts 260
D. K. Steakhouse 260
Da Crawfish & Crab
 Shack 300
Dave & Buster's 270
Dave's Ice Cream 284
Down to Earth 298
Duc's Bistro 279
Duke's Waikiki 261

Eating House 1849 298
Eggs'n Things 261
El Burrito 277
Ethiopian Love 279
Famous Kahuku Shrimp
 Truck 292
Fete 279
Fiji Market & Curry
 Kitchen 292
Flour & Barley 267
Foodland Farms 270
Fumi's Kahuku Shrimp 293
Giovanni Pastrami 261
Giovanni's Aloha Shrimp
 Truck 291
Golden Palace 280
Gordon Biersch 271
Hale'iwa Joe's at Haiku
 Gardens 290
Hale'iwa Joe's Seafood
 Grill 295
Hank's Haute Dogs 271
Hannara Restaurant 300
Happy's Fast & Fresh 262
HI-BBQ 292
Honolulu Chocolate
 Company 278
House Without a Key 262
Hula Dog 262
Hula Grill 262
Hy's Steak House 262
Il Lupino Trattoria & Wine
 Bar 268
Island Snow 287
J.J. Dolan's 280
Just Tacos Mexican Grill &
 Cantina 298
K & K BBQ Inn 287
Kai's Island Korn 292
Kaka'ako Kitchen 276
Kalapawai Café & Deli ..288
Kan Zaman 280
Karai Crab 271
Keneke's 284
Killer Tacos 296
Kobe Japanese Steak
 House 268
Koko Head Café 284
Kona Brewing
 Company 284
Kono's 296
Kua 'Aina Sandwich 296
L&L Hawaiian Barbecue ..285
La Cucaracha 269
La Mariana Sailing
 Club 272

La Mer 267
La'ie Chop Suey 291
Lanikai Juice 288
Legend Seafood 280
Lei Lei's Bar & Grill 293
Lemongrass Vietnamese &
 Thai Cuisine 288
Leonard's 278
Liliha Bakery 276
Little Village Noodle
 House 281
Loco Moco Drive Inn 285
Longboards Bar & Grill ..298
Los Chaparros 277
Los Garcia's 288
Lucky Belly 281
Luibueno's 299
M's Oceanfront
 Restaurant 263
Mai Tai Bar at the Royal
 Hawaiian 263
Makahiki 299
Maria Bonita 281
Marukame Udon 269
Matsumoto's 296
Maui Brewing
 Company 263
Maui Mike's 297
Maui Tacos 288
Maunakea Marketplace 281
Mexico Lindo 289
Michel's 267
Moké's Bread &
 Breakfast 289
Monkeypod Kitchen 299
Moose McGillycuddy's ..263
Morton's Steakhouse 272
Murphy's Bar & Grill 281
Nashville Waikiki 272
Nico's Pier 38 276
Nobu 275
North Shore Kula Grille ..293
North Shore Tacos 291
O'ahu Market 282
'Olelo Room 299
Opal Thai 282
Original Pancake
 House 273
P. F. Chang's 266
Pa'akai 293
Papa Ole's Kitchen 290
Pint + Jigger 273
Prima 289
Rainbow Drive-In 277
Restaurant 604 297
Rock Island Café 264

Romy's Kahuku Shrimp
 Hut 292
Roy's Beach House 293
Ruffage Natural Foods/
 Ahi Bowl 264
Rum Fire 264
Saeng's Thai Cuisine 289
Saigon Noodle House 289
San Lorenzo's 296
Sansei Seafood & Sushi ..269
Scoop of Paradise 296
Serg's Mexican Kitchen ..277
Seven Brothers 291
Seven Brothers at
 the Mill 292
Shark's Cove Grill 294
Shirokiya Japan Village
 Walk 275
Shrimp Shack 290
Siam Garden Café 278
Snow Factory 278
South Shore Grill 285
Spaghettini 297
Sunny Days Café 285
Surf n Turf Tacos 270
Sweet E's Café 273
Tacos & More 301
Taormina 268
Tchin Tchin 282
Ted's Bakery 294
Teddy's Bigger Burgers ..290
Thai Lao 300
The Beach Bar 264
The Greek Corner 274
The Pig & The Lady 282
Tiki's Grill & Bar 265
Tô-Châu 283
Top of Waikiki 265
Town 273
Tropics Bar & Grill 265
Two Scoops Ice Cream
 Parlor 300
Waialua Bakery 297
Wailana Coffee House ..265
Waiola Shave Ice &
 Bakery 278
Whole Foods Market 285
Wiki Wiki Market 266
Willows 277
Wolfgang Puck Express ..266
Wolfgang's Steakhouse ..266
Yard House 266
Dinner Cruises 307
Dinner Shows 308
Island Nightlife 301
Lu'au 301

It's hard to beat this romantic table at La Mer.

By their very nature, restaurant reviews are the most subjective part of any guidebook. Nothing strains the credibility of a guidebook more. No matter what we say, if you eat at enough restaurants here, you will eventually have a dining experience directly in conflict with what this book leads you to believe. All it takes is one person to wreck what is usually a good meal. You've probably had an experience where a friend referred you to a restaurant using reverent terms, indicating that you were about to experience dining ecstasy. And, of course, when you go there, the food is awful and the waiter is a jerk. There are many variables involved in getting a good or bad meal. Is the chef new? Was the place sold last month? Was the waitress just released from prison for mauling a customer? We truly hope that our reviews match your experience. If they don't (or even if they do), please drop us a line. Readers help us *tremendously* to keep tabs on the restaurants, and we read and digest (so to speak) every e-mail.

We often leave out restaurant hours of operation because they change so frequently that the information would be immediately out of date. These decisions are usually made quite capriciously in Hawai'i. If you're going to drive a long way to eat at an establishment, it's best to call first. Restaurants that stand out from the others in some way are highlighted with this *ono* symbol.

In some restaurants around the island you'll see guidebook recommendation plaques, guidebook door stickers and signed guidebooks, but you won't see ours.

The reason? We *never* tell them when we're there. We review everything on the island *anonymously*. We're more interested in being treated like everyone else than copping a free meal. How could you trust our opinion if the restaurant *knew* who we were?

By their reviews, many guidebooks lead you to believe that every meal you eat in Hawai'i will be a feast, the best food in the free world. Frankly, that's not our style. O'ahu, like anywhere else, has ample opportunity to have lousy food served in a rotten ambiance by uncaring waiters.

There are *tons* of restaurants on O'ahu, and we could only include so many. If you have a favorite you want to recommend, send us an e-mail and we'll check it out. We love finding new places.

For each restaurant, we list the price *per person* you can expect to pay. It ranges from the least expensive entrées to the most expensive, plus a beverage and sometimes an appetizer. You can spend more if you try, but this is a good guideline. *The price excludes alcoholic beverages since this component of a meal can be so variable.* Obviously, everyone's ordering pattern is different, but we thought that it would be easier to compare restaurants using actual prices than if we used symbols like different numbers of dollar signs or drawings of forks or whatever to differentiate prices between restaurants.

When we give **directions** to a restaurant, *mauka side* of highway means "toward the mountain" (or away from the ocean). The shopping centers we mention are on the maps to that area.

Most restaurants don't care how you dress. A few discourage tank tops and bathing suits. Some restaurants have dress codes requiring **resort wear**, meaning covered shoes and collared shirts for men (nice shorts are *usually* OK), dressy sportswear or dresses for women. Only a few require jackets.

It's legal to bring your own alcohol to restaurants in Hawai'i, and many restaurants, especially inexpensive ones, have no objections to letting you BYOB.

Local food can be difficult to classify. Basically, local food combines Hawaiian, American, Japanese, Chinese, Filipino and several other types and is (not surprisingly) eaten mainly by locals.

Some restaurants have the annoying and presumptuous habit of including the tip on the bill automatically. Be on the alert for it, or you may double-tip. And what if you get horrible service and don't *want* to tip? Then you're left in the awkward position of making them remove it.

Dining at the resorts is expensive, but you probably aren't being gouged as much as you think because their costs are exorbitant. One resort GM we know confided that they had over $7 million in revenue for their food and beverage department one year, but they only made $100,000 in profit. (And this was the first year they had ever made *any* profit on food.)

When we mention **parking**, you should assume it'll cost you money. Free parking is uncommon and is mentioned when it's available.

The Dept. of Health displays placards outside the entrance of restaurants following surprise inspections. Green means the establishment passed inspection, yellow means up to two violations were observed and red means…the inspector probably didn't stay for lunch. We wouldn't necessarily walk out on a yellow restaurant. Might mean they did something minor or ticked off the wrong guy. Though we stand by our dining reviews, we won't always know when a restaurant fails an inspection. Just keep an eye out for these placards when going out to eat to help ensure a safer meal, and please let us know if you see a red placard at a place we recommend.

Many of the restaurants in the Waikiki area make their entrées available to delivery services, such as **Bite Squad Hawaii** (www.bitesquad.com). For under $11 (depends on where you're staying), they'll pick up your order and bring it to you, which can be *waaay* convenient.

ISLAND FISH & SEAFOOD

Below are descriptions of various island foods. Not all are Hawaiian, but this might be of assistance if you encounter unfamiliar dishes.

'Ahi–Tuna; raw in sashimi or poke, also seared, blackened, baked or grilled; good in fish sandwiches. Try painting ahi steaks with mayonnaise, which *completely* burns off when BBQ'd but seals in the moisture. You end up tasting only the moist ocean steak. Generally most plentiful April through September.

Lobster–Hawaiian spiny lobster is quite good; also called "bugs" by lobster hunters. Maine lobster kept alive on the Big Island are also available.

Mahimahi–Deep ocean fish also known as a dolphinfish; served at lu'au; very common in restaurants. Sometimes tastes fishy (especially if frozen), which can be offset in the preparation.

Marlin–Tasty when smoked, otherwise can be tough; the Pacific Blue Marlin (kajiki) is available almost year round.

Monchong–Excellent-tasting deepwater fish, available year round. Usually served marinated and grilled.

Onaga–Also known as ruby snapper; excellent eating in many preparations.

Ono–Wahoo; *awesome* eating fish and can be prepared many ways; most plentiful May through October. "Ono" is also the Hawaiian word for "delicious."

Opah–Moonfish; excellent eating in many different preparations; generally available April through August.

'Opakapaka–Crimson snapper; great-tasting fish cooked several ways. Common October through February.

'Opihi–Using a special knife, these must be pried off rocks at the shoreline, which can be hazardous. Best eaten raw mixed with salt.

Poke–Fresh raw fish or octopus (tako) mixed with seaweed (limu), sesame seed and other seasonings and oil.

Shutome–Swordfish; dense meat that can be cooked several ways. Most plentiful March through July.

Shrimp–Kahuku shrimp or prawns are farm-raised on the North Shore.

Walu–Also goes by other names such as butterfish and escolar. Be careful not to eat more than 6 ounces. The Hawaiian nickname for this oily fish is maku'u, which means—*ahem*, this is awkward—"uncontrollable bowel discharge." Eat too much, and you may pay more dearly than you intend.

LU'AU FOODS

Chicken lu'au–Chicken cooked in coconut milk and taro leaves.

Haupia–Coconut milk custard. Tasty, but too much will give you the… *ahem*.

Hawaiian sweet potatoes–Purple inside; not as sweet as mainland sweet potatoes but very flavorful.

Kalua pig–Pig cooked in an underground oven called an imu, shredded and mixed with Hawaiian sea salt (outstanding!).

Lomi salmon–Chilled salad consisting of raw, salted salmon, tomatoes and two kinds of onions.

Pipi Kaula–Hawaiian-style beef jerky.

Poi–Steamed taro root pounded into a paste. It's a starch that will take on the taste of other foods mixed with it. Consider dipping your pipi kaula in it. (Now *that* sounds bad if you don't read it right.) Visitors are encouraged to try it at least once so they can badmouth it with authority.

OTHER ISLAND FOODS

Apple bananas–A smaller, denser, smoother texture than regular (Cavendish) bananas and a bit tangy.

Barbecue sticks–Teriyaki-marinated pork, chicken or beef pieces barbecued and served on bamboo sticks.

Bento–Japanese box lunch.

Breadfruit–Melon-sized starchy fruit; served baked, deep fried, steamed or boiled. Definitely an *acquired* taste.

Crackseed–Chinese-style spicy preserved fruits and seeds.

Guava–About the size of an apricot or plum. The inside is full of seeds and tart, so it is rarely eaten raw. Used primarily for juice, jelly or jam.

Hawaiian supersweet corn–The finest corn you ever had, even raw. We'll lie, cheat, steal or maim to get it fresh. Kahuku-grown corn is often available from stands around the North Shore.

Huli huli chicken–Hawaiian BBQ style.

Ka'u oranges–Big Island oranges. Usually, the uglier the orange, the better it tastes.

Kim chee–A Korean relish consisting of pickled cabbage, onions, radishes, garlic and chilies.

Kona coffee–Grown on the Kona coast of the Big Island. Smooth, mild flavor.

Kulolo–Steamed taro pudding. (Tasty.)

Laulau–Pork, beef or fish wrapped in taro and ti leaves, then steamed. (You don't eat the ti leaf wrapping.)

Liliko'i–Passion fruit.

Loco moco–Rice, meat patty, egg and gravy. A hit with cholesterol lovers.

Lychee–A reddish, woody peel that is discarded for the sweet, white fruit inside. Be careful of the pit. Good, small seed (or chicken-tongue) lychees are so good, they should be illegal.

Macadamia nut–A large, round Australian nut grown on the Big Island.

Malasada–Portuguese donut dipped in sugar. Best when served hot.

Manapua–Steamed or baked bun filled with meat.

Mango–Bright orange fruit with yellow pink skin. Distinct, tasty flavor.

Manju–Cookie filled with a sweet center.

Musubi–Cold steamed rice rolled in black seaweed wrappers, sometimes with sliced Spam.

Papaya–Melon-like, pear-shaped fruit with yellow skin; best eaten chilled. Good at breakfast. Don't eat too much or you'll...be sticking close to home.

Plate lunch–An island favorite as an inexpensive, filling lunch. Consists of "two-scoop rice," a scoop of macaroni salad and some type of meat, either beef, chicken or fish. Sometimes called a box lunch. Great for picnics.

Portuguese sausage–Pork sausage, highly seasoned with red pepper. Tastes weird to some people.

Pupu–Appetizer, finger foods or snacks.

Saimin–Noodles cooked in either chicken, pork or fish broth. Word is peculiar to Hawai'i. Local Japanese say the dish comes from China. Local Chinese say it comes from Japan.

Sea salt–Excellent (and strong) salt distilled from seawater.

Shave ice–A block of ice is "shaved" (*never* crushed) into a ball with flavored syrup poured over the top. Best served with ice cream on the bottom. Very delicious.

Taro–Found in everything from enchiladasto breads and rolls to taro chips and fritters. Tends to color foods purple. Has lots of fluoride for your teeth.

WAIKIKI AMERICAN

Included in this category are **Pacific Rim** (sort of a fusion of American and various cuisines from around the Pacific, including Hawaiian and Asian) and **Seafood**. This is because so many restaurants on O'ahu blend these categories, and it just doesn't make sense to try to separate them.

A special note on breakfasts: Many of the resorts in Waikiki will be happy to hose you with sickeningly overpriced breakfasts—often buffets—with the assumption that you won't want to venture too far first thing in the morning. $20–$30 breakfast buffets of mediocre food, or $10–$15 pancakes are common. Our philosophy is if you're gonna get your pockets picked in the morning, let it at least be at an oceanfront location, where the sounds of the surf might drown out the groans of fellow patrons discovering that the check isn't really a typo after all. We've tried to present you with viable options to the usual hotel fleece job.

Atlantis Seafood & Steak
2284 Kalakaua Ave, Waikiki • (808) 922-6868
The signs on the sidewalk make the prices seem oh, so reasonable, but the ultimate experience is a bit less so. If you're expecting lots of beef options and fresh island fish, you're likely to be disappointed. The steak is mostly their prime rib or the crazy expensive filet. Seafood is frozen mahi mahi, shrimp, salmon, or fish and chips. (Their web site says it's "fresh island caught," but even our waiter agreed with us that it's frozen.) You're paying for the prominent Kalakaua location, not quality food ingredients, which taste cheap. (Hey, at least the mai tais are fairly good.) Mostly indoor with a few outdoor tables on the lanai overlooking Kalakaua Avenue (though the tiki torches warm up two of those tables). $15–$20 for lunch—burgers, a couple of pastas, and fish and chips—$25–$55 for dinner. Near Duke's Lane and Kalakaua.

Chart House
1765 Ala Moana Blvd, Waikiki • (808) 941-6660
ono Dinner is a real treat here. Not part of the national Chart House chain, they have a classic steakhouse style (gas lamps on each table, polite service

and high prices) with great seafood and a killer pupu menu. Their prime rib borders on perfection and sells out nightly. Some worthy alternatives are the stuffed 'ahi or the famous garlic steak. For more intimate seating, try to get one of their booths. We like to sit on the lounge side with the soft live Hawaiian music nightly. Seating is first-come first-served and has the same elevated view of the harbor. They have an enormous pupu menu, plus they offer some of the expensive entrées in a smaller portion size and price. $10–$30 in the lounge. The dinner menu is $30–$120. On the corner of Hobron and Holomoana overlooking the Ala Wai boat harbor.

Cheeseburger in Paradise
2500 Kalakaua Ave, Waikiki • (808) 923-3731
A bamboo-laden restaurant that looks like a South Seas/Caribbean hoarder's closet, minus the cats. We counted over 20 'ukuleles on the walls and shelves among the countless other interesting artifacts. They started on Maui in 1989 as Cheeseburger in Paradise. (Jimmy Buffett sued them because he has a song by that name. They settled and changed the name of future locations, and Buffett launched his own chain by the same name, but it's unrelated to the Hawai'i locations.) The menu is the same at all three locations. Burgers start at $14 and include fries. Lots of burger options plus other sandwich and salad choices. The burgers are mediocre, and they will *only* cook them medium-pink. $16–$25 for lunch and dinner. On Kalakaua near the Alohilani Resort. The other Kalakaua location, called **Cheeseburger Waikiki**, at the corner of Ala Moana, has parking. For the Lewers location, called **Cheeseburger Beachwalk**, park at the Embassy Suites Waikiki Beach Walk and have your ticket validated.

Chuck's Cellar
150 Kaiulani Ave, Waikiki • (808) 923-4488
Perfectly named. Located in a dark, thick,

jazz-filled cellar, the atmosphere really works. The food is steak and seafood and includes their soup and salad bar, baked potato or rice. We didn't give them an ono because it feels like they're cutting corners. And when you're in a cellar in Waikiki—even one with a cool atmosphere—you gotta be firing on all cylinders for this price. Chuck's ain't right now. $35–$50 for dinner. Park at the Ohana East on Kuhio Avenue. Don't drive too far into their garage; it dead ends with no place to turn around.

Cream Pot
444 Niu St, Waikiki • (808) 429-0945
Ya gotta start with the ambiance. It's like being inside a French fairytale cottage house. You'll either love it or hate it. If only there were some soft surfaces to soak up some of the loud, ambient noise. Next, no description would be complete without warning you that there's usually a wait. Sometimes really long, or as they'll put it, "Just a few minutes," even when tables are empty. Earlier arrivals may get luckier. Don't hesitate to remind them you exist. We've seen people forgotten and *visually age* in the process.

Last comes the food. Not your typical Denny's breakfast. Crêpes, Belgian waffles, hand-rolled omelets, baked eggs and usually some creative specials. Sweet items abound as do more savory dishes. It's not about heartiness here; it's about quality. The soufflé pancakes are delicious but take approximately *one lifetime* to deliver. The menu is what you get in a French dream from a Japanese chef from Southern California. If you can forgive the thin service and the time it'll take to complete your meal (don't say we didn't warn you), you'll be happy with the results. $12–$22 for breakfast or brunch. Closed Tuesdays. At Niu and Ala Wai. Open 6:30 a.m.–2:30 p.m. Park in their building, and they'll validate.

Cuckoo Coconuts
333 Royal Hawaiian Ave, Waikiki • (808) 926-1620
These guys are really trying here. They've taken an old parking lot and created an almost comically stereotypical tiki bar (which is something you don't actually see very often in Hawai'i—sorry to shatter illusions) illuminated by colorful rope lights. But they embrace the tacky, and it kinda works, especially at night when the dark helps make it look more charming and less dingy. Nighttime also brings live music. The problem is the location. Instead of a nice sandy spot on the beach, they are a half-block inland from the main drag through Waikiki, surrounded by the city and city noise. And food quality is mixed. The Hawaiian burger tastes very standard—all of the flavor comes from the pineapple. But the fish and chips is good. Instead of big chunks they serve little filets, soft as can be. $10–$20 for lunch and dinner. People seem to like the piña colada served in a hollowed-out pineapple, but it's $16, so you have to decide how badly you want that Instagram pic. On Royal Hawaiian and Lauula Street.

d. k. Steakhouse
2552 Kalakaua Ave, Waikiki • (808) 931-6280
Part of the same restaurant, owner and kitchen as **Sansei Seafood & Sushi.** Typical surf-and-turf dinner options for $35–$85, but they actually dry age their beef on-site. What's dry-aged beef? Oh, so glad you asked. First thing to know—all beef is aged. The usual method (because it's cheaper and faster) is called wet aging, which is done in a sealed bag that keeps in moisture. The process of dry-aging involves hanging it in a freezer to let it dry out for a longer period of time to concentrate the flavor and give the enzymes time to break down the meat to make it more tender. (Other fancy steakhouses in Waikiki also offer dry-aged

beef.) Here, you've got the option of a 15-day or 30-day dry-aged ribeye. If you've never tried it before and aren't sure what you're getting into, go for the 15-day. Most of the tenderization happens in the first two weeks, and the flavor, while more intense than wet-aged, won't be too much of a departure from what you are used to. (After two weeks, the difference is marginal at best, but the cost keeps going up the longer it's aged.) On the third floor of the Waikiki Beach Marriott Resort.

Duke's Waikiki
2335 Kalakaua Ave, Waikiki • (808) 922-2268

ono As legendary as its namesake here in the islands, Duke's has the sort of dreamy atmosphere that's synonymous with Waikiki, and it's one of our favorite places to eat breakfast. Some of the tables overlook a pool, while others overlook the famous surf spot. (Duke Kahanamoku was the sport's first ambassador, the guy who introduced surfing to the American mainland.) Most, however, overlook other tables. Get there close to their 7 a.m. opening time to get a coveted railing table. Koa wood is everywhere, and the ambiance, though it can get a bit loud and crowded, is pleasing.

As for the food, it's dependably well prepared and generously portioned. Fresh fish, steak, pizzas, sandwiches and burgers. Many items have an Asian or Pacific twist. They make a decent mai tai, too. You can eat at the restaurant or the **Barefoot Bar**; each has separate menus. The breakfast buffet with an omelet station, at $18, is a no-brainer to recommend. What a great way to start the day! Lunch is either a $19 (plus beverages) buffet or off the menu for $12–$18. Dinner is $20–$36. Consider the fish sautéed and herb crusted—excellent! Try the huge hula pie for dessert. Reservations recommended for dinner. In the Outrigger Waikiki Beach Resort.

Eggs'n Things
343 Saratoga Rd, Waikiki • (808) 923-3447
2464 Kalakaua Ave, Waikiki • (808) 926-3447
451 Piikoi St, Honolulu • (808) 538-3447

ono They've been around since 1974, and there's probably been a line outside from day one. Expect a wait no matter which of their three locations you choose. That's because they have a good breakfast selection with huge portions for relatively cheap prices. (The pancakes, though, are surprisingly flavorless. Same with the French toast. Best to stick to the eggs instead of the things.) Open at 6 a.m. for breakfast, there's usually no wait during the first hour. They're also open for dinner, but their breakfast fingerprints are all over items like steak and eggs or chicken fried steak. $10–$18. On Saratoga just off Kalakaua.

The menu is mostly the same across locations, but the atmosphere is completely different at each. The one on Saratoga is the flagship, and the inside is cramped and worn in a charming kind of way. The restaurant on Kalakaua Avenue is across the street from Waikiki Beach. They'll have you order and pay before being seated so they can move a higher volume of people through. (Expect subtle hints that they want the table if you take too much time to enjoy your food.) The location on Piikoi, just outside Waikiki, is the least crowded and most relaxed.

Giovanni Pastrami
227 Lewers St, Waikiki • (808) 923-2100

It's kind of a cross between an upscale sports bar and a Roman bathhouse. Italian glass-covered columns line the entry to a central bar surrounded by plasma screens. If you like Reuben sandwiches, they make a seriously juicy one. Many of the items are priced tightly between $16 and $18—omelets, salads, etc. Breakfast is served all day. Though pricey, portions are large. You'll spend $12–$25 no matter what you order. Happy hour is your best bet. You get a free slice of cheese pizza with every drink (Mon.–Fri. from 3–6 p.m. and nightly 10 p.m. until last call). On Lewers Street across from the Waikiki Beachwalk.

Happy's Fast & Fresh

2055 Kalia Rd, Waikiki • (808) 955-0555

ono Although Hale Koa is a military hotel restricted to active duty and retired military, a little-known loophole in the rules allows *anyone* from the beach to walk onto their property and eat at their snack bar by the pool (Barefoot Bar) or Happy's Fast & Fresh farther into the resort (where burgers are under $5). This means the cheap food and drinks at the bar (with no sales tax) are available to *you*. So if you're irritated at the thought of $20 burgers at other resorts lining Waikiki, head over here and pay around $5. Burgers, hot dogs, chicken sandwiches and similar items at the cheapest prices around. (Their other restaurants are not available to the general public.) Grab a bite, plop yourself onto the beach, and pat yourself on the back for your ingenuity. $4–$9 for lunch and dinner at the pool. The mai tais at Barefoot Bar are pretty good, though perhaps we've been influenced by what a sweet deal this place is.

House Without a Key

2199 Kalia Rd, Waikiki • (808) 923-2311

A serene, mostly outdoor setting beside Waikiki Beach (which you can't really see from your table—just the ocean). Dinner features well-dressed, well-lit live musicians performing low-key Hawaiian music. The menu is small (as is the wine list), and it doesn't really appear to have a theme. The service is excellent, but the quality of food and preparation doesn't justify a $22 burger. The coconut cake is a great way to top things off, though. The mai tai (which isn't on the menu) is topped off with 151 rums to take the pain out of the prices. $20–$40 for dinner, lunch is $15–$25. Resort casual attire required.

They don't take reservations. In the Halekulani resort.

Hula Dog

2442 Kuhio Ave, Waikiki • (808) 256-7008

ono Similar to pigs in a blanket, it's an unusual way to deliver polish or veggie dogs. They are inserted in a bread sleeve with their "secret sauce" (though I'm partial to their spicy garlic pepper cheese sauce) with a number of tropical relishes on top. Pretty tasty. To drink, you have fresh squeezed lemonade, water or whatever you brought with you. $7–$11 for lunch and dinner. Located in a food truck at the corner of Kuhio and Kapuni.

Hula Grill

2335 Kalakaua Ave, Waikiki • (808) 923-4852

ono On the second floor of the Outrigger Waikiki hotel, the restaurant has seating that mostly overlooks the beach. The atmosphere is breezy and relaxed, with bamboo and koa wood everywhere. A great spot to get breakfast if the buffet line at Duke's downstairs is too long. (And it probably is….) All the classic meat, eggs and pancakes with a local twist. They don't churn you through the way so many other Waikiki restaurants do, and they serve breakfast late, which is great if you want to start your day by going to the beach first. *Breakfast and lunch* prices are reasonable for what you get and where you're getting it. Dinner (steak, seafood, salad) is far pricier. Good vegetarian options. Excellent service. $10–$15 for breakfast, $10–$26 for lunch, $25–$56 for dinner. You can also find it by strolling along the Royal-Moana stretch of Waikiki Beach.

Hy's Steak House

2440 Kuhio Ave, Waikiki • (808) 922-5555

ono A wonderfully elegant steak house that serves the best steak on the island, *bar none*. They clearly use top-notch ingredients, and their preparation skills are superb. The excellent steak selection is augmented by some seafood, including lobster. The staff seems happy and relaxed, not stuffy. (They wear tuxedos, but you'll be fine in collared shirts and long pants—or dresses, if you prefer.) The glassed-in grill room is a beautiful addition to an upscale yet comfortable atmosphere with music some nights. Overall, though the price is almost as high as Morton's, we don't feel gouged here and look forward to re-reviewing whenever we can justify the price. $35–$60 for dinner, with a few pricier items. Reservations recommended. Valet parking only. On Kuhio Avenue near Uluniu.

M's Oceanfront Restaurant
2476 Kalakaua Ave, Waikiki • (808) 971-1766
OK… we lied. Forgive us. It's not *really* called M's. If we called it by its real name—*McDonald's*—you'd never read this review. But these golden arches, on Kalakaua and Liliuokalani Street, are across the street from Kuhio Beach. Grab your McMuffin and coffee and take it to one of the beachside tables. Two people—for $16—eat on the beach. Yeah, works for us. A similar option at "Royal Burger" (ahem, Burger King) exists at Kalakaua and Ohua Street. Open 24 hours.

Mai Tai Bar at the Royal Hawaiian
2259 Kalakaua Ave, Waikiki • (808) 923-7311
A place for an afternoon cocktail since it's right next to the beach. (Oddly, their mai tais are wildly inconsistent—sometimes way too sweet, sometimes like nasty gasoline.) Nothing's great here. Not the food (overpriced thin pizzas and burgers), not the service and not the drinks. (Overall, we've had bad luck with their tropical drinks here, though out of a sense of duty we'll keep trying.) But what a great location—at least if you're on a royal budget. At the Royal Hawaiian, Waikiki. $22 burgers, $16 salads, $30 for a novelty drink in a hollowed-out pineapple, about double the rate of most elsewhere else that sells 'em—that's the pricing scheme here.

Maui Brewing Company
2300 Kalakaua Ave, Waikiki • (808) 843-2739
Hoppy people will be happy here; lager lovers might be unimpressed. The beer is brewed on Maui, and they have a huge selection. (The coconut porter is our favorite.) If you can't get a table, the enormous bar is open seating. The food is pricey but tasty—pizza, burgers, seafood and other bar fare with a local twist. Many ingredients come from local farmers, though some dishes are described in a way that makes them *sound* better than they are in reality (we're looking at you, breakfast bowls). They have some creative cocktails as well, especially the breakfast-themed ones. Speaking of which, there are plenty of items that cater to those looking to soak up alcohol from the night before, and you can order from any menu, any time of the day. (Going to a brewery to nurse a hangover sounds like a recipe for trouble. Just sayin'.) The open-air, modern feel makes for a comfortable spot to escape the hustle and bustle of the street. Like all good breweries, they also have some games like shuffleboard and foosball. Breakfast is $10–$25, lunch and dinner is $14–$32. Across from the Royal Hawaiian Center on Kalakaua Avenue.

Moose McGillycuddy's
310 Lewers St, Waikiki • (808) 923-0751
ono A pretty hoppin' place at night with live music and dancing upstairs. The food is ordinary pub food—nothing special. Burgers, sandwiches and lots of pupus (appetizers) at lunch; add some Mexican, chicken and beef at dinner. They have a long happy hour from 4–7 p.m. with ever-changing drink specials after 7 p.m. Go for the music and nightlife

or for breakfast. $9–$15 for breakfast (unless you order their *12-egg* omelet for $24), and the bloody mary is a good choice here. $12–$22 for lunch and dinner. On Lewers Street just mauka (toward the mountain) of Kalakaua.

Rock Island Café
131 Kaiulani Ave, Waikiki • (808) 923-8033

It's a totally manufactured, hit-you-over-the-head-with-nostalgia, 1950s-themed diner, but the colorful retro setting is kinda fun, if you enjoy a place decorated with a life-size statue of Elvis, old Marilyn Monroe movie posters, vinyl records, a barbershop chair, Coca-Cola memorabilia and whatever other sentimentality they can cram in, plus there are lots of collectibles on display available for purchase. The food is standard American fare: hot dogs, sandwiches, burgers (including one with ham and pineapple on top to make it Hawaiian), personal pizzas, milk shakes, sundaes, root beer floats. They've got a small bar with beer and a variety of quintessentially Hawaiian cocktails: mai tai, pina colada, lava flow, blue Hawaiian. The food is *adequate*, nothing more, nothing less. The waitresses wear pink dresses, and they've got oldies playing, but they are clearly aware that demographics are changing: You're just as likely to hear the theme song to *Frasier* or the *Facts of Life* as you are the Beatles. A little cheaper than the other places to eat around here at $7–$15. Order and pay first at the cashier up front. At the King's Village Shopping Center, on Kaiulani Avenue at Koa, one block inland from the Waikiki Beach Center.

Ruffage Natural Foods/Ahi Bowl
2443 Kuhio Ave, Waikiki • (808) 922-2042

ono A longtime natural food store that has a number of very tasty hot items ranging from the gluten-free (very tasty curry chicken) to vegetarian items (good veggie chili dogs or grab their breakfast tofu scrambler) to sandwiches (not all of which are flavorful) to great poke (a *very* local dish). $7–$17 for lunch or early dinner. Just a few tables overrun with traffic noise—might want to get it to go. On Kuhio Avenue between Uluniu and Liliuokalani.

Rum Fire
2255 Kalakaua Ave, Waikiki • (808) 922-4422

ono A cool, trendy upscale bar atmosphere (lots of rum, lots of fire) with tons of well-conceived drinks and a killer rum selection. Check out their "rum bible" with 101 selections from around the world. (We're *plowing* our way through that list—just for you—still loving the *Ron Zacapa* and the *Zaya*.) Also a good beer and wine by-the-glass selection. Oh, yeah, and food. The selection is modest, and there's no real theme. Think of it as high-end bar food with a definite local flair. Portions aren't huge, and the appetizer list is pretty meager. But the food's tasty. $12–$20 for lunch, up to $30 for dinner. In the Sheraton Waikiki. Friday and Saturday nights it turns into a dance club at 9 p.m. with a cover charge and bottle service.

The Beach Bar
2365 Kalakaua Ave, Waikiki • (808) 922-3111

ono Expensive drinks, but this is probably the most perfect beach bar location in Waikiki. And sure, service is scant, but the live entertainment, good mai tais and intimacy with the beach help to slow you down anyway. So relax under the shade of the sprawling banyan tree, feel the ocean breeze on your face, and get carried away by the soft Hawaiian music. Look for the corner table on the left side to be as close to the sand as possible. Burgers, sandwiches, salads and pricey appetizers with a few ever-changing entrées added for dinner. $18–$25 for lunch and dinner. At the Moana Surfrider hotel next door to the Waikiki Beach Center.

Tiki's Grill & Bar

2570 Kalakaua Ave, Waikiki • (808) 923-8454

Their trademark is the retro-Hawaiian décor—sort of a '50s look. The food's so-so—not great, not bad—but their love of salt is apparent in *everything*. Even some of the dessert selections include a salted caramel sauce. Maybe it's so you can choke down their gasoline-like mai tais. Huge menu of fresh fish, sandwiches, pasta, fish tacos, short ribs, fish and chips, and burgers at lunch. Add prime rib, steak and shrimp at dinner. Some tables have nice views of the Kapahulu Ponds across the street. Breakfast is continental-style for $15 and nothing to write home about . Lunch is a touch better at $13–$18. It's $26–$35 for dinner. At the corner of Kalakaua and Paoakalani at the Waikiki Beach Hotel. Go up the escalator.

Top of Waikiki

2270 Kalakaua Ave, Waikiki • (808) 923-3877

ono Every table here gets the best views—eventually. That's because the whole restaurant slowly turns to give you a 360-degree view of the city, ocean and Diamond Head. It takes one hour to make a full revolution, and the views are excellent, though a small number of people will find the movement unsettling when suddenly looking up. They advertise sunset specials, but, unfortunately, the sunset view isn't as spectacular as they would have you believe. (There are a couple buildings that block the horizon where the sun sets during parts of the year.) $40–$65 a plate—more for surf and turf—with top-notch service and expertly prepared seafood, beef, poultry and some vegetarian options. The ginger pesto crusted monchong with soy mustard sauce literally melts in your mouth. We also like the kurobuta pork chop. The centrally located bar is a great place to come for $5–$9 happy hour drinks and $8–$16 pupus. Look around for the exit before you leave. It's probably going to be in a different spot than when you entered, and you may end up doing a lap before you leave. Dinner only. No beach attire, and reservations recommended. If you park at Waikiki Shopping Plaza or Waikiki Business Plaza, they will validate.

Tropics Bar & Grill

2005 Kalia Rd, Waikiki • (808) 952-5960

Let's start with something positive. They have a great location on the beach. Also… well, that's it. The food is overpriced, bland and poorly presented. The service is unfriendly, and they seem understaffed every time we've been there. We hit places like this multiple times—because everyone has a bad day now and then—but these guys are consistently bad all around. Expect to wait 60–90 minutes for dinner and close to an hour at lunch. For that wait you can get a $21 burger that tastes like a formerly frozen patty. If you'd rather come for breakfast, you'll find a $26 omelet. They have a decent mai tai, but you may have to wait until it snows in Hawai'i before you get it. You have better options on the beach. Dinner will run you $20–$49, lunch is mostly $23 sandwiches. In the Hilton Hawaiian Village.

Wailana Coffee House

1860 Ala Moana Blvd, Waikiki • (808) 955-1764

A longtime landmark since 1970. Despite the reputation among locals, the food's merely average—nothing more—but the price is right. The breakfast selection is pretty good (the Jamboree is a good deal and includes coffee) and the portions are huge. Lunch and dinner (served any time) is a large selection of steak, seafood, burgers, soups, local dishes and salads. At Ala Moana and Ena in north Waikiki—parking is in the public parking garage on Ena Road and is only $1 with validation. $7–$12 for breakfast, $9–$16 for lunch and $9–$20 dinner. Open 24-hours daily, except for Tuesday night when they close at 9 p.m. and reopen at 6 a.m. Wednesday.

Wiki Wiki Market
2005 Kalia Rd, Waikiki • (808) 949-4321

Handy location to grab some simple grinds while you're hanging at the Kahanamoku section of Waikiki Beach. Their best offering is the tasty Italian panini. They also have sandwiches, teriyaki chicken and burgers. They also have overpriced, dry scrambled eggs for breakfast. We can't give an ONO to any place that charges $10 for a hot dog (and still look ourselves in the mirror). It's comparable to convenience store fare, and the location is convenient for a grab and go. Just behind Tropics at the Hilton Hawaiian Village. $12–$18.

Wolfgang Puck Express
2570 Kalakaua Ave, Waikiki • (808) 931-6226

Ol' Wolfgang probably has a lot going on, but we wonder if he's ever actually visited this place. It's supposed to be fast food on the beach, but service is often achingly slow and rude. It took a half hour to get a salad and some overcooked mahimahi. On another occasion we tried the pizza and found it so-so and overpriced. You can do better. $10–$13 for breakfast, $10–$15 for lunch or dinner. Underneath Tiki's Grill and Bar at the Waikiki Beach Hotel.

Wolfgang's Steakhouse
2301 Kalakaua Ave, Waikiki • (808) 922-3600

First of all, this does not refer to Wolfgang Puck. This guy was the head waiter at a famous New York steakhouse and came out to Hawai'i to open his own. The atmosphere *looks* classy (especially with the huge wine room), but it's loud inside, and the service is not particularly responsive. You'll be paying big bucks (their cheapest steak, NY, is $66), but their menu stresses family-style steak—for two, three or four—so hopefully everyone likes it cooked the same way. Everything is à la carte and sides are crazy expensive. ($12 for mashed potatoes or steamed spinach?) Overall, it's the kind of experience where you walk out saying, "For that kind of money I expected a lot more." $70–$90 for dinner. In the Royal Hawaiian Shopping Center.

Yard House
226 Lewers St, Waikiki • (808) 923-9273

ONO A small chain with a powerful trademark. They have 130 beers on tap. (Mainland locations have over *200* on tap, so ignore the sign out front saying they have the largest selection in the world here.) They use some impressive technology and infrastructure to keep the beer cold here. The chain is named after the 3-foot-tall glasses they *used* to offer. (You'll now have to settle for two *half*-yards of beer.) As for food, they have a huge selection of steak, rib, seafood, burgers, pizza and more, and the quality is pretty good. Try the mac 'n' cheese with chicken, bacon, and truffle oil. Expect it *loud* in here. Happy hour from 2:00–5:30 is *all* the beers on tap. $12–$25 (plus a few pricier items) for lunch and dinner. Easy to spot on Lewers mauka of Kalia Rd.

WAIKIKI CHINESE

P. F. Chang's
2201 Kalakaua Ave, Waikiki • (808) 628-6760

ONO Part of a nationwide chain, but this *super*-prominent location and their two stories of usually full tables command attention. Expect to wait for a table during peak times. The gourmet Chinese food is consistently tasty and the selection more than ample. Portions are mostly large enough to allow one per person plus a side or appetizer. The best secret here is their happy hour food. Come in before 6, and you can feast on their cheaper lettuce wraps, crispy beans and more and make a meal of it. Too bad their adult beverages are often disappointing. $19–$31 for dinner. At the Royal Hawaiian Shopping Center. Entrance on Lewers Street.

WAIKIKI FRENCH

La Mer
2199 Kalia Rd, Waikiki • (808) 923-2311

ONO One of the most expensive meals you'll find in Waikiki. But it also has a dreamy, romantic atmosphere, excellent service and well-crafted French food with local ingredients. A great place to propose to that someone special. Reservations recommended as are long sleeves or jackets for men. The menu is a seven-course sampler that takes about 3 hours and costs $205 *per person*. There are also three- or four-course options available for $125 or $155 respectively. In the Halekulani resort.

Michel's
2895 Kalakaua Ave, Waikiki • (808) 923-6552

ONO So let's get something straight at the start: You're going to spend a lot tonight. This top shelf dining experience is plopped right on a cozy chunk of beach with exceptional views looking down the whole of Waikiki. You're going to get delicious food served by an attentive staff. They label themselves as French food, but we're... how do we say this? We're happier than we would be in a classic French restaurant. The food is a bit more substantial, the service more accommodating and empathetic, and the portions on many items more generous. (Not desserts, though, which are off the scale in terms of quality—especially the creme brûlée and the warm chocolate soufflé—but portions are mercifully small.) Many of the entrées are prepared tableside—even the lobster bisque—and we've found these selections to be their best offerings. They also have a tasting menu for around $100 (add $40 for wine pairing). You can reserve a table right at the edge, next to the beach, but those are usually spoken for a month or two in advance. The good news: Nearly all tables have good views. From the seafood en papillote to the châteaubriand (for two) to the warm seafood salad—we haven't had a bad meal yet. And, when we look around, most people seem pretty happy—until they get the bill. Then the crushing reality may make them wish they'd had one more of those tasty martinis to kill the pain. $50–$100 for dinner. At the Diamond Head end of Waikiki behind the Lotus Hotel near Sans Souci Beach. Reservations recommended.

WAIKIKI ITALIAN

Arancino
255 Beachwalk, Waikiki • (808) 923-5557
A small Italian café with a half-dozen or so pastas and some 12-inch pizzas with thin crust and more traditional Italian toppings. The prices are reasonable for what you get, and the place is always full by 7 p.m.—often 6 p.m.—and they don't take reservations. Your best bet is to put your name on the list and then stroll around Waikiki until they call you. They're pretty efficient at turning the tables—perhaps too efficient. $15–$35 for dinner. On Beachwalk. Paid parking at the Bank of Hawai'i building at Beachwalk and Kalakaua. There are also locations at the Waikiki Beach Marriott Resort and the Kahala Hotel & Resort.

Flour & Barley
2330 Kalakaua Ave, Waikiki • (808) 892-2993

ONO There are lots of opportunities to spend big bucks on food at the International Marketplace. After walking by a $90 piece of beef at Strip Skirt, this, happily, ain't one of them. The flour refers to their thin crust 11-inch pizzas. The barley refers to the beer. Though the draft selection is not that big, they make up for it with lots of bottled beer and tasty cocktails. They also have a few pastas and chicken, which are a lot pricier—almost as if they really want you to stick with the pizza. So we have. And the results are pretty darned good. (We like the Gianna, which makes good use of pine nuts.) Red sauce and garlic cream sauce with more plant selections than animals. If you're solo, the bar is a good place to *grind* your pizza (a local word for eating). $16–$30 for lunch and dinner.

Il Lupino Trattoria & Wine Bar
2233 Kalakaua Ave, Waikiki • (808) 922-3400

ono The dining room is dimly lit and has a romantic feel, but try to get a table outside, in the Royal Hawaiian courtyard. Classic Italian dining with excellent service and delicious food. They offer lots of simple dishes that are meant to be shared, similar to tapas, and many entrees can be ordered family style. They do seafood well here, and you may lean toward those dishes when you see the price of their steaks (usually over $100—enough to exclude from our price averages). Despite an extensive selection of liquor, the bartending skills here aren't the best, so stick with something from their massive wine list. Parking is in the Royal Hawaiian garage, and they'll validate. $12–$20 for breakfast, $15–$40 for lunch and $25–$50 for dinner, with a few more expensive items on each menu, including a monster Porterhouse steak for $120.

Taormina
227 Lewers St, Waikiki • (808) 926-5050

A vast menu bolstered by a huge wine selection (by the bottle) with lots of great Italian reds. Food flavors are bold and memorable and, being Sicilian, lean more toward red sauces. The crema di mascarpone con gamberetti e capasante (a seafood bruschetta) appetizer is amazing and makes us want to come back just for that. Entrées are bursting with flavor here, especially the lasagna. When the food is this tasty—even when you're not hungry—you know you've hit a home run. Service is attentive, but the outside patio table ambiance is not as good as the indoor seats. They can be a bit stingy on the wine pours. On Lewers Street makai of Don Ho Lane. Parking at the Embassy Suites and Wyndham Hotel, and they'll partially validate. $22–$45 with a couple of pricier steaks and some cheaper items at lunch.

WAIKIKI JAPANESE

Benihana of Tokyo
2005 Kalia Rd, Waikiki • (808) 955-5955

Part of the Benihana chain of teppan-yaki restaurants (where the food is prepared in front of you by a knife-wielding chef). The sushi is not the best, but the cooking show is kind of fun, and the chefs are sometimes pretty engaging. It's expensive, but if you've never done teppan-yaki, it's an interesting experience. Overall, the food's not bad, but not remarkable. Steak, lobster, shrimp and vegetables on a sizzling grill. At the Hilton Hawaiian Village $12–$25 for lunch, $22–$80 for dinner. Reservations recommended.

Kobe Japanese Steak House
1841 Ala Moana Blvd, Waikiki • (808) 941-4444

When we contemplated this review, it sounded so close to Benihana's that we decided to focus on their differences. Mostly teppan-yaki, with sushi and a large pupu menu, Kobe has been open since 1972, has fewer choices on the menu and valet parking. The building really shows its age compared to Benihana's facilities. The food is pretty good, but the chefs weren't very entertaining or engaging. For the price you'd expect more. They also have annoying photographers who solicit each table before and after your meal. Kobe is behind the Hilton Hawaiian Village on Ala Moana Boulevard. Try nearby Benihana first. If you can't get in for some reason, go to Kobe. $25–$55 for dinner.

Marukame Udon
2310 Kuhio Ave, Waikiki • (808) 931-6000

ono This review is predicated on the concept that long lines don't scare you. (They definitely scare me.) This Japanese noodle house draws a steady crowd, even when there aren't tour buses lining up out front. You'll immediately see noodles being made from scratch. Grab a tray and a tempura plate and pick your udon—sauce, curry, seasoned beef, etc. Choose hot or cold and large or small, and watch 'em prepare your meal. Continue through the cafeteria-style line to select your tempura and musubi options. Everything tempura is à la carte and cheap. Lines might be long, but they are quick, efficient and clean. The udon noodles are delicious. The broth might be a tad weak if you were raised on packets of cheap ramen noodles. Feel free to add an extra cup of salt if that's the case. The tempura chicken is borderline addictive. $3.75 to $7.25 covers all udon options. Expect to spend about $10. Don't forget to bus your dishes, and feel free to leave yourself a generous tip. On Kuhio near Nohonani Street.

Sansei Seafood & Sushi
2552 Kalakaua Ave, Waikiki • (808) 931-6286
An impressive sushi-making machine, this local chain is famous for its 50 percent off early bird special on Sunday and Monday. The doors open at 5:15 p.m., but you'll want to be there an hour early to get in line. They slash their food prices in half until 6 p.m., so grab a to-go menu while you wait, and be prepared to order when you sit down. The sushi rolls come out lightning fast. The menu has some inventive rolls and entrées, and the service is fantastic. The signature drinks are pretty good here, and they pack a punch. Try the apple tart for dessert. $14–$35 for dinner. On the third floor of the Waikiki Beach Marriott Resort. They were just shy of an ONO because many of the rolls were too small and a bit underwhelming for the price. But it's a good place to go for the early bird special.

WAIKIKI MEXICAN

Buho Cocina
2250 Kalakaua Ave, Waikiki • (808) 922-2846
Modern Mexican served on a rooftop setting in the heart of Waikiki. This isn't where you want to come if you're looking for a standard burrito. Instead you'll find dishes such as wagyu beef nachos, smoked brisket tacos, avocado tacos, Mexican-flavored poke (raw, cubed and seasoned ahi), and carne asada fajitas. $12–$24, with most dishes at the high end of that range, plus pricey appetizers. Pricey but creative drinks, many with a Mexican twist on classic Hawaiian cocktails. The cantina is open late. Awnings provide shade, and they've got fire pits at night. At the corner of Kalakaua Avenue and Royal Hawaiian. Take the elevator from the street to the fifth floor of the Victoria's Secret building. Dress sharp and make a reservation, or you can expect a long wait during peak times.

La Cucaracha
2446 Koa Ave, Waikiki • (808) 924-3366
It's a bit gutsy naming a restaurant La Cucaracha (which literally means *the cockroach*). The atmosphere is bright and festive, but the food leaves something to be desired. They have all the classic dishes—tamales, carnitas, chile rellenos etc.—but the ingredients and preparation seem rather unenthusiastic and boring. The margaritas are decent, and this may be a good place to get a drink and a snack, but go elsewhere to dine. Lunch and dinner are $18–$30. On Koa Avenue near Kalakaua and Ulunui Avenue.

Surf n Turf Tacos

2310 Kuhio Ave, Waikiki • (808) 922-8226

Simple menu with burritos, nachos, quesadillas, tacos and salads. Service is is gruff and uncaring, so wipe that *I'm-so-glad-to-be-in-Hawai'i* smile off your face. Some things have a definite Hawaiian twist, like the poke tacos. They also have some breakfast options served until 1 p.m. Order at the counter and take a seat at one of the four small indoor tables, or grab one of the two uncovered outdoor tables. **$9–$15** for breakfast, lunch or dinner, which are *muy bueno* prices for Waikiki. On Kuhio near Nahua.

HONOLULU AMERICAN

a place to eat

1035 University Ave, Honolulu • (808) 941-4554

ono These guys are too modest. (Heck, a *vending machine* is "a place to eat.") This is tasty, inexpensive, gourmet cuisine in a clean, well-lit modern atmosphere. They're hard to put into a category, but comfort food done island-style probably comes close. The small menu includes dishes like macadamia nut mahimahi with ginger cream sauce, sweet and sour ribs, and the popular blue New Yorker, a N.Y. strip steak smothered in bleu cheese herb butter on a bed of rice with caramelized onions. Portions are savory and generous for the price. (The homemade Oreo brownie-wich dessert is best shared.) **$10–$12** for lunch or dinner. Service is fast and friendly. Open 11 a.m.–midnight, they close from 2–5 p.m. on weekdays. BYOB. On University south of the H-1.

Alan Wong's

1857 S King St, Honolulu • (808) 949-2526

ono This is one of those places about which much hype exists. It's one of the *in* places. Sometimes *in* places are good at nothing *but* hype. But not in this case. Simply put, the food's excellent. It's unclassifiable with a Pacific Rim bent. What does that mean? The menu changes often with items such as ginger-crusted onaga (snapper), steak, an appetizer called da bag (hard to explain but effective), macadamia nut coconut-crusted lamb chops (the *best* lamb we've ever had), and more. Menu changes constantly. The restaurant's small but fairly loud. When you make reservations (which you'll need—they even call you back the day before to confirm), ask for a lanai table, if possible, which has nice views of Manoa Valley in the distance. Alan Wong's is pricey, but the food's top notch. **$30–$60** for dinner. Come out of Waikiki on Kalakaua and turn right on King—it's on your right.

Dave & Buster's

1030 Auahi St, Honolulu • (808) 589-2215

ono You gotta restaurant floor (with bar), a vast game floor (also with bar) augmented by the rooftop (bar) at night with great views (and pretty generous happy hours). The menu is a good mix of steak, ribs, pasta, fish and chips, burgers, sandwiches, fish, and signature items such as short rib and cheesy mac sandwich, lawnmower salad and a half-pound buffalo wing burger. Most items are good, and portions tend to be ample. Service is friendly but sometimes slow, and waits are common at dinner. (They don't take reservations.) **$15–$28** for lunch and dinner. Lunch specials can bring it down a couple bucks. Things are muted during lunch but are usually banging at dinner. On Auahi between Kamakee and Ward.

Foodland Farms

1450 Ala Moana Blvd, Honolulu • (808) 949-5044

ono Yeah, it's a local version of Whole Foods, but this is an awesome place at Ala Moana to grab food to go. They have a huge selection from a hot bar, salad bar, pizza stand to a rotisserie & grill, sushi and poke station, bakery and a wicked mochi ice cream station. (You may not have had mochi before, but you'll want it again after you try it.) Huge juice selection, lots of fruits—it's an easy place to love if your wallet is getting sore from Waikiki's pricey restaurants. It's not cheap-cheap, but it's pretty reasonable. They have some tables near the wine bar and at the back of the store. Most of the food is surprisingly good, and the variation is unexpectedly vast for the setting. It's a bit hard to find, hiding in plain sight at Ala Moana Center. Take Ala Moana Boulevard and enter from Piikoi Street. It's near Nordstrom. $5–$15 for breakfast, lunch and dinner.

Gordon Biersch
1 Aloha Tower Dr, Honolulu • (808) 599-4877

ONO A well-run restaurant with a diverse selection of fish, steak medallions and flat iron frites, pizzas (which make a nice appetizer for two), great burgers, stir fry, salads and sandwiches. The sauces that go with their steaks are all pretty good, but it's the gorgonzola-garlic that keeps us coming back. The lobster and shrimp mac and cheese is really likable if you can get past the $22 price. They brew their own beer here (the Märzen is excellent), but the cocktail selection is bigger (although the mai tai could use some work). The views overlook busy Honolulu Harbor, but they're occasionally blocked by a large ship if it docks in front. Good desserts. Live entertainment some nights. Not cheap, but you get your money's worth, and the food quality is better than what you'll get in Waikiki for the same price. $12–$28 for lunch and dinner. A couple miles north of Waikiki at Aloha Tower Marketplace at Ala Moana and Bishop Street. They validate parking, but only for the first hour, so it will probably cost a couple bucks.

Hank's Haute Dogs
324 Coral St, Honolulu • (808) 532-4265

ONO Haute means *elegant* or *high-class*, and ol' Hank ain't kidding. These aren't your typical Oscar Mayer wieners. They get very creative here. Not only dogs, but also sausages, brats, chorizo and even a burger called the Hank Burger, which is Hank's only miss. Try the Hawaiian—a Portuguese sausage with mango mustard and pineapple relish. The aptly named Fat Boy is a BLT on steroids—a hot dog wrapped in bacon and deep fried, topped with lettuce, tomato and mayo. Consider using that as your wiener in a chili dog for more decadence. The truffled mac 'n' cheese is pretty different. Order at the counter and take to one of the few seats inside or out. Everything is cooked to order, and it sometimes takes some time for them to craft these babies. You may find the prices a bit steep—about $7 per specialty dog—but it's worth it. Lobster dog and lobster fat boy are more expensive. Open daily for lunch and dinner. Just outside of Waikiki; take Ala Moana Boulevard north (keeping the ocean on your left). Take Coral Street on the right. Hank's is a couple hundred feet on the left.

Karai Crab
901 Hausten St, Honolulu • (808) 952-6990

ONO This is a sister restaurant to the Willows, an intimate dining area with only seven tables, so it's a good idea to make reservations. You're here for one reason—seafood. This is how it works: Pick your critter, choosing from mussels, clams, crawfish, crab or lobster. Next, select your seasoning from their seven options. We like the Karai special—it's a cajun garlic sauce. Then choose the spice level. If you like it hot, go for the three star, but be warned: It's made with ghost chillies. Your food will come in a big bowl. (The combo comes with mini corn on the cob and potatoes mixed in.) They have some tasty sides, too. The jalapeño cornbread is moist and delicious. This ain't your typical salty crab house by the wharf, although they do have the plastic bibs, napkin dispensers and throw-away paper tablecloths. The atmosphere is bright and clean, and the service is friendly and attentive. They have beer and wine on hand, and if you want a cocktail, they will get one for you from the Willows, though it may take a little longer. The whole thing will run you $20–$35, possibly more for the crab and lobster, depending on the market price. Open for dinner at 5 daily. From Waikiki, get on McCully Street and at the first traffic light, go right onto Kapiolani Street. Then take a left onto Hausten Street and park in the valet lot for $3 if there's no street parking. Or you can self-park in the lot next to the Willows for $2.

La Mariana Sailing Club
50 Sand Island Access Rd, Honolulu
(808) 848-2800

ono A real find. This blast from the past is the last vintage tiki restaurant in Hawai'i and worth checking out for that reason alone. (It dates back to *pre-statehood*.) The walls are decorated with bamboo and carved wooden tikis with an indoor waterfall and fish tank, colorful glass globes hanging from the ceiling, and lamps made from translucent puffer fish. Much of the décor was salvaged from other famous, now-closed tiki bars (Sheraton's Kon Tiki Bar and Don The Beachcomber). The atmosphere is best at night, when they have live music.

If they put more effort into the kitchen, this place would be great, but unfortunately, the food quality just seems to be getting worse over the years. Fried appetizers, chewy nachos, uninspired burgers, overcooked and over-seasoned seafood. Best to avoid at lunchtime. Dinner is better, particularly the prime rib. The mai tais taste like fuel—*cheap* fuel. If you go, do so for the experience of stepping back in time to a bygone era, when the pace on

O'ahu was slower. (You'll remember the experience more than the meal when you get home anyway.) $10–$16 for lunch, $14–$31 for dinner with most prices on the high side of that range.

Take Ala Moana to Sand Island Access Road and look for a sign on the right. Mosquitos can be a problem here. They're right next to a marina, and you may find some salty dogs at the bar, which can really add to the experience, depending on which dogs are there. The ONO is only for the genuine *nighttime* tiki experience, not for the food.

Morton's Steakhouse
1450 Ala Moana Blvd, Honolulu • (808) 949-1300

ono This is a chain that features *insanely* expensive steaks. Here's how it works: You spend $60 for a steak, and you get… a piece of meat. Nothing else. Want veggies or a potato? It's $14 extra, and they're rather rigid when it comes to toppings. We went with someone who asked for sour cream and chives, and he was told, "We don't offer chives." (Fourteen bucks for a potato, and they won't sprinkle some measly chives on it?) Service is friendly and competent, but they seem to go for long stretches when they forget about you. Pardon us, but for this kind of money we'd like a bit more attention and perhaps even a bit of… groveling. (You know, where even if you order peanut butter on your steak, it's an *excellent choice, sir.*) $50–$75 for dinner. Happy hour in the bar is a much better deal. In the Ala Moana Shopping Center.

Nashville Waikiki
1 Aloha Tower Dr, Honolulu • (808) 926-7911

Not in Nashville and not in Waikiki. It's at the Aloha Tower Market, downtown Honolulu, by the harbor. The Nashville part feels pretty accurate, though. Aside from the toasted taro bun on the burger, there's almost no trace of being in Hawai'i. Country music, classic rock, pool tables, blackjack (just for fun), line dancing in the evenings. Good food: brisket, pulled pork, smoked meats. $10–$25. Lots of drink specials at the bar. Avoid the high-top tables—the stools are much too low for the height, which may make your back ache. Ask them to validate parking.

Original Pancake House
1221 Kapiolani Blvd, Honolulu • (808) 596-8213
Part of a national chain, this place makes good pancakes. They have some—like the apple pancake and the Dutch Baby—that are *baked* and take 45 minutes. (Call ahead to order.) This place fills up fast, so get there early. They have omelets, crêpes and the usual breakfast items. The menu is small and very basic, and the service seems rushed. $8–$13, open 6 a.m.–2 p.m. On Kapiolani between Piikoi and Pensacola. (Their other location is forgettable.)

Pint + Jigger
1936 S King St, Honolulu • (808) 744-9593
ono A hip place with a large selection of whiskeys and scotch. This gastropub, with the windows blacked out and so much brick and wood, feels less like Hawai'i and more like a basement pub or a microbrewery on the mainland. They take pride in their constantly changing, specially crafted drinks with unusual ingredients, and they might look at you disapprovingly if you order a mai tai here. The food is best described as gourmet bar food—fish and chips alongside dishes such as brandy and bacon strawberries (sounds strange, but it works). But the *best* reason to come here is their burger—always a contender for the title of best on O'ahu. The Pint + Jigger stout burger is a local beef patty with garlic aioli, beer cheese, lettuce and pickle. Consider it with bacon and avocado. Definitely worth upgrading to the mesquite BBQ fries. $8–$14 for brunch, $10–$17 for dinner; they're open at 4:30 p.m. on weekdays and 8 a.m. on weekends for brunch. (Got to get up early

here if you want to watch live sports due to the time difference.) Take McCully Street out of Waikiki, left on Young, left on Artesian, then left on King. Park in the lot on the left, just before the traffic light. No minors allowed to enter after 8 p.m.

Sweet E's Café
1006 Kapahulu Ave, Honolulu • (808) 737-7771
ono Sweetie's—get it? A popular place for breakfast in Honolulu. Everything on the menu begins with the letter E. No one could say why—it's a mystery. They're known for the Enchanting French toast stuffed with blueberry cream cheese. They also make something called the Extreme Mess—hash browns topped with three eggs, sausage, ham, bacon, onions, peppers and cheese. Two people can easily make a full meal from this alone. Attention to detail seems to be slipping lately, so if your meal comes out burned, send us note to let us know. There is a large parking lot behind the restaurant, but you can only use it on weekends. During the week, parking is limited in the small lot in front. They also serve sandwiches and pizza for lunch, but breakfast is the real attraction here. $10–$16 for breakfast or lunch. A short car or bus ride from Waikiki on the corner of Kapahulu and Kaimuki avenues.

town
3435 Waialae Ave, Honolulu • (808) 735-5900
Farro, tatsoi, polenta, mizuna… If these foods sound appetizing, or even familiar, then you might be interested in town. (Yes, you *have* to spell it with a lowercase *t*.) We put it under American cuisine because we don't have a category for *Pretentious Organic*. town prides itself on exclusive use of local and organic ingredients. The menu changes often due to the availability of fresh items, and there are usually just 10 entrées to choose from. One tasty regular dish is the pan-fried monchong with steamed vegetables. The food is actually

very good here, well seasoned and healthy, but the experience is slightly out of our comfort zone. For instance, there's no salt and pepper on the table, presumably because you aren't welcome to mess with their concoctions. The artsy atmosphere, plus the pricey menu full of unrecognizable ingredients, is certainly an acquired taste. Service is weak—they tend to keep you waiting even when they aren't busy. **$15–$25** for lunch, **$22–$35** for dinner. On the corner of Waialae and 9th avenues. Parking is in the lot behind the building. Closed Sundays.

HONOLULU FRENCH

Chef Mavro
1969 S King St, Honolulu • (808) 944-4714

ono Well, here it is—the most expensive restaurant we've ever reviewed in Hawai'i. A couple can easily spend $500 for the evening. Which begs the question—is the food worth $500? Of *course* not. *No* food is worth that much. But a better way to approach it is, *if you have $500 to blow, is this a good place to blow it?* Answer: yes.

Let's start with the downside. There's no view, it's on a busy street in a marginal neighborhood, and the interior is a nice, modern Hawaiian, but not *that* nice. Oh, and their mixed drink bartending skills are pretty bad. (But it's all about the wine here.) So far not so good.

But here's where they soar. You start with the premise that you have to trust them. You have two choices—four courses or six courses. You can substitute a little, usually for an extra fee. (They *love* extra fees.) Then you choose between wine pairing or no wine pairing. We strongly encourage the pairing, because they do it really, really, really well. The menu changes every season, and the staff gathers to do blind taste testing of the wine. (I'll bet *nobody* calls in sick on *that* day.) They have a small plates menu on the lower

level but it's not the reason to eat here.

The table will be yours for the evening. It'll take about 3 hours—it's slow by design here. About half their customers are local clientele who come to treat themselves. Chef George Mavrothalassitis is a friendly and approachable Frenchman. (I was gonna take a good-natured jab at the French by saying, first one of *those* I ever met, but thought the better of it.) He often visits many tables during the evening. On the corner of King and Mc-Cully. Reservations recommended (and they take your credit card, so don't stand 'em up). Closed Sun. and Mon. **$100–$280** for dinner.

HONOLULU GREEK

The Greek Corner
1025 University Ave, Honolulu • (808) 942-5503
Traditional Greek food like baba ganoush and gyros. The portions are decent, and the prices aren't bad at **$8–$15** for lunch or dinner. The gyro plate is a little short on pita bread, and the baba ganoush is a little too sweet for our liking. But overall, this place isn't bad, and the food is acceptable. Open seven days for lunch and dinner. Located just outside of Waikiki. Take McCully Street north (away from the ocean), then right onto Kapiolani Boulevard and left onto University Avenue. Once you get to the intersection of University Avenue and King Street, look up and to the left, and you'll see a sign on a blue building that says "Puck's Alley." Parking is behind this building. Go straight through the intersection, and look for the poorly marked entrance to the lot on the right. They will validate.

HONOLULU ITALIAN

Assaggio
1450 Ala Moana Blvd, Honolulu • (808) 942-3446

ono Huge lunch and dinner menus, including lots of seafood, pastas, chicken and sandwiches with large portions. The ambiance is restful, if slightly dressy. Items such as the fish arrabbiata (which is good) and stuffed baked eggplant (also good) supplement more expected pasta items. Service is adequate, and it's not too horribly priced at lunch. Ask for a table near the fountain at the Ala Moana location. Dinner also works well here, with a massive menu of authentic Italian food (including bad bread, just as it does in Italy.) The mai tai is pretty tasty. The Ala Moana location can be loud because of the lack of soft surfaces. At Ala Moana Shopping Center just outside Waikiki on Ala Moana Boulevard. (Park near Macy's.) At the Hawai'i Kai location ask for a window seat for a nice view. $11–$25 for lunch, $17–$35 for dinner. Reservations recommended.

Auntie Pasto's

1099 S Beretania St, Honolulu • (808) 523-8855
This family-friendly restaurant is reasonably priced for the quality, but it can get a bit loud due to the open kitchen. The dinner menu has a nice selection of pastas, chicken and eggplant. The carbonara is soupy—they serve it with a spoon. If you like seafood, try the red pepper calamari appetizer. They also have a dish called cacciucco (an Italian seafood stew composed of nearly every critter that lives in the ocean—it's pretty good). The pasta is a better bet than the disappointingly bland pizza. Lunch ($11–$18) is mostly hot sandwiches and pasta, but the dinner menu ($12–$27) is also available. Wine available by the glass, and $4 drafts on special during happy hour. At Pensacola and Beretania in downtown Honolulu.

Boston Style Pizza

515 Pepeekeo St, Hawaii Kai • (808) 394-8001
3506 Waialae Ave, Kaimuki • (808) 734-1945
ono Not to be confused with the many other Boston Pizza restaurants on the island. Or go ahead and confuse them—they were once affiliated and are still pretty much the same. So is our review. 19-inch pizzas for $21–$29 or by the slice for $6–$8. (What they call a slice is really two pieces—it's an entire quarter of the 19-inch pizza.) Many specialties to choose from. We like this pizza and eat it way too often (we especially like stopping at the Hawaii Kai location for lunch after building up an appetite snorkeling at Hanauma Bay). But we won't recommend grabbing a full pizza from the Kaimuki location (closest to Waikiki) and taking it back to your hotel room until they get boxes that are big enough to actually *enclose* the pizza, instead of having part of it stick out of the box, letting the heat escape it. In fact—avoid the Kaimuki location altogether. They seem less focused on customer service there.

HONOLULU JAPANESE

Nobu

1118 Ala Moana Blvd, Honolulu • (808) 237-6999
ono Absolutely epic flavors in an ultra chic ambiance. Japanese food with a *Peruvian* influence. The selection is vast and overwhelming, and it's not practical to list individual items. But honestly, we haven't had *anything* here that wasn't off the charts. Flavors are not Japanese subtle but rather finely infused. Whether it's fish or salads or steak, they serve some of the best food in the state. Don't get me wrong. It's pricey. And if we have a complaint, it's that the service might not be attentive enough. But if you're looking to splurge on wicked food, this is the place to do it. $40–$90 (or more if you go all out) for dinner. In the Ward Village across from Kewalo Harbor. Reservations recommended.

Shirokiya Japan Village Walk

1450 Ala Moana Blvd, #1360, Honolulu
ono A surprisingly authentic replication of what you might actually

experience on a visit to Japan. This 65,000-square-foot indoor venue is a collection of individual vendors selling every type of Japanese comfort food as well as burgers, shave ice and the ever-important $1 pints of beer. It's worth the experience even if you don't like Japanese food. (Contrary to American perceptions, the Japanese fry a large portion of their meals.) Artificial cherry blossoms and paper lanterns hang everywhere, and the deluge of choices may seem bewildering. Don't get overwhelmed. Wander around for a bit. Then lock onto a vendor, try something and move on. Some will be delicious, some won't. But hey, you're getting a twofer—a mini trip to eat in Japan on your Hawaiian vacation. Price is all over the place from $5–$40 for lunch and dinner. In Ala Moana Shopping Center.

HONOLULU LOCAL

Kaka'ako Kitchen
1200 Ala Moana Blvd, Honolulu • (808) 596-7488

ono Very popular with locals. A huge menu of local items, such as Chinese five-spice shoyu chicken, tempura fish, sandwiches, 'ahi wraps, salads and a lot more. Reasonable prices for the quality. Order at the counter, and they'll bring it to your table in a take-out container. Their coconut mochi is a wonderful, dense-as-lead dessert, and their pumpkin bread is outrageously pumpkin-y. (Is that a word? It ain't in my spell checker. Then again, neither is Kaka'ako…) Avoid the eggplant Parmesan. Even if you don't eat your meal here, the desserts (to go) are great. On the Auahi Street side of Ward Centre near Kamakee. Parking is free in the Ward Center garage. $12–$17 for lunch and dinner.

Liliha Bakery
515 N Kuakini St, Honolulu • (808) 531-1651

ono This place feels like a time machine. They've been a-round since 1950, and we doubt that it's changed much. A classic greasy spoon diner with a Hawaiian twist. The cooks are dressed in all white, complete with paper hats, and the waitresses have long aprons and a take-no-prisoners attitude. There's one long bar with about 20 seats, and everything is cooked directly in front of you on a grill with lots of butter. A simple breakfast menu with all the fixin's, including loco moco. Lunch and dinner is local-style grinds and sandwiches. The food's pretty good and *very* cheap. You can get out of here for under $10.

Don't leave without trying their most famous bakery item. It's a puff pastry filled with chocolate and a dab of chantilly frosting on top—it's amazing. They call it a coco puff, and they claim to make 5,000–7,000 *daily*.

Closed from 8 p.m. Sunday to 6 a.m. Tuesday, but open 24 hours a day the rest of the week. To get there from Waikiki, get on H-1 east and take exit 21A, then take a right onto Liliha Street and a left onto N. Kuakini. The bakery is on the corner to the left. They also have another location on Nimitz Highway that seats 170.

Nico's Pier 38
1129 N Nimitz Hwy, Honolulu • (808) 540-1377

The only way to get fish fresher than Nico's is to catch it yourself. They're located next door to the Honolulu fish auction where all the commercial fishing boats bring their catch to be sold to local markets and wholesalers. Needless to say, *order the fish here*. Seating is in an open-air dining room overlooking the boats that caught your meal. Lunch is cafeteria-style. To avoid looking like a rookie, walk in and pick any empty table, then go up to the counter, and order your sandwich or local-kine plate lunch. You'll get a ticket and a pager. Dinner is more traditional service. It's $5–$10 for breakfast, lunch runs $9–$17, slightly more for dinner at

$14–$28. Don't forget to try one of the 20 different dessert choices. Follow the signs off Nimitz Highway near Alakawa. Parking is free at the harbor.

Rainbow Drive-In
3308 Kanaina Ave, Honolulu • (808) 737-0177

ono This Oʻahu icon has been churning out ono grinds at cheap prices for more than half a century. Plate lunches are the staple here with "two scoop rice" or fries and macaroni salad. Offerings change daily, but the shoyu chicken and the loco moco (beef patty covered with an egg and smothered in gravy) are highly revered. Lots of options involving chili. At breakfast, try the sweetbread French toast if they haven't run out. $5–$12. Open 7 a.m.–9 p.m. daily. Just outside Waikiki on the Diamond Head side, on the corner of Kapahulu and Kanaina.

Willows
901 Hausten St, Honolulu • (808) 952-9200

ono Old-time Oʻahu visitors may be familiar with Willows. It goes back to 1944, when Waikiki was a sleepy, fairly unknown place that had few dining options. The natural springs on the property were incorporated into a beautiful pool. In the '90s it closed and later reopened. Today its pond and waterfall have been cement-lined, and the menu is all buffet. But if you're looking to slip (just slightly) out of Waikiki and want an excellent buffet with local-style flavors, such as lau lau, kalua pig, curries, teri chicken, poke and a prime rib carving station, as well as some delicious housemade desserts, the Willows still works pretty well. The atmosphere is relaxing and peaceful. It's tucked away in a residential neighborhood. From Ala Wai Boulevard take McCully, right on Kapiolani, left on Hausten. $28 for the weekday lunch buffet ($35 on Saturday). The Sunday brunch buffet is $40 and includes an omelet station, as well as some extra goodies. Dinner buffet is $45. (Children and seniors get a discount.)

HONOLULU MEXICAN

El Burrito
550 Piikoi St, Honolulu • (808) 596-8225
We like the tamales here, and that's about it. The carnitas consists of dry chunks of pork, the salsa is cheap, and the beans and rice taste burnt. You can actually hear the microwave being used in the kitchen. Only eight tables inside this hole in the wall, but you're sure to find a seat. $10–$17 for lunch and dinner. On the corner of Piikoi and Kapiolani. Closed Sundays.

Los Chaparros
2140 S Beretania St, Honolulu • (808) 951-6399

ono Good Mexican food can be elusive on Oʻahu. We like the atmosphere, bright colors and upbeat Mexican music here. We love the salsa, the enchiladas and the super burrito. (We guessed its weight to be at least 2 pounds.) Their red and spicy green sauces go great with everything, and the fajitas are reasonably good. The pozole is flavorful with plentiful, tasty chunks of meat, and the margaritas are excellent. The tamales are the one thing we could pick on here. The taste is good, but the shells need work. The banana flautas for dessert are excellent. The servers are very attentive and friendly. You may have to wait for a table if you don't get here early—this place ain't a secret. The parking lot is small—only six spaces—so you may have to park on the street. On Beretania just past Isenberg. $10–$24 for lunch and dinner. Closed Monday.

Serg's Mexican Kitchen
2740 E Manoa Rd, Honolulu • (808) 988-8118

ono Fresh local ingredients, tasty Mexican flavors, good prices and large portions. Serg's is located 3.5 miles up mauka from bustling downtown Waikiki. Place your order at the window and take a seat at a picnic table under their covered dining area. It won't take too long. The rajas con queso is an appetizer, but it could easily be a meal, and the chimichangas don't disappoint. For dessert try the tostada de plantano, a large, wonderful treat. Weekends have breakfast until noon featuring several egg dishes, Mexican-style pancakes, and breakfast burritos. $7–$12 for breakfast, $8–$16 for lunch and dinner.

HONOLULU THAI

Siam Garden Café
1130 Nimitz Hwy, Honolulu • (808) 523-9338

ONO Good Thai food, but they've been slipping lately, and the ONO is marginal. We like the green curries, great pad thai and flavorful panang. Even if you don't like spicy, the vegetable stir fry bursts with flavor, and they have lots of Thai salads. (Summer rolls are fairly tasteless, though.) $10–$18 for lunch and dinner. At Nimitz Center Shopping Center on Nimitz near Alakawa. Open till 10 most nights. They can be fussy about substitutions.

HONOLULU TREATS

Honolulu Chocolate Company
1200 Ala Moana Blvd, Honolulu • (808) 591-2997

ONO Expensive but well-made chocolates, truffles, pralines and other candy treats. Try a peanut butter praline truffle. $3–$8. In Ward Centre at Ala Moana Boulevard and Kamakee. Parking accessed from Auahi Street.

Leonard's
933 Kapahulu Ave, Honolulu • (808) 737-5591

ONO The best place on the island to try malasadas (Portuguese donuts). Fresh, hot and insanely good. Get them filled if you want. (We're predictable and usually get chocolate filling.) Technically, it's just outside Waikiki, but close enough. A little over a buck each. Outside Waikiki on the Diamond Head side on Kapahulu and Charles. They also have a couple of red and white trucks that wander the island. If you see one, their malasadas are just as good and made fresh on the trucks.

Snow Factory
1960 Kapiolani Blvd, Honolulu • (808) 946-7669

ONO This stuff is hard to describe. It's like a cross between shave ice, cotton candy and ice cream with a texture that is really unusual. You'll either love it, or it'll leave you flat. Can't really say more. They are just barely outside Waikiki near the intersection of McCully and Kapiolani behind the Taco Bell. $5–$8. Give it a try if you're in an adventurous mood.

Waiola Shave Ice & Bakery
3113 Mokihana St, Honolulu • (808) 735-8886

ONO Also just outside Waikiki, this is the place for shave ice. The fineness of the ice depends on the sharpness of the blade and the pressure, and this place has the finest ice we've ever seen. Frankly, we didn't know you could *make* ice this fine. Add to that the fact that they chill their syrup (keeping it from chunking), and you get an easy-to-recommend shave ice, even if it *is* served without a smile. They claim to be a bakery, but besides a couple pre-packaged brownies and cookies, don't expect much. Go for the shave ice. Just mauka of Waikiki. Driving up Kapahulu, when the Safeway store is on your left, Mokihana Street is on your right. $4–$6. Cash only.

CHINATOWN DINING

Chinatown is a cultural and dining destination. Here you will find the most authentic Chinese food on the island, as well as other international flavors. In addition to what we reviewed, there are innumerable opportunities to eat your heart out here. Look at the map on page 153 to orient (if you'll pardon the expression) yourself.

Brick Fire Tavern

16 N Hotel St, Honolulu • (808) 369-2444

Italian—Neapolitan-style pizza cooked in a wood-fired brick oven. The oven heats to 900 degrees, so it only takes 90 seconds for your pizza to cook, and they urge you to finish eating within 10 minutes of your pizza coming out of the oven to properly experience the flavor. Too bad the service isn't that fast—your drinks may come out after you're done eating. (Especially if you order the alcohol-infused Italian milkshake.) The personal pizzas ($14–$19) taste good, but don't expect many standard combinations. They like to experiment with gourmet toppings and seasonal flavors. (Some of the weirder ones like cranberry work surprisingly well.) For an extra dollar they'll crack an egg yolk on top, but we'd pay them a buck not to. A few beer and wine options to pair with your pizza. In Chinatown on Hotel Street. Open from 11 a.m.–10 p.m., they close from 2–5 p.m. Closed Sunday. Between Chinatown's Smith and Nuuanu.

Duc's Bistro

1188 Maunakea St, Honolulu • (808) 531-6325

ono ♪ **French/Vietnamese**—This is another great option for fine dining in Chinatown in a restaurant that has been here for over 20 years. The menu is a mix of French and Vietnamese cuisine, and they do both categories well. All items come à la carte, and sharing is encouraged. We like the filet of basa with capers and dill-lemon sauce. Also popular is the lamb tenderloin with turmeric and garlic, as well as the fire-roasted eggplant. The escargot is very tasty. There's no written

dress code, but the service and atmosphere dictate that you shouldn't come here looking like you just walked off the beach. For dessert, if they have it, the chocolate ganache flourless cake is deadly. $15–$25 for lunch and dinner. Live Hawaiian music on Thursday, and jazz or contemporary music on Saturday evenings. Dinner only on Saturdays and Sundays. On Maunakea near Beretania. Park in the self pay parking lot across the street, but don't pay. Remember your stall number, tell the host, and they will validate.

Ethiopian Love

1112 Smith St, Honolulu • (808) 725-7197

Ethiopian—A small, laid-back Ethiopian café in Chinatown. Great for vegetarians and vegans, or try mixing a meat dish with a vegetarian item—they pair well. Served with traditional injera (spongy, sour flatbread.) There's a lot of pride in presentation both with the food and how clean they keep the place (they swap tablecloths and reset tables almost immediately after diners leave). The honey and peanut tea has a frothy texture and is a surprisingly satisfying dessert. A little pricey for what you get. $9–$18, dinner only. BYOB.

Fete

2 N Hotel St, Honolulu • (808) 369-1390

ono ♪ **American**—In an area dense with good restaurants, this one is on a whole different level. (The price is also upper level, so take that into consideration.) It's a toss-up whether you want to categorize it as New American or Contemporary French (*fête* is French for party or feast), but that's really a distinction without a difference since the menu is globally inspired. You'll find a wide range of dinner entrées ($18–$55), but it's hard to say exactly what since they change regularly. Expect items such as roasted duck breast, Mexican lasagna, salmon, and lamb cavatelli. The grilled pulpo (octopus) is perfectly seasoned and not chewy or fishy. The steak puts other restaurants' cuts to shame. Slice it thin to savor as much of the flavor as possible. The olive oil cake for dessert is an acquired taste that will leave you craving more by the end. The lunch menu ($11–$28) has many of the same options as the dinner menu, as well as sandwiches. In Chinatown, at the intersection of N. Hotel Street and Nuanuu Avenue. The atmosphere is simple, perhaps a little generic. Brick walls, large windows and a well-stocked bar.

Golden Palace
111 N King St, Honolulu • (808) 521-8268

ono **Chinese**—Here you are surrounded with dim sum carts stocked with dumplings of every kind: steamed, baked, boiled or fried. Don't be afraid to ask questions of the servers, though the response might be in broken english. This is an eating adventure, and at the end you will have dined on a range of dishes you won't remember. Take your time, and don't get hung up on a single cart. The dim sum is so cheap ($2.69) that if you don't like one, leave it and order from the next cart. The regular menu's not bad, but the dim sum is what we like. On King Street between Kekaulike and Maunakea streets.

J.J. Dolan's
1147 Bethel St, Honolulu • (808) 537-4992

Italian/Irish—A lot of people here (especially transplants from the East Coast) *swear* that this dimly lit Irish pub serves the best pizza on O'ahu. We don't, *but* if you like paper-thin, fold-in-half-to-eat slices, you'll probably love it. Fans of a thicker crust might think it's overhyped. What's *not* debatable is that the place is popular with the *pau hana* (after work) crowd. Whole 14-inch pies are $17–$19. They offer a few classic combinations as well as house specialties. The breaded chicken wings ($9) are a good complement to the pizza, and better than the fries. Long bar with plenty of whiskey and beer on tap. You can find this Irish pub that serves New York-style pizza in Honolulu's Chinatown. Open 11 a.m.–2 a.m. Closed Sunday. On Bethel mauka of Pauahi Street.

Kan Zaman
1028 Nuuanu Ave, Honolulu • (808) 554-3847

ono **Mediterranean**—Where does a person go to get Lebanese and Moroccan food in Hawai'i? Glad you asked. Chinatown, of course…. If you peek inside on a slow weeknight, the empty dining room may discourage you from going in. If it's so good, why is no one here? Don't hesitate—everyone is probably in the patio area hidden in back. Lunch ($13–$15) includes expected items like falafel, shawarma (yummy) and kebabs in sandwich form. Dinner plates ($16–$29) are larger and more complex. The grilled rack of lamb will make your tongue dance with flavor. Prices are a bit high, but portions are large and filling, and if it's too pricey you can always hit one of the other Lebanese/Moroccan places in the area. (Sorry, shawarma always brings the smart aleck out in me.) Dining in Chinatown requires venturing outside the Waikiki tourist haven, so you probably won't run into too many other visitors, but you may run into some in-the-know Hollywood types, on-island to work on their latest production. No alcohol, but you're welcome to bring your own bottle of wine. Closed Sunday. On Nuuanu near King Street.

Legend Seafood
100 N Beretania St, Honolulu • (808) 532-1868

ono **Chinese**—Absolutely epic Chinese seafood and crisp service. A giant menu of common and uncommon but well-conceived Chinese dishes, including stir fry, prawns in a taro basket appetizer (*highly* recommended), stuffed duck, tofu stuffed with shrimp and ham, braised whole shark's fin soup, etc. The food is fantastic and the ingredients top quality. Lunch is dim sum, which is also good, but if you're looking to treat yourself, go for dinner. $8–$18 for lunch, $13–$25 for dinner. At River and Beretania.

Little Village Noodle House
1113 Smith St, Honolulu • (808) 545-3008

ono **Chinese**—Ironically, it's one of the few decent Chinese restaurants in Chinatown. The food is closer to Chinese-American, but they do it well. They also have something extraordinarily rare here—*free* parking. The selection is large, but portions are on the small side. Their signature item is the fried rice, and it won't disappoint. $12–$20 for lunch and dinner. BYOB. Corkage fee is $1 per person if you use their glasses, free if you bring your own. On Smith near Pauahi Street.

Lucky Belly
50 N Hotel St, Honolulu • (808) 531-1888

ono **Japanese**—Hard to classify these guys. Think Japanese with a focus on bacon. In addition to pork entrées, lunch offers salads, a few plates and massive bowls of specialty in-house-made ramen. We liked the lamb lumpia for an appetizer. The shrimp tacos make a delicious lunch plate that we highly recommend. The dining room is small but very well laid out and covered in dark wood, giving it a hip, comfortable feeling. The staff is friendly and attentive. They also serve a number of specialty drinks that you've never heard of, such as the tasty *Fade to Red*. $11–$21 for lunch or dinner. Closed Sundays. On N. Hotel and Smith Street.

Maria Bonita
15 N Hotel St, Honolulu • (808) 536-6185
Mexican—In Chinatown on North Hotel Street, it's a pre-gentrified hole in the wall.

Not as busy as you'd expect for Mexican food in a bar-heavy area. They mostly cater to the downtown lunchtime rush, and they're sometimes open at night. Food is authentic, but it's not a home run. $7–$12. On Hotel near Nuuanu Avenue.

Maunakea Marketplace
1120 Maunakea St, Honolulu • (808) 524-3409
Asian—The vicinity around Kekaulike pedestrian mall is the center of the Chinatown universe. All the best markets are within two blocks of this point. But on the other side of Hotel Street, Maunakea Marketplace is the only one with a food court. To get to it, you must run through a gauntlet of veggie, meat and seafood vendors, from the unusual to the downright scary. Look for the fish tanks full of crabs next to the bizarre seafood on ice. The level of exoticness depends on what local fisherman hauled from the deep that morning. Then follow the salty fried smells to the narrow food court with cuisine from all over Asia: Thai, Vietnamese, Korean, Filipino, Chinese, Japanese and some local. Most of the dozen vendors serve one-, two- or three-choice plate lunches for $4–$8. Cash only. There's seating inside for 80 and 20 more in an outdoor courtyard. Visiting this market is a must-do in Chinatown.

Murphy's Bar & Grill
2 Merchant St, Honolulu • (808) 531-0422

ono **Irish**—This bar has had its liquor license on O'ahu for 150 years, and has been an Irish pub since 1987, annually hosting the St. Patrick's Day block party. If that's not Irish enough for you, may we suggest the corned beef and cabbage? Their Blarney Burger is the one of the best burgers on the island. They also have steak, salad, fish and chips, and a really good open-face turkey sandwich. Lots of stained glass, an ornate wooden bar and real Irish beer on tap make this a popular place to bend an elbow. $13–$25 for lunch and dinner. On the corner of Merchant and Nuuanu.

O'ahu Market
145 N King St, Honolulu
Seafood—An open-air market with the freshest poke (see *Island Fish & Seafood* on page 257) around. Be sure to ask if it's fresh or frozen. Expect to pay $9–$12 per pound. You may see pigs being butchered on the street. On N. King and Kekaulike Street in Chinatown.

Opal Thai
1030 Smith St, Suite 6, Honolulu • (808) 381-8091
ono Thai—If you allow it, a meal at Opal Thai can be the equivalent of being a guest in Opal's home. Opal is the owner. You won't miss him because he'll likely be your host, maitre d', server, busboy and cashier. He'll provide you with a menu, but if you're expecting to pick what you want, go elsewhere. Opal takes time with every table to inquire about his guests' Thai tastes and preferences, then creates a customized family-style meal based on your responses. The flavor balances, the temperatures and preparation, the presentation—everything here is exceptional. Come with an open mind, and be prepared for the entire experience—you won't be disappointed. The space is on the small side but works well thanks to the personalized service. Choose a spot at the bar for a good view of the cooking action. With seating for 30–35, expect a wait. Reservations are recommended for peak seating times. BYOB. $16–$24 for lunch and dinner. They close between meals. On Smith between Hotel and N. King Street.

Tchin Tchin
39 N Hotel St, Honolulu • (808) 528-1888
American—There's no sign marking this trendy Chinatown wine bar—you have to know it's there. On North Hotel Street, look for the neon Club Hubba

Hubba sign and then to the right until you find No. 39. There's an open doorway with a steep set of stairs leading up. Hidden bar—sounds exciting, right? For most visitors, probably not. Polished concrete floor, brick walls, exposed ceiling—a novelty in Hawaii for sure, which is probably why it's so popular with the downtown professional set, but commonplace elsewhere.

It's from the same people as nearby **Lucky Belly** and Livestock Tavern, though, so you know it's good. No entrées, just tapas meant for sharing. Choose from the small plates or the smaller plates (their wording, and it's accurate). Crab, anchovies, $10 truffle fries with aioli.

A couple can easily drop $100 with food and wine, which comes in 2-ounce and 6-ounce servings as well as in bottles. Don't wait for them to seat you; the place is designed for mingling. You'll see a few dudes in T-shirts, but most everyone else will be dressed to impress. If you're planning to imbibe, remember that you'll have to negotiate that same steep set of stairs on the way back down. Open Tuesday–Saturday nights.

The Pig & The Lady
83 N King St, Honolulu • (808) 585-8255
ono Vietnamese—We don't know why the swine got top billing over the lady. Not as pork-heavy as the name leads you to assume; in fact, there are few dishes with meat. It's primarily Vietnamese with inspiration from across the Pacific Rim. The vegetable pho is very good but not exactly authentic—they definitely put their own spin on things. Experimenting with flavors and combinations is a hallmark of this trendy Chinatown restaurant, so ask for recommendations—they'll talk you through the menu and give honest assessments based on your likes and dislikes. The LFC (Laotian Fried Chicken) is the only menu item that has never changed. It's

sweet and savory and spicy at the same time. Only three entrées on the dinner menu ($31–$35), and they can run out. Several appetizers or small plates are good for sharing, such as Samoan sweetbread or ahi on Spanish toast. They are as creative with the drink concoctions as they are with the menu. Might not be a good option for less adventurous diners, or if you've been out snorkeling and hiking all day and need something hearty—portions can be *teeny*. But if you're looking for culinary excitement, this is it. No dress code, but most dress to impress. Reservations are a good idea. Closed Sunday. On N. King between Smith and Mauna Kea Street.

Tô-Châu
1007 River St, Honolulu • (808) 533-4549

ono **Vietnamese**—Incredibly popular with locals, they specialize in pho, a noodle dish served in beef broth with vegetables and your choice of meat. There's usually a line out the door the entire time they're open. If you go, you'll find yourself scraping the last drop of soup out of your bowl. Yeah, it's *that* good. $9–$11 for lunch only. On River Street between Hotel and N. King streets.

EAST OF WAIKIKI DINING

Once you leave Honolulu and Waikiki behind, heading toward the sunrise, there are quite a few dining choices before you get to Kailua. There are almost as many categories as restaurants in this area, so we mention their category in the description.

Azteca
3617 Waialae Ave, Kaimuki • (808) 735-2492

ono **Mexican**—You'll have to drive to get here from Waikiki, and there's no scenic view. But they've got some of the better Mexican food on O'ahu, and sometimes that's exactly what you want when traveling—good food without having to pay a fortune. The items are mostly basic—tacos, burritos and enchiladas—but they are delicious and authentic. In fact, the main language spoken in the restaurant is Español. The specialty items seem a bit overpriced for the portions, but they're well prepared. $9–$21 for lunch and dinner, but the lunch specials are only available until 3 p.m. On the corner of Waialae and Koko Head Avenue. Closed Sunday.

Bogart's Café
3045 Monsarrat Ave, Honolulu • (808) 739-0999

ono **American**—One of the best cafés on O'ahu. Open for three meals, but breakfast is their specialty. The waffle with Nutella (chocolate hazelnut spread) and strawberries is a personal favorite (hey, Nutella and strawberries in *roofing tar* would still be tasty), and the omelets are packed with gourmet ingredients. Nobody beats their roasted potatoes. Two drawbacks: no bathroom, and there aren't many tables, so you may be left standing while you wait for your food. $10–$16, cash only. You can walk to it from the east side of Waikiki if you don't mind a stroll. See map on page 49. At Monsarrat and Kanaina Ave.

Bubbies Ice Cream
7192 Kalanianaole Hwy, Hawaii Kai
(808) 396-8722

ono **Treats**—Locally made ice cream, plus an unusually good selection of ice cream-related items like the wonderful hand-dipped mochi (you gotta get one) and cookie ice cream sandwiches. Flavors like *dark dark chocolate chocolate chip* are delicious, and prices are more reasonable than many gourmet ice cream places. They sell by weight (69¢ per oz.), starting with a "fetal-dip" at 2 ounces, going all the way up to a whole bucket. $2–$5. In Koko Marina Center off Hwy 72, Hawai'i Kai.

Dave's Ice Cream

41-1537 Kalanianaole Hwy, Waimanalo
(808) 259-0356

Treats—Pretty good locally made ice cream. Love the sweet potato ice cream. They also have changing local flavors like mango, haupia and lychee. In Waimanalo Town Center on Hwy 72 in Waimanalo. $4–$7. They also have other locations. Cash only.

Keneke's

41-857 Kalanianaole Hwy, Waimanalo
(808) 259-9800

Local—In Waimanalo, this is the first restaurant you'll come to after rounding the southeast corner of O'ahu heading north toward Kailua. Their specialty: cheap local plates. The $6 all-day breakfast special includes choice of meat plus two eggs, rice, toast and a medium soft drink. For $8 the lunch special includes choice of meat (garlic shrimp, several styles of chicken, beefsteak) with rice or fries, and macaroni or tuna salad, plus a drink. Lots of other options and combination plates to choose from here, most of them only a few bucks. How good the food is entirely depends on how hungry you are by the time you hit this place. This is classic local food. The loco moco sits heavy, as it is designed to do. Sit at the picnic tables out front or get it to go—birds have marked nearly every inch of the covered dining area as theirs. On Kalanianaole Highway (72), the prominent red-and-white-checkered building is hard to miss.

Koko Head Café

1145C 12th Ave, Kaimuki • (808) 732-8920

ono American—A bright and up-scale American brunch café, with heavy Asian and local influences on flavor. This is no greasy spoon; food falls on the gourmet side of the spectrum. Take the breakfast bibimbap. It's bacon, Portuguese sausage, ham, kimchi, shiitake mushrooms, ong choy, sesame carrots and bean sprouts covered with an egg sunny-side up, served over garlic rice in a hot skillet. (Don't even *tell* me you had one of those last week.) There are simpler options, but most everything has a twist. Attentive service. Entrées are $9–$16, but you can easily spend quite a bit more than that indulging in the creative (and strong) mixed drinks from the bar. A short drive from Waikiki, on Koko Head Avenue by H-1, not to be confused with the southeast corner of the island. Open until 2:30 p.m.

Kona Brewing Company

7192 Kalanianaole Hwy, Hawaii Kai
(808) 396-5662

ono Italian—We have a lot of affection for the original Kona Brewpub in Kailua-Kona on the Big Island. This one isn't as good as the Kona location, but it's still good enough to merit an ono, with some caveats. Pizza and beer—that's why you come here. The draft beer is brewed on the Big Island, and most of the permanent and seasonals are very good. (Bottles come from the mainland.) The pizza comes with a variety of sauces. We like the cajun for its spiciness (Pele's Own is a good combination). The Kau Pesto pizza is a nice mix of pesto-based sauce, artichoke hearts, chicken and sun-dried tomatoes, but it doesn't have quite the level of flavor you might expect, and other combinations, like the Greek, are also a bit light on the flavor. Some of the tables have nice views overlooking the waters of Hawai'i Kai, and they have surprisingly good meatloaf, of all things. With tasty beer and mostly tasty pizza, it's a likeable experience. In Koko Marina Center, Hawai'i Kai. Look for the movie theater, and go directly across the parking lot until you come to the docks, then hang a left. Pizza for $13–$27.

L&L Hawaiian Barbecue
41-1610 Kalanianaole Hwy, Waimanalo
(808) 259-6888

ono **Local**—We don't normally bother to write about chain restaurants (you *know* what to expect at a Burger King). But in this case we are making an exception, because even though L&L does have some locations on the mainland, it's considered a Hawaiian chain and fairly ubiquitous here. In fact, there are more than 40 locations on O'ahu alone. This is the local version of fast food: a mix plate with two scoops of rice, macaroni salad, and beef, chicken or fish. Quick, filling, cheap and satisfying. Price and quality seem to be pretty consistent across the state. $7–$13. You'll find this one on the mauka (mountain) side of the road as you pass through Waimanalo.

Loco Moco Drive Inn
7192 Kalanianaole Hwy, Hawaii Kai
(808) 396-7878

Local—First of all, it's not a drive-in. This place is designed to appeal to locals, and visitors might not find the flavors rewarding. Stay away from the sandwiches. (The teri beef sandwich has so little meat it could almost be classified as homeopathic.) If you're hungry after snorkeling, consider a generously portioned plate lunch—the selection is vast. Otherwise, forget it. In Koko Marina Center. $6–$12.

South Shore Grill
3114 Monsarrat Ave, Honolulu • (808) 734-0229

ono **American**—Some interesting burgers, sand-wiches and tacos, including good fish tacos. The SSG burger is a 6-ouncer topped with their homemade slaw and served on a bed of shoestring onion rings on ciabatta bread. If that's not good enough, try the East Coast West Coast—a chicken sandwich piled high with pastrami and cheese. The heaping portions on the plate lunches are great. They bake their own desserts daily. Order and pay at the window, then wait for your name to be called in the dining area, if there's room—it's small with only a few tables. You may have a wait—this place can get busy. $9–$18 for lunch and dinner. From Waikiki, head toward Diamond Head on Kalakaua Avenue. Turn onto Monsarrat between the zoo and Kapiolani Park. Look for it on the left just after Kanaina Avenue.

Sunny Days Café
3045 Monsarrat Ave, Honolulu • (808) 792-2045

American—Simple café just outside the eastern boundary of Waikiki, on the far side of the zoo (toward Diamond Head). Delicious, beautifully presented food, but priced as if you've got an ocean view, despite being several blocks inland. $16 for eggs Benedict, $17 for very berry pancakes. (The caramel banana pancakes with nuts for $10 is filling and their best value, although it's mostly banana and nuts and very little pancake.) Lunch is mostly sandwiches plus whatever the entrée of the day is, which might be steak, might be lomi lomi salmon. Add $4 to upgrade from rice to quinoa. $9–$18 for breakfast, lunch and early dinner. The beverages are pricey too.

Whole Foods Market
4211 Waialae Ave, Kaimuki• (808) 738-0820

American—If you come from a town with a Whole Foods, you already know about the cornucopia of healthy and organic foods they offer. Sandwiches, sushi, BBQ, Asian cuisine, soup and salad bar and a hot bar. Their pizza might have the best crust on the island. The hot bar regularly has spicy Indian dishes right next to turkey with all the fixin's. It's pricier than other supermarket food, but the quality and selection make it worthwhile. $9–$21 for lunch and dinner. In the Kahala Mall.

KAILUA DINING

Aloha Salads
600 Kailua Rd, Kailua • (808) 262-2016

ono **American**—A cubbyhole with fantastic salads, subs and wraps with great ingredients for darned reasonable prices. Yeah, that's what we like to hear. Their selection is imaginative, often including various fruits, local vegetables and produce as well as island fish. We've had good luck with their soups of the day, and even kids will love their PB&H sub with bananas. If all this seems too healthy, top it off with the Nutella, strawberry and honey wrap. An easy place to like, unless you want to sit down. (Just a few seats.) $9–$13. In Kailua Shopping Center.

Big City Diner
108 Hekili St, Kailua • (808) 263-8880
American—A small, local diner-*ish* chain. The seating is really uncomfortable, especially the vertical booths—pick a chair. The super-varied breakfast menu has typical entrées along with items such as Mama's breakfast bread pudding (a tasty guilty pleasure), unusually adorned pancakes, and kimchee fried rice. Lunch and dinner have just as much variety with lots of salads, sandwiches and burgers, local items and a hodgepodge of assorted selections. With such a broad appeal, there's something for everyone. We liked the tangy guava spice chicken wings. Overall passable, but not memorable. Full bar and some open-air seating at the Kailua location (stay away from the margaritas). $7–$13 for breakfast, $11–$27 for lunch and dinner. In Kailua Town Center on Hekili Street.

Bob's Pizzeria
130 Kailua Rd, Kailua • (808) 263-7757
Italian—The price of a greasy slice might be startling—$6—but so is the acreage. It's a quarter of a 19-inch pie. At the corner of Kailua and Kalaheo in Kailua.

Boots & Kimo's Homestyle Kitchen
151 Hekili St, Kailua • (808) 263-7929

ono **American**—Our endorsement presumes something that probably *won't* happen: that there won't be a ridiculous wait. 'Cause frankly, we don't think *any* breakfast is worth cooling your heels for an hour (or more). This place is popular with locals and visitors. We could almost have classified them as local food. Their specialty is awesome macadamia nut pancakes with a marvelous creamy mac sauce. Definitely try them, if you can bear the wait. Lots of omelets, so-so hash browns and local dishes in a local sporty environment. Love their strawberry waffles. Breakfast until 2 p.m.; plate lunch and sandwiches also served after 11 a.m. Service can be less than loving. Between Hahani and Hamakua. $9–$14 for breakfast or lunch. Cash only. Closed Tuesdays.

Boston's North End Pizza
25 Kaneohe Bay Dr, Kailua • (808) 245-8055
Italian—Not to be confused with the many other Boston Pizza restaurants on the island. Or go ahead and confuse them—they were once affiliated and are still pretty much the same. So is our review. 19-inch pizzas for $21–$29 or by the slice for $6–$8. (What they call a slice is really two pieces—it's an entire quarter of the 19-inch pizza.) Good for grabbing a quick bite to eat, but there's no sign of being in Hawai'i here—it's as if you stepped off the island and into a standard mainland pizza joint. In the Aikahi Park Shopping Center near the north end of Kailua Beach. See map on page 72.

Buzz's Original Steakhouse
413 Kawailoa Rd, Kailua • (808) 261-4661
American—Across the street from Kailua Beach, and also the closest restaurant to Lanikai Beach. Convenient (and correspondingly crowded), but its location doesn't take advantage of the potential views. Lunch is burgers, fish burgers,

chicken and lots of salads. Dinner is steak and seafood. The steak and lobster combo is pretty good, though beef cuts could be a better quality. Love the Chinese-style fish. When they have it, the stuffed 'ahi is amazing. The artichoke surprise appetizer can be awesome, but it's also quite variable. The dessert tray has deliciously sweet, ever-changing selections. Their "legendary mai tais" are very strong—like gasoline. Their "BFRD" adds pineapple to a taller glass. Same gas mileage, lower octane. Service is attentive, but they try to rush you through to take advantage of the high volume of people. $11–$17 for lunch entrées, $18–$44 for dinner. Reservations recommended. Go early or go late. Prime time is pretty hectic. No tank tops allowed after 4:30 p.m.

Champa Thai
306 Kuulei Rd, Kailua • (808) 263-8281
Thai—If you're looking for Thai food in Kailua, this isn't the place to find it. You're better off checking out **Saeng's Thai Cuisine** (or even just going hungry). $10–$25 for lunch and dinner. At Kuulei and Malunui Avenue.

Cinnamon's
315 Uluniu St, Kailua • (808) 261-8724
ono ⌐ **American**—Open since 1985, you'll want to bring your sweet tooth and your stretchy pants. Open-air seating abounds in the atrium of the Kailua Square on Uluniu. The owner makes all the cinnamon rolls, biscuits, cornbread and coffee cake in her home. Known locally more for breakfast and brunch, you can definitely expect a crowd. Arrive early, or they could run out of cinnamon rolls. Try the red velvet pancakes or the mac nut cinnamon roll. We also loved the lox Benedict, but their corned beef hash can be avoided. The lunch menu consists of salads, soups, sandwiches and assorted plates. But it's breakfast that is the star. They will accept

your reservation if there are five or more in your party. We were told with a wink and a nod that if you made a reservation for 5 and showed up with 4, your reservation would still be honored. Breakfast is $10–$14, lunch $12–$14.

Crêpes No Ka 'Oi
143 Hekili St, Kailua • (808) 263-4088
ono ⌐ **American**—Novel food for relatively cheap cheap. So far, so good. All items come on their fresh crêpes with a few breakfast combinations along with their "savory" items, such as the Popeye (lots of spinach, of course), Haole Boy (ham, cheese and pineapple—ironically, on a pizza that's called Hawaiian) and others. Also lots of dessert crêpes, many with the highly addictive (in a good way) Nutella. A huge tea selection. Simple surroundings, ample portions and reasonably quick service. $8–$10 for breakfast, lunch and dinner unless you snag one of the desserts. Closed Tuesdays and no dinner on Sundays. Near Hahani and Hamakua streets. They also have a location in Kahala Mall.

Island Snow
130 Kailua Rd, Kailua • (808) 263-6339
Treats—Good shave ice, though they can be overly generous with the syrup. Get ice cream on the bottom. This is a convenient treat after a hard day of beachgoing at Kailua or Lanikai Beach. Often served with indifference, even if you burst into flames from spontaneous human combustion. At Kailua Beach Center near Kalaheo; walkable from Kailua Beach Park. $2–$3.

K & K BBQ Inn
130 Kailua Rd, Kailua • (808) 262-2272
Local—It's a hole in the wall with a disheveled look, and the food quality varies considerably, but the selection is huge, and they are within walking distance to Kailua Beach Park. Local foods such as

chicken katsu, teri steak, sweet and sour spare ribs, saimin and other noodle dishes, plus burgers, fish sandwiches, etc. In short—not great food, but it's convenient for Kailua beachgoers. Nothing more. In Kailua Beach Center on Kailua Road near Kalaheo Road. $7–$12.

Kalapawai Café & Deli
750 Kailua Rd, Kailua • (808) 262-3354

ono You can't beat the quality of food for the price. They use mostly locally sourced ingredients, and their pride shows. Tasty breakfast sandwiches, juicy sandwiches for lunch (try the French dip) and delicious seafood and steaks for dinner. For breakfast and lunch, place your order at the counter and pay at the register. Dinner after 5 p.m. brings table service. Consider the jidori chicken breast with roasted mushrooms. The salads are enormous here. No matter what you order, you'll leave happy and full. They have a large wine list and a good selection of craft beers. Our gripe with these guys is the cramped dining room and small parking lot. Be prepared to park on the street and pay the meter. $4–$8 for breakfast, $8–$15 for lunch and $14–$27 for dinner. On the corner of Kailua Street and Kainehe. They have another location in Kapolei.

Lanikai Juice
600 Kailua Rd, Kailua • (808) 262-2383

ono Treats—Expect to wait in line at this locally famous juice bar. Their smoothies are great, and they focus on all-natural ingredients. All orders include your choice of supplement. Try their Mango Sunrise with bee pollen for strength and endurance, or their strawberry shaka with echinacea for an immune boost. It's hard to go wrong, no matter what you get. $4–$10 In the Kailua Shopping Center. They also have locations in Honolulu—one in Waikiki, one in Kapolei and one in Haleiwa.

Lemongrass Vietnamese & Thai Cuisine
20 Kainehe St, Kailua • (808) 261-0222

Thai/Vietnamese—Saying you have the best Thai food in Kailua is like saying you have the best prison food west of the Rockies. That's a pretty low bar. They win, but there are no bragging rights. Thai and Vietnamese with a menu that has noodle dishes, sandwiches, lots of curries and lots of pho. The interior and exterior aren't much to speak of, though the food is acceptable and the service quick but snippy. If you order Thai hot, be prepared to tell them how many peppers you want. (Four won't do the job.) Acceptable red curries and Pad Thai; avoid the papaya salad. Pho is fairly tasty. If we sound less than enthusiastic with our praise, that's because we are. $10–$20 for lunch and dinner. On Kainehe off Kailua Road.

Los Garcia's
14 Oneawa St, Kailua • (808) 261-0306

Mexican—Huge menu of traditional and non-traditional Mexican items, including fajitas, steak and seafood, plus vegetarian items and a full bar. Service is lightning fast. The flavors don't work for us, but they have an unusually loyal customer base who no doubt think we're full of beans. They do, however, have good margaritas and a good selection of tequilas. On Oneawa near Kailua Road in Kailua. $8–$20 for lunch and dinner. Consider parking a block over at the municipal building on Aulike.

Maui Tacos
539 Kailua Rd, Kailua • (808) 261-4155

Mexican—This small, local chain is a good place to go for tacos and burritos. It's not overly expensive (though it ain't exactly cheap), portions are large, and they're totally flexible when concocting items. Don't neglect the sauces to the right of the soda machine to spice things up the way you like them. In Kailua Village Shops at Kailua and Hahani in Kailua. $7–$10 for breakfast, $7–$15 for lunch and dinner.

Mexico Lindo
600 Kailua Rd, Kailua • (808) 263-0055
Mexican—Good looking—that's the theme. The interior is good looking, the food is good looking, even the menu is good looking. But that's where it ends. It's skin deep. Beyond the looks, everything disappoints. The festive Mexican ambiance gets dampened by the noise inside. The menu is broad and varied, but tastes so bland you may be grateful for that bottle of Tapatío on the table. They have a good selection of tequilas, but avoid the gasoline-like margaritas. Service is either with a smile or with a snarl. $12–$28 for lunch and dinner. In the Kailua Shopping Center.

Moké's Bread & Breakfast
27 Hoolai St, Kailua • (808) 261-5565
ono Local—This is a great little offbeat, family-operated restaurant. In- and outdoor seating and a *Mom's cooking* feel. They bake their own bread here and braise their own beef brisket for making Reubens and corned beef hash, and it is rockin' delicious. The usual suspects show up for breakfast: loco moco, liliko'i pancakes, waffles and French toast, as well as pork chops and gravy and a house-cut ribeye with eggs for $13.50. Lunch is sandwiches on their fresh baked bread, soup du jour and fresh green salads. Good service, good ingredients, good folks. Expect a wait, especially on weekends. Breakfast is $9–$14, lunch is $8–$11. By the way, it's Moké, *not Moke*. In Hawai'i, if you're not from here, and you call someone a moke (especially if he *is* a moke), bad things will happen to you and your bones. See definition in *Basics* on page 40. Closed Tuesdays. On Hoolai off Kailua Road.

Prima
108 Hekili St, Kailua • (808) 888-8933
American—A "hip" feeling place with tapas and brick oven pizzas. Decor is sparse, modern and simple, as is the menu. A few interesting tapas such as maitake mushroom with cauliflower puree or Brussels sprouts with prosciutto and bordelaise. From their genuine Naplese brick oven come pizzas that are thin and flavorful, if a bit salty. Lunch is just the pizzas—no tapas. Tapas-style share plates from $8 to $22, pizza $16–$22 plus any extra toppings you choose. Service is friendly and eager to please, but it's a bit pricey for food that's merely acceptable. Next to Foodland.

Saeng's Thai Cuisine
315 Hahani St, Kailua • (808) 263-9727
Thai—If you're in Kailua and looking for excellent Thai food… you're outta luck. The food's not exactly good, the service is not exactly good—the restaurant's not exactly good. Guess that about covers it. But if you're craving Thai in Kailua, it's not exactly bad (and it's better than another Kailua Thai restaurant, the terrible **Champa Thai**.) Nice vegetarian selection. $11–$25 for lunch and dinner. On Hahani Street at Kailua Street.

Saigon Noodle House
1020 Keolu Dr, Kailua • (808) 261-2466
Vietnamese—Large Vietnamese menu that does a pretty good job of explaining your options. All kinds of noodles, rice dishes and Vietnamese sandwiches with most items under $10. Service is lightning fast, portions generous and flavors are good. They don't fish from the usual stream of visitors. Nearly all their customers are residents of Enchanted Lakes subdivision, yet it's only a few minutes from Kailua Beach. We ain't saying it's the best food on the island; we're saying it's a heck of a deal. In Enchanted Lakes Shopping Center.

Teddy's Bigger Burgers

539 Kailua Rd, Kailua • (808) 262-0820
134 Kapahulu Ave. Waikiki • (808) 926-3444
66-111 Kamehameha, Haleiwa • (808) 637-8454
46-021 Kamehameha, Kaneohe • (808) 247-0000
4850 Kapolei Pkwy, Kapolei • (808) 674-2447

ono **American**—A retro burger joint with the look and feel of a fast food place, but the food is much higher quality, and you'll have to wait while they make it. Build your own (choose from 5-, 7-, or 9-ounce patties, or absolutely kill it by ordering the 18-ounce monster double), then add toppings, or pick one of the many specialties. Burgers are their signature item (they use ground chuck instead of the typical ground beef), but they also have a really good crispy chicken sandwich, as well as fish sandwiches. The shakes are just barely liquid enough to drink with a straw. You can skip the upgrade to the butter garlic fries. Veggie burger available as well as a cheaper kids' menu. They have 11 locations scattered across O'ahu. $7–$18.

KANE'OHE DINING

Hale'iwa Joe's at Haiku Gardens

46-336 Haiku Rd, Kaneohe • (808) 247-6671

ono **American**—Located in a lush garden setting at Haiku Gardens, it's nice to do a pre-meal stroll in the garden and pond area if you arrive before sunset. In fact, we *strongly* recommend getting there for an early dinner— the bar and lounge opens at 4:30 p.m. with dinner service starting at 5 p.m (and they don't take reservations). The views of the Ko'olau Mountains are exquisite in the afternoon, but the open-air garden setting might bring flying bugs later in the evening. We like the tables near the railing the best. The food is generally pretty good. Try the Thai calamari for an appetizer or the expertly prepared escargot. Dinner is steak and seafood, plus ribs, pork chops and sometimes lobster. The decor includes lots of attractive koa wood. Drinks are very good here—not too boozy with good flavor. The ONO is for the setting and drinks—the food is good but doesn't quite carry it alone, and the service can be slow at times. $20–$40 for dinner. Brunch on Sundays 9 a.m.–2 p.m. for around $30. From Hwy 830 (Kamehameha Highway), turn toward the mountain onto Haiku Road near the Windward Mall in Kane'ohe. You'll see it on the left not long after Haiku Road crosses Hwy 83.

BETWEEN KANE'OHE & KAHUKU

Once you drive north of Kane'ohe on Hwy 83, your options dwindle until you get to Hale'iwa 40 miles away. Here we've listed the restaurants *in the order that you'll see them*, not in alphabetical order.

Shrimp Shack

53-360 Kamehameha Hwy, Hauula
(808) 256-5589

Pacific Rim—On the side of the road at Ching's Punalu'u Store in Punalu'u, this yellow truck serves classic O'ahu garlic shrimp (head off), coconut shrimp, spicy shrimp (we're starting to sound like Bubba in *Forrest Gump*), plus some mahi mahi, crab and New York steak. Prices run $11–$16 unless you dig into the whole snow crab or start mixing things. You can also go cheaper with hot dogs, chili rice or popcorn shrimp. Nice folks, but flavors are underwhelming. Keep going unless you're real hungry.

Papa Ole's Kitchen

54-316 Kamehameha Hwy, #9, Hauula
(808) 293-2292

Local—They may have styrofoam plate service, but the grinds are cheap, flavorful, fatty and abundant. It's literally dripping with unhealthinesss. If you get a plate lunch, expect a heaping plate of kalbi ribs or teriyaki chicken, for instance, along with two huge scoops of rice and mac salad. Burgers are priced similar to Mc-Donald's but taste better. Avoid the fries. $5–$13 for lunch and dinner. In the Hau'ula Kai Center. Closed Wednesday. Cash only.

North Shore Tacos
54-296 Kamehameha Hwy, Hauula
(808) 293-4440
Mexican—They aren't modest about claiming to have the No. 1-rated fish tacos on O'ahu. In fairness, we agree that they're good, but they're not the best. Almost everything is made in house—the horchata, the decadent liliko'i chocolate mousse and even the hot sauce. Order at the counter and sit in the open, breezy, surfing-inspired dining room, and watch the surfing videos playing on two TVs. You won't have to wait long. The price is a little steep for the portion size, the reason for no ONO. $10–$13 for lunch and dinner. In front of the Hau'ula Shopping Center, heading north on Kamehameha Highway.

La'ie Chop Suey
55-510 Kamehameha Hwy, Laie • (808) 293-8022
Chinese—They are fast, efficient, friendly and priced right. An endless, sprawling menu confronts you, but at lunch most opt for either the pre-chosen lunch plate or the larger dinner plate (available at lunch—spring for that one). We're talking around $7 for a large portion. If you want to go off the menu, there's almost certainly something for everyone. Not the best food, but it doesn't take much to rise above others in La'ie. Consider the Doctor's Special if you like veggies. Off-the-menu items will cost you $6–$15. Closed Sundays. Near Foodland.

Seven Brothers
55-510 Kamehameha Hwy, Laie • (808) 744-6440
ono ⌐ **American**—This is a family-owned burger joint in the La'ie Village Center next to Foodland. Besides the creative burgers and salads, they have some delicious fries with a unique twist.

Get 'em plain or try the paniolo fries. It's a combination of fresh-cut fried potatoes, bacon, fried pineapple, cheese, BBQ sauce and onion rings. (And it's only a *trillion* calories per serving.) They have a long bar inside and the only thing missing is… liquid aloha. La'ie is a dry town. The family also owns Seven Brothers at the Mill, and they serve the same delicious home-made banana bread-based desserts. In a strip mall with no view, but for $6–$15 you can't beat the price.

KAHUKU SHRIMP & MORE

On the side of Hwy 83 in Kahuku, 25 miles north of Kane'ohe. The northern tip of the island has become synonymous with shrimp—shrimp trucks, shrimp shacks and shrimp farming. (Though not all get their shrimp from the nearby farm.) These businesses are listed in the order that you will encounter them in the *North Shore Sights* chapter.

Giovanni's Aloha Shrimp Truck
56-505 Kamehameha Hwy, Kahuku
(808) 293-1839
Pacific Rim—The most famous of all the Kahuku shrimp trucks, this may have once been an unassuming spot in the middle of nowhere, but it's become so well-known and heavily visited that long lines and equally long waits can be a real problem. Three shrimp dishes (and a scampi hot dog) comprise the menu with shrimp scampi the most popular item. They use a delicious (and very garlicky) marinade. Though tasty, many people object to dealing with the shells and the shrimp legs (which you tear off), not to mention burning your fingers in the process. It's $14 and includes rice. The spicy shrimp is so strong it could probably be used to clean hard water spots off your shower. If you feel inclined, they will give you a marker and you can sign the truck with your initials or leave a comment. Definitely

avoid the bathrooms ('nuff said about that), and use the wash bin near the tables. This is our second favorite shrimp truck *in Kahuku* (we prefer Romy's), though the service is incredibly indifferent. They also have another location in the Pit in Hale'iwa on Kamehameha. Same menu, same service. Cash only.

Kai's Island Korn
56-505 Kamehameha Hwy, Kahuku
(484) 529-6307

ono **American**—This ain't shrimp but a tiny corn stand behind Giovanni's on Burroughs and Kam Highway. Flavors are good. We love the Island Style, but it's the Baja that we dream about. $5, cash only. If you've never tried locally grown Hawaiian Supersweet corn, this place will knock your socks off.

Seven Brothers at the Mill
56-565 Kamehameha Hwy, Kahuku
(808) 852-0040

ono **American**—In Kahuku, and it's *not* only about shrimp. Order your food at the window and take a seat outside at the picnic tables, or sit inside, which gets hot. Owned by seven brothers operating out of an old sugar mill, they serve tasty burgers, fish and salads with locally grown greens. Their coconut mac shrimp is pretty good. They advertise it as "life-changing." We can verify that this advertising claim is a bald-faced falsehood. Our lives didn't change one bit after we ate their shrimp (but the awesome chocolate chip coconut banana will change at least an hour of your life). You'll spend $7–$18 for a filling lunch or dinner. Closed on Sunday. In Kahuku just after Burroughs Road on the right in the old sugar mill.

Fiji Market & Curry Kitchen
56-565 Kamehameha Hwy, Kahuku
(808) 293-7120
Indian—Hard to find behind the gas station at the Kahuku Sugar Mill center. It's like visiting a real market in Fiji, complete with an aunty in back churning out tasty beef, lamb and chicken curries for about $13 and delicious roti wraps for $9. Portions are generous. A no-brainer if you like curries.

HI-BBQ
56-565 Kamehameha Hwy, Kahuku
(808) 724-2341

ono **American**—Unabashed meat lovers, it's about brisket, pulled pork and other meat items. Portions are hefty—you will not walk away hungry. Their bacon-infused baked beans are not as flavorful as they sound, but the meats are mighty tasty. The brisket works without their barbecue sauce, but we like to drizzle a little on anyway. Pulled pork already comes with the sauce. Don't count on any seating; consider this to go only. Most items are $13 or $15, but they have a huge plate for $25. In Kahuku near the Sugar Mill.

Famous Kahuku Shrimp Truck
56-580 Kamehameha Hwy, Kahuku
(808) 389-1173
Pacific Rim—*Infamous* might be more appropriate for these guys. There's a reason that people are lined up at the nearby Giovanni's Shrimp Truck and not here—it's junk. The shrimp, squid and fish plates all taste pretty similar, which is not a good sign. The truck is in such rough shape that you'd be forgiven if you thought it had been vandalized at some point. You can do much better, and luckily the better choices are right next door. $10–$14, cash only.

Romy's Kahuku Shrimp Hut
56781 Kamehameha Hwy, Kahuku
(808) 232-2202

ono **Pacific Rim**—Located 0.75 miles past Kahuku Town (toward Hale'iwa) after you've driven by their competitors. They harvest their shrimp and prawns that day, and the freshness shows. Garlic butter (No. 1) or the sweet and hot (No. 2) are even harder to peel than Giovanni's, but the eggroll shrimp (No. 3) eliminates the work. Expect to wait 20–40 minutes unless you call it in. (They take the phone off the hook when it gets busy, though.) You get shrimp and rice for about $15. Make it prawns or sunfish, and the price goes up. The tables can be windy, so you might want to eat in the car. Cash only. (There's an ATM there.) Might want to avoid the fresh sunfish. We've seen 'em dead in the holding tank.

Fumi's Kahuku Shrimp
56-777 Kamehameha Hwy, Kahuku
(808) 232-8881
Pacific Rim—Just past and similar to, but not as good as Romy's, they raise their own shrimp and cook it fresh or sell it live. Ten different styles (some peeled and fried if you don't want to deal with the shells). $13.

Lei Lei's Bar & Grill
57-049 Kuilima Dr, Turtle Bay • (808) 293-2662
American—Located at the golf course at Turtle Bay Resort. Sit inside the large dining area, at the well-stocked bar, or outside at one of the covered tables overlooking the golf course. Only a few breakfast items (but a tasty croissant sandwich), sandwiches, burgers and salads for lunch, and steak, prime rib, seafood and chicken for dinner. The potato mac salad is pretty good, but overall, the food is unremarkable. Avoid the mai tai. $10–$13 for breakfast, $14–$20 for lunch, $28–$45 for dinner.

North Shore Kula Grille
57-091 Kamehameha Hwy, Turtle Bay
(808) 293-6000
Local—It's hard to classify these guys (In the Turtle Bay Resort on the North Shore) as anything besides local/American with a Hawaiian twist. The food, although presented very well, lacks the flavor you

expect, and it's coupled with unenthusiastic service. Turtle Bay has a captive audience here—they're the only resort in the area—and it shows. It's hard to get warm and squishy about any place that charges $21 for a burger and fries. We *understand* that they use locally sourced ingredients (they start beating that into you as soon as you walk in), but the prices don't match the product or the service. Our favorite thing here was the Maui Wowie Tai, made with Maui rums and honey, as well as ginger liqueur. $20–$45 for dinner. They also have a $31 breakfast buffet. That said, it's better than the **The Point** near the pool, which consists of unimpressive bar food with poor service.

Pa'akai
57-091 Kamehameha Hwy, Turtle Bay
(808) 293-6000
ono **Pacific Rim**—Pa'akai is the Hawaiian word for sea salt and they pride themselves on using local ingredients, including locally produced salt. We like the pork tenderloin and black truffle mashed potatoes for an entrée or the pan-seared kampachi with roasted butternut squash. The dining room is surrounded by soft surfaces and has a beautiful ocean view. The drinks are strong but flavorful. Service is a bit awkward. But overall, a great place to impress your date. $35–$70 for dinner. At the Turtle Bay Resort near the northern tip of the island.

Roy's Beach House
57-091 Kamehameha Hwy, Turtle Bay
(808) 293-7697
ono **Pacific Rim**—It's hard to say anything bad about this place—except the price. Great food, killer beachfront location and well-conceived dishes. You're right next to Kuilima Cove at the Turtle Bay Resort with ocean breezes and a restful, wood-filled ambiance at the covered and uncovered tables. Lunch items such as mac nut mahi mahi, mis-

oyaki salmon, kobe burgers and short ribs rarely disappoint. Dinner is steak and seafood along with lamb. They pour some mean tropical drinks that can be sneaky, so beware if you're not staying at the resort and having to drive a ways. But all of this comes with a price—a pretty big one. It's $20–$30 for lunch, $30–$50 or more for dinner, and appetizers are profoundly expensive.

Ted's Bakery
59-024 Kamehameha Hwy, Waialee
(808) 638-8207

ono **American**—They have pies and cakes, whole or by the slice. Breakfast is simple and cheap at $6–$11. Lunch is great plate lunches, large burgers, shoyu chicken (which always sells out) and good garlic shrimp for $7–$17. Sit at the outside covered tables, or better yet, grab your food and head to nearby Sunset Beach, which is just to the southwest on Hwy 83. Open daily 7 a.m.–8 p.m. (8:30 p.m. on weekends). Located just before Sunset Beach if coming from Kahuku.

Shark's Cove Grill
59-712 Kamehameha Hwy, Pupukea
(808) 638-8300

Super convenient if you're on the beach at Shark's Cove or Three Tables (and parking is safer). A white truck with plenty of outdoor seating and a decent view of Shark's Cove. Burgers, salads, sandwiches or kabobs and pretty good cookies. Overall, it's not bad. (Of course, we usually review this place after we've been diving or snorkeling at these two beaches, and even cat food would taste good after we've come out of the ocean.) Breakfast available from 8–11 a.m. with just a few egg dishes, pancakes and a breakfast sandwich. $7–$12 for breakfast, $9–$15 for lunch and dinner. Across from Shark's Cove on Highway 83 north of Waimea Bay.

HALE'IWA DINING

You'll notice a disproportionate number of ONOs on the North Shore. It's not that we hand them out like candy up here; it's just that the caliber of food and competition seems higher.

Banzai Sushi
66-246 Kamehameha Hwy, Haleiwa
(808) 637-4404

ono **Japanese**—Hale'iwa's only sushi bar has a strong North Shore vibe, including surfing movies playing on a projector. Seating under a lanai is half western (tables), half Japanese (floor). Some of the combo options are a pretty good value. And the sushi tastes nice and fresh. (Love the Maui Wowi roll.) $15–$35 (or more—it's easy to spend a lot on sushi) for lunch and dinner. In the North Shore Marketplace.

beach house
62-540 Kamehameha Hwy, Haleiwa
(808) 637-3435

ono **American**—Also called the Hale'iwa Beach House, this is one of the first restaurants you'll come to in Hale'iwa if you're approaching town from the northeast (a good thing if you're hungry—you'll hit it before the major traffic snarl). It's also one of the only restaurants on the north shore with an ocean view. Unfortunately, it's across the highway, so there's a good chance you'll still be looking at a slow-moving line of vehicles crawling by, but the open-air architecture helps give the place more of a beachside feel. It's a pricier option ($12–$29 for lunch entrées, $30–$40 for dinner), but the price is in line with the quality. (That's reviewer code for *the food is really good*.) The focus is steak and seafood, but which is superior depends entirely on what you are in the mood for. Awesome lobster and shrimp curry. Limited vegetarian options (basically a fettuccini pasta or salad). Kids' menu items for $8. Extensive (and expensive) bar, which is their biggest disappointment. They aren't shy with the salt in their dishes here, so if you're sensitive, ask them to go easy and tweak it yourself. The place has an upscale feel, but casual clothes are fine—*it's the north shore, brah*. Some of the wait staff seem to have a bit of an attitude, as if they resent having to serve you because they'd rather be out surfing. But maybe if we lived in Hale'iwa, we'd feel the same way.

Big Wave Shrimp
66-521 Kamehameha Hwy, Haleiwa
(808) 366-2016
Pacific Rim—A shrimp option in Hale'iwa that has more seating at picnic tables than some of their competition. The garlic butter shrimp is fairly tasty and served with abundant garlic sauce for dipping. Their spicy version is not as hot as many of the other shrimp trucks on the island. Remember that you'll have to peel your shrimp, but it's not served with the head. In all, not a bad choice. In Hale'iwa on Hwy 83 just north of the traffic circle. $13–$16 for lunch or early dinner.

Breakers Restaurant & Bar
66-250 Kamehameha Hwy, Haleiwa
(808) 637-9898
ono ✓ **American**—A good menu, good food and a funky Polynesian/surfer atmosphere. An easy place to recommend. Bar fare that mixes some Mexican- and Asian-inspired dishes, plus steak, seafood, burgers, and their popular fish and chips. Breakfast items are hearty (love the short-rib hash) as well as sweet with pancakes, waffles and French toast. We've never had a bad meal here, but their menu has been in flux lately—stick with burgers and seafood for the safest bet. In the North Shore Marketplace on Kamehameha Highway (83). Breakfast is $10–$15, lunch is $11–$18, dinner is $16–$27, plus pricey appetizers.

Café Hale'iwa
66-460 Kamehameha Hwy, Haleiwa
(808) 637-5516
ono ✓ **American**—This is a long-time North Shore landmark. Breakfast is a hit with surfers who prefer the "dawn patrol" special (eggs and pancakes for $7.50 before 8 a.m.). The red and green sauces can spice up your morning here. Lunch is simple burgers, sandwiches and salads. Service is fast and friendly. $8–$14 for breakfast and lunch. At the mauka end of town near Paalaa Road.

Cholo's Homestyle Kitchen
66-250 Kamehameha Hwy, Haleiwa
(808) 637-3059
ono ✓ **Mexican**—No frills, but flavorful food at reasonable prices. Most entrées have a pretty decent spicy bite to them. Typical Mexican items, plus fish tacos and burritos. Service is often slow and indifferent, but not rude. They make a good mojito. In the past they have been a little unkempt, but they cleaned up the place. Some outdoor seating, but not much of a view. Takeout is available. At the North Shore Marketplace on Kamehameha Highway (83). $9–$18 for lunch and dinner. (More for fajitas.) They also have a roving food truck during surfing season.

Hale'iwa Joe's Seafood Grill
66-011 Kamehameha Hwy, Haleiwa
(808) 637-8005
ono ✓ **American**—A nice menu of fresh fish, half-pound burgers, coconut shrimp, fish sandwich, a good fish taco, steak and more for lunch, plus pupus of sushi, ceviche, ribs, etc. The sizzling mushrooms are a great appetizer (ask for some parmesan on the side). Dinner is a bit more steak- and seafood-oriented. Consider the covered outdoor tables if it's not too windy. Flies might be a problem, but this is a Hale'iwa-wide problem. This place serves potent mai tais

that come in a souvenir glass you get to keep. They would *not* have gotten an ONO if they were in Honolulu because of inattentive service and inconsistent food preparation on occasion, but this about as nice as it gets in Hale'iwa. $11–$20 for lunch, $16–$35 for dinner. At the corner of Hale'iwa Road and Kamehameha Highway (83) across from the harbor.

Killer Tacos
66-560 Kamehameha Hwy, #1, Haleiwa
(808) 637-4573
Mexican—It's the place for simple, flavorful Mexican food without high prices. They season things reasonably well here, and you can mix and match to create your own burritos or tacos. In Hale'iwa town on Kamehameha Hghway near the traffic circle at Waialua Beach Road. $4–$8 for lunch and early dinner.

Kono's
66-250 Kamehameha Hwy, Haleiwa
(808) 637-9211
ONO American—Simply a great place for breakfast in Hale'iwa. Their burritos are justifiably famous. Each starts with eggs, cheese and potatoes, then branches off from there. We recommend Wendy's burrito with sautéed onions, peppers and bacon. And always add gravy; you never know when you'll get your next fix. Prices are relatively cheap. They sell their own salt rub, which they are generous with on some of their items, such as the kalua pork. Their baked sandwiches at lunch are *so* hot they need a warning label. Stick with breakfast. $8–$12 for breakfast and lunch. At the North Shore Marketplace on Kamehameha Highway (83).

Kua 'Aina Sandwich
66-160 Kamehameha Hwy, Haleiwa
(808) 637-6067
ONO American—A well-known burger joint that makes great burgers

(with third- and half-pound patties), nice, thin house-cut fries and fairly good sandwiches (which are outshined by the burgers). The fries grow on you as you continue to gobble them up. The place can get pretty crowded. Place your order at the counter and wait for them to call your name. $8–$17 for lunch and dinner. In Hale'iwa on Kamehameha Highway across from the Hale'iwa Shopping Plaza.

Matsumoto's
66-111 Kamehameha Hwy, Haleiwa
(808) 637-4827
ONO Treats—There are two good sources of shave ice in Hale'iwa. Matsumoto's is the legendary source with high name recognition (they've been here since 1951), and 50 yards down the road is **San Lorenzo's**. *Insanely* long lines are the norm at Matsumoto's, and we've seen it at times with a 45-minute wait and only a handful of people at San Lorenzo's. Frankly, San Lorenzo's isn't as good (somewhat underwhelming flavors and slightly coarser ice), but it beats the wait. Both companies are cheap—$4–$5 with ice cream on the bottom. And be careful of bees and wasps that seem to thrive on the dropped shave ice at both locations. In Hale'iwa on Kamehameha Highway between Hale'iwa Road and the Hale'iwa Shopping Center.

Scoop of Paradise
66-145 Kamehameha Hwy, #5B, Haleiwa
(808) 637-3456
Treats—They have two dozen housemade flavors. The ice cream is kind of dry—as is the service. They also sell Bubbie's Ice Cream, which is better. There's much more going on here than just ice cream, though. There is delicious nostalgia, and the shop has toys for kids of all ages. In Hale'iwa Shopping Plaza on Kamehameha Highway across from Ace Hardware. $4–$8.

Spaghettini
66-200 Kamehameha Hwy, Haleiwa
(808) 637-0104
Italian—Pizza and pasta. The food is filling, and portions are large for the price, but flavors are on the dull side—you won't be fantasizing about it later. The pizza by the slice is marginally better than the pasta. $4–$16 for lunch and dinner. On the highway in Hale'iwa. An OK option for a quick stop if you're hungry and don't want to spend a lot.

Waialua Bakery
66-200 Kamehameha Hwy, Haleiwa
(808) 341-2838
ONO **Treats**—Consummate bakery with authentic surf-town style offering fresh baked cookies and pastries as well as sandwiches with excellent house-made bread and buns. Try their Parmesan garlic bun or the pesto wheat bun for your sandwich, only two of the many delicious options baked fresh daily. Or grab a smoothie or healthy shot of wheatgrass, make yourself at home on their patio, and people watch. $3–$12. Cash only. Closed Sunday. Bring in your own cup or to-go container and they'll give you a free cookie.

CENTRAL O'AHU DINING

Maui Mike's
96 S Kamehameha Hwy, Wahiawa
(808) 622-5900
ONO **American**—This is a great place to get your hands dirty while dismantling a half-chicken cooked in a fiery rotisserie. They claim to use fresh (never frozen), hormone-free, organically fed chickens, and we have to admit they taste better than the rotisserie chickens you find in the supermarket. Your choice of seven different dipping sauces customizes the whole experience. If only they had a bathroom (or pressure washer) to remove the sticky mess from your hands. $7–$15 for lunch and dinner. On the highway in Wahiawa town.

Restaurant 604
57 Arizona Memorial Dr, Honolulu • (808) 888-7616
ONO Despite winning our *least interesting restaurant name* award, this is a *great* place to relax and get something to eat after visiting Pearl Harbor. (Or before, if you've got a lot of time to kill before your tour starts. But make sure you go get a ticket first since they run out early.) This place is next to the WWII Valor in the Pacific Monument parking lot but hidden from view; walk up the road and go under the bridge. The restaurant is right on the water, with a *fantastic* open-air view of the harbor's east loch and a small marina. That bridge you went under to get here is the bridge to Ford Island, which, unfortunately, blocks the view of the military ships. The burgers here are perfectly moist and made with grass-fed beef from The Big Island. (The deluxe makes good use of bacon and avocado.) Good fish tacos. Creative drinks from the bar. Dinner is fancier with steak and more seafood. The place is usually crowded with uniformed military personnel due to the proximity to the base, so service can be a little slow. Lunch prices ($12–$16) are very reasonable for Hawai'i. Dinner is more expensive at $19–$31, but they'll let you order a burger off the lunch menu if you ask. Eat here during daylight hours since you lose the view after dark. Don't try to to figure out the significance of how the number 604 in the restaurant's name relates to Pearl Harbor. Was it the time of the start of the attack? Number of Japanese Zeros? Nah, 604 is the building number.

KO OLINA & KAPOLEI DINING

Ama'ama
92-1185 Aliinui Dr, Ko Olina • (808) 674-6200
ONO **American**—You're paying for an awesome beachside location

at the Aulani, Disney Resort. When the sun goes down, so does the view, making dinner—as delicious as it is—overpriced. The ONO is for breakfast and lunch. The small breakfast menu is gourmet, an example being the breakfast sandwich—a lobster claw, egg, avocado, tomato, lettuce, and truffle oil on a brioche bun. Yeah, this ain't no McBreakfast. Sandwiches at lunch get a similar treatment. Dinner is steak and seafood (including a darn fine cioppono). Love the crispy Singaporean pepper shrimp. And the kurobuta pork shoulder is impossibly tender and delicious. The food here is top-notch and you won't regret a single morsel—until you get the bill. **$15–$30** for breakfast, **$20–$30** for lunch, **$35–$65** for dinner. Reservations recommended for dinner. Disney validates up to four hours of parking if you spend at least $35.

Bic Tacos
4450 Kapolei Pkwy, Kapolei • (808) 200-1181

ONO **Mexican**—We like finding places like this: cheap prices, good food, great flavors. Tacos burritos and bowls. Pick the stuff you want, pick what you want to put it in, and get to it. Their motto is spot on—simple, fresh and bold. If you like spicy, gotta try the pork chorizo. Love the steak, too. The atmosphere is simply a long counter, and a long row of tables—but you can take yours to go and find a nicer spot. In Kapolei Commons Shopping Center. **$5–$10** for lunch and dinner.

Down to Earth
4460 Kapolei Pkwy, Kapolei • (808) 675-2300
American—Part of a local chain of health food stores with a hot and salad bar (sold by the pound) that makes a pretty decent place to stop and grab a quick and healthy bite. They also have wraps and hot and cold sandwiches. Several types of kombucha available on tap. **$8–$16** for lunch and dinner. At the corner of Kalaeloa Boulevard and Kapolei Parkway, Kapolei.

Eating House 1849
4450 Kapolei Pkwy, Kapolei • (808) 447-1849

ONO **American**—A rustic chic atmosphere that is open and loud with good food and mostly good service. Menu is seafood and steak with some Asian. In fact, the kamameshi (hot pot rice bowl) with butterfish is incredible, and the crispy cauliflower and Brussels sprouts—which I dreaded as a kid—are awesome. Flavors are bold. They make a mean blackened ahi. Nice selection of wines (including 50 under $50), good signature cocktail (love the Hawaiian martini, which is better with Hangar One than Skye) and beer choices. Consider the warm apple volcano dessert. This is part of small local chain started by chef Roy Yamaguchi after he sold his namesake restaurants. **$25–$60** for dinner. At the Kapolei Commons. Reservations recommended. Their Waikiki location isn't as good.

Just Tacos Mexican Grill & Cantina
92-1046 Olani St, Ko Olina • (808) 677-7782
Mexican—The name is strange. They've got a lot more than "just tacos," including queso, ceviche, fried calamari, fajitas, enchiladas, taco salads and steaks. Tacos include The Ultimate Taco (which is actually a burrito) along with the usual chicken, steak, fish, etc. The food is adequate but not very memorable, especially for the price. **$16–$35** for lunch or dinner. Margarita pitchers are $30–$35. Indoor and outdoor seating with an attractive bar presentation and almost *400* tequila choices. *Olé!* Located at Ko Olina Center.

Longboards Bar & Grill
92-161 Waipahe Pl, Ko Olina • (808) 679-4700

ONO **American**—If prices seem high—hey, look around—you're open-air right next to lagoon No. 3 with wicked sunset views. The food is reasonably good, certainly not great. Unimaginative fish, steak, a pasta or two at dinner, sandwiches, wraps and large, tasty burgers plus salads at lunch. Good poke if you're up for a uniquely local dish. Portions are ample—get an appetizer or an entrée, not both. Drinks are delicious but taste weak. Extensive and selfless research, however, has led us to conclude they aren't as weak as they seem. (That's our Wizard thoroughness peeking through.) The food by itself wouldn't get them an ONO, but this is the sunset view you dreamt of when you imagined Hawai'i. Breakfast is a buffet for $23, lunch is $17–$20. Dinner has the lunch menu plus entrées up to $35 and occasional buffets. Take the road to lagoon No. 4 and valet park at the Marriott's Ko Olina Beach Club.

Luibueno's
91-5431 Kapolei Pkwy, Kapolei • (808) 637-7717
Mexican—This place had a lot more charm when it was on the north shore. Now it's in the mall in Kapolei, and it *feels* like a mall restaurant. The prices went down, as did the quality. They can still make a decent margarita, but it's the kind of place that is better for drinks and pupus rather than a full-on dining experience. It's also a popular place on Saturday nights when they clear the floor for salsa dancing at 10 p.m. Most of the clientele are local folks in the service industry, and they tend to keep the dance floor going till closing time. Be warned that the bathroom is a shared space for men and women, and the shortage of doors can make things awkward. $12–$32 for lunch and dinner. In the Ka Makana Alii Mall in Kapolei.

Makahiki
92-1185 Aliinui Dr, Ko Olina • (808) 674-6200
ONO **American**—This *ain't* the place for a relaxing breakfast, but kids will love it. If you make a reservation, they will have Mickey Mouse personally greet you. "Aunty's Breakfast Celebration" is a party with Goofy and Minnie Mouse

circulating through the dining room entertaining and taking pictures, while Aunty plays the 'ukulele to dancing and activities for the kids. The buffet itself doesn't disappoint, and it shouldn't for this price. There is something for everyone—American, Chinese, Japanese and local dishes. There's also an omelet bar and a special kids' buffet. It's gonna cost $39 ($20 for kids 9 and under.) The characters have an early bedtime, so dinner is more relaxed with live music, and the buffet is prime rib and seafood with a huge dessert selection. $52 for grownups and $25 for kids 9 and under. Located in the Aulani, Disney Resort & Spa.

Monkeypod Kitchen
92-1048 Olani St, Ko Olina • (808) 380-4086
ONO **American**—Part of a small, local chain from well-known chef Peter Merriman, the food is usually excellent, and the menu wanders from type to type. Fish coconut stew (which is awesome) is featured next to gnocchi with sausage, pizzas, steak, saimin and bulgogi pork or fish tacos. (So we just classified it as American because… well, it is.) Service at this location can be a bit slow for these prices. They have more than two dozen beers on tap, lots of wine and a pretty good bar. The unusual mai tais come with a foam float, and we're not sure what we think of them. (We'll just have to keep trying them until we form an opinion.) Appetizers are *very* pricey. Lunch is $18–$30, dinner is $20–$55. The menu urges you to "save your fork for pie." Sorry, but at $10 a slice, I want a new fork. In fact, can I take it with me? Reservations recommended. In Ko Olina Station.

'Olelo Room
92-1185 Aliinui Dr, Ko Olina • (808) 674-6200
Hawaiian—A cool lounge with pupus and cocktails, where Hawaiian is spoken, and even the tables and chairs are labeled with their Hawaiian names. So here's

your chance to immerse yourself. (For the record, the ancient Hawaiians never had a word for mojito—or mai tai, for that matter.) $10–$20. Located in the Aulani, Disney Resort & Spa. Disney validates up to four hours of parking if you spend $35 or more.

Thai Lao
91-563 Farrington Hwy, Kapolei • (808) 674-2262

ONO **Thai**—Located in the Halekuai Center, the dining area is small and cramped, but it has a very clean and modern feel. The service is friendly and attentive. Expect to wait—this place is very popular, and for good reason. The food's outstanding, and the portions are generous. A large menu with traditional Thai dishes, as well as some Laotian dishes. Lots of curries here. Try the panang, and, if you like heat, make *sure* you ask, otherwise, they will prepare it really mild. The summer rolls are very fresh and include a couple of shrimp in each one. $11–$15 for lunch and dinner. They also have a location in Pearl City.

Two Scoops Ice Cream Parlor
92-1049 Olani St, Ko Olina • (808) 489-4350
Treats—Serves a relatively unremarkable ice cream. $4–$8. At Ko Olina Center.

WAI'ANAE DINING

Coquito's
85-773 Farrington Hwy, Waianae • (808) 888-4082

ONO **Puerto Rican**—This little gem is a small house that's been converted to a restaurant. Sit at one of the tables inside, or ask for a spot outside on the covered porch. To add some authenticity to the atmosphere, they play salsa music. It's a simple menu, almost everything has plantains in it, and it's very reasonably priced. The food is hearty and delicious but doesn't leave you feeling heavy. Try the mofongo, a mashed plantain dish with your choice of meat on

top. There is also a vegetarian option. Save room for the tasty in-house-made tres leche cake. BYOB. $10–$25 for lunch and dinner. Closed Monday. On Farrington Hwy north of Army Street.

Da Crawfish & Crab Shack
87-064 Farrington Hwy, Maili • (808) 679-9080

ONO **rican**—Directly across from Ma'ili Beach Park, there's a brightly colored banner advertising a crawfish and crab shack. It's a bit loud and everything echoes inside, especially when there is a sporting event on one of the three large TVs. They also have outdoor tables. The menu has a little of everything from inexpensive bar food, a steak with poi and corn, crab, crawfish, lobster, clams, shrimp, or any combination of the above. You order your ocean critter, choose your seasoning (they only offer three), and then choose your spice level. (Mild really is mild.) Prices here are all over the place. If you stick to the bar menu, you'll spend $6–$10. More prepared meals or seafood will run you $15–$30. You're on the second floor overlooking the beach to the west, where the whole wall is glass, so from anywhere in the dining area you have an amazing sunset view. The food alone wouldn't get them an ONO. But for this part of the island and with this sunset view, it's worth recommending.

Hannara Restaurant
86-078 Farrington Hwy, Waianae • (808) 696-6137
Local—Cheap grinds are the draw here. It's a Hawaiian-style greasy spoon diner serving local plate lunches along with traditional Hawaiian foods, such as poi and lau lau. If the local flavors don't do it for ya, they also have American diner food, including chicken fried steak and cheeseburgers, and they serve breakfast all day. $6–$13 for breakfast and $5–$16 for lunch and dinner. On the highway in downtown Wai'anae.

Tacos & More
85-993 Farrington Hwy, Waianae • (808) 697-8800
Mexican—No. Is that succinct enough? Trust us, and just say no.

ISLAND NIGHTLIFE

While it's true that the neighbor islands are a bit lacking in nightlife, no one would ever make that comment about O'ahu. From simple lounges with a single musician playing Hawaiian music on an acoustic guitar to full-blown dinner shows to seedy strip clubs—Waikiki has something for just about everyone.

But people's taste in nightlife varies *tremendously*. This is a section where we feel a little vulnerable, because things change weekly in the world of nightlife. The Friday edition of the *Star-Advertiser* newspaper has an entertainment section (called *TGIF*) that lists what's going on in the coming week. It's *extremely* comprehensive. (It's also online.) Also look for *Midweek* and *Weekly* magazines. Nightlife is one area where the free stuff (seen at news racks everywhere) can come in handy because of the ads. By the way, if you learn about something playing at the **Hawai'i Theatre** (808-528-0506) that sounds interesting, jump on it. This has got to be one of the most beautiful theaters you'll ever see. The restoration is incredible, and it looks like what an upscale theater must have looked like in the 1920s, which is when it was built.

Legendary to Waikiki, **Duke's Waikiki** (808-922-2268) at the Outrigger Waikiki Beach Resort is always ringing with live music and good drinks. Every Sunday afternoon, master guitarist Henry Kapono plays until sunset, drawing quite a crowd. Also in Waikiki, **The Beach Bar** (808-922-3111) at the Moana Surfrider has Hawaiian entertainment each night until 9. Inside the Halekulani is the hidden gem, **Lewer's Lounge** (808-923-2311). Nightly jazz piano and top-of-the-line cocktails

in a classy lounge make this a favorite place for a relaxing libation.

Chinatown is home to numerous bars that draw people of all types and flavors. Most are found along Nuuanu and Hotel streets. The dueling Irish pubs of **O'Toole's** (808-536-4138) and **Murphy's** (808-531-0422) on Nuuanu Street are sharp contrasts. The rowdier O'Toole's boasts live music and a large selection of beers, while Murphy's is a landmark establishment known for their pau hana (after work) time and sports bar scene. Hotel Street offers a few more choices from seedy to artsy—something for everyone.

While there's literally no end to the number of bars and lounges in Waikiki, there are also several notable dinner shows and lu'au available.

LU'AU

Hula dancers in grass skirts and coconut bras bend and sway to the music. Smiling people in their finest aloha wear sit together at a table with a mai tai in hand and a plate of kalua pig in front of them. A performer on stage twirls a torch lit at both ends to an urgent drumbeat. The idea of a lu'au that you probably already have in your head isn't that far off from reality. The pig is baked in an underground oven called an imu all day, creating succulent results when prepared right. Shows feature dance styles from across Polynesia, and they are usually exciting and fast-paced. Sure, it's one of the most touristy things you can do, but going to a lu'au can be a real blast, and if time allows, it's highly recommended.

Different lu'au are held on different nights, and the schedules change with the whims of the managers, so verify the days before making plans. Prices listed in this section are pre-tax, but most places don't expect you to leave a tip. (You can upgrade to VIP packages that include perks like better seats, more drinks and a real flower lei.) The buffets are all-you-can-eat, and there's also a cash bar where you can have the bartender make something more to your liking if the watered-down mai tai they hand you on your way in the door doesn't satisfy you. If you are a vegetarian or have food allergies, be sure to let them know when you book. And be sure to remember the golden rule at the buffet line—the cheapest stuff comes first, so reserve enough plate real estate for the good stuff at the end.

Compared to the neighbor islands, the lu'au experience on O'ahu tends to be heavily processed and can leave you feeling a little bit like cattle led to the slaughter. But the economics of larger crowd sizes mean that O'ahu shows can afford bigger casts with more elaborate production values.

There are four options to choose from in Waikiki, which is convenient, but they are flawed or terribly expensive. (And of these, one is both flawed *and* terribly expensive.) Your choices are the **Diamond Head Lu'au**, **Waikiki Starlight Lu'au**, **Te Moana Nui Tales of the Pacific**, and **The Royal Hawaiian's 'Aha'aina Lu'au**.

Most lu'au outside Waikiki offer transportation if needed, for an additional charge. Of those that require travel, **Ka Moana Lu'au at Sea Life Park** in East O'ahu is the closest, and it has a beautiful natural setting.

The biggest and most popular lu'au on O'ahu is the **Polynesian Cultural Center Ali'i Lu'au** on the North Shore, but there are some tradeoffs to consider, not least that it's the farthest away.

There are three classic lu'au (all of them pretty good) on the west side of the island, where it is drier with less chance of rain: **Germaine's Lu'au**, **Paradise Cove**, and **Chief's Lu'au**. (**Ka Wa'a Lu'au at the Disney Aulani Resort** and the **Fia Fia Lu'au** are also on the west side, but you'd probably only add those to your list to consider if you are staying in the Ko Olina resort area.)

Be sure to read the full reviews to pick the one that is best for you, since there are some important differences.

Waikiki

Diamond Head Lu'au
2777 Kalakaua Ave, Waikiki • (808) 926-3800

This is a great choice if you aren't scared off by the price. The smaller, more intimate setting on the grounds of the Waikiki Aquarium helps give it a backyard barbecue feel, closer to what you'd experience at a lu'au on a neighbor island. (They limit it to 250 seats max, so reserve a spot well in advance.) Good aloha and plenty of fun pre-show cultural activities to explore, such as lei making and learning how to play various musical instruments. Not as many performers (or as scantily clad), but the young cast seems to be having the most fun compared to other shows. Lots of genuine smiles and very entertaining. The menu features shrimp appetizers, poke (raw, cubed and seasoned ahi), ribs, huli huli chicken, vegan vegetable curry, and a kalua pork carving station, and many of the ingredients are locally sourced, farm-to-table.

A few complaints: The buffet closes almost immediately after the show starts, so if your table is one of the last to go through the line the first time, you'll have to eat fast if you want seconds. The fire knife display is only OK. And we'll say it again: the price. It's $159 for adults, $89 for kids 4–12, $139 for ages 13–17. Pretty steep for a lu'au that is only marginally better than some of the other top choices, but that price at least includes a mai tai greeting plus two additional drinks, and everyone gets a flower lei. Shows Sunday, Monday, Thursday and Friday. The (dimly lit) aquarium stays open for a half hour after the show ends exclusively for lu'au guests. Another nice thing: no long drive back to your hotel afterward. You can walk.

Waikiki Starlight Lu'au

2005 Kalia Rd, Waikiki • (808) 941-5828

This one is frustrating. The high-caliber dancers here are arguably the most talented and technically proficient on the island. The Polynesian revue is fast-paced and energetic, and the near-constant whoops and calls are infectious. The vigorous Tahitian dancing is especially captivating. But no amount of rapid hip gyrations can distract from the fact that this lu'au takes place *on top of a parking garage* at the Hilton Hawaiian Village. And that's just inexcusable, considering that the resort sits on a beautiful piece of oceanfront property. (Of course, down there, anyone strolling on the beach could just watch for free.) Six stories up, flanked by hotel towers, you're exposed to the wind (so bring a light jacket if you tend to get chilly) and a good amount of street noise.

The long buffet has more and better options than almost any other lu'au on O'ahu, and they keep it open throughout almost the entire show so you can keep going back. They also have a children's buffet for picky eaters. But the food can get cold because of the wind. And they start things off by forcing everyone to stand up and learn to hula before the crowd has a chance to loosen up and get into it. Guests get one weak drink on the way in, plus one drink ticket for the bar. The four-man fire knife finale is intense (although they put up a wire screen to protect the audience, slightly reducing the excitement.) If you're looking for a traditional lu'au setting with cultural activities and more of an interactive show, go elsewhere. If watching great dancing is your main criterion, this is a good pick. **$111** for adults, $67 for kids 4–11. Sunday through Thursday.

Te Moana Nui Tales of the Pacific

120 Kaiulani Ave, Waikiki • (808) 921-4600

Here's a good option to keep in your back pocket in case of a torrential downpour. Te Moana Nui is more or less the same kind of performance as you'd see at a traditional lu'au, but it's held indoors at the Sheraton Princess Kaiulani Hotel in Waikiki. The show itself is good, with highly skilled dancers and elaborate costumes. And despite being indoors, they even have a fire knife display. (The Sheraton must have great confidence in their fire sprinkler system.) But the venue really dampens the experience (it feels like a hotel conference room), so, unless you have the misfortune of visiting during a rare rainy stretch that makes choosing a lu'au with an outdoor location impossible, you're better off going elsewhere.

Dinner is the buffet at the hotel restaurant, so you won't get to sample many traditional Hawaiian foods. Instead, you'll dine on sushi rolls, shrimp, crab legs, miso yakitori chicken, prime rib, and a dessert bar featuring some exceptional pies. No need to rush through dinner. Once you head up the escalator to the second floor showroom, you'll find yourself spending a lot of time just waiting with only a few mildly amusing pre-show activities (like lei making) to keep you entertained. And once you're finally let into the showroom, you'll spend a lot more time waiting for the main show to begin. It's **$105**, including the buffet and one drink ($70 for kids 5–12), or $60 for a cocktail ticket, which includes the show and one drink. Performances Sunday, Wednesday and Friday.

The Royal Hawaiian's 'Aha'aina Lu'au

2259 Kalakaua Ave, Waikiki • (808) 923-7311

This is a smaller, more upscale affair with higher quality food than your typical lu'au. And its enviable setting on a grassy lawn at the iconic Royal Hawaiian hotel, right next to Waikiki Beach, can't be beat. But the price is an *I-must-have-misheard-you* **$188** *per person*. ($106 for kids 5–12.) That takes the prize as the most expensive dining event in the state.

And even if money is no object, the current show is hard to recommend. Much of it involves a rather low-energy parade of performers walking across the stage dressed as various members of the Hawaiian royal family while an emcee narrates the history of the monarchy. Slow and not terribly engaging. The dancing is not altogether authentic either. Other vignettes include a rifle drill team routine, WWII-era music, and a musician rocking out hard on an ukulele. Price includes a mai tai greeting, plus two additional drinks from the bar. Mondays only.

East O'ahu

Ka Moana Lu'au at Sea Life Park
41-202 Kalanianaole Hwy, Waimanalo
(808) 926-3800

Of the lu'au options that require traveling, Ka Moana is the closest. The grassy grounds are tucked into the Ko'olau mountain range on the east side of the island, about a 30-minute drive from Waikiki. There's a simple stage with a long canoe, and behind that, you've got a commanding view (until the sun goes down) of the ocean and two offshore islands. Great setting, but remember: this is the *windward* side of the island, and sometimes that breeze can get chilly in the evening, so bring a jacket.

This is a more affordable sister-program to Waikiki's Diamond Head Lu'au. Both shows are entertaining and feature lots of dancing and a (so-so) fire-knife display, but the menu here is standard lu'au fare, and it's a little more gourmet there. But the food is decent, and the pork isn't too salty. They've also got more room here to spread out—there's plenty of space to wander around the grounds and check out the pre-show activities like lei-making, headband weaving and learning how to play various instruments, making this lu'au feel less processed than most of the others. **$99** for adults, $74 for kids 4–12, $87 for ages 13–17. One drink included. It's an additional $16 for bus transporta-

tion from Waikiki, or $5 (cash) to park. No shows Thursday or Saturday.

All tickets include admission to Sea Life Park. That bonus may seem like you're getting a whole lotta bang for your buck, but before you get too excited, just remember that to make good use of the pass you'll want to arrive at the park early enough in the day to see the 12:30 p.m. dolphin show, and, since it's a small park, you'll likely run out of things to see while waiting for the lu'au to start. (Plus the park closes an hour before the lu'au begins.) If your schedule allows, come back and use the pass within seven days instead.

The North Shore

Polynesian Cultural Center Ali'i Lu'au
55-370 Kamehameha Hwy, Laie • (800) 367-7060

The one is a juggernaut—definitely the biggest and most popular lu'au on the island—but only consider it if you're already planning to spend the afternoon exploring the Polynesian Cultural Center. It's not worth driving this far just for the lu'au.

The PCC is a gem worth seeing. Many people who go choose to add on the optional Ali'i Lu'au. Doing so more than doubles the price (not an insignificant jump), but you *may* still save *a little bit* of money compared to visiting the cultural center one day and then separately paying for a different lu'au elsewhere another night. But as the No. 1 paid attraction on O'ahu (Pearl Harbor is No. 1 overall, but that's free), the PCC's capacity has grown to staggering proportions, and as a result the dining portion is crowded and heavily processed. Ironically, the lu'au is the *least* authentic part of the day's experience, and depending on what you are looking for in a lu'au, it may or may not be the right fit. Don't choose it just because so many other people do.

The **$146** ticket price ($116 for kids 4–11) includes admission to the cultural center, a dinner buffet with a mini lu'au show while you eat, and then a spectacular after-dinner show on top of that.

The buffet is good and has plenty to choose from, including traditional Hawaiian foods and other standard dishes like chicken and fish. There's light entertainment, including a procession of the royal court, and music and dancing to enjoy while eating. Seating is cramped, though, and depending on when your table is called, the experience might seem a little rushed (but you can keep eating and making trips to the buffet even after the show is over—you've got time.) One thing to remember is that this whole operation is run by the Mormon Church, so *don't expect anything in your drink other than fruit juice.* If potent mai tais are your reason for taking in a lu'au, look elsewhere.

After dinner, everyone gets shuffled into the 2,700-person, multi-tier Pacific Theater for an evening show called "Ha: Breath of Life." This is the main event. The show has the highest production values of any in Hawai'i, and the singing and dancing from different countries and in several different Polynesian languages is fantastic. Because it's a church production, you may notice some strong religious overtones, and there are parts where the storyline moves a little slowly, but if you find yourself getting restless, hold on. The fire knife climax is by far the largest display you'll see anywhere, and it's a great, dramatic way to end the show.

After everything is done, it's a 60- to 90-minute drive back to Waikiki from La'ie going by the windward side, which can make for a very long day (especially if your internal body clock hasn't adjusted to the time zone change). Consider taking their bus ride for an extra $25. Open every night but Sunday. They usually have discounts on their website.

Important note: They've got a dizzying array of meal packages to choose from on their website. The price in this review is for the *ambassador level* lu'au package,

which they force you to upgrade to if you want to eat at a normal dinner time. Their standard lu'au ticket costs about 20 bucks less, but that has you eating mid–afternoon, which seriously cuts into your time exploring the cultural center, leaving you with a lot of dead time before the after-dinner show starts.

Wai'anae (West O'ahu)

Germaine's Lu'au
91-119 Olai St, Kapolei • (808) 425-9166

Germaine's is one of the better shows overall, and the best if you're excited to get up on stage and learn to hula (something that's always more popular with the women in the audience than the men, despite the fact the hula was originally a dance practiced exclusively by male warriors). Don't worry—they won't force you to get up on stage if you don't want to. At **$85** for a standard ticket it's also the least expensive. ($65 for kids ages 4–12, $75 for ages 13–20). The oceanside grounds are pretty, sandy and full of palm trees, and the shoreline has good sunsets most of the year (except during the weeks around the summer solstice when it sets over land).

Up to 800 people a night during peak times, but 400–500 is average, and the high-energy and enthusiastic performers do a good job of fanning out on stage and playing to all parts of the audience. One drink included with admission, and here again prices are lower than at other lu'au; it's $5 for a mai tai (not the strongest, not the weakest), $10 for a specialty drink. A tip—if you find the size of the mai tais too small, you can purchase a large glass for $10 in the souvenir shop, and they'll fill *that* each time instead. Also, you can always ask the bartender to add more *seasoning* to your drink. Last call is after the fire knife, which comes midway through the program instead of the finale.

One major complaint is that the food quality isn't as good as elsewhere (perhaps that's a tradeoff they made to keep prices low), but if you're looking for a classic lu'au that doesn't cost a fortune, this is probably the one you should choose. Located near the Ko Olina Resort at the southwest corner of the island, it's about four hours at the site and two hours of travel time (round trip) from Waikiki. (Add $16 per person if you need transportation.) Check-in is at 5:15 p.m. Closed Mondays.

Paradise Cove Lu'au

92-1089 Aliinui Dr, Ko Olina • (808) 842-5911

On the west side of the island, Paradise Cove ranks slightly behind nearby Germaine's, but the two are almost interchangeable, and both are good choices. This one is bigger (the max capacity is 1,200 people), but they do an excellent job of directing everyone on the grounds, so you never feel crowded. And the setting is beautiful. The gates open at 5 p.m. nightly, but here's a tip—arrive at 5:30. You'll still have plenty of time to see all the demonstrations such as coconut husking, and you'll avoid the lines from the tour buses. On the way in you're handed a mai tai, but it's more like mildly alcoholic POG juice. (The $6 mai tais from the bar are much better.) You'll also get a cash card with credit to spend on additional drinks, which mostly accounts for the price difference between this one and Germaine's.

Beside the typical lu'au pre-show activities such as tattoos, hula dancing and spear throwing, they also perform a hukilau ceremony at the beach with some lucky/ unlucky volunteers. This is what a lu'au should be—standing on the beach, mai tai in hand, watching an ancient traditional fishing ceremony with the sun setting in the background. The food includes typical poi, fish, lomi lomi salmon, vegetables and kalua pig. They do a good job keeping the lines short, and you have plenty of time to grab seconds. During dinner there's

a quiet show with soft Hawaiian music. Afterward, the real show starts with talented hula dancers, pounding drums and, of course, a fire knife dancer. $97 ($75 kids 4–12, $85 ages 13–20). Add $16 for roundtrip transportation from Waikiki.

Chief's Lu'au

400 Farrington Hwy, Kapolei • (877) 357-2480

This is a great option for couples and families alike. It's hosted by the colorful Chief Sielu, who makes this lu'au feel less like a show and more like an informal gathering of friends. Before dinner (traditional lu'au foods), they've got fun activities to keep you entertained, including spear throwing, fire making, headband weaving and (temporary) tattoos. The show itself is really quite enjoyable and funny, but the momentum slows to a crawl during the too-long audience participation part in the middle. (This show has the most audience interaction, but they will leave you alone if you don't want to participate.) The thrilling eight-man fire knife show at the end is the most exciting on the island and the top reason to choose this lu'au.

The big knock against this one compared to the other west-side competitors is that the location isn't nearly as romantic. Instead of a nice sandy beachside location, it's on the grounds of the Wet 'n' Wild Hawai'i waterpark, on an "island" surrounded by the lazy "river" with waterslides in the background. The space was specifically designed with this lu'au in mind, so that helps keep things running smoothly, and it's nicely landscaped with a waterfall with two giant wooden tikis behind the large stage, but it feels very artificial (because it is). It's also crowded when at maximum capacity of 550 people. Still, the strength of the show makes this a good alternative to the other players. It's $95 for a standard adult ticket, which includes one drink. ($75 for children 5–12, $85 for ages 13–20). It's about an hour from Waikiki. Add

$18 for bus transportation or $5 to park. Closed Tuesday and Saturday.

Fia Fia Lu'au

92-161 Waipahe Pl, Ko Olina • (808) 679-4700

Fia Fia is held Tuesdays on the grounds of the Marriott Ko Olina (southwest corner of the island). It's put on by the same crew as the nearby Chief's Lu'au. The stage here is smaller and the seating more crowded, but the experience and show is basically the same: fun pre-show cultural activities, lots of dancing, an exciting fire knife display, and a humorous host. The price is a little bit higher here than there, but that's partly because a standard ticket includes two drinks. $110 for adults, $63 for kids 4–11. On the lawn next to the lagoon, but you're oriented looking toward the hotel towers. 400-person maximum.

Ka Wa'a Lu'au at the Disney Aulani Resort

92-1185 Aliinui Dr, Ko Olina • (808) 674-6320

This lu'au is at the Disney Aulani Resort—it's got to be the best for kids, right? Not necessarily. Aside from a brief cameo by Mickey and Minnie Mouse, this is more or less a traditional lu'au. Just about everything is executed well: the buffet is among the best you'll find (including a kids' station that isn't just loaded with junk food), the setting is lush and green (although there's no ocean view, and you're backed by hotel towers), the staff is welcoming, and the music and production values are higher than at any other show. The program itself is family-friendly, mostly tame. There are a few intense parts, but nothing too scary for little kids. There's just one problem and it's a biggie: The script is dull. The cast performs it well, and the dancers are talented, but there's just not enough dancing and far too much narration. It's hard to understand how Disney, a company that created so many magical movies with elaborate song and dance numbers, green-lit this show.

If you're a parent with small kids staying at the Disney Aulani Resort (or one of the other nearby Ko Olina resorts on the southwest corner of the island), you'll probably be happy with the results, especially since your keiki can be in bed asleep 15 minutes after the show ends. But otherwise, you're better off choosing a different lu'au. It's $129 for an adult ticket that includes a mai tai greeting, and $79 for kids 3–9. Lu'au days vary, so you'll have to contact them to ask for the schedule, and seating is first come, first served, so be sure to arrive right at the start of check-in. It can be hard to see from the back, but multiple small stages in addition to the main platform help bring performers closer to the audience. Free valet parking if coming from off-site.

DINNER CRUISES

Majestic

Pier 6, Aloha Tower Marketplace, Honolulu (808) 973-1311

The Majestic from Atlantis Cruises can be summed up like this—great boat, mediocre food and show. The boat is amazingly smooth using Seakeeper technology—basically gyrostabilizers, similar to what they use in Steadicams. Spinning gyros are used to cushion some of the rock 'n' roll the ocean sends your way. The buffet has scant choices. Another deck is for drinks, and the top deck is open. In all, Majestic has the potential to be a really great product—if only they'd try harder on the food. $99 ($109 for Friday fireworks cruise). Alcohol is available for extra at the bar. They leave from Pier 6 near the Aloha Tower Marketplace, and transportation is free from *some* Waikiki hotels.

Star of Honolulu

Pier 8, Aloha Tower Marketplace, Honolulu (808) 983-7827

The Star of Honolulu is a huge, 232-foot, rock-steady (most of the time) ship with four decks that can hold 1,500 passengers. (Don't worry, it won't have that many, and it doesn't feel as crowded as some smaller boats.) The top deck is what they call their five star offering with a seven-course meal (they rotate the menu), live jazz, air conditioning and a wallet-choking $201 price. Below they have a steak and lobster dinner (no A/C) for $151, a crab and steak deck for $115 and a buffet deck that's $97. They don't guarantee anything below the top deck because they often host large groups and other things that can get in the way. (They charge $10 more on Fridays because you'll get to see fireworks that they aren't paying for.) Overall, though, they do a good job, and the crew is professional. In short, a very good cruise at super-premium prices, which leaves from Honolulu Harbor next to the Aloha Tower Marketplace. Parking is by the hour at Pier 5 and 6.

DINNER SHOWS

Magic of Polynesia
2300 Kalakaua Ave, Waikiki • (808) 672-2520

Magic of Polynesia is a fun, unabashedly Vegas-y magic show, although much of it seems to be the same trick done several different ways. A curtain goes up, and when it comes down, poof! The guy is gone or has switched objects. Impressive the first few times, but it stops being surprising after a while because modern audiences are savvy enough to inherently distrust props. And there's little personality from the illusionist—as if he, too, is a prop. But don't let this dissuade you. The tricks come rapid-fire without a lot of setup, so your brain doesn't have time to process what you just saw and critically dissect it. Sit back and enjoy the ride, and you'll still feel a sense of wonder. The close-up magic portion is more engaging—you won't be able to trust your own eyes—and the Polynesian dancing is as good as you'll find at a lu'au. It's $61 for

the show alone ($46 for kids 4–11). They also offer it as a dinner/show combo, but you're better off eating elsewhere first. Drinks available for purchase during the show. At the Waikiki Beachcomber hotel. Reserve in advance.

Rock-A-Hula Legends in Concert
2201 Kalakaua Ave, Waikiki • (808) 629-7469

OK, OK, the whole idea of celebrity impersonators is kinda lame, but Rock-A-Hula Legends in Concert is a *thoroughly* enjoyable experience. Besides, how else can you see Elvis and Michael Jackson together live in concert? Add in some Hawaiian hula and Tahitian dancing, and this is a wildly entertaining show that never fails to get people dancing in their seats.

The show is held in a 750-person theater on the fourth floor of the Royal Hawaiian Center in Waikiki. Elvis is a permanent fixture, as is Michael Jackson. The third slot is usually a current pop star, such as Katy Perry, but the lineup changes periodically, so you'll have to check the website. The production value is over the top, and all of the performances are live (no lip-synching.) There's also a fire-knife dancer.

It's $69 ($41 ages 3-11) for the show only, or they have an $89 cocktail option that comes with one drink and better seating. (You can always buy drinks at the bar.) If you would rather get the dinner-and-show combo, splurge and upgrade to the $149 VIP package, which includes two drinks, a four-course meal of beef tenderloin, Alaskan salmon and lobster, and seats next to the stage. The $109 lu'au buffet seems mostly oriented toward tour groups from overseas and is a poor offering compared to other lu'au options on the island. Check in by 7:30 p.m. unless you're also getting dinner, in which case you'll need to arrive earlier. You'll get a chance to meet the performers and get your picture taken with them after the show. No shows on Friday.

About the Author

More than two decades ago, I bought a one-way ticket to the island of Kaua'i after another venture failed spectacularly. (That's a *really* good story… for another time.) I was devastated, broke, and working in the construction industry as an unskilled laborer just to survive, thinking that I had peaked at such a young age, and it was all downhill from there. But at least I was living in Hawai'i. I spent my free time exploring, but I got frustrated when weekend after weekend I couldn't find a particular beach I'd heard about that I wanted to go to. I looked at a couple of guidebooks, but they all referred to a road that hadn't existed in a long time. And I dreamed that maybe I could find a way to do it better.

Within days of of entertaining that dream, however, I had to return to the mainland due to the declining health of my mother, who passed away shortly thereafter.

It was while I was away that a plan emerged—I would return to Kaua'i and start writing guidebooks. There were just a few problems with this plan: I had no writing skills, I didn't know how a book was published, I wasn't good at photography, I didn't know how to use a computer, *and I had no money.*

So I spent a year on the mainland and applied for every credit card I could and tried to acquire the skills I would need to make my dream come true. Just when I was ready to return to the islands in 1992, I watched in horror as a category 4 hurricane smashed into Kaua'i, causing widespread devastation. I couldn't pick another island because Kaua'i was the one I knew, the island I had fallen in love with. Knowing that hurricanes clear out old growth, giving sunlight (and a chance) to encourage younger foliage, I figured that the same might be true in business. So with a huge stack of credit cards and two suitcases, I moved back to a ravaged island and got to work.

I completely covered one of the walls of my 290-square-foot rented room with highly detailed topographic maps of the island, so I could study them while drinking my morning coffee (gotta have coffee). This was before Google Earth, after all.

Over the next year, I spent my mornings exploring the island and checking out various visitor activities like helicopter rides and snorkel tours (which I did anonymously and paid for with my credit cards—*at 22 percent interest*). I'd review a restaurant at lunch, and then I'd spend my afternoons doing a hike or swimming a beach in multiple conditions to assess its safety, before returning to my room to have a simple dinner of canned chicken and rice (because it was so cheap), then worked into the evening making my own maps of the island. Before going to bed each night, I would read every book about Hawaiian history I could get my hands on.

The first edition of "the blue book" came out in March 1994. I paid to print the first 10,000 books (with cash advances from that stack of credit cards) and mailed free copies to newspapers for review. The first order was for only one case, but a year later a nationwide bookstore chain agreed to stock the book. It took off from there. Next came Big Island, then Maui and O'ahu. I packed up my equipment and lived for two years on each island researching, mapping, writing and photographing.

Today the *Revealed Series* is no longer a one-man show. I have an awesome team that has expanded over the years, but ultimately the books and the apps are an expression of what I think about Hawai'i and comes from the experience of actually *doing* all the things you'll read about. And our ability to keep current and find new things is greatly helped by feedback from our incredibly enthusiastic readers. Please keep it coming.

Once in a while, if you are *really* lucky in this life, you find the place and circumstance to which you belong. I hope you will fall in love with Hawai'i the way I did, and return often. But wherever you travel in life, take chances, embrace the uncertainty of outcome, go with an explorer's heart, and most importantly, share what you find with others.

—One lucky buggah, *Andrew Doughty*

INDEX

Island Dining Index on page 254

Aaron's Dive Shop **229, 247**
About the Author 309
Acroflight International **178**
Activity Booths 173
Activity Cancellation Policies 174
Adventure on 2 Wheels **24**
Aerial Photos 41
Ahupua'a O Kahana State Park 83
Aikau, Eddie 92
Air Tours 174
Airplane Tours 176
Airport Lei Greeting 44
Ala Moana Area 63
Ala Moana Beach 62
Ala Moana Regional Park 127, 244
Ala Moana Shopping Center 63, 229
Ala Wai Canal 47
Ala Wai Municipal Golf Course . . .**188**
Alamo Rent a Car **23**
Alan Davis Beach 132
Albatross Habitat 214
Alcohol on the Beach 57
Ali'i (Chiefs) 15
All Hawai'i Cruises **183**
Aloe Vera Gel 30
Aloha 38
Aloha 'Aina Cab **23**
Aloha Beach Services **52, 181**
Aloha Jet Ski **217**
Angel Wings Painting 96
Area Code for Hawai'i 44
Art on the Zoo Fence 58
Atlantis Submarine **235**
Atoll 11
Attractions, Cultural & Educational . . .152
Attractions, Fun 167
Attractions, Historical 156
ATV Tours 178
Avis Rent A Car **23**

BYOB **256**
Banzai Pipeline 89, 147
Barbers Point 110
Barnes & Noble Bookstore **40**
Basal Springs 54, 130
Bathtub Beach 140, *141*
Bayonet Constitution 164
Beach Access 10, 119
Beach Cabins 142, 185
Beach Conditions 119
Beach Path, Waikiki 53
Beach Safety 117
Beaches, 'Ewa & Leeward 126

Beaches, 15 Best . . . . . . *Back cover flap*
Beaches, Leeward 117
Beaches, North Shore 116, 145
Beaches, Wai'anae 120
Beaches, Windward 116, 133
Bees 32
Bellows Beach 75, 134
Best Bets 63, 81, 100, 115
Big Island 12, 14, 17
Big Kahuna Rentals **24**
Bike Hawai'i **179**
Biki (Bikeshare Hawai'i) **26, 179**
Biking 179
Birthing, Royal Hawaiian 104
Birthing Stones, Kukaniloko *15*, 104
Bishop Museum 154, *155*
Bishop, Princess Bernice Pauahi 154
Bite Squad Hawaii **257**
Black Point 129, 130
Blue Hawaiian Helicopters **176**
Blue Nun Sport Fishing **187**
Boat Tours 179
Bodysurfing .131
Boogie Boarding 55, *173*, 184
Books About Hawai'i 40
Boom Boom Sportfishing **187**
Box Jellyfish 31, 67
Breadfruit 14
Breakfast Buffets 259
Breakout Waikiki **185**
Brigham Young University–Hawai'i . . .84
Bruddah Iz 40
Budget Rent a Car **23**
Bugs 32
Buses 26, 47
Byodo-In Temple *78*, 81

Cabin Rentals **86, 142, 185**
Camping 184
Camping Permits 184
Cane Spiders 32
Car Break-ins 26, 111, 118
Caucasians, First 17
Cell Phone Law 26
Centipedes .32
Chief's Lu'au **306**
Child Restraint Law 25
Chinaman's Hat
  (Mokoli'i) 83, *84*, 137, 245
Chinatown 153, *154*
Chun's Reef .150
Chupu Sportfishing Fleet **187**
Climbworks Keana Farms **240**

Cockroach Bay 133
Cockroaches 32
Coconut Island (Moku-o-lo'e) 81
Cook, Captain James 16, 18
Coral 31
Coral Crater
  Adventure Park 171, 178, 241
Coral Creek Golf Course **188, 189**
Coral Reefs 11, 13, *33*, 228
Corona Project 99
Costco **34**
Crouching Lion 83
Cycle City Harley **24**

Damien Tours **253**
Day trip to Moloka'i 252
DEET 22
Dehydration .33
Department of Health Placards 256
Dews of Ka'ala 108
Diamond Head 55
Diamond Head Beach Park 128
Diamond Head Harley **24**
Diamond Head Hike 190
Diamond Head Lu'au **302**
Dillingham Airport 96
Dillingham, Benjamin 63, 167
Dinner Cruises 307
Dinner Shows 308
Discount Hawai'i Car Rental **23**
Dole, James 101
Dole Pineapple **103**
Dole Plantation **35, 103**
Dole, Sanford 20
Dollar Rent A Car **23**
Dolphin Excursions **183**
Dolphin Quest **168**
Dolphin Star **183**
Dolphins 112, *167*, 168
Dolphins, Swimming With *167*, 168
Doris Duke's Shangri La **156**
Double-hulled Voyaging Canoe 14
Dragon's Nostrils *198*
Driving Around Honolulu 60
Driving Around O'ahu 24
Driving Times Chart . . . .*Inside*
  back cover
Driving Tours 45
Drowning 117

E-mail Address **4**
Eddie Would Go 92

INDEX

Island Dining Index on page 254

'Ehukai Beach Park 90
Electric Beach 125
Emperor Seamounts 11
Enterprise Rent-A-Car **23**
Escape Rooms 185
'Ewa 109
'Ewa Beach .126
'Ewa-bound, Definition 25
Exotic Car Rentals 24

Falls, Likeke **36, 202**
Falls, Lulumahu 193
Falls, Manoa 192
Falls, Maunawili 203
Falls, Waihe'e 208
Falls, Waimano 210
Falls, Waimea 42, 92, 223
Farmers Markets 41, 59
Fia Fia Lu'au **307**
Fiber Balls From Pineapple Cores . . .103
Fire Coral 31
Fireworks Over the Ocean 58, *59*
Fish & Seafood 257
Fish Feeding 231
Fishhooks 15
Fishing 186
Flash Floods 33
Flat Island .220
Flyboarding Hawai'i **218**
Food Pantry **34**
Ford Island .108
Fort DeRussy Beach *46*, 53
Freebies in Waikiki 57
Fresh Water Hazards 32
From Here to Eternity Beach 70, 131

Garden, Foster Botanical **224**
Garden, Ho'omaluhia Park
  Botanical 80, 224
Garden, Koko Crater Botanical . . .224
Garden, Lili'uokalani Botanical . . .225
Garden, Wahiawa Botanical 225
Garden Tours 223
Gardens, Lyon Arboretum 224
Gardens, Senator Fong's
  Plantation 225
Gardens, Waimea Valley
  Botanical 223
Geckos 32
Germaine's Lu'au **305**
Getting In & Out of Waikiki 44
Gilbert Islanders 40

Gilligan's Island 81
Giovanni's Aloha Shrimp Truck **86**
Gliders 177, *178*
Go Bananas **222**
Go Fishing Hawaii **187**
Go-kart Racing 170
Goat Island 86, 141, *142*, 246
Gods 16, 17, 20
Golden Plover (Kolea) 13, 14
Golfing 187
Gray's Beach 54
Great Mahele 20
Greeters of Hawai'i **44**
Grocery Stores 34
Gun Clubs .189

H-3 Highway **77**
H-3 Tunnel .78
H2O Sports Hawai'i 217, 218, 225
Haiku Stairs 78, 248
Haleakala 12
Hale'iwa 96
Hale'iwa Beach Park 150
Halona Blowhole 70, 131
Halona Cove 70, 131
Hanauma Bay Nature
  Preserve *66*, 67, 131, 226, **233**
Hang Gliders 132
Haole, Definition of 35
Happy Trails **216**
Hau'ula 84
Hau'ula Beach Park 139
Hawai'i Beach Time 22, **220**
Hawai'i Children's
  Discovery Center **34**
Hawaii Escape Challenge **186**
Hawaii Glider &
  Sailplane Academy **178**
Hawaii Gun Club **189**
Hawai'i Institute of
  Marine Biology 81
Hawai'i Kai 221
Hawai'i Luxury Car Rentals **24**
Hawai'i Nautical **227**
Hawai'i Pirate Ship Adventures **35**
Hawai'i Polo Trail Rides **215**
Hawaii Revealed App 21, 29, 45
Hawai'i Shark Encounters **243**
Hawai'i State Art Museum **156**
Hawai'i State Fish 37
Hawai'i Theatre **301**
Hawai'i Water Sports Center **239**
Hawaiian Airlines **21**

Hawaiian Alphabet 37
Hawaiian Canoes 16
Hawaiian Culture 15, 18, 20
Hawaiian, Definition of 35
Hawaiian Diving
  Adventures **227, 247**
Hawaiian Hoary Bat 15
Hawaiian Homelands 74
Hawaiian Islands 12, 18
Hawaiian Language 37
Hawaiian Monk Seal 119
Hawaiian Music 40
Hawaiian Ocean Promotions **68**
Hawaiian Parasail **225**
Hawaiian Railway Society **35, 167**
Hawaiian Style Band 40
Hawaiian Style Rentals **24**
Hawaiian Time 36
Hawaiian Volcanoes 12
Hawaiian Watersports **184, 220,**
  222, 236
Hawai'i's Last King 162
Hawai'i's Last Monarch 165
Hawai'i's Plantation Village **166**
Hazards 30
He'eia State Park 219
Heiau 36
Heiau, Ku'ilioloa (Nene'u) . . .113, 124
Heiau, Luakini 91
Heiau, Pu'u o Mahuka 90
Heiau, Ulupo 77
Hele Huli Adventure Rentals **222**
Helicopter Tours 175
Hertz Rent A Car **23**
Hidden Beach 96, *97*, 151
Hikes, Around Kailua 201
Hikes, Central O'ahu 210
Hikes, Eastern O'ahu 196
Hikes, Near Honolulu 190
Hikes, North Shore 209
Hikes, Top of the World 195
Hikes, Wai'anae 211
Hiking 189
Historic Buildings 162
Hokule'a 92
Holokai Catamaran **180**
Holokai Kayak & Snorkel **219**
Honolulu 60
Honolulu City Hall 165
Honolulu International Airport 21
Honolulu Kite School **222**
Honolulu Museum of Art **156**
Honolulu Polo Club **75**
Honolulu Soaring **178**

INDEX
Island Dining Index on page 254

Honolulu Zoo 35, 170
Horseback Riding 215
Hukilau 141
Hukilau Beach/La'ie Beach 85, 141
Hula 40
Hula 'Auana 40
Hula Kahiko 40
Human Pets 104
Human Sacrifice 16, 19, 91, 161
Humidity 28
Humpback Whales 239
Humuhumunukunukuapua'a 37
Hurricane 'Iniki 28
Hurricanes .28

Identifying Sea Life 231
International Marketplace 47
Internet Access 41
'Iolani Palace 57, 162
Island Divers 227
Island Foods 258
Island Seaplane 176
Islandview Hawai'i 243

James Campbell Company 87
Japanese Fishing Shrine 69
Jellyfish .31, 67
Jet Skiing .216
Jetlev 218
JN Exotics .24
JN Rentals .23
Judd Trail to Jackass Ginger Pool 193
Judicial Building 164

K1 Speed Hawai'i 35, 170
Ka Moana Lu'au at
   Sea Life Park 304
Ka Wa'a Lu'au at the
   Disney Aulani Resort 307
Ka'a'awa 83
Ka'a'awa Beach Park 137
Ka'alawai Beach 129, 233
Ka'ena Point 88, 97, 115, 213
Ka'ena Point Hike 212
Ka'ena Point Natural Area Reserve . . .214
Ka'ena Point State Park 120
Kahala Avenue 64
Kahala Beach 129, 233
Kahana Bay 83
Kahana Bay Beach Park 137, 138
Kahana River 221

Kahanamoku Beach 53
Kahanamoku, Duke 53
Kahe Point .125
Kaho'olawe .12
Kahuku 86
Kahuku Golf Course Beach 143
Kahuku Municipal Golf Course . . .188
Kahuku Shrimp 153
Kahuna 104
Kailua 76
Kailua Bay 220, 246
Kailua Beach 75, 77, 80, 136
Kailua Beach Adventures 184, 220
Kaiona Beach Park 75, 133
Ka'iwa Ridge Hike 207
Ka'iwi Scenic Shoreline Park 71
Kaka'ako Waterfront Park 127
Kalae'o'io Beach 137
Kalakaua Avenue Shopping 229
Kalakaua, David 162
Kalaniana'ole Beach Park 125
Kalaupapa Guided Mule Tour 253
Kalaupapa Leprosy Settlement 252
Kaluahole Beach 128
Kaluanui Beach 138
Kaluanui State Park 84
Kama'aina 35
Kamakau 93
Kamapua'a (Demigod) 79
Kamehameha The Great 14, 18, 20
Kamehameha the Great Statue 163
Kanaenae 35
Kanaka Maoli 35
Kaneana Cave 115
Kanenelu Beach 137
Kane'ohe 79
Kane'ohe Bay 33, 81, 208, 218
Kane'ohe Bay Pillbox 207
Kane'ohe Marine Corps Base 79
Kaohi-ka-ipu Island 74
Kapahulu Groin 53, 55
Kapiolani Park 54
Kapu System 16, 20, 91, 104
Kaua'i 12, 17
Kaupo Beach Park 133
Kawaiaha'o Church 165
Kawaiku'i Beach Park 131
Kawailoa Beach (Leftovers) 150
Kawainui Marsh 77
Kawainui Marsh Path 207
Kawainui Regional Park 77
Kawela Bay 116, 144
Kayaking 218
Kayaking Destinations 220

Kea'au Beach Park 122
Kealia Beach 150
Keawa'ula Beach 120
Ke'ehi Lagoon Beach Park 126
Kekaulike Market 153
Kepoikai II 180
Kewalo Basin 179, 186, 187
Kilauea Vocano 12
King Kamehameha 14, 18, 20
Kingdom of Hawai'i 162
King's Village Shopping Center . .58, 229
Kiteboarding/Kitesurfing 222
Ko Nau Lani 182
Ko Olina 112, 233
Ko Olina Golf Club 188
Ko Olina Lagoons 112, 124, 125
Ko Olina Ocean Adventures 182
Koko Crater 64, 65
Koko Crater Arch 70, 198, 199
Koko Crater Railway Trail 199, 200
Koko Head .65
Koko Head-bound, Definition 25
Kokololio Beach Park 139, 140
Kolea (Golden Plover) 13, 14
Kona Winds 28
Konahuanui 75
Ko'olau Golf Club 188
Ko'olau Mountain Range . . .28, 75, 108,
   175, 195, 204
Ko'olau Volcano 29
Ku (War God) 17
Kualoa 82
Kualoa Beach Park 83, 136, 245
Kualoa Ranch 83, 137, 172,
   178, 179, 216, 240, 241
Kualoa Sugar Mill Beach 137
Kuhio Beach 43, 54
Kuilei Cliffs Beach Park 63, 128
Kuilima Cove 143, 233, 244
Kukaimanini Island 145
Kukaniloko Birthing Stones 15, 104
Kuli'ou'ou Ridge Trail 195, 197
Kunia Regional Signals Intelligence
   Operations Center 105
Kure Atoll 11

Lahilahi Point 123
La'ie 84
La'ie Beach Park (Pounders) 140
La'ie Point 85, 86
Lana'i .12, 101
Lana'i Lookout 68
Laniakea Beach 150

Lanikai Beach 76, 134, *136*
Lanikai Pillbox Trail 207
Laniloa Beach 140
Laniwai Spa 233, 234
Leaping Place for Souls *16*, 98
Leeward Side 28
LeiGreeting.com 44
Leina-a-ka'uhane *16*, 98
Leptospirosis 32
Lifeguards .119
Light Rail Constuction 25
Likeke Falls Hike 202
Likelike Hwy 79
Living Ocean Scuba 226
Local Food 256
Local Resident 35
Lo'ihi Volcano 12
Lono (Land Fertility God) 17
Lu'au 301
Lu'au Foods 257
Lulumahu Falls Hike 193
Lunalilo 165
Lyft 22

Mac Nut Farm 82
Maggie Joe Sport Fishing 187
Magic Island 127, *128*
Magic of Polynesia 308
Magic Sport Fishing 187
Ma'ili Beach Park 124
Mainland .35
Maita'i 180
Majestic .307
Makaha 95, 114
Makaha Beach Park 122
Makaha Caverns 122
Makahiki 17
Makai 45
Makai Research Pier 74
Makalei Beach 128
Makani Catamaran 181
Makani Kai Air 253
Makani Kai Helicopters 175
Makao Beach 138
Makapu'u Beach Park *70*, 71, 133
Makapu'u Head 71
Makapu'u Lookout 71
Makapu'u Hike to the Dragon's
  Nostrils 196
Makaua Beach 137
Makua Beach *101*, 115, 120
Makua Cave 115, 121
Malaekahana Beach 142

Malaekahana Beach
  Campground 185
Malaekahana State Recreation Area . . .86
Mana 76
Mana Kai 181
Manana Island 74
Mandara Spa 234
Manoa Falls Trail 192
Manu Kai *58*, 180
Map, Island Overview . . . .*Inside
  back cover*
Map, Quick Reference . . . .*Inside
  front cover*
Maps, Explanation of 10, 25
Marine Life 30
Marquesan Carvings 15
Marquesas Islands 14
Marriage License Requirements 26
Matsumoto's 96
Maui 17
Mauka 45
Mauna Lahilahi Beach Park 123
Mauna Loa Volcano 12
Maunakea Marketplace 154
Maunalua Bay Beach Park 131
Maunawili Demonstration Trail 204
Maunawili Falls Hike 203
Maunawili Valley 204, *205*
Maze, Dole Plantation 35, 103, *105*
Mele 40
Menehune .15
Mermaid Cave
  (The Tunnels) 125, 247
Mighty Mo
  (USS Missouri) 109, *158*, 159
Mile Markers 10
Military Bases 104, 105
Mission Houses 165
Moana Lani Spa 234
Moanalua Valley 248
Modern Hawai'i 19
Moepu'u 76
Mo'i (King) 17
Moku'auia Island 86, 141, 142, 246
Mokule'ia Beach Park 96, 150
Mokulele Airlines 21
Mokulua Islands 135, 220
Mokulua Nui Island 246
Moku-o-lo'e (Coconut Island) 81
Moku'ume'ume 108
Mole Crabs 136
Moloka'i 12, 19, 252
Monastery Tag 146
Monk Seals 119, *144*

Mosquito Repellent 22
Mosquitoes 32
Motorcycle Rentals 23
Mount Ka'ala 29, 105, 108, *215*
Mount Ka'ala Summit Hike 214
Mount Olympus 250, *251*

Na Hoku II 180
Nanakuli .112
Nanaue (Shape-shifting God) 115
Natatorium 56
National Car Rental 23
National Memorial Cemetery
  of the Pacific 161
Naval Radio Transmitter Facility 114
Navy Blimps 110
Night Marchers 99
Night Shipwreck Dive 246
Night Snorkeling 244
Nightlife 301
Ni'ihau 12, 17
Nimitz Beach 126
North Shore 88
North Shore Catamaran 183, 240
North Shore Shark
  Adventures 243
North Shore Shopping 220, 229
North Shore Sportfishing 187
Northern Tip Empty Beach Walk 209
Northwest Passage 17

O'ahu 12
O'ahu Airport Express 23
O'ahu's Volcanoes 29
Ocean Conditions 117
Ocean Hazards 30, 117
Ocean Joy Cruises 183
Ocean Safety Tips 117
Ocean Temperatures 28
Off-island .35
Offshore Islets *19*, 135
'Ohi'a Trees 105
'Ohikilolo Beach 115, 121
'Ohikilolo Point 115
'Ohikilolo Point Hike 211
'Okina 37
Old Nu'uanu Pali Road 79
One Ocean 243
One'ula Beach Park 126
Ono Rating 255
Original Glider Rides 178
Outrigger Canoe Rides 52

INDEX

Island Dining Index on page 254

Pacific Aviation Museum **160**
Pacific Rim Cuisine 258
Pacific Skydiving Center **231**
Packing, What to Bring 21
Paddle, Hike & Jump Adventure 246
Pali Golf Course **188**
Pali Highway 79
Pali Lookout 14, *76*, 79
Pali Puka Lookout *201*
Pali Puka Trail 201
Papa'iloa Beach 150
Papale o Kane 114
Papaoneone Beach 122, *123*, 233
Paradise Air **177**
Paradise Cove Lu'au **306**
Paradise Helicopters **175**
Paradise Rent-A-Car **23, 24**
Parasailing 225
Parenting, Ancient Hawaiian 104
Parking 47, 256
Pearl Country Club **188, 189**
Pearl Harbor 108, 111, 156
Pearl Harbor Avenger 159
Pearl Harbor Day, First Attack 80
Pearl Oysters 108
Pedal Power Bike Tours **179**
Pele's Chair 132, *133*
Personal Responsibility 42, 117
Pest Hotline 32
Pidgin Words & Phrases 39
Pigs 14, 33
Pineapple Industry 20, *41*, 101
Pipi (Hawaiian oysters) 108
Planetarium (Bishop Museum) 155
Plantation Life 166
Plate Lunch 258
Pleasant Holidays **21**
Po Pau 'Ole o Milu 99
Pohaku o Kaua'i 214
Poka'i Bay Beach Park 113, 123
Polynesian Cultural Center **85, 152**
Polynesian Cultural Center
    Ali'i Lu'au **304**
Portuguese Man-of-War 31
Pounders (La'ie Beach Park) 140
Powered Hang Gliding 176
Private Property Access 42
Pua'ena Point 88
Public Beaches 119
Pulemoku Rock 141
Punahou School 62
Punalu'u Beach Park 138, *139*
Punchbowl Cemetery 161
Pupukea Beach Park 147

Pu'u Ma'eli'eli Trail 207
Pu'u Ualaka'a State Wayside Park 62
Pu'u-loa 108
Pu'u-o-hulu Kai 112, *115*
Pu'u-o-hulu Kai Hike 212
Puowaina 161

Queen Lili'uokalani **20**
Queen Lili'uokalani Statue 165
Queen's Beach 53, 55

Rabbit Island **74**
Rainfall Map 27
Rainfall Patterns 28
Red Hill 111
Reefs 11, 13, *33*, 228
Rental Cars 22
Renting a Kayak 222
Republic of Hawai'i 20
Resort & Condo Reviews 29
Resort Wear 256
Restaurant Delivery Services 256
Restaurant Dress Codes 256
Rip Currents 117
Rock-A-Hula Legends in Concert ...**308**
Rocketman 217
Rogue Waves 117
Round Top 61
Royal Hawaiian Band 58
Royal Hawaiian Golf Club **188**
Royal Hawaiian's
    'Aha'aina Lu'au **303**
Royal-Moana Beach 54
Rule Your Own Island 245

S. Tanaka Store Antique
    & Bottles **87**
Sacred Falls Park 84
Safety Tips, Ocean 117
Sam's Club **185, 233**
San Lorenzo's **96**
Sand Island 127
Sandy Beach 70, 131, *132*
Sans Souci Beach 56
Sashimi Fun Fishing **187**
Satellite Tracking Station 99
Scaventour **186**
Schofield Barracks 104, 105
Science Adventure Center 155
SCUBA Companies 227
SCUBA Diving 225

SCUBA, Introductory 227
SCUBA Sites 225
Sea Anemones 31
Sea Arch (La'ie Point) *86*
Sea Drops 31
Sea Life Park **35, 74, 168, 169**
Sea Life Park Dolphin Encounter ...**35**
Sea Urchins 31
Seasickness 187
Seat Belt Law 25
Secluded Cove *34*, 97
Segway of Hawai'i **223**
Segway of Hawai'i Kailua **223**
Segway Tours 222
Settlers, First Wave 14
Settlers, Second Wave 15
Shaka 36
Sharks 30, 124, 242
Shark's Cove *89*, 90, *146*,
    147, *232*, 233
Sharks, Swimming With 242
Shave Ice 96, 258
Sherwood Forest 75
Shipwrecks 226
Shopping 229
Shrimp Trucks 86
Silver Guys 59
Skydive Hawai'i **231**
Skydiving 230
Skywave **41**
Smartphone App 21, 29, 45
Snakes 32
Snorkel Gear 233
Snorkel Sites 233
Snorkeling 30, 231
Snowden, Edward 105
Sobriety Checkpoints 26
Spas 233
Speed Limits 26
Spirit of Aloha **179**
Spitting Cave of Portlock 65
Stairway to Heaven 78
Stand Up Paddling (SUP) 237
Star Beach Boys **52, 181**
Star of Honolulu **240, 307**
State Capitol Building 165
Street Performers 59
Submarine Museum **160**
Submarine Tours 234
Sugar Industry 20
Sugar Mill 83
Sugar Plantation Camp 166
Sunburn 30, 118
Sunday Showcase 59

INDEX

315

Island Dining Index on page 254

Sunken Island 218, 219
Sunscreen 22, 30, 118
Sunset Beach
   (Pau-malu) 89, 145, 233
Sunset on the Beach Movie Night 58
Sunset Point .88
Sunset Suratt 236
Sunset Walk .47
Sunset Watching 125
Surf, Dangers of 117, 119
Surf HNL (Girls Who Surf) 237
Surf N' Sea 222, 227
Surf Report .117
Surf Season 88, 94
Surfing *98*, 236, *237*
Surfing Houses 94
Swanzy Beach Park 137

Taboos (Kapu) 16
Tahiti 15, 16
Tamura's Market 85
Tantalus Drive *60*, 61
Taro 14
Taxis & Shuttles 23
Te Moana Nui
   Tales of the Pacific Lu'au 303
Ted's Bakery 89
The Ponds 54
TheBus 26, 47
Theft 118
Three Tables *147*, 149, 233
Thrifty Car Rental 23
Throw-net Fishing 15
Torch Lighting Ceremony 58
Tracks Beach 125
Trade Winds 28
Traffic 34
Traffic Pattern, Honolulu 25
Train Ride Tour 103
Travel Packages 21
Traveler's Checks 44
Traveling with Children 34
Trespassing .42
Tropical Farms 82
Tsunami, 1946 85
Turtle Bay 88, 143
Turtle Bay Golf Course 188
Turtle Bay Golf Fazio Course 188
Turtle Bay Golf Palmer Course 188
Turtle Bay Horseback Rides 216
Turtle Bay Resort 143
Turtle Beach
   (North Shore) 94, 150, 233

Turtle Beach (Wai'anae) 123
Turtle-watching 94
Turtles *44, 95*, 144
Turtles, Interacting with 94
Twogood Kayaks 220

Uber 22
Ulehawa Beach Park 124
Ultralights 71
Ulupau Head 80
Uncle Bobo's 83
Updates to Book 4, 41
US Army Museum 59
USS Arizona Memorial *109*, 157
USS Bowfin 159, *160*
USS Missouri
   Battleship 109, *158*, 159
USS Oklahoma Memorial 159

Valley of the Temples **81, 208**
Vancouver, George 93
VIP Car Rental 23
Volcanoes 29, 65

Wa'ahila Ridge **250**
Wahiawa 105
Wai'alae Beach Park *130*, 131
Waiale'e Beach Park 144
Waialua Estate Coffee
   & Chocolate Plantation 101
Wai'anae 110, 113, 114, 116
Wai'anae Coast 221
Wai'anae Regional Park 183
Wai'anae Volcano 29
Waihe'e Falls Hike 208
Waikiki 2, 46, *52*
Waikiki Aquarium **35, 56, *166*,**
   167
Waikiki Bboys 59
Waikiki Beach 53, *54*, 128
Waikiki Beach Center 54, 236
Waikiki Beach Services **52, 181**
Waikiki Beachwalk 47
Waikiki Climate 28
Waikiki Diving Center 227
Waikiki Exits 44
Waikiki Gun Club 189
Waikiki Resort Index & Map 48
Waikiki Shell 56
Waikiki Shuttle 23
Waikiki Starlight Lu'au 303

Waikiki Starry Skyline Viewpoint 62
Waikiki Trolley **26, 52**
Wailupe Beach Park 131
Waimanalo .74
Waimanalo Bay Beach Park 75, 134
Waimanalo Beach Park 75, 134
Waimano Falls Hike 210
Waimea Bay 91, 148, 149, 233
Waimea Falls Adventure Park . . .93, 223
Waimea Valley **42, 93, 223**
Walls (Queen's Beach) 55
Walmart/Sam's Club **34, 185, 233**
Washington Place 166
Wasps 32
Water Shoes 117
Watercraft Connection 217
Waterfall Hazards 33
Waterfalls, see also Falls 36
Waterproof Box 118
Waterskiing 239
Wave Runners (Jet Skis) 216
Waves 101 238
Weather 27, 78
Website Updates Page 4
Website, Hawaii Revealed 4, 41
Weddings on O'ahu 26
Wet 'n' Wild Hawai'i **35, 169**
Whale Watching Tours 239
Whale Watching from Land 71
Where to Stay, Deciding 29
Where to Stay in Waikiki 52
White Plains Beach Park 126
Wi-Fi 41
Wild Bunch Sport Fishing 187
Wild Side Specialty Tours 183
Willie K 40
Wind Turbines 88
Windward Side 28
Windward Watersports **220, 222**
WWII Armistice 159
WWII, 1st Japanese POW 134
WWII Valor in the Pacific 156
www.hawaiirevealed.com 4, 41

X-treme Watersports **218, 225**

YMCA Camp Erdman **96**
Yokohama Bay 115, 120

Ziplines **240**
Zombie Apocalypse Tour 171

Your Vacation from **Start** to *Amazing!*

Brutally honest, anonymous reviews. No paid advertisements accepted—ever.

Start with our **best-selling guidebooks.**

*Trusted for over **two decades by millions of travelers**.*

Companion website with helpful travel information and links.

Look for our ALL NEW REDESIGNED APP "HAWAII REVEALED"

All the features you loved in our old apps PLUS new ones you will love even more!

Visit our website for more details.

"A must for any serious visitor."
—The New York Times

"The best guidebook. Every nook and cranny is explored by long-time residents."
—Conde Nast Traveler

"...the authors are continually updating the content with new gems, taking into account reader feedback."
—The Discovery Channel

Look for our books, eBooks and apps in your favorite bookstore or online.
Visit our website for recent updates, travel information, local events, weather information
and so much more to plan and have your best vacation—ever!

www.hawaiirevealed.com • aloha@hawaiirevealed.com
Follow us on Facebook & Twitter @hawaiirevealed

WIZARD PUBLICATIONS INC *Believable Guides for Unbelievable Vacations*®